THE POWER OF POLITICAL ART

THE POWER OF
POLITICAL ART

THE 1930S LITERARY LEFT RECONSIDERED

ROBERT SHULMAN

THE UNIVERSITY OF NORTH CAROLINA PRESS   CHAPEL HILL AND LONDON

Parts of this study have appeared in " 'I Was Marching': The Radical Reportage of Meridel Le Sueur," *NST* 1 (1988): 221–31; "Political Art and Ethnicity: The Radical Discourse of Meridel Le Sueur," in *The Future of American Modernism: Ethnic Writing between the Wars*, edited by William Boelhower (Amsterdam: Free University Press, 1990), pp. 217–42; and "Subverting and Reconstructing the Dream: The Radical Voices of Le Sueur, Herbst, and Wright," in *Deferring a Dream: Literary Sub-Versions of the American Columbiad*, edited by Gert Buelens and Ernst Rudin (Basel: Birkhauser, 1994), pp. 24–36.

© 2000 The University of North Carolina Press

Designed by April Leidig-Higgins
Set in Minion by Keystone Typesetting, Inc.
Manufactured in the United States of America

The paper in this book meets the guidelines for permanence and durability of the Committee on Production Guidelines for Book Longevity of the Council on Library Resources.

Library of Congress Cataloging-in-Publication Data
Shulman, Robert, 1930–   The power of political art: the 1930s literary left reconsidered / Robert Shulman.
p. cm. Includes bibliographical references and index.
ISBN 0-8078-2540-9 (cloth: alk. paper)
ISBN 0-8078-4853-0 (pbk.: alk. paper)
1. American literature—20th century—History and criticism. 2. Communism and literature—United States—History—20th century. 3. Politics and literature—United States—History—20th century. 4. Authors, American—20th century—Political and social views. 5. Communism—United States—History—20th century. 6. Right and left (Political science) in literature. 7. Power (Social sciences) in literature. 8. Radicalism in literature. 9. Nineteen thirties. I. Title.
PS228.C6 S58 2000   810.9'358—dc21   99-055916

04 03 02 01 00   5 4 3 2 1

To the usual suspects—

Sandy, David, Natasha, Smadar, and Talia

Rereading *Native Son* is an experience of renewing the dialectical awareness of history and society, but is not in itself an aesthetic experience.

Harold Bloom, introduction to *Richard Wright's Native Son*

It is clear from this history that *aesthetic*, with its specialized references to art, to visual appearance, and to a category of what is "fine" or "beautiful," is a key formation in a group of meanings which at once emphasized and isolated *subjective* sense-activity as the basis of art and beauty as distinct, for example, from *social* or *cultural* interpretations. It is an element in the divided modern consciousness of *art* and *society*.

Raymond Williams, *Keywords: A Vocabulary of Culture and Society*

We must come back to where we started, to the critic's primary function. He must judge the work of art as work of art. But knowing form and content to be inseparable, he will recognize his duty to both. Judgment of art is unavoidably both an aesthetic and a social act, and the critic's sense of social responsibility gives him a deeper thirst for meaning.

F. O. Matthiessen, "The Responsibilities of the Critic," 1949

CONTENTS

ACKNOWLEDGMENTS

At the University of Washington I have benefited from the involvement, response, and questioning of the students in a series of graduate and undergraduate special topics and honors courses on the 1930s left. At an early stage the encouragement of Iris Tillman Hill and Alan Trachtenberg was exceptionally valuable. At the end Alan Trachtenberg helped me significantly refocus *The Power of Political Art*. My late colleague, Malcolm Brown, provided a model of intelligence, persistence, and engagement that was important to me, as were his controlled passion and questioning of received orthodoxies. My colleagues, Joe Butwin and Ross Posnock, gave early drafts a careful reading. The comments of an anonymous reader for the press helped me clarify my assumptions and especially to make my treatment of 1930s communism much more precise and well developed than it had been. In 1988, 1991, and 1994 the participants in American Studies Association, European Association for American Studies, and Modern Language Association panels on the 1930s and on the changing literary canon provided a welcome sense of shared concerns, including inevitable differences in emphasis and approach. Sabbatical leave and a Graduate School research grant from the University of Washington were indispensable. David Haugen was an exemplary research assistant.

INTRODUCTION

In literature departments in America during the early Cold War "political art" was either a contradiction in terms or a reminder of the discredited work of the 1930s left, a literature that was generally dismissed as doctrinaire and party line, lacking in linguistic and imaginative energy and committed to a dated and dangerous Communist ideology.[1] Although "political" has favorable associations in current discourse and "subversive" art is valued, not rejected, the power of the political art of the 1930s left has still not been fully explored, has still not fully emerged from the shadow of its earlier neglect and denigration. By examining the careers and creative work of Meridel Le Sueur, Josephine Herbst, Richard Wright, Muriel Rukeyser, and Langston Hughes, in my view among the best of the talented artists of the 1930s left, I hope to show that their political art has a continuing power to engage contemporary readers.[2]

Although a significant body of post-1930s left theory and criticism has been an invaluable resource, I am a critic and scholar interested in Marxism, not a Marxist critic or scholar.[3] Like any critic, I view my material from a point of view. Rather than providing a descriptive label or abstract summary, I would prefer to allow its characteristics to emerge in the course of this book. From my perspective what I offer are interpretations. My aim is to bring alive and to stimulate interest in the still contested history and literary history of the 1930s and the Cold War and to engage the primary literature of the 1930s left in depth and detail. Other readers can then build on or challenge my interpretations but what is really important to me is for the radical political art of the 1930s to receive active, intelligent criticism and classroom exposure. I hope readers coming to my work from the vantage points of current poststructuralist, feminist, or Marxist positions will find something of value, even though I am not working within and extending their critical paradigms. Although I have tried not to read back present-day concerns into the thirties or to fault writers of an earlier decade for not being really up-to-date contemporary theorists, from the start I was nonetheless interested in finding imaginatively realized work that might speak to present-day readers. I also wanted to break down the barrier between the "aesthetic" and the "political," particularly as this distinction continues to be used against politically engaged writing.[4]

Meridel Le Sueur, Josephine Herbst, Richard Wright, Muriel Rukeyser, and Langston Hughes illustrate the range and quality of work done by left writers during the 1930s. Along with other committed, gifted men and women, they helped make the cultural dialogue of the thirties left one of the most vital in American history. Their work, and not theirs alone, has continuing power to engage and challenge readers. To understand fully their creative achievements, we need to consider the cultural dialogue of the thirties left, because the meaning and resonance of each individual voice is amplified by its involvement in a complex, energizing discourse. The reverse also holds: when the left movement was stigmatized as vulgar and un-American before and during the Cold War, individual achievements were diminished. Writers like Le Sueur and Herbst, who had earlier been seen as part of the vanguard contributing to the new American literature, disappeared from public view. When they were rediscovered in the 1970s and 1980s, their radical politics were typically overlooked or criticized.[5]

Instead of being an asset, moreover, Wright's complex politics in *Native Son* was reduced to ritual denunciations of "the prolixity and dubiety of Max's courtroom speechifying."[6] The entire genre of the protest novel was stigmatized and turned against Wright in James Baldwin's influential "Everybody's Protest Novel."[7] The process continues into the 1990s. Houston Baker holds Wright's Marxism responsible for his "in effect murdering" women in *12 Million Black Voices*. For Baker, Max, the Marxist lawyer in *Native Son*, is "the ideologue attorney Boris Max."[8] Baker is only one of the talented contemporary critics who combine poststructuralist and feminist concerns to reinscribe the Cold War narrative to the disadvantage of the writers of the 1930s.

For her part, in 1938 Muriel Rukeyser dedicated her *U.S. 1* to the left poet and critic Horace Gregory. In the changed political climate of 1946, in his *A History of American Poetry, 1900–1940*, Gregory devoted less than a paragraph of negative comment to Rukeyser's 1930s poetry, "conceived in terms of slogans and commands," effectively and symptomatically dismissing her radical work and characterizing the movement as doctrinaire.[9] Rukeyser nonetheless continued as a well-respected poet until her death in 1980, but her radical poetry of the 1930s has been generally ignored or, when considered, either dismissed or presented as politically moderate.[10]

Langston Hughes, for his part, depended on public readings for his income. He organized his autobiographies to avoid or downplay his 1930s political radicalism, he publicly distanced himself from his earlier politics after he privately testified before the McCarthy Committee in 1953, and he did not include his left poetry in his *Selected Poems* (1959), so that for most readers his radical poetry does not exist.[11] The point is not to criticize Hughes, who continued to write and who would otherwise have been silenced. But his self-censorship is a reminder of the pressures writers and critics were subjected to during the Cold War as they engaged the cultural dialogue of the thirties left.

Although all five of the writers I concentrate on were either members of the Communist Party or closely identified with it, I have referred to their work under the general term "political" rather than "proletarian," "Communist," or "revolutionary." In discussions of the most commonly used term, thirties critics and writers did not agree on what constituted "proletarian" literature.[12] As Joseph Kalar accurately observed, "we have not yet had a clear formulation of what proletarian esthetics is. . . . Somebody has said we have no proletarian literature, we have only revolutionary literature."[13] Mike Gold, who supposedly mandated an iron "law of genre" for proletarian fiction, instead supported his own fictional practice by arguing that "there is nothing finished or dogmatic in proletarian thought and literature. We cannot afford it," Gold went on. "It would be fatal for us to have fixed minds. Proletarian literature," Gold stressed, "is taking many forms. There is not a standard model which all writers must imitate, or even a standard set of thoughts. There are no precedents. Each writer has to find his own way." The one requirement for Gold, "all that unites us, and all we have for guide, is the revolutionary spirit. If this spirit does not exist in a book, that book has no place in proletarian literature." Gold concluded with a reaffirmation of the thrust of his 1921 "Towards Proletarian Art" by arguing that "to my mind, it is the task of each proletarian writer to describe that portion of proletarian life with which he is most saturated. It is such an immense new field that he simply cannot even do as he ought, but as he must. I do not believe any good writing can come out of this mechanical application of the spirit of proletarian literature. In America, where everything is confused, we must begin humbly with the things we know best."[14]

Particularly when we focus on the actual creative work of the thirties left, including Gold's *Jews without Money*, the range and diversity explode stereotypes about a monolithic "proletarian realism" or proletarian literature and aesthetics. Because I am interested in the ways writers engage the full range of political concerns, moreover, I do not want to limit myself to a terminology implying an official set of positions, however contested. Similarly, "Marxist" and "Communist" are overlapping but not identical terms. "Communist" in thirties and even more in Cold War discourse connotes official party positions and is distractingly loaded with associations of un-American subversion. It is tempting to set up a drama that opposes a few writers to "the orthodox strains of proletarian writing with its facile convictions and two-valued perspective."[15] This drama, however, overlooks the lack of consensus; reinforces the Cold War view of the period; and, in the process of recovering one group of writers, makes it difficult for us to read and value the creative achievements of writers who supported, were supported by, and often actively contested "proletarian orthodoxy," which is to say, the pressures and positions of the party.

During the depression the Communist Party was at the center of the cultural dialogue of the thirties left. Although they took the party into account, however, the writers in my study did not create with a set of directives on the desk, and their political concerns are not limited to those of the party. As Barbara Foley indicates, moreover, its authoritarian reputation to the contrary, official party positions on literature typically took the form of advice and sharply phrased criticism, not commands and dogma.[16] In practice, people in the movement often did feel under pressure to accept the judgment of such party cultural officials as Alexander Trachtenberg and V. J. Jerome.[17] Although in their public statements authors like Richard Wright could endorse party views about which they had reservations, on my observation, in their creative work the writers attracted to the party typically made up their own minds. As writers in their writing, as a group they were intelligent, independent, and radical, active participants in a creative dialogue to which the party contributed significantly. In left fiction, in particular cases intense drama results as authors like Le Sueur and Wright imaginatively render conflicts with or within party positions. Working closely with the fiction and poetry of five engaged writers has impressed on me how active their imaginations were, how frequently they either probed, challenged, or convincingly confirmed received positions, as in Hughes's playful, irreverent use of slogans.

At the center of my book are works conceived and written as integral contributions to the culture of the Popular Front (1935–39). Important exceptions are Meridel Le Sueur's "I Was Marching" (1934) and "Women on the Breadlines" (1932), Langston Hughes's poems of the early 1930s, and, chronologically, Josephine Herbst's *Pity Is Not Enough* (1932) and *The Executioner Waits* (1934), works published during the Comintern's Third Period (1928–34). The connection between individual creations and official, and often controversial, contested positions is not simple and not always possible to establish convincingly. When party positions are pertinent, I bring them into focus, as in the bearing of the line on "the Negro Question" on Max's speech in *Native Son* or the conflict between the militant and moderate tendencies in Le Sueur's "Tonight Is Part of the Struggle," written in 1935 at a moment of transition between the revolutionary Third Period and the more accommodationist Popular Front. For its bearing on cultural policy, the 1930 Comintern-inspired Kharkov conference on literature, a major influence on American criticism and theory during the Third Period, has been carefully examined by Barbara Foley.[18]

On the political front, during the late 1920s in what the Communist International defined as capitalism's third period after World War I, even before the depression the Comintern stressed the intensifying internal contradictions of global capitalism.[19] "The main characteristics of the third period," in Earl Browder's words, are the "sharp collision between expanding productive forces and strictly limited markets, rising revolutionary tide of the working class revolt, maturing national revolutionary struggles in the colonies, sharpening imperialist rivalries— all against the background of the unprecedentedly swift rise of socialist economy in the Soviet Union."[20] Intensified by the depression, "the revolutionary upsurge" gave urgency to the contest for leadership of the working class.[21] Because from the point of view of the Communist International it was important for Communists to lead the proletariat, the international party defined its main enemies not as the German and Italian fascists but rather the social democrats in Europe and the New Deal in America, the left competitors for the allegiance of the working class. For the same reason, in America the American Federation of Labor, the Socialist Party, particularly the Muste wing, and such former Communist leaders as Jay Lovestone, James Cannon, and Bertram Wolfe all received scathing treatment in the *Communist*, the theoretical journal of the Communist Party.[22]

In Germany the party saw the Social Democrats as "the auxiliary police to fascism" in that they co-opted into parliamentary forms the revolutionary tendency of the workers and directed their energy "away from the revolutionary class struggle and from Communism."[23] During the early thirties the Comintern also emphasized that "the supreme test for Communist Parties is the struggle against imperialist war."[24] Instead of the danger of German Nazism, Japan's invasion of Manchuria and Shanghai was central, partly because of the huge losses the Chinese Communists suffered, partly because of the threat of war against the adjacent Soviet Union.[25] In making the rise of fascism in Germany and Italy a secondary consideration to the danger to the Soviet Union and the threat of colonial and imperialist war, particularly in China, and in blocking cooperation with German "social fascists," the party and its Third Period analysis also blocked cooperation that may have prevented the Hitler takeover in 1933.

As the threat of fascism became more obvious, after 1935 the Comintern shifted to a policy advocating a United Front or People's Front or Popular Front to oppose fascism and work for peace.[26] Communists were now encouraged to work with other left groups within unions, for example, or within the many political and cultural organizations aimed at supporting antifascist causes, such as the Spanish loyalists and the related opposition to racial oppression centering on the Scottsboro Boys. Within these groups and in magazines, newsletters, documentary films, novels, poems, and murals, sometimes as engaged individuals, sometimes together, Communists and non-Communist leftists and liberals worked, argued, publicized, and criticized each other and, in the process, succeeded in creating a recognizable Popular Front political culture with shared, contested concerns, values, images, and ideas. Culturally, the Kharkov conference emphasis on writing by and about workers and its stress on the key role of the party relaxed to welcome work from a range of class positions, often by established rather than young, unknown authors.

On the Communist side, politically the Popular Front in America contained conflicting tendencies: the moderate "Communism Is Twentieth-Century Americanism" emphasis coexisted with undercurrents of the earlier revolutionary strain. "In a very special sense," moreover, "the Popular Front allowed Communists to combine two sometimes contradictory beliefs and sets of images: a kind of populist patriotism and an international sense of solidarity that was ultimately attached to Soviet interests. American Communists," Paul Lyons continues, "were able to balance, at least until 1939, attacks on 'Tories' and 'Copperheads' in the name of a crusading New Deal, efforts to create an alliance of all democracies against fascist aggression in Spain, and defenses of the Soviet Union against 'Trotskyite' and 'fascist' slander and counter-revolutionary plots. As second generation Americans, sensitive about being indigenous," Lyons concludes, "thirties Communists could attack convention while remaining true to their nation."[27]

As for its literary accomplishments, for me one of the surprises of my study was to realize how much good work was done during the Popular Front. I had been trained to look down on Popular Front literature as reductive, middlebrow, and simplistic, the epitome of the worst features of the left literature of the 1930s.[28] All five of my writers, however, produced first-rate work as an integral part of the Popular Front, and they are not alone. I hope my study will complement Judy Kutulas's analysis and contribute to the reassessing of the culture of the Popular Front.[29]

In the course of my work I also discovered a left avant-garde that has been obscured by the prestige of high modernism, particularly as interpreted by Clement Greenberg and other *Partisan Review* critics in the decade before and during the crucial period of canon formation after World War II. The left avant-garde has also been overlooked because surveys of the period often focus on, or use as interpretive lenses, such theoretical positions as pronouncements about socialist realism or the polemics of Stalinism and anti-Stalinism instead of putting at center stage the actual creative work of the 1930s left.

As I was reading the primary imaginative literature of the 1930s, I gradually began to see a left avant-garde that includes writers as diverse as Le Sueur, Herbst, Rukeyser, Wright, Dos Passos, Farrell, Gold, Rollins, Algren, Dahlberg, Fearing, Funeroff, and West. They were avant-garde in the sense that they combined a vanguard critique of the middle class, a probing of relatively unexplored areas of American experience, and vital experiments in form and language, sometimes modernist, more often within the conventions of realism-naturalism.[30] They saw themselves as politically engaged vanguard writers whose revolutionary commitments and formal innovations placed them at the forefront of artistic creativity in America. They saw themselves as breaking new ground and helping to create a new American literature. The avant-garde status of these writers and the dialogue they animated and were energized by, however, was lost sight of, particularly because left literature generally and left realism-naturalism specifically were elided into a form of party line, middlebrow kitsch in the view that came to prevail during the 1950s—Robert Warshow accurately represents the received position.[31] I hope my study will help us recover as avant-garde the energy and qualities of individual writers and the dialogue they distinguished and were stimulated by. With regard to terminology, I would like to reserve the words "modernism" or "high modernism" for writers like Eliot and Joyce but not to allow them sole property in the term "avant-garde." Another avant-garde, politically left, frequently nonmodernist, and grounded in the traditions of realism-naturalism, also has a claim on our allegiance, despite the almost automatic contrary usage of the past several decades.

Although knowledgeable academics currently teach and discuss my five writers, their radical 1930s political art has fared less well, partly as a continuing result of its neglect and dismissal during the early Cold War period. The earlier marginalizing of the 1930s left, including the left avant-garde, did not take place in a political vacuum. I also learned during the course of my work that the political and cultural repression of the Cold War period was even deeper and more pervasive than I had imagined at the outset. This discovery may simply comment on the limits of my imagination and my own susceptibility to the hegemonic processes of the Cold War period. It is nonetheless worth stressing that, the impact on academic critics aside, all five of the writers in my study were the objects of official persecution—

persecution, not harassment, "dirty tricks," or some other euphemism. Official intimidation played a central role in the complex cultural politics of the Cold War. Gramsci tended to downplay or rule out the role of official force in the process of cultural hegemony. Based on my reading of the post–World War II American experience, however, we need to keep that role very much in mind as an integral part of the process, inseparable from real or threatened loss of jobs and the undermining of intellectual credibility.

Coda: A Note on Criticism

As recent criticism indicates, and as I suggest in my opening chapter, "The Cultural Dialogue of the Thirties Left," the writers and works I concentrate on are not the only ones meriting attention. James Bloom has written persuasively about Mike Gold and Joseph Freeman.[32] In his admirable *Worker-Writer in America: Jack Conroy and the Tradition of Midwestern Literary Radicalism, 1898–1990*, Douglas Wixson recovers a neglected, noncanonical tradition of worker writing based on oral and folktale sources and traditions of worker solidarity. Constance Coiner has carefully examined Meridel Le Sueur and Tillie Olsen's relation to the Communist Party, although she is more perceptive about Olsen than Le Sueur.[33] Agnes Smedley's *Daughter of Earth*, Fielding Burke's *Call Home the Heart* and *A Stone Came Rolling*, Tess Slesinger's *The Unpossessed*, Grace Lumpkin's *A Sign for Cain* and *Make My Bread*, and Myra Page's *Moscow Yankee* are among the other talented women writers who have received critical reappraisal.[34] Dos Passos has been the subject of continuing critical and biographical interest, as has Farrell.[35] Although they have been generally overlooked, for the most part noted in passing, Robert Cantwell's *The Promised Land* (1934) and Edward Newhouse's *You Can't Sleep Here* (1934) and *This Is Your Day* (1937) deserve further consideration, as does the poetry of Edwin Rolfe and the poetry and film criticism of Kenneth Fearing.[36] As a representative man of letters, Isidor Schneider wrote poetry, novels, and criticism, was an editor of *New Masses*, and was active in the League of American Writers. His work, too, warrants further study.

Beginning with Walter Rideout's indispensable *The Radical Novel*, the period has been surveyed, the poetry by Cary Nelson's ground-breaking *Repression and Recovery*, the criticism and literature of the anti-Stalinist left by Alan Wald's important *The New York Intellectuals*, the genres of proletarian fiction and criticism in revealing fashion by Barbara Foley's *Radical Representations* and more problematically by Paula Rabinowitz's *Labor and Desire*.[37] Paul Lauter's "American Proletarianism" is a concise, reliable overview.[38] In his historically precise revisionist study of Wallace Stevens and modernism, Alan Filreis shows in convincing detail the extent to which left discourse and poetics significantly influenced even those like Stevens who were not part of the organized left.[39] Filreis confirms Cary Nelson's insight that during the thirties, for radicals and conservatives, "the range of poetry marked as 'political' in this period was so diverse, its style and subject matter so varied, that the nature of the 'political' is, in fact, itself continually being extended and called into question."[40]

It is not creative work, however, but the literary and political criticism of the 1930s left that has been most frequently examined, beginning with Daniel Aaron's *Writers on the Left*.[41] The New York intellectuals of the *Partisan Review* are frequently cast as the exceptions to the prevailing dogmatism, reductionism, and party line criticism that supposedly characterize the period and the *New Masses*.[42] David Peck, James Bloom, and Barbara Foley have challenged this widely shared denigration of the *New Masses* "Stalinist" group, which in addition to Gold and Freeman includes such gifted writers and critics as Isidor Schneider, Edwin Seaver, Granville Hicks, Edmund Burgum, and Joshua Kunitz. I see both the *New Masses* and *Partisan Review* groups and critics like Edmund Wilson, Kenneth Burke, Malcolm Cowley, Newton Arvin, and F. O. Matthiessen as contributing to an exceptionally vital, intelligent cultural dialogue.

My emphasis, however, is not on criticism but on the period's creative work and particularly on what I see as the best of that work, so that I also stress a different set of concerns from those considered by Walter Rideout, Cary Nelson, Alan Wald, and Paula Rabinowitz, who are surveying the spectrum of left fiction, poetry, or criticism. Instead, I do the kind of detailed, in-depth, contextualized analysis I believe works need if they are to be read for their insights into the past and for their power to engage us in the present.

From a Marxist point of view, not in *Radical Representations* but in a suggestive article on proletarian fiction, Barbara Foley addresses the question, Is it any good? Foley stresses that the ideology of bourgeois individualism underlies the "typicality and narrative transparency" of classic realist-naturalistic fiction. In contrast, proletarian writers who to a greater or lesser degree rejected and sought to replace this ideology created a poetics that disrupts the transparency—Max's speech in *Native Son* is an example. Foley argues that instead of being evaluated as significant alternatives to conventional realism-naturalism, however, the formal features of proletarian fiction designed to disrupt and replace bourgeois norms get read as aesthetic evidence of inferiority. Foley's emphasis on shared formal features as well as the revolutionary content of proletarian fiction and her recognition of the role of the reader's expectations ("the author-reader contract") point to an approach that complements the one I have followed in reading and evaluating the left literature of the 1930s.[43]

In addition to the studies I have cited, Richard Pells's *Radical Visions and American Dreams*, Walter Susman's "The Culture of the Thirties," Walter Kalaidjian's *American Culture between the Wars*, and Judy Kutulas's *The Long War* provide valuable contexts for understanding the thirties left.[44] Pells and Kalaidjian, however, also contribute to the prevailing anti-Stalinist narrative, which stresses a few writers who stand out against the reductionism and dogmatism said to characterize the period. Robert Warshow catches the prevailing tone and content when he writes in 1947, "it was the Communist party that ultimately determined what you were to think about and in what terms. There resulted," Warshow continues, "a disasterous vulgarization of intellectual life, in which the character of American liberalism and radicalism was decisively—and perhaps permanently—corrupted," so that in Warshow's representative view, "for the serious intellectual, something more than an error of taste or judgment was involved when he accepted the pretensions of 'proletarian literature.' "[45] Michael Denning counters such views and significantly reorients our understanding of the thirties by placing the Congress of Industrial Organizations (CIO) and worker culture at the center of his comprehensive, revisionary *The Cultural Front*.[46]

Lawrence Schwartz, Maurice Isserman, James Murphy, M. J. Heale, and Barbara Foley have done the detailed intellectual work that clears the air of the 1930s anti-Stalinist and Cold War constructions of the role, character, and negative influence of the Communist Party.[47] They counter the views of historians like Harvey Klehr, Theodore Draper, and Ronald Radosh, who stress the dominance of the Soviet Union over the Communist Party U.S.A. (CPUSA), present the party as an authoritarian and highly disciplined agent of the Soviet Union, and see the party through its leadership as acting primarily in the interests of the Soviet Union.[48] Ellen Schrecker and Victor Navasky are among the most recent critics of this interpretation of the party.[49] For Schrecker and Navasky, "at the top the party was responsive to the Soviet-led international apparat, with all its arbitrary twists and turns. Yet simultaneously, at the bottom and in the middle—which is where, after all, most of its members were—it was," in Schrecker's words, " 'genuinely dedicated to a wide range of social reforms.' "[50]

The autobiographies of Al Richmond and Steve Nelson, moreover; the interviews in Vivian Gornick's *The Romance of Communism*, Victor S. Navasky's *Naming Names*, and Griffin Fariello's *Red Scare*; Mark Naison's detailed *Communists in Harlem during the Depression* and Robin D. G. Kelley's *Hammer and Hoe* and *Race Rebels*; Roger Keeran's *The Communist Party and the Auto Workers' Union*; and

Paul Lyons's *Philadelphia Communists, 1936–1956* similarly correct the view of a monolithic, authoritarian party laying down a line the rank and file, including intellectuals, routinely followed.[51] Russell Reising and Barbara Foley have called attention to recent work on the 1930s in the Soviet Union, work that qualifies the Cold War image of a monolithic dictatorship.[52] The extensive work of revisionist historians has also taken us beyond the Cold War narrative about both the foreign and domestic policy of the 1940s and 1950s, a narrative inseparable from the denigration and near disappearance of the left literature of the 1930s during the post–World War II period.[53] Critics like Hilton Kramer who believe on metaphysical grounds that a 1930s Communist or Communist sympathizer is by definition a liar will of course not be persuaded.[54]

CHAPTER 1

THE CULTURAL DIALOGUE OF THE THIRTIES LEFT

To recover a sense of the pre–World War II vitality and range of commitments of the 1930s left, we need to recall that in America the left dialogue that became a major cultural force in the 1930s emerged from the energies released by the Russian Revolution in 1917 and from grass-roots American sources, particularly the irreverent protest culture of the International Workers of the World (IWW or Wobblies) in the wheat fields, logging camps, and textile factories of the 1910s.[1] The Wobblies not only advocated one big union and the power of the general strike; they also satirized the pie-in-the-sky promises of the bosses. Their songs and poems energized the loggers and farm laborers of the Northwest and Midwest and the mill workers of Massachusetts and New Jersey. Sometimes humorous, sometimes blasphemous, almost always defiant, their slogans, poems, and songs in hundreds of thousands of copies of *The Little Red Song Book*—on the title page, *I.W.W. Songs to Fan the Flames of Discontent*—voiced "solidarity forever" and the irreverent knowledge that "you haven't a pot in which to spit, / Or a window to throw it out."[2]

In 1917 the IWW's success at organizing workers in the timber, farming, mining, and textile industries, however, coincided with its opposition to World War I. The Wobblies were vulnerable to the charge of striking to subvert the war effort rather than to improve the substandard conditions of underpaid laborers. Prosecuted under the Sedition Act of 1917, 101 leaders were sentenced to terms of up to twenty years. The IWW was also devastated by the 1919 Palmer Raids. Further undercutting the movement were internal divisions about Russia and the Communist Party. Despite these conflicts and however stimulated from Soviet and European sources, the left cultural discourse of the 1930s was an integral part of an American radical tradition that for Meridel Le Sueur, Josephine Herbst, Jack Conroy, John Dos Passos, and countless others included the IWW.[3]

In the immediate aftermath of the 1917 revolution, John Reed's *Ten Days that Shook the World* (1919) brought together both the American radical and Russian revolutionary movements in a book that resonated through the left reportage of the 1930s. Granville Hicks, at the height of his prestige, wrote *John Reed*.[4] Reed's importance in the cultural life of the 1930s left is further testified to by the John Reed Clubs, named in his honor. Between 1929 and 1935 this Communist-sponsored organization of young, radical writers and artists attracted writers as different as Richard Wright, Jack Conroy, and Philip Rahv and published such journals as *Left Front* (Chicago), *Midland Left* (Indianapolis), and the early *Partisan Review* (New York).[5]

Although Trotsky was later vilified as a traitor, during the twenties his *Literature and Revolution* (1924) was an eloquent, nuanced probing of the possibilities of radical art, a powerful cultural force for left intellectuals before the depression. Radical writers as different as Dos Passos and Wright, Sol Funaroff and Alfred Hayes and such left intellectuals as Philip Rahv and William Phillips, moreover, responded to the modernist innovations of Eliot and Joyce. Dos Passos was also stimulated by the futurists, particularly Fernand Lèger and the French poet, Blaise Cendrars.[6] Looking back on the twenties after World War II, Josephine Herbst noted that "artists of the vanguard welcomed the revolution—a few years of electrifying activity under the illusion that revolutionary politics and advanced art were moving in the same direction. A sense that the esthetic ideals of modernism could be fully realized under a social system that was a kind of political analogue to these ideals. Malevich had said, 'Cubism and futurism were the revolutionary forms of art foreshadowing the revolution in political and economic life of 1917.'"[7] Both as precedent and antagonist, the energies of high modernism played an active role in the cultural dialogue of the thirties left, a dialogue that became acrimonious after Rahv and Phillips split with the Communist Party and *New Masses* and in 1937 turned *Partisan Review* into a modernist journal fiercely critical of the party and those associated with it.

During the 1920s and 1930s, left discourse was vitalized not only by modernist writers and disputes but also by the creative achievments of such realist-naturalist writers as Dreiser, Sherwood Anderson, and Jack London. For Mike Gold and Joseph Freeman, Whitman was a continuing source of inspiration for the radical American art they were committed to.

In the years immediately preceding the 1930s, the cultural dialogue in America thus accelerated during the twenties with works like Mike Gold's "Towards Proletarian Art" in the *Liberator* (1921), Langston Hughes's "Rising Waters" in *The Workers Monthly: The Communist Magazine* (1925), and Mike Gold and Joseph Freeman's reactivating of the *Masses* into the *New Masses* in 1926.[8] Jack Conroy's experiences with "the other twenties," the twenties of strikes, unemployment, and hobo camps, animated his valuable contribution to the left cultural dialogue, as did his and other worker-writers' response to "unionism, Debsian socialism, 'wild jackass' populism, and folk expression."[9] Meridel Le Sueur, grounded in the same traditions, participated when she joined the Communist Party in 1923 or 1924. Between 1921 and 1927, moreover, the fight to save Sacco and Vanzetti compelled writers like Dos Passos, Gold, and Josephine Herbst.

Moving from quite different origins in the Garveyite movement of the 1920s, Cyril Briggs and Richard B. Moore became effective Communist organizers and street speakers in the Harlem of the early 1930s.[10] By the mid-1930s, "awakened by Italy's invasion of Ethiopia, . . . Black Communists and sympathizers fought Franco as a backhanded response to Mussolini. But their unexpected experiences in the Spanish Republic and as members of a radical International Brigade changed them forever. In both cases," Robin D. G. Kelley stresses, "these black radicals created a kind of hybrid movement that combined Garveyism, Pan-Africanism, African American vernacular cultures and traditions, and Euro-American Marxist thought."[11] Drawing on these traditions, by the late 1930s the party contributed to an active cultural dialogue. "The Party's concern with black culture," Mark Naison shows, "extended far beyond its involvement with black artists whose work normally frames the debate—Richard Wright, Langston Hughes, and Paul Robeson. It involved support for black theatre, WPA-sponsored and independent; efforts to encourage the teaching of black history in colleges and schools; the sponsorship of concerts and musical theatre aimed at winning recognition for black musicians; and campaigns to end discrimination in amateur and professional sports."[12]

Well before these developments, as early as 1919 in the midst of the coal and steel workers' strike, Josephine Herbst had written her parents, "the more I see of the poor—of the underlying population—the more I believe in revolution & the class war. I never used to believe in that—the hope seemed somewhere else—but now it's the underdog's only salvation."[13] Between ten and fifteen years later, under the pressure of the Great Depression and the rise of European fascism, hundreds of other writers, painters, musicians, and film makers increasingly came to share the hope of revolution. When Joseph Freeman assessed the status of revolutionary literature in 1930, he concluded that "outside of Michael Gold and, of late, Paul Peters, there is no solid achievement to boast of."[14] The situation had changed dramatically by 1935, marked by the Communist-sponsored American Writers'

Congress and the publication of an impressive anthology, *Proletarian Literature in the United States*.[15]

In the most controversial speech at the American Writers' Congress, Kenneth Burke challenged the use of "the symbol of the worker" and proposed instead the use of "the people" as more in touch with American values.[16] Most Americans, he argued, do not "really want to work, let us say, as a human cog in an automobile factory, or as gatherers of vegetables on a big truck farm. Such rigorous ways of life enlist our *sympathies*, but not our *ambitions*. Our ideal is as far as possible to *eliminate* such kinds of work" (p. 89). Anticipating the Popular Front, Burke proposed instead using "the people," because it is a positive symbol connoting unity and common purpose (pp. 87–94). Burke offended orthodox party people still committed to a revolutionary posture focused on workers. Although he was subjected to a powerful, unsettling barrage of criticism, he was not silenced but along with Henry Hart, Joseph Freeman, and Edwin Seaver edited *American Writers' Congress*, the collection that presented the public image of the congress (p. 17).[17]

Burke, Farrell, Wright, Le Sueur, Langston Hughes, Jack Conroy, Malcolm Cowley, and hundreds of other writers and critics agreed and disagreed, tangled with and supported each other and the party organizers they sometimes cooperated with and sometimes satirized. In the process, both at the congress and throughout the decade they collectively contributed to an exceptionally lively cultural dialogue. In the received narrative the Communist Party nonetheless had "unfortunate or even stultifying effects for art, art theory, and artists alike."[18] Although Communist Party pressures eventually alienated such gifted writers as Horace Gregory and Richard Wright, at best, however, during the 1930s Communist Party politics also energized the creative work of writers, painters, composers, and film makers even as their art animated their politics. For those like Wright who experienced a conflict between the demands of politics and their own creative work, moreover, the process often strengthened, not weakened, their art.

The still influential anti-Communist denigration of the 1930s left obscures much of what a gifted generation of radicals achieved in literature, painting, film, photography, music, and literary and cultural criticism. In-depth analysis is provided in the following chapters, but to appreciate the accomplishments of an entire movement, at the outset we need to recall the panorama of left creative work and the challenges artists were responding to.

Although conflicts, rivalries, and later in the decade basic political and artistic antagonisms were integral to left discourse, during the thirties young left writers and artists nonetheless had a sense of shared purpose, of working together toward political and artistic goals they were in the process of creating. Both during the

Third Phase and the Popular Front, the party's political and cultural positions were an important part of a creative dialogue, not the single voice of unquestioned authority. In the anti-Communist view, an authoritarian party imposed its commands on naive, dangerous, or deluded followers. During the thirties young American writers and artists, however, may not so much have followed Marx as discovered that Marx was on their side. In any case, throughout the decade there was a widely shared enthusiasm to bring alive a new, equalitarian society and to experiment with new forms of writing, film, and music that would do justice to neglected areas of personal and American experience. Stimulated by the Communist Party, energies were galvanized by causes like Scottsboro and the Spanish Civil War and pervasively by the breakdown of the depression. For some, the sense of solidarity with millions of other ordinary Americans mitigated the feeling of alienation characteristic of American artists and intellectuals. For others, the commitment with like-minded associates strengthened their sense of avant-garde separation from the dominant society.

In the cultural world, in the Middle West Jack Conroy and his *Rebel Poet* and *Anvil* and the Communist-inspired Chicago John Reed Club provided centers for like-minded writers—Le Sueur, Algren, Wright, H. H. Lewis, Joe Kalar—who were in touch by mail if not in person and whose efforts were mutually supportive. For East Coast radicals, since the New York left was predominantly Jewish, beneath art and politics there was a shared culture, often but not always immigrant and familiar with poverty and the experience of the outsider. The film maker Leo Hurwitz and the poet Edwin Rolfe (Solomon Fishman), friends since high school, shared apartments, a common background, and a commitment to artistic excellence and radical political change. A decade before he helped found the Group Theatre, Harold Clurman roomed in Paris with Aaron Copland. "As Odets is my playwright, Copland is my composer," Clurman wrote. "His world is parallel with mine."

Politically, artistically, and socially these composers, playwrights, and directors shared concerns with the film makers of the Workers Film and Photo League and later with the members of the Nykino group and Frontier Films. Copland and Marc Blizstein wrote music for innovative left documentaries. For May Day 1935 Copland also wrote the music for Alfred Hayes's poem, "Into the Streets May First." Through his wife, May Wolfe, the poet Edwin Rolfe met the playwrights Albert Maltz, Clifford Odets, and the other members of the Theatre Union and the Group Theatre. Left poets, composers, dramatists, and film makers stimulated each other and worked together in their art and politics.[19] Their creativity was intimately related to a vital left culture that especially but not only in New York involved theater, film, music, and lectures. Many left writers and artists were grounded in an immigrant socialist culture with close ties to the union movement and later the stimulus of radical politics in the City College cafeteria.

During the 1940s and 1950s, for such representative anti-Communist New York intellectuals as Clement Greenberg and Robert Warshow, accepting artists like Odets, Copland, and Clurman reflected a Stalinist politics and amounted to support for the philistine and middle-brow.[20] But Greenberg's widely accepted un-nuanced binary opposition between the modernist avant-garde and kitsch is at least as reductive and doctrinaire as the work Greenberg and the other New York intellectuals rejected on reinforcing political and aesthetic grounds. Rather than doctrinaire, wholesale rejection or celebration, what is called for is a careful reassessment of the entire range of left creative work, a reassessment open both to the work itself and to the social-political context within which the artists functioned.

The need for such a detailed, nuanced appraisal is illustrated by Anthony Dawahare's recent misrepresentation of a totalized "proletarian literary movement" and "proletarian" critics as either "blind" or hostile to "mass culture."[21] The complex left probing and critique of "mass culture" is the subject for a book. To indicate the range of possibilities, we might recall from many instances the subtle film criticism and film theory of Harry Alan Potamkin; the film theory and practice of such left documentary film makers as Leo Hurwitz; the pioneering discourse on film and theater in New Theatre; the film and theater criticism of Kenneth Fearing and James Farrell in New Masses and Partisan Review; the history and theory of the Group Theatre; the innovative Living Newspaper and other accomplishments of the left theater of the 1930s; and the centrality of folk music, folklore, and the blues in the culture of the Popular Front.[22]

The movie, theater, sports, and book sections of the Daily Worker during the late 1930s correct the view of the organized left's indifference or programmatic hostility to "mass culture." Similarly, the ads for lectures, concerts, books, and rallies in the Daily Worker and New Masses illuminate an active involvement in that culture. Popular or mass culture, moreover, self-consciously pervades such left works as Dos Passos's U.S.A., Farrell's Studs Lonigan, Wright's Native Son and Lawd Today!, the poetry of Kenneth Fearing, Langston Hughes, Horace Gregory, Edwin Rolfe, and Alfred Hayes, Le Sueur's The Girl, sections of Rukeyser's Theory of Flight and U.S. 1, Mike Gold's Jews without Money, and Jack Conroy's The Disinherited and his journals, the Anvil and Rebel Poet.

As for the Cold War critics' view of the aesthetic weakness of the radical art of the 1930s left, in the years immediately preceding and following the American Writers' Congress and Proletarian Literature, Edward Newhouse, a young writer with a Hungarian background, published two novels whose urbane style played off against their Hooverville and strike-organizer subject matter. Newhouse's *You Can't Sleep Here* (1934) and *This Is Your Day* (1937) and Robert Cantwell's *Land of Plenty* (1934) represent the kind of talent that animated and was animated by the discourse of the thirties left. Because these two writers are neither the best or worst of those involved in the movement, they give a sense of the very respectable quality of work created as part of the dialogue of the thirties left, as does Dalton Trumbo's well-received antiwar novel, *Johnny Got Your Gun* (1938).[23]

By the end of the decade during the Popular Front between 1936 and 1940, as vital parts of the dialogue on the left, a series of impressive works appeared, one reinforcing and amplifying the significance of the others. In 1938 Muriel Rukeyser's *U.S. 1*, for example, was reviewed in the same issue of *Time* as Wright's *Uncle Tom's Children*.[24] Langston Hughes had been publishing politically radical poems throughout the decade. A collection of these poems aimed at ordinary workers, *A New Song*, also appeared in 1938. Josephine Herbst completed her Trexler trilogy with *Rope of Gold* in 1939, the same year as her friend Nathaniel West's *The Day of the Locust*. West's novel was as brilliant and deeply grounded in the imagery and concerns of the thirties left as it was deconstructive and disillusioned. Kenneth Fearing's *Collected Poems*, the summation of a decade's work, came out in 1940, the same year as Wright's *Native Son* and Le Sueur's *Salute to Spring*.

On the fringes of the movement, energized by its concerns and the genre of reportage, James Agee's *Let Us Now Praise Famous Men* was finally published in 1941. Also on the fringes of the movement, John Steinbeck's revealing strike novel, *In Dubious Battle* (1936), and later *Grapes of Wrath* (1939) both showed the animating power of the radical and moderate tendencies of Popular Front culture. After speaking of the relation between *In Dubious Battle*, other "proletarian literature," and such New Deal documentary films as *The Plow That Broke the Plains* and *The River*, Malcolm Cowley concluded that "a whole literature is summarized in this book, and much of it is carried to a new level of excellence."[25]

These and other works contradicted and supported each other, the support as active in stylistic and substantive disagreement as in agreement. The conflicts about the revolutionary as distinct from the accommodationist strains within the Popular Front, for example, are as revealing in Le Sueur's "Tonight Is Part of the Struggle" as they are in the conflicts within Wright's Boris Max in *Native Son*. Le Sueur's lyric prose-poetry, moreover, complements and contradicts Wright's naturalism, a naturalism strongly inflected with expressionist probing. The hard-won affirmations in the concluding strike in Herbst's *Rope of Gold* are in dialogic opposition to West's inversion of the left iconography of the protest march in the concluding riot scene in *The Day of the Locust*. Hughes's irreverent critique of the pain of exploitation and his celebration of "the red flag of revolution" are as accessible as Rukeyser's powerful critique is obscure.[26]

Cumulatively, in the work of these and the other writers associated with the movement, the creators of the thirties left engaged in a complex dialogue, a discourse with images, values, and goals sufficiently in common so that the writers could explore serious divergences and dissents. What needs to be stressed is that the movement, the dialogue, intensified and deepened the significance of all of those who participated in it. In the 1950s, when the movement was either stigmatized or ignored, the value of each individual writer was also diminished, in many cases to the point of invisibility.

What we have also lost sight of is the extent to which these exploratory, dissident left writers constituted not only a political but also a cultural vanguard. Many of them—Le Sueur, Rukeyser, Herbst, Wright, Dos Passos, Farrell, Gold, Rollins, Algren, Dahlberg, Funaroff, Fearing, West, and Agee, for example—were avantgarde writers in the sense that they powerfully challenged middle-class values, probed relatively unexplored areas of American life, and actively experimented formally, often within those conventions of realism-naturalism now and during the Cold War so much in disrepute.[27] In claiming the status of the avant-garde for significant left writers, I am invoking values from both sides of the Brecht-Lukács dispute.[28]

As part of the 1950s marginalizing or denigration of the thirties left, the political-literary culture of the Popular Front received especially harsh treatment. What the 1950s construction obscures is the vitality, range, and complexity of a discourse that animated and includes *Native Son* and *Uncle Tom's Children*; *Rope of Gold* and *The Day of the Locust*; Langston Hughes and Muriel Rukeyser; Meridel Le Sueur, James Agee, and John Steinbeck. The cloud over the Popular Front, however, is inseparable from the fact that all of those involved had to deal with the accusations of betrayal against Trotsky and with the treason trials of the heroes of the Bolshevik Revolution. The Moscow Purge trials, the mass executions in the Soviet Union between 1936 and 1938, and the excoriation of Trotsky as a traitor split the American left so that even those who remained loyal to the party had to overcome doubts and reservations. For many, what compelled continued allegiance was the strong antifascist stand of the Soviet Union. When the Soviet Union abruptly changed course, turned foe into friend, and tried to buy time by signing the Hitler-Stalin Pact in 1939, left intellectuals like Granville Hicks finally gave up, although, as Maurice Isserman has shown, the party continued to engage creative Americans throughout the 1940s.[29] For all its positive results, the Popular Front was nonetheless characterized by the equivocations and compromises related to the changing needs of Soviet policy.

Opposition to the fascists and support of the loyalists in the Spanish Civil War, on the other hand, were central features and achievements of the Popular Front. In Spain, after six years of intense class and political conflict, including the brutally suppressed Asturias miners' revolt, a right-wing Catholic government was defeated in the election of February 16, 1936. On July 17, 1936, army leaders who had been in touch with Italian and German fascists led a well-organized revolt against the moderate left-center Popular Front government, which was also opposed by the church and the large landowners. For complex reasons—ideology, investments, misperceptions of the danger of German and Italian fascism—Britain and a reluctant Popular Front government in France adopted a nonintervention policy, refused to honor treaty obligations to Spain, blockaded arms shipments to the loyalists, and allowed Germany and Italy to violate the embargo. Ten thousand well-equipped Italian troops and the most advanced German tanks and the planes of the German Condor Division fought with Franco. Only the Soviet Union and its arm, the International Brigade, sided with the loyalists to counter the right-wing attack.[30]

Americans on the left supported the Soviet response, were inspired by the resistance of the Spanish workers, and were deeply threatened by the fascist aggression.[31] They saw the fight in Spain as the last chance to defeat the fascists and prevent another world war. As one member of the Abraham Lincoln Brigade said, the fight in Spain allowed him to bring together all of his commitments in one principled action. Herbst and Dos Passos, Hughes and Rukeyser were only a few of those on the left to go to Spain as reporters committed to the loyalist cause. Edwin Rolfe, a neglected left poet, and Alvah Bessie, later a blacklisted script writer, are among the many from the creative community who fought in Spain. The Popular Front also attracted to Spain non-Marxist celebrities like Hemingway and Dorothy Parker. In *Homage to Catalonia*, however, George Orwell acutely analyzed the twists of Soviet policy—support of the war but suppression of the revolution in Barcelona, a project that exposed a dark side of the Popular Front.[32] Like Scottsboro, the Spanish Civil War nonetheless mobilized the best energies of the left. For those who fought and reported from Spain and for those who worked actively in America, the war was a pivotal event in the decade and in their lives.

At home the movement actively supported racial equality. In 1931 at the start of the most significant American political trial of the decade, the Communist Party had taken the lead in defending the Scottsboro Boys, nine (later eight) black youths between thirteen and twenty-one, convicted of rape by an Alabama jury after a hasty trial on suspect evidence. During and in the aftermath of the Harlem Riot of 1935, after Manhattan district attorney William Dodge had accused the Communists of starting the riot, the party had gained further credibility as a radical movement committed on interracial grounds to addressing the underlying causes of the riot—strained relations with the police, inadequate schools (no schools had been built in Harlem for over twenty years), substandard conditions at Harlem Hospital, high unemployment even by depression standards.[33]

Culturally during the Popular Front, Mark Naison stresses that, functioning in a principled and effective way, "writers close to the party spoke of the attraction whites historically displayed toward black music, dance, and theatre—or even black language and the black sense of style—as the affirmation of a democratic impulse rather than a journey to the heart of darkness. In doing so, they helped give the struggle for racial equality the aura of a movement of cultural regeneration." In emphasizing "the uniqueness of this perspective," Naison goes on to indicate that "historically, opponents of civil rights had argued that racial equality meant cultural degeneracy, that black culture embodied a barbarism that would undermine American civilization if blacks were not prohibited from 'social intercourse' with whites and excluded from positions of political power. Popular Front critics turned this argument on its head, arguing that the distinctive culture of blacks contributed to much that was vital and original in American life and that their full emancipation would strengthen the entire nation."[34]

Politically the official party position on "the Negro Question" was that in the Black Belt Negroes constituted an oppressed nation within a nation, on the model of the national minorities in the Soviet Union. The party was committed to work to establish an independent nation to give blacks the control and self-determination they deserved. The official "Resolution on the Negro Question" (1930) was characteristically debated and interpreted in more than one way, not accepted as a monolithic entity.[35] In the reliable view of Philip S. Foner and Herbert Shapiro, the main features of the Comintern position were that "the Negroes in the Black Belt constituted a nation; they were not a colony, but had 'semi-colonial' status; 'bourgeois nationalism' should be opposed, and the slogan for equal rights was applicable to those Negroes in the North, but in the Black Belt the main slogan should be the right of self determination."[36]

In the North the party understandably downplayed this slogan. Although the party did effective work in the South, the nation within a nation position did not really appeal to Southern blacks, who saw themselves as American. Because American blacks did not have a separate language, moreover, the analogy with the Soviet national minorities had a serious theoretical flaw. The self-determination position had the further potential of arousing the racial animosity of white workers, who in the new nation would be subordinated to black control, not the most effective platform for a party intent on recruiting ordinary workers.[37] During the Popular Front, although the party never formally changed its official position, in practice leading black spokesmen like James. W. Ford stressed Scottsboro, the CIO, the Sharecroppers' Union, and "the fight against the whole Jim-Crow set-up," not self-determination and the nation-within-a-nation slogan.[38]

More generally, as it merged into the concerns and imagery of the New Deal under the slogan "Communism Is Twentieth-Century Americanism," the discourse of the Popular Front stressed the importance of the common man, of the ordinary worker and farmer, of the immigrant, African American, and Native American. As with the New Deal, democratic heroes like Lincoln and Jefferson had an honored place in the discourse, along with Tom Paine and Whitman. During the 1950s, however, despite—or because of—these commitments, the Popular Front became associated with sentimentality, mushiness, and lack of intellectual rigor. For its influential critics, the cultural mediocrity of the Popular Front was inseparable from its suspect Communist Party–fellow traveler politics. As a movement what was lost sight of were the achievements, diversity, and avant-garde versions of an exceptionally vital cultural dialogue, a tribute to the force of the 1950s negative interpretation.

CHAPTER 2

REPRESENTATIVE CAREERS AND REPUTATIONS

Meridel Le Sueur

One of the gifted radical writers who lost public visibility during the early Cold War is Meridel Le Sueur (1900–1996). Le Sueur emerges from the midwestern radicalism of Eugene Debs, the International Workers of the World (IWW or Wobblies), and her crusading parents, Marion and Arthur Le Sueur. Marion Le Sueur was lecturing on birth control before World War I. Arthur Le Sueur, a lawyer and the first Socialist mayor of Minot, North Dakota, was a friend and political ally of Eugene Debs. Both of Le Sueur's parents remained active on the left until their deaths in the 1950s, at that time opposing and suffering the consequences of Cold War political persecution. At the beginning of the 1930s Le Sueur gave a powerful account of her Midwest cultural origins in "Corn Village," which in 1931 won the *Scribner's* "Life in America" contest.[1] Recognized as one of the most talented writers on the left, during the 1930s Le Sueur was publishing regularly in *Scribner's*, *Yale Review*, *Pagany*, and *Harper's Bazaar* as well as in Communist Party publications like the *New Masses* and the Sunday *Worker*. A selection of her politically engaged prose-poetry appeared as *Salute to Spring* (1940).

Le Sueur joined the Communist Party during the early twenties and throughout the 1930s and in the decades that followed she was active in the radical cultural politics of the Midwest. During the early thirties like Nelson Algren and Richard Wright, she was committed to the party-sponsored John Reed Clubs, whose Chicago branch published *Left Front*. Like Algren, Wright, and Langston Hughes, Le Sueur also contributed to Jack Conroy's *Anvil*, a vital left magazine open to new work "bitter and alive from the furnace of experience—and from participants, not observers, in most instances."[2] In 1935 in the *Anvil* Le Sueur published two of the episodes from her novel in progress, *The Girl*. The episodes grew out of and validated her sensitive interest in the lives and speech of the unemployed working-class women whose stories she recorded in Minneapolis as a Workers' School teacher and Workers' Alliance comrade.

In the male-dominated cultural politics of the party, Le Sueur was independently at odds with the party, as evidenced by the emphasis in her fiction on the empowering of women. Working cooperatively within and for the party, Le Sueur was one of the writers who called for and addressed the 1935 American Writers' Congress. In the *New Masses* she affirmed her commitment to the party in her response to Horace Gregory's reservations about party discipline and the need for the middle-class writer to stay true to his own deepest emotional experience.[3] In the late 1930s, after Le Sueur's agent, Maxim Lieber, had unsuccessfully submitted *The Girl* to a single publisher, Le Sueur did not send the novel out again, so that this feminist and politically radical novel was unavailable to deepen and complicate the sense of the 1930s for the postwar critics who were deciding who and what counted in twentieth-century American literature. In *The Girl* Le Sueur, inspired by *Studs Lonigan*, intended to do for the world of marginalized working-class women what Farrell had done for lower-middle-class men but not, as with Farrell, at the expense of her point-of-view character.

When her collection of a decade of creative work, *Salute to Spring*, appeared in 1940, the public response was favorable but muted. With the war approaching and the cultural prestige of the movement in decline, the radicalism of Le Sueur's vision did not have the resonance it would have had in 1935 when Farrell completed his trilogy. But in *North Star Country* (1945) Le Sueur was nonetheless able to flesh out her reportage and pay tribute to her region in a work that is part prose, part radical history, and part mythmaking poetry. *North Star Country* is one of those neglected works of cultural history like William Carlos Williams's *In the American Grain*, works that give us a new way of seeing the nation.

For over thirty years it was also the last of Le Sueur's works to reach a mainstream audience. During the Cold War she was blacklisted and hounded by the FBI. Except for her children's books, her works were simply unavailable. During the 1950s her best job, Le Sueur recalls, was as a lavatory attendant at a bus terminal. Two weeks into the job, after a visit from the FBI her boss reluctantly fired her. In Minneapolis Le Sueur and her parents ran a boardinghouse inhabited, she remembers, by drug dealers and others who could not lose their jobs as a result of pressure from the FBI. For two years the FBI had a surveillance car and two agents outside the house of this threat to American complacency. For a period during the 1950s Le Sueur lived in a bus on an Indian reservation. She was not subpoenaed before any of the investigating committees, partly because the Indians warned her when the authorities were coming.[4]

For Le Sueur and thousands of others the Cold War was not remote but immediate and personal. Le Sueur continued to write in her journals and in party publications but she had become a nonperson and the movement she belonged to was being treated as a dangerous threat to national security.[5] Growing out of the changed political-cultural climate of the antiwar and civil rights movements, during the 1970s a politically engaged, maverick publisher, John Crawford, began making Le Sueur's work once again available to contemporary readers. Responding to and helping create feminist interest, the Feminist Press also published a comprehensive Le Sueur anthology, *Ripening* (1982).

The arc of Le Sueur's critical reception graphically illustrates the connection between literary reputation, politics, and cultural politics. During the era when proletarian or revolutionary writing was seen as the vanguard literature of America, Le Sueur was a highly visible, well-respected writer. *Salute to Spring* appeared in 1940 as the cultural prestige of the movement was declining and too late to benefit from the cultural authority the movement had commanded during the middle 1930s. *The Girl* was unknown because unpublished. Under the pressure of blacklisting, active political suppression, and the ahistorical literary criticism of the 1950s, to mainstream readers and critics Le Sueur became invisible during the Cold War. In the context of contemporary feminism, Le Sueur again became visible, viable, and also open to a feminist negative criticism remarkably similar to the Cold War narrative.[6]

Josephine Herbst

Like Le Sueur, Josephine Herbst (1893–1967) is grounded in the small-town life of the pre–World War I Midwest but she also has personal and literary ties to the expatriate and New York literary and political worlds of the 1920s and 1930s.[7] Herbst's father lost his small farm machinery business in Sioux City, Iowa, and during her childhood he worked for others for low pay as a watchman in a warehouse. Her mother stimulated Herbst's reading and fed her imagination with romantic stories about the handsome, lost Uncle Joe Frey, the model for Joe Trexler of *Pity Is Not Enough*, the first novel in the Trexler trilogy. Before she was ready to come to her own terms with her mother's myth of the family past, Herbst taught school, worked as a secretary in Seattle, and spent a year as a part-time student at the University of Washington. During World War I she took courses in beekeeping and received a B.A. in English at Berkeley.

In 1919 Herbst took her passion for literature and politics to New York. Through her friend, Genevieve Taggard, she immediately became part of a vital Greenwich Village. In 1920 Herbst had an intense affair with Maxwell Anderson. She also had an abortion. In 1922 she left her job with the *Smart Set* and lived for three years in Germany, Italy, and France. She met her future husband, John Herrmann, at La Dôme in Paris in 1924. When they returned to America they lived in the country in Connecticut and, under pressure from Herrmann's parents, they were married in 1926. Along with periods of isolation in the country, Herbst also had a lively intellectual and social life in New York, Connecticut, and Erwinna, Pennsylvania. In her memoirs, however, her account of an idyllic winter in Connecticut is complicated by the haunting sound of an owl in the night, a sound Mary Anne Rasmussen perceptively interprets as the ignored cry of a lonely woman.[8] For Herbst, this undercurrent strain of loneliness, of being cut off and ignored as a woman and as a woman writer, goes along with the vitality of her creative and social involvements.

As a writer Herbst was grounded in the traditions of the realistic novel, but she was intimately familiar with the modernism of Joyce and Eliot and she had a lively, sophisticated awareness of the experimental writing and music of the twenties. Katherine Anne Porter, Allen Tate and Carolyn Gordon, Holger Cahill, Nathan Asch, and Edmund Wilson all figure in her memoirs of the period. A little later she became close friends with writers as different as Nathaniel West and James Farrell. She and John Herrmann visited Hemingway and Dos Passos in Key West. She had known Mike Gold since her arrival in New York in 1919. Gold and Dos Passos were only two of the friends who shared her and John Herrmann's involvement in the protest against the 1927 execution of Sacco and Vanzetti.

Based on her personal experience, inclinations, and her view of working-class oppression, Herbst shared the rebelliousness and openness to experiment of the vanguard art and politics of the early 1920s. Unlike her left fiction of the thirties, however, the two novels Herbst published during the late 1920s, *Nothing Is Sacred* (1928) and *Money for Love* (1929), were political only in the important sense that the personal is political and that issues of class, money, and gender were alive in her imagination from the start of her writing career.

Her shift to an overt concern with class politics was stimulated in 1930 when Mike Gold arranged for her and John Herrmann to attend, not as delegates but as observers, the Second International Conference of Revolutionary Writers in Kharkov, USSR. In her Trexler trilogy she fused her personal concerns with what she had learned—or relearned—at Kharkov about "the Marxist theory of class."[9] From a left perspective she drew on her immediate and extended family history to give a radical rendering of America from the 1870s through the mid-1930s. The successive volumes of the trilogy—*Pity Is Not Enough* (1933), *The Executioner Waits* (1934), and *Rope of Gold* (1939)—were regularly reviewed in the influential, mainstream publications, including the Sunday *New York Herald Tribune Books*, the *New York Times Book Review*, the *Saturday Review of Literature*, and *Time*, as well as in liberal journals like the *Nation* and *New Republic* and radical journals like the *New Masses* and *Partisan Review*. Although not all of the reviews were favorable, her critical reputation as one of the most significant writers of the decade was firmly established after the publication of *The Executioner Waits*.

When Herbst left Harcourt, Brace for Scribner's after the publication of *Rope of Gold*, an indication of her prestige is that her new editor was the legendary Maxwell Perkins. Herbst's sales, however, did not match her critical reputation. None of the Trexler novels sold more than fifteen hundred copies and she lived very close to the bone, sometimes at the supportive artist's colony, Yaddo, sometimes in her unimproved farmhouse in Erwinna. In 1936 a Guggenheim gave her more financial security than she had had for years.

During the decade in addition to a major trilogy, through her personal ties and her reportage on Scottsboro, Cuba, Nazi Germany, and the Spanish Civil War, Herbst contributed meaningfully to the cultural dialogue of the thirties left. For Herbst and others the late 1930s were a troubled period. It is important, then, to stress that in contrast to Hemingway's view that "love is more important than politics," for Herbst "those of us who had become involved in politics were led there also through the devious ways of trying to find the more human community. Politics had engulfed the world, and might devour the writer too, but before he could recognize it as the dragon, he had to attempt to find the way to the lair."[10]

Love may or may not be more important than politics, but during the thirties for Herbst love complicated politics. During the early thirties she had a troubled affair with Marion Greenwood, a young sculptor she had met at Yaddo, and in 1934–35 she experienced the breakup of her marriage to John Herrmann. Her trips to Germany, Cuba, and Spain were partly to get over the pain of separation. The dislocations of her personal life were reinforced by the demoralizing defeat of the Spanish loyalists. For Herbst and others on the left the defense of Spain was crucial. By 1938, however, the war in Spain was going badly and by 1939 the loyalists were defeated. Tensions between "Stalinists" and "Trotskyites," moreover, had intensified during the last half of the decade. The show trials in Moscow were unsettling, friends were at odds, the sense of community was eroding, and Herbst was pulled in opposing directions. Although the period of the Popular Front also has frequently overlooked positive, creative energies, for Herbst it was a time of acute personal and political disturbances. Drawing on and transforming them, Herbst completed her trilogy with *Rope of Gold* in 1939.

Her response to the reviews of *Rope of Gold* indicates how important serious criticism was to her. "I am very tired," she wrote a friend, "and the clippings of reviews of my book Rope made me sick. With the exception of one or two there was no attempt to get what the book was about especially in relation to the long complicated pattern of the other two books. Some of the reviewers did not even know there were two books preceding. It is a pretty terrible thing. I put ten years of my life into those books, and one wants at least to be a little understood." As a woman writer of limited means, moreover, she was not one of the boys. "In all this time," she went on,

> I never managed to get a little crowd of rooters and cheerers around me like most of the boys who have done half as well or as much as I. I have never had money to hang around the city and fawn on the reviewers or on those boys who cheerfully gave up writing for Fortune, Time, Hollywood and all the rest. Of all the people writing creative stuff I have never alibied . . . that this was 'no time to write.' It may be a hard time but it is a time to write, any time is. Books flow over the reviewers like water year in and year out and our country is literally the only country in complete anarchy where there is no sense or reason to the reviews and where the serious writers are not protected by the slightest support or understanding. They are protected by nothing.[11]

Although in the *New Republic* Rebecca Pitts gave *Rope of Gold* one of its most perceptive reviews, for the most part Herbst was on her own.[12] In the circle she might have expected the most support, she was not protected by either the cultural apparatus of the Communist Party or by the anti-Communist *Partisan Review.* Her feelings about the cultural politics of the party emerge in her criticism of the League of American Writers, especially Richard Wright's puffing of Edna Ferber and others as "topnotch writers."[13]

In the era of the Hitler-Stalin Pact, with the western democracies on the defensive against fascist attack and with the United States about to enter the war, Harcourt, Brace had second thoughts about republishing the Trexler trilogy as a single volume. Works that only a few years earlier had been praised as vital parts of a vanguard literature now seemed, if not risky at least out of step with the cultural demands of the times. What was called for in wartime was a more affirmative, less critical, and less politically radical fiction than Herbst had written. Whatever the reasons for Harcourt's decision, unlike Dos Passos's *U.S.A.* and Farrell's *Studs*

Lonigan, Herbst's Trexler trilogy never received contemporary attention either as a whole or as an important part of the thirties cultural dialogue that extended and deepened the significance of all of its participants. At a crucial moment in her career Herbst was denied the reinforcement of full-scale critical appraisal.

Herbst, however, did receive critical appraisal of another sort. In 1942 she was fired from her job at the German desk of the Office of the Coordinator of Information and subjected to a full-scale FBI investigation of her political beliefs and activities. Although she was eventually cleared of disloyalty, she did not return to government service.[14] Herbst was not alone; at the same time Malcolm Cowley, for example, was pressured into resigning from the Office of Facts and Figures; Muriel Rukeyser was forced out of her job with the Office of War Information; and the FBI was investigating Richard Wright to see if it could prosecute him under the sedition statutes for writing *12 Million Black Voices*.[15] During the period when the United States and the USSR were allies, the Cold War assault on the thirties left was gathering momentum long before journalists named the movement after Senator Joseph McCarthy in the early 1950s.

Elinor Langer has exposed Katherine Anne Porter's role in giving the FBI false, distorted, or unverifiable evidence against Herbst, one of the most disgraceful episodes of literary-political betrayal in our history.[16] Hilton Kramer and Steven Koch have revived these charges, in Koch's case using guilt by association as a main tactic. Kramer places heavy emphasis on the subversive nature of Herbst's refusal to implicate John Herrmann and, through him, Alger Hiss for their connections with a man she saw once and came to realize was Whittaker Chambers. Kramer believes this refusal could only result from Herbst's acceptance of Communist orders from above. Both Kramer and Koch view matters through the lens of debatable assumptions about "Stalinism," assumptions that make almost every move of the accused into a sinister act.[17]

Herbst published two novels during the 1940s, *Satan's Sergeants* (1941) and *Somewhere the Tempest Fell* (1947). Neither novel advanced her reputation. By the early 1950s Herbst was practically unknown to younger readers and writers. The pattern is a familiar one. Because her more recent novels were variously diminished in scope or not fully realized imaginatively, she lacked stature as a contemporary writer. Her role as a powerful political-social novelist intimately engaged with the movement counted against, not for her, because the movement was stigmatized when it was not simply ignored. At the end of her life, looking back on Spain and on the vitality of the 1930s, Herbst felt that for her "most of the time since then has been lived on buried treasure of earlier years, on a kind of bounty I could still take nourishment from, and I suspect that the kind of dwindling I have come to feel is due to the lack of enough vital elements streaming in events and circumstances."[18]

As a writer Herbst thrived on the "vital elements streaming in events and circumstances." To value her creative work, critics and readers have to respond positively to the vital elements composing it. None of the approaches that energized literary criticism in the 1950s, however, could do justice to Herbst's probing of "events and circumstances" in the social, political, and historical panorama of the Trexler novels. Herbst's special sensitivity to the dilemmas of the twentieth-century "new woman," moreover, was not of primary interest to the men who were deciding who and what counted during the 1950s. The Trexler novels were in any case if not out of print, at least out of circulation.

Herbst's post–World War II critical neglect was compounded by continuing governmental intrusions, although she eventually managed to get a passport. Although Herbst had drifted away from the party, she did not lose her interest in politics. In 1954 she wrote a pamphlet defending Harvey O'Connor from McCarthyite attacks and during the 1960s she opposed the Vietnam War. She also continued writing. She published "Hunter of Doves" in the prestigious *Botteghe Oscure* (1954), and in "The Ruins of Memory" (1956) showed her critical and polemical powers at their best in her celebration of the realistic tradition that gave dignity to the disparaged political art of the 1930s.[19]

Herbst's main energy, however, went into her memoirs, writing as good or even better than her novels. Herbst attracted the attention of younger writers like Philip Roth and Saul Bellow, who published "A Year of Disgrace" in his *Noble Savage* (1961), so that, although Herbst was not widely known, she had influential support. Walter Rideout wrote an essay of rediscovery in 1983, and Elinor Langer published her exceptional biography the same year. Warner Books reissued the Trexler trilogy as a mass-circulation paperback and Feminist Press published *Rope of Gold* as part of its series recovering neglected women writers of the 1930s.

Although Herbst is no longer unknown, the Warner paperbacks went out of print, indicating that she is not a mass-circulation author, and because the Feminist Press *Rope of Gold* is no longer in print, either, Herbst is unavailable for classroom use. Despite her well-respected sponsorship, during the 1960s she did not have a critical breakthrough and in the 1980s Saul Bellow did not have the kind of cultural authority Alice Walker exerted on Zora Neale Hurston's behalf. Herbst is also a demanding writer whose twists of style, radical politics, and complex feminism have not elicited the same approval as Hurston's do.[20] The challenge, then, is to show that far from being defects, these qualities are basic to the power of Herbst's political art.

Richard Wright

Richard Wright's career and reputation are revealingly different from Le Sueur's and Herbst's—and from Hurston's. Wright was born into rural Mississippi poverty in 1908. His father deserted the family when Wright was five, and he was raised by a mother and grandmother who practiced strict religion and severe discipline, the latter in their view to protect Wright from getting in trouble with whites. The threat of lynching pervades Wright's account of his childhood. In his autobiographies, *Black Boy* and *American Hunger*, Wright continues the African American narrative of self-making and self-education initiated by Frederick Douglass. In the tradition of Douglass's ingenuity in learning to read, for example, Wright tells of thwarting the white authorities by forging a note to the librarian: "Dear Madam: Will you please let this nigger boy . . . have some books by H. L. Mencken?," signed in the name of a white friend.[21] Dreiser was central for Wright and in *Black Boy* and the interviews he gave in Paris he also stresses the importance to him of Mencken, Sherwood Anderson, Sinclair Lewis, D. H. Lawrence, Dostoevski, Zola, Conrad, Maupassant, Flaubert, Chekhov, and later Joyce, Henry James, Stephen Crane and, in Chicago, Proust, T. S. Eliot, Pound, and Huxley.[22] His practice was to read everything he could by the writer who compelled him.

After leaving the South for Chicago in 1927, at his post office job he fell in with a group of radical writers and artists, joined the John Reed Club in 1933, and, inspired and supported by his party friends, Wright became a genuine writer, first of Communist poetry and between 1935 and 1938 of Communist reportage, the prize-winning, politically and racially charged short stories of *Uncle Tom's Children* (1938), and the posthumously published *Lawd Today!*. This unsparing, experimental novel combines the corrosive detachment of *Studs Lonigan*—Farrell was a Chicago friend—with the influence of T. S. Eliot, the left communal novel, and the call and response of the African American tradition. Wright joined the Communist Party in 1934 and, though he had conflicts with the blacks in the Chicago branch, he was active in the cultural politics of the party throughout the thirties and early forties. After he moved to New York in 1937 he wrote over two hundred articles as Harlem editor of the *Daily Worker*. His "Blueprint for Negro Writing" (1937) is an important theoretical essay combining Wright's independent and Communist Party Marxism and his awareness of what was vital in the African American tradition.

In *Native Son* (1940) Wright brought these strains to imaginative life in a way that animates the dialogue of the thirties left and allowed him to explore his attraction to and conflicts with the party, as well as to create within the naturalistic, left, and African American traditions an expressionist, avant-garde master-piece. After Wright made some changes to satisfy the Book-of-the-Month Club, *Native Son* became a critically acclaimed best seller whose canonical status was almost immediately ratified in a way that confirms Richard Ohmann's analysis of the way books enter the twentieth-century American canon, although *Native Son* is much more radical than the post–World War II works Ohmann focuses on.[23] Despite his serious reservations about the party's support of Roosevelt's war pol-icy—Wright believed it reinforced the segregation of blacks—he nonetheless pub-licly and actively supported the party during the early 1940s. Partly because of these reservations, partly to oppose party influence on his writing, in 1942 Wright privately broke with the party and in "I Tried to Be a Communist" in the *Atlantic* in 1944 he did so publicly. Wright's independent Marxism and his persistent oppo-sition to American racial practices, however, continued until the end of his life.

Not by coincidence, although Wright was no longer a Communist, in 1942 the FBI began what was to be a nearly twenty-year campaign against him. Wright was included on a secret list of those to be rounded up and sent to internment camps in the event of a national emergency.[24] Arthur Rampersad notes that the FBI "began an investigation in December 1942 to determine if *12 Million Black Voices* was pros-ecutable under the sedition statutes. Although the sedition investigation is con-cluded in 1943, the FBI will continue to monitor Wright's activities, chiefly through the use of informers, for the remainder of his life," which is to say that, in the guise of looking for spies, the FBI spied on a writer whose seditious crime was that he exposed American racism and later took a nonaligned position in the Cold War.[25]

The 1940s surveillance was secret; in public Wright's reputation was furthered by his autobiographical *Black Boy* (1945). *Native Son* and *Black Boy* never disap-peared from view the way Le Sueur and Herbst did but after Wright moved to Paris in 1947 he was gradually displaced as America's most prominent African American writer. When his next novel, *The Outsider*, appeared in 1953 the reviews were "mixed" and the sales "disappointing."[26] Wright's Pan-African nonfiction, more-over, although it invites reassessment, did not have the same impact on readers in the 1950s as *Native Son* and *Black Boy* had a decade earlier.[27] A combination of current work that could be dismissed, the powerful attacks on *Native Son* and *Black Boy* by an articulate cultural critic, James Baldwin, and the prominence of new work by younger writers, Baldwin and Ellison, contributed to the relative marginalizing of Wright's radical work of the 1930s.

In particular, Ellison's sophisticated symbolism, modulated views on race, and his Cold War treatment of the Brotherhood in *Invisible Man* (1952) fit in well with the prevailing literary and political opinions of the 1950s, in contrast to what was taken as the dated naturalism and Popular Front politics of *Native Son*. In the hopeful era of *Brown vs. Board of Education* (1954), moreover, for Wright to be accurate about race in *Native Son*, the improvement *Brown* signified had to be wrong. If they bothered with it at all, Americans had a strong incentive to treat *Native Son* as a historical curiosity hardly pertinent to a period when Cold War antagonisms discouraged taking seriously Wright's probing of the racial hatreds that undercut the claims of American democracy in its conflict with Soviet tyranny.

As an instance of the return of the culturally and politically repressed, under the pressure of the black urban uprisings of the 1960s, *Native Son* again came into prominence. More recently, for an important group of contemporary readers Wright's fictional treatment of women has been a source of controversy that has affected his current reputation.[28] On the traditional set of issues, what is surprising is the persistence into the 1990s of the caricature view of *Native Son* as seriously flawed by its supposedly dated, unenlivened naturalism and Communist Party politics.

In this view, art and politics or literature and political-racial beliefs are opposed, with left and racial politics and ideas the villains, as in Louis Menand's claim that "Wright's convictions flatten out the 'literary' qualities of his fiction, and lead him to sacrifice complexity for force," in contrast, as in the 1950s, to Ellison.[29] Menand himself is writing in a tradition initiated by Clement Greenberg, Alfred Kazin, and James Baldwin within the anti-Stalinist, high modernist New York intellectual discourse of the 1940s and 1950s. Although they are of course disputed and perhaps beleaguered, his judgments and the assumptions they emerge from continue to claim the allegiance of many in and out of the contemporary academy.[30]

In the 1950s Wright may have been ignored by critics but he continued to be the object of FBI, State Department, and CIA attention. The organizations he belonged to were infiltrated and spied on; his passport applications were repeatedly questioned, a source of serious anxiety to Wright; false stories about his speeches were planted in *Time*; political pressure dried up funding for his *Native Son* film project; in Paris false stories were circulated in the black community to discredit Wright and to isolate him at a time when he badly needed companionship. Addison Gayle makes a strong case for the view that sustained government persecution significantly hastened Wright's death by intensifying his high blood pressure and deepening his anxieties.[31]

Muriel Rukeyser

From a very different class, religious, and regional milieu than Wright, Herbst, and Le Sueur, Muriel Rukeyser (1913–80) was born into a wealthy New York Jewish family. Her father owned sand quarries and, for all her ambivalence, Rukeyser was proud that his concrete trucks poured the cement that helped build New York. Rukeyser had governesses and was driven to private school in a limousine. She went to the Ethical Culture School, graduated from Fieldston in 1930, and for two years attended Vassar when it was a symbol of elite privilege. Of her earlier years, "there were a few sets of books at home," she recalls, "but after I had gone through these, I read whatever the maids recommended. This was the sheltered life, this was a life of comfort. All I knew was that it was not comfortable to me. I was beginning to care about a set of things which poetry was giving me."[32]

In her formative years "there was not a trace of Jewish culture that I could feel— no stories, no songs, no special food—. . . except for a silver ceremonial goblet, handed down from a great-grandfather who had been a cantor, and a legend that my mother's family was directly descended from Akiba" (p. 5). Later, however, after Rukeyser's mother "turned to religion . . . I began to go to Temple with my mother, instead of to the Museum, and I went every Saturday for seven years" (p. 6). Rukeyser criticizes the complacency of the organized congregation but during services she responded powerfully to the Bible, to "its clash and poetry and nakedness, its fiery vision of conflict resolved only in God" (p. 7). In her view "my themes and the use I have made of them have depended on my life as a poet, as a woman, an American and as a Jew" (p. 8). In focusing on her Jewish heritage, Rukeyser concludes that "to me, the value of my Jewish heritage, in life and in writing, is its value as a guarantee. Once one's responsibility as a Jew is really assumed," Rukeyser affirms, "one is guaranteed, not only against fascism, but against many kinds of temptation to close the spirit. It is a strong force in oneself against many kinds of hardness" (p. 9). In contrast to organized religion, for Rukeyser her Jewishness is inseparable from her political radicalism, her politics of resistance, and is integral to her imagination: "the imagination moves, the spirit opens, one knows again what it is to be Jewish; and what it will always be at its best in one's life and one's writing: memory and fire and poetry and the wandering spirit that never changes in its love of man" (p. 9).

Because of her father's bankruptcy and in accord with her vision of political involvement, Rukeyser left Vassar in 1932 to work on the staff of *Student Review*, sponsored by the National Student League, "the militant vanguard of student revolt against war and reaction."[33] In March 1933 she and two friends drove South to cover the Scottsboro trial. Her poem on Scottsboro, "The Trial," came out in *New Masses* the next year, so that Rukeyser was appearing with Langston Hughes, Edwin Rolfe, and Kenneth Fearing, who were publishing in *New Masses* during the same period.[34] During 1934 she also reviewed writers as diverse as Faulkner,

Wheelwright, and Hamsun for *New Masses*.[35] She edited *Housatanic*, a New England literary journal, and during spring 1935 as associate editor of *New Theatre* she was working with other left writers and intellectuals involved in theater, film, and music.

Leonard Bernstein recalls that as an undergraduate in 1937, when he came from Cambridge to New York for Anna Sokolow's New York debut, he sat in the first row of the balcony of the Group Theatre with a group that included Muriel Rukeyser and Aaron Copland. Afterward Copland invited everybody in the row to a birthday party at his loft, an event Bernstein associates with Rukeyser, the beginning of his long friendship with Copland, and his introduction to New York and to an elite artistic community of "poets and literary people, musicians" and photographers. Rukeyser already had a reputation as a "poet, and a very good one."[36] She had been seriously writing poetry since Vassar and, to help with her collection, *Theory of Flight*, she had taken flying lessons. Her left commitments animate the modernist verse of *Theory of Flight*, which won the Yale Younger Poet's Award in 1935.

In early 1936 for "The Book of the Dead" in *U.S. 1*, Rukeyser did firsthand research on Union Carbide's abuses at Gauley Bridge, West Virginia, where thousands of workers were dying of silicosis. Later that year she went to England and then to Spain to cover the antifascist Olympics. She crossed the border on the first day of the war, experienced the anarchist victory in Barcelona, and stayed to work with the Spanish Medical Bureau. Her reports on Barcelona for *New Masses* and *Life and Letters Today* and her long poem, "Mediterranean" in *U.S. 1* are examples of the depth of her involvement.[37]

Unusual for difficult, radical modernist poetry, her 1938 collection, *U.S. 1*, was reviewed in the major mass circulation publications as a representative of the promise of left literature, a promise several reviewers saw in her case as flawed but significant.[38] Her commitment "to extend the documentary" led her not only to the formal innovations of "The Book of the Dead" but also to her own documentary, *A Place to Live*, produced by the Philadelphia Housing Authority in 1941. In addition to the 1935 Yale Younger Poet's Award, in 1940 Rukeyser won the Oscar Blumenthal *Poetry* Prize, in 1942 an award from the American Academy of Arts and Letters, and in 1943 a Guggenheim Fellowship.

In 1942, however, in an unsigned editorial and two subsequent additions, *Partisan Review* attacked her as "a poster girl" of the left, as an opportunistic poet who "plumped with romping vigor for the Revolution, rode the bandwagon of proletarian literature, . . . and cried Yes like Molly Bloom to the working class." In *Partisan Review*'s wickedly unfair satire, Rukeyser was a "poster girl" partly because she advocated using poetry on posters and billboards to support the war effort, partly to undercut her as a prominent woman in the limelight.[39] In keeping with its anti-Stalinist discourse on the thirties left, the *Partisan Review* editors made Rukeyser into a symbolic representative of what they saw as the unprincipled expediency and superficial kitsch of the orthodox left, in contrast to what they saw as their own independent radicalism and principled reasons for qualified support of the war. The editorial attacks were also designed to block Rukeyser's appointment as librarian of Congress, a position she was alleged to be angling for.

In separate letters, Rebecca Pitts and F. O. Matthiessen responded. Pitts wrote a vigorous, nuanced appraisal of Rukeyser's attempt to integrate disparate realms of experience—politics, science, and mysticism—and to derive meaning from them, in contrast to the venom of the *Partisan Review*'s personal attack, which for Pitts variously ignored or distorted Rukeyser's poetry.[40] Matthiessen systematically went to Rukeyser's poems to refute each of the editorial charges and to show "that, instead of criticizing an author's work, you have made unjustifiable charges about her character. You have made her sound like a slick careerist, whereas her writing shows her to have been throughout the past decade a convinced anti-fascist and radical democrat."[41] For Rebecca Pitts and F. O. Matthiessen in 1942, Rukeyser's status as an important twentieth-century writer depended on her 1930s left poetry and the contexts it emerged from and illuminated.

The next year, however, in a substantial essay on Rukeyser in *Poetry*, John Malcolm Brinnin struck a note that anticipated the post–World War II view of the 1930s left. Without citing evidence he presented "The Book of the Dead" as a "failure," "flat and prosaic," one of the works in which "the poet spoke in the single-mindedness of a political program," "in slogans," in contrast to her successful use of private language in several other poems.[42] In 1946 Horace Gregory reinforced this view of "slogans" in his *History of American Poetry, 1900–1940*.[43] These views had practical results: during 1943–44, under the pressure of the *Partisan Review* attack, policy disagreements, and the "*New York World Telegram* exposé [of Rukeyser] as 'Communist,'" she left her Office of War Information position, one of several left writers similarly driven from wartime government service.[44]

In the immediate post–World War II period, although her own productivity diminished—she was a single mother raising a son—Rukeyser nonetheless continued to be recognized as a significant contemporary poet. She was one of the poets represented in the 1950 anthology *Mid-Century American Poets*, her work appeared in Kimon Friar and John Malcolm Brinnin's discriminating anthology, *Modern Poetry: American and British* (1951), in Oscar Williams's *A Little Treasury of*

Modern Poetry (1952), in George Elliott's *Fifteen Modern American Poets* (1956), and in Bradley, Beatty, and Long's influential *The American Tradition in Literature* (1956), and she was on the Bollingen Prize Committee in 1954.[45] Her left poetry, however, was either excluded or minimally reprinted in these anthologies. Rukeyser continued as a well-respected poet, and her productivity increased after her son reached college, but, with the exception of M. L. Rosenthal's 1953 essay, her radical work of the 1930s was for the most part ignored along with the left movement itself.[46] As late as a 1974 retrospective essay on Rukeyser, Virginia R. Terris negatively criticized Rukeyser's political poetry as marked by "a veil of abstractions" and "theorizing" in contrast to "her personal voice" and "her greatest creative strengths [which] have manifested themselves in her poems of intimate human relationship and myth-making."[47] Even Louise Kertesz, who deals at length with Rukeyser's political poetry, minimizes her radical politics, as does Walter Kalaidjian.[48] Kate Daniels's biography in progress and recent dissertations suggest a promising change in this neglect, although for Anne Herzog "radical politics" does not refer primarily to the left politics of the 1930s.[49] Rukeyser herself continued her political involvement—she was a member of a peace mission to Vietnam in 1972 and in 1975 she went to South Korea to protest the threatened execution of the poet, Kim Ch-Ha.[50]

In contrast to the marginalizing of her politics in the post–World War II view of Rukeyser, however, near the end of the American Inquisition, in 1958, the American Legion tried to get Rukeyser fired from her position at Sarah Lawrence. Dr. Harold Taylor, Sarah Lawrence's president, stood his ground and responded that "none of the faculty took intellectual orders from outside authority, Communist or otherwise."[51] Rukeyser has the distinction of being publicly vilified both from the left by the *Partisan Review* and from the right by the American Legion.

Langston Hughes

Within his family tradition Langston Hughes (1902–67) had a powerful precedent for his own radicalism: his grandmother's first husband died at Harpers Ferry as one of John Brown's raiders. His financially successful father, on the other hand, left the family for Mexico when Hughes was a baby and was critical of the lack of ambition he felt characterized most blacks. When they briefly became reunited immediately before and after Hughes graduated from high school, as a practical businessman his father disapproved of Hughes's literary interests. Until he was twelve Hughes was raised by his grandmother in Lawrence, Kansas, and then in Topeka and Cleveland by his impoverished mother, a former schoolteacher.

Hughes began his career as a poet with perhaps his best-known poem, "A Negro Speaks of Rivers" (1921), which he wrote when he was eighteen on his second trip to Mexico to visit his father. After his father paid for a year at Columbia—they broke off relations because Hughes did not take engineering—Hughes shipped out as a mess boy on a freighter to Africa and later to Rotterdam. He worked as a cook at a Paris nightclub, visited Italy and Spain on a shoestring, lost his money and passport in Genoa, and finally worked his way home on a freighter.

Hughes made his early reputation as a race poet and he is still known primarily as the creator of "The Negro Speaks of Rivers," of the bittersweet jazz poems of *The Weary Blues* (1926), and of the vernacular prose of the Simple collections (1950ff.). As a poet, Hughes is closely identified with the Harlem Renaissance and with the argument of his 1926 essay, "The Negro Artist and the Racial Mountain," in which Hughes opened up a space for writing "my own poems [which] are racial in theme and treatment, derived from the life I know." These poems are not genteel but are alive with the cabaret milieu and rhythms of jazz. In accord with his insight that the racial assimilation of genteel "high-class" blacks served the interests of white capital, as early as 1925 Hughes was also drawing on "the life I know" in militant poems of political, racial, and social exposure, poems he was publishing in the *Workers' Monthly*, "The Communist Magazine."[52]

For a decade after the Crash in 1929, at the center of his creative life during the 1930s, Langston Hughes, in his full creative maturity, wrote—and later suppressed—a body of politically radical poems. These poems appeared in, for example, *International Literature*, the journal of the Soviet International Union of Revolutionary Writers, and the *New Masses*, the political-cultural journal of the American Communist Party. Although Hughes did not join the party, for over a decade he was closely associated with its political and cultural positions. He was on the masthead of *New Masses* as contributing editor and he either addressed or had his speeches read at the four biannual meetings of the American Writers' Congress. The Congress, it bears repeating, was organized by the Communist Party but included and appealed to influential non-Communists who supported the Spanish Loyalists, were opposed to "war and fascism," and were "drawn together by the threat, implicit in the present social system, to our very lives as creative men and women."[53]

In 1932–33 Hughes spent a year in the Soviet Union as part of an abortive film project, *Black and White*. During the 1930s and as late as 1946 he wrote sympathetically about the Soviet Union, particularly about what he saw and experienced as the absence of racial bias.[54] In the face of State Department obstruction, Hughes went to Spain to report on the African Americans who were fighting Franco and the Moors who were forced to fight for the Spanish dictator. On the way he addressed the militant Second International Writers' Congress in Paris in 1937. Hughes had earlier been deeply moved by the Scottsboro case and the way the party defended the nine young black men in the most highly charged political trial in America during the 1930s.[55]

Although specialists are familiar with Hughes's political poetry, with the notable exception of the *Heath Anthology*, this phase of his career has still not entered the anthologies or the public view of Hughes. One reason is that as early as 1940 he organized his autobiography, *The Big Sea*, so that it ends before he wrote his most radical poetry. Symptomatically, he omitted the exuberantly militant red "CHRIST-MAS CARD" from the version of "Advertisement for the Waldorf-Astoria" he used in *The Big Sea*. In 1946 Hughes nonetheless published his second tribute to Lenin, the same year he wrote a series of sympathetic essays on the Soviet Union.[56] In 1949 *Life* identified Hughes as one of America's fifty most representative "dupes and fellow-travellers."[57]

In response, as the Cold War intensified Hughes worked out an accommodation with the official anti-Communists of the post–World War II period. After a discreet private meeting with the staff of the McCarthy Committee, who agreed not to ask him to "name names," Hughes in return testified publicly that he had completely changed his ideology and preferred his more recent work.[58] The experience led Hughes to write—but to delay publishing—a hard-hitting satire of the committee, "Un-American Investigators."[59] Hughes filtered out his political radicalism from the second volume of his autobiography, *I Wonder as I Wander* (1956). He similarly excluded his left poetry from *The Selected Poems of Langston Hughes* (1959). Because with a single, recent exception his radical political poems are absent from the standard anthologies, readers who grew up in the fifties or later are familiar with a Langston Hughes created under the special pressures of the Cold War. Although he never publicly and forcefully did justice to the full depth, intensity, and complexity of the radical political poetry he wrote between 1925 and 1938, in the last year of his life Hughes did include a few of his powerful, suppressed poems in *The Panther and the Lash*, the 1967 collection in which he responded to the political energies of the 1960s.[60]

As a young poet, Hughes graduated from college at the start of the depression. He broke his ties with his patron, Mrs. Charlotte Mason, and determined to support himself as a writer. Throughout his adult life, on his slender income he was also responsible for supporting his mother and a mentally retarded brother. Instead of turning out commercial work, however, Hughes put his best energies for a decade into committed political poetry, hardly the way to fortune. During the thirties

Hughes did receive help from a wealthy patron, Noel Sullivan. But Hughes also depended on the income from public readings, many of them in black churches. In 1933 a group of influential African American ministers attacked Hughes because of what they saw as the blasphemies in "Goodbye, Christ."[61] No wonder that after this controversy, he avoided religiously incendiary work. He nonetheless continued to write and publish intense, idiomatic, irreverent political poetry. During the Cold War as during the 1930s, he was dependent on income from writing and readings. Hughes chose to suppress and survive, so that he could continue to publish and to maintain his public credibility in support of the racial causes he was committed to.

In an attempt to make up for that suppression, in 1973 Faith Berry brought together a generous selection, *Good Morning Revolution: Uncollected Social Protest Writings by Langston Hughes*. Although it went out of print, this collection has been reissued. It gives us easy access to poems that are otherwise hard to come by and in a context that stresses Hughes's political art through commentary and the reinforcing power of related poems and essays. Like most public, political art, Hughes's radical work benefits when it is presented in historical, political, and literary context rather than in a collection as a series of discrete poems unrelated to others or to the passions of history and politics.[62]

During the 1930s, in his political poetry Langston Hughes came into his own as a mature poet. Occasionally critics recognize that "the body of writing which resulted from these turbulent years contains the most searing, ironic, and powerful poetry and prose that Hughes ever wrote."[63] The standard view, however, is that with a few exceptions during the 1930s Hughes "abandoned his poetic muse to preach politics" and that "Hughes was not the only talented black writer who usually achieved miserable results when he attempted political poetry."[64] Even when, like Onwuchekwa Jemie, critics value Hughes because he "held on to his Marxist vision," those who deal with Hughes's radical work nonetheless confine themselves to brief overviews.[65] The left poetry of Langston Hughes, however, deserves and responds to the kind of detailed attention we are accustomed to giving Hughes's modernist contemporaries.

The same applies to the 1930s left fiction, poetry, and reportage of Le Sueur, Herbst, Wright, and Rukeyser. To establish the power of their political art, we now need to look closely at their works and the contexts they emerge from and illuminate.

CHAPTER 3

THE RADICAL ART OF MERIDEL LE SUEUR

From the left discourse of the 1930s and 1940s, a discourse centering on but not confined to the cultural politics of the Communist Party, Meridel Le Sueur developed the idea of "people's culture." "People's culture" is rooted in the left's concern with proletarian literature, in the Popular Front's commitment to folk culture and the study of folklore, and in what at best was the left's sensitivity to black culture and to the importance of immigrants, ethnicity, and regions in the America of the 1930s and 1940s.[1] Le Sueur explores, criticizes, and celebrates people's culture as a counter to the predominantly male, capitalistic, WASP culture of official America. As part of the dialogue on the left, moreover, Le Sueur challenged the male-dominated cultural politics of the Communist Party as well as the European-oriented preferences of such left intellectuals as Philip Rahv and William Phillips. Sacvan Bercovitch persuasively argues that within the ideological hegemony of the myth of the American nation, "differences did not count. Nation meant *American*, *American* meant *the people*, and *the people* meant those who, thanks to the Revolution, enjoyed a commonplace prosperity: the simple sunny rewards of American middle-class life."[2] In opposition to this influential cultural myth, Le Sueur offers her version of people's culture. Finnish labor organizers, Polish peasants displaced from the Old World to Minneapolis, and characters like Stasia, Hoinck, and Amelia in *The Girl* all give the vitality of their language, suffering, and impudence to Le Sueur's radical art.

"Corn Village"

People's culture is one of the recurring concerns in Le Sueur's neglected work from the 1930s. Ethnicity, feminism, and Marxism, moreover, contribute different, reinforcing, sometimes conflicting accents to her voice and language. Take an early achievement, "Corn Village" (1931). Its quality was recognized immediately—it was a prize-winning essay, the first one *Scribner's Magazine* published in its series, "Life in America." At the end of the decade, Le Sueur used "Corn Village" to open her collection, *Salute to Spring* (1940). In "Corn Village" Le Sueur combines autobiography, regional history, essay, social criticism, and fiction, a fusion of genres that makes it difficult for traditional critics to value her work.[3]

From the vantage point of 1930, at the start of the new depression decade, in "Corn Village" Le Sueur initiates a dialogue with the old America, with the Kansas heartland she grew up in before World War I. As early as "Corn Village" Le Sueur's preliminary, intuitive sense of people's culture animates her work and conditions her selection, treatment, and organization of her material. Playing off against her midcontinent Yankees—the hard, spare bodies, the nasal speech, the people "all frightfully alone and solitary"—Le Sueur brings alive the ethnic alternatives of the Irish evangelical preacher and the full-bodied Polish prostitutes.[4] The Yankees, the land, and the foreigners weave in and out of the nonlinear flow of Le Sueur's poetically heightened discourse. Combined with the authenticating voice and responses of the "I" of the essay, they organize and body forth a vision of America, of a people's culture. In this early version, the need for change is urgent. Except for the foreigners, "the people" are too tight, too hard, too empty, too repressed to satisfy Le Sueur. They are nonetheless her people. For all Le Sueur's reservations, her people help constitute her even as she draws on the resources of American scenes, values, and languages to suggest alternatives to the dominant culture. Her own discourse is a primary alternative. Nonlinear, open to metaphor and symbol, and receptive to ethnic, radical, and feminist vitality, Le Sueur's discourse is a model of the people's culture she celebrates, criticizes, and strives to actualize. Le Sueur has an underlying faith that, however flawed, the people and the land contain the possibilities of an America growing from precisely delineated conflicts, energies, and history.

In "Corn Village" through her language and sensibility Le Sueur thus transforms the old Middle West. She shows the nourishment it fails to provide and the fear and love it inspires. Working in the tradition of Sherwood Anderson and Sinclair Lewis, she goes beyond them to once again make commonplace America a special place in the imagination. To say that she writes about Kansas when she was growing up there is thus misleading, because her Kansas is simultaneously personal and public, particular and an embodiment of America itself. Le Sueur is almost always conscious of America. Because a widely shared view locates left discourse in New York, Le Sueur's version of the continent is a necessary corrective. Her vision of America is darker and deeper than the stereotypical optimism and superficiality *Partisan Review* and even more recent critics attribute to the writers of the 1930s left. In the face of right-wing Americanism, moreover, we need to stress Le Sueur as an American writer fully conscious of America as a central subject. In *North Star Country* (1945) she gives her fullest expression to the project she initiates in "Corn Village." *North Star Country*, usually classified as regional history, is actually an ambitious probing of the meaning of America. Using the perspectives of folklore, ethnic, radical, and regional history, in *North Star County* Le Sueur goes beneath the consensus myth of America to bring alive the overlooked people's culture she sees at the center of the nation.

From "Corn Village" to *North Star Country* and beyond, for Le Sueur a crucial failing of the dominant society is what she elsewhere calls "the rot of a maggoty individualism."[5] In "Corn Village" she shows this individualism grounded in the essential isolation and "the terrible insecurity at the bottom of every man's soul" in the town she lived in. The town itself is "falling to pieces with its rotten wooden houses, and the grey shredded faces," the physical embodiments of all that fails to nourish a person (p. 9). "In the mid-center of America," she stresses, concentrating on the symbolism of the center, "a man can go blank for a long, long time. There is no community to give him life. . . . No fund of instinct and experience has been accumulated, and each generation seems to be more impoverished than the last" (p. 8). In a reversal of the life imagery of the American pastoral, Le Sueur focuses on the symbolic significance of the winter solstice in order to place in sweeping perspective her sense of "the dim, dim faces, the blank interior of the continent, the winter madness coming on, the winter death, the sun leaving the great dark continent, the blank, cold prairies, the shocks of corn desolate in the fields, the earth upturned in the cold sunlight" (p. 9).

Here is Le Sueur's dominant organizing image for the old America, an America she presents as in need of radical transformation. By the early years of the 1920s, the consensus myth of American possibility centering on the virgin land and the American individualist had lost its power to compel a range of American writers. Le Sueur's vision of the winter void at the center of America is her independent version of Eliot's wasteland, of Fitzgerald's sense of the blighting of the fresh green breast of the New World, and of Dreiser's rendering of the forest as a malignant, destructive setting for the murder in *An American Tragedy*. Like Eliot, Fitzgerald, and Dreiser, Le Sueur works within and subverts an influential hegemonic myth. For her part, writing in 1931 about the early years of the century, Le Sueur conveys a sense of the continent that became increasingly convincing as the depression deepened to give her account an exceptionally contemporary resonance. In "Corn Village" she sets the stage for the series of conversion experiences that structure *Salute to Spring*. Especially in "Annunciation" and "I Was Marching," she provides radical alternatives both to the old hegemonic myth and its grim mid-1920s antitype.

In "Corn Village," her prologue to her radical work of the 1930s, Le Sueur asks "what does an American think about the land, what dreams come from the sight of it, what painful dreaming?" In opposition to her own communal dream she continues, "are they only money dreams, power dreams? Is that why the land lies desolate like a loved woman who has been forgotten? Has she been misused through dreams of power and conquest?" (pp. 10–11). Le Sueur's imagery and vision thus anticipate Annette Kolodny's feminist revisionism of the myth of the virgin land.[6] Le Sueur's feminism is inseparable from her sense of the Indian's veneration for the land, a view that informs her critical insight that "the guilty white spirit" has violated something sacred (p. 11).

To deepen and sharpen the basic issues, Le Sueur invokes Lincoln as a major organizing presence. Lincoln functions as a quintessential embodiment of people's culture, particularly of the patriarchal, Yankee version about which Le Sueur has deeply mixed feelings. "Remember the sadness and innate depression of Lincoln as symbolic," she writes. "He was naturally a lover, but he never loved the land, though he walked miles over it, slept and lived on it, and buried the bodies of those he loved in it; and yet he was never struck with that poetry and passion that makes a man secure upon his land, there was always instead this convulsion of anxiety, this fear" (p. 11).

Le Sueur's mind weaves in and out, bringing together personal experience, personal observation, and representative characters and episodes, all aimed at uncovering the meaning of America, "trying to get you alive with significance and myth" (p. 24). As much as any of the myth and symbol critics of the Cold War period but from a radical perspective, Le Sueur is explicitly concerned with meaning, myth, and symbol. As opposed to the hegemonic myth of America, her own myth of Lincoln and the myth of the land merge with accounts that under the pressure of her language and interpretation assume deepened significance. The isolation of the townspeople is momentarily relieved, and "they stand close together, welded together in the lines of their bodies" (p. 18). What brings them together is the violence of two lovers, the girl shot dead, her lover a suicide. The violence and shattered love are cathartic and function the way the violence and love of the revivals do to bring people together around a love they ordinarily deny. What distinguishes Le Sueur's account is the way her sensitivity to the body reinforces her view of the need for a cohesive sexual love her townspeople only rarely manage to express. As pioneers they have been too busy, moving, moving.

As men and women caught up in a false ideology of success as money and power, they have worked too hard and enjoyed too little. The men—"these meaty men live in this delicate world, their bloody lives, and are looked upon by the rabbit, the prairie dog, and the deer" (p. 10).

The woman's equivalent of Lincoln as a significant organizing center is Le Sueur's own grandmother. Le Sueur details her spare grandmother's unwillingness to touch another body, her discipline, and her release only in the ecstasy of the revival (pp. 20–21). Le Sueur knows from the inside the extent to which women are instruments of colonization, even as she herself resists. Just as in "Corn Village" Le Sueur is searching for a counterideology, she shows that her grandmother does everything in her considerable power to transmit to her descendants her own intense, repressive dedication to the dominant ideology. The contrast between the grandmother and Le Sueur is as marked as that between the grandmother and the foreign women who come alive in this narrative. Le Sueur typically fuses her versions of feminism and ethnicity. In "Corn Village" it is the foreigners who bring some flesh and color to the drab town and the hard Yankee bodies. Le Sueur celebrates "the great Polish woman who kept a 'house' . . . I liked her body, so rich and loose, and her broad-hipped lazy walk. The acrid Yankee body is a hard body to live with, always ungiven, held taut for some unknown fray with the devil or the world or the flesh. These illicit women, so menacing, were the only ones at that time who could wear bright colors" (p. 14).

Their counterpart is the Irish revival preacher, his red hair a little longer than the rest, "a man of monstrous amorous vitality which he threw into his sermons, a great, wild vitality wonderful to behold and a silver Irish tongue too, so that he broke all the bitterness asunder, the silvery words breaking over the landlocked, corroded people. He was a fine actor, and had a fine roll to his words and a great sonorous natural cadence that added richness to our terse Yankee speech for many days after" (p. 22). Le Sueur's own voice responds as she enters into and brings alive the cadences and amorous vitality of this alternative to Yankee restraint. In Le Sueur's discourse, the Polish prostitute and Irish preacher are as integral to her vision of people's culture as they are at odds with the decorum of official culture.

In "Corn Village" as the precise details accumulate, they enlarge to characterize an entire "landlocked, corroded people." In a dozen different contexts the Yankee emerges with his hard, acrid body and terse speech, men and women held in, not quite able to break out, isolated in the center of the continent in the dead of the winter storm that for Le Sueur captures the essential meaning of the continent. Her vignette of breaking down in the car in the country near Simonson's farm, a storm coming on, epitomizes her sense of their bleak, enclosed situation. Everything about the episode becomes an occasion for reflections that carry the meaning beyond Simonson to the deepest meaning of America. Simonson's body reminds her of Lincoln's and she reflects on "the mystery of the slim tenuous Yankee body, hard and gawky like a boy's, never getting any man suavity in it, but hard and bitter and stubborn, always lanky and ill-nourished, surviving bitterly." She knows there is tenderness there, too, but it is held back, not easy for Simonson to express. Le Sueur repeatedly probes Lincoln's meaning to convey Simonson's full significance. They share "a despondency from lack of nourishment," a lack of nourishment that goes beyond food to what are for Le Sueur the communal and sexual sources of life (p. 12).

Le Sueur's version of American hunger is rooted in the midcontinental America of her youth and extends from there into the city of "Women on the Breadlines" and "Women Are Hungry," into the central drama and imagery of story after story, and back to the countryside in a whole series of reports on ravaged depression farms.[7] In these reports 1930s America emerges as a Third World country in the grip of famine and drought. She forecasts later developments in her concluding image of Simonson. "We went toward the tumbling buildings so temporary and lost," she remembers. "There were no stars now the darkness had come, no North Star, no guide, and Simonson talking in a void, the last man on the frontier, a far, lone man at an outpost, waiting to move on, to move back, to move . . ." (pp. 14–15). Le Sueur's own alternative is the concluding, cohesive movement of "I Was Marching," her narrative of her own Marxist conversion, and, appropriately, the concluding work in *Salute to Spring*.

As prologue, "Corn Village" exemplifies Le Sueur's practice of political art and her sense of ethnicity. None of the key terms—"political," "art," and "ethnicity"—can be seen in isolation. The nonlinear form, the metaphorically heightened language, the sensitivity to the body, to the landscape, and to the need for love and community as well as the reliance on an "I" and a personal voice to radically criticize conventional middle America and move toward a countermyth and meaning—as early as "Corn Village" these defining characteristics of Le Sueur's avant-garde art body forth a politics in the deep sense of alternative power relations and an alternative ideology, or, rather, in "Corn Village" they register Le Sueur's sense of the need for these alternatives. The ethnic figures, the Indian veneration for the land, and the probing vitality and values of the "I" develop Le Sueur's alternative through contrasts with the prevailing Yankee restraints, isolation, and rigidities. In her discourse itself, however, Le Sueur does not deny or segregate. The free-flowing form, the fusion of genres, and the reliance on metaphoric language constitute Le Sueur's avant-garde political art as much as her increasingly radical overt statements.

In *Salute to Spring* Le Sueur traces a birth out of the loneliness and the void she had brought to a focus in "Corn Village." She organizes *Salute to Spring* around the power and eloquence of three first-person narratives, "Corn Village" at the start, "Annunciation" at the center, and "I Was Marching" at the end. Cumulatively they develop her feminist sense of birth as the prototype and promise of the new revolutionary self and world in "Annunciation" and "Tonight Is Part of the Struggle" and of her own Marxist conversion inseparable from a radicalized people's culture, all culminating in "I Was Marching." The contrast between the dead winter landscape and isolated American lives of "Corn Village," the reanimated fecundity of "Annunciation," and the conversion and fusions of "I Was Marching" give an affirmative organizing rhythm to *Salute to Spring*. The move from "Corn Village" to "I Was Marching" also measures the distance between a rendering of the dead end of the consensus myth of America and Le Sueur's radical, Marxist alternative, a myth of a cohesive, activist people's culture.

The tensions between Third Period militancy and Popular Front radicalism in "Tonight Is Part of the Struggle" and "Salute to Spring" and the role of Le Sueur's feminism throughout her work are reminders that as a 1930s Marxist writer Le Sueur drew on and transformed the pressures she experienced as the politics and cultural politics of the party shifted. For the light it throws on the complexities of left cultural politics, it is worth stressing that "I Was Marching" (1934) emerges from and expresses a version of the revolutionary militancy of the Third Period, not of the more accommodationist Popular Front that dominated official policy until almost the time the party press, International Publishers, brought out *Salute to Spring* in 1940.

"Women on the Breadlines"

What was unacceptable to the party in 1940 as it was open to criticism in 1932, however, was the Marxist-feminist art of "Women on the Breadlines" (1932), Le Sueur's second piece in the *New Masses* but excluded from *Salute to Spring* at the end of the decade. In this early achievement of Le Sueur's political art, the simple declarative sentences pile up with the force of poetry, each detail charged and moving. In describing the women sitting and waiting for work in the city free employment bureau, Le Sueur uses the painful imagery of "hunger like the beak of a terrible bird" to twist the idiomatic language into a statement of heightened poetic intensity focusing on one of her central preoccupations throughout the report and the decade—the destructive power of hunger, of starvation in the midst of plenty.[8] Le Sueur brings alive the immediacy of hunger and all it stands for—no jobs, the endless waiting, the physical, mental and spiritual impact of a system that produces the conditions she highlights. Starvation, as in "Arise, ye prisoners of starvation," is basic to Marxist discourse. Le Sueur rediscovers for herself the full meaning of starvation. For her it is not a dead metaphor or an empty piece of rhetoric. The prisoners of starvation are those John Reed calls "the Dark People," the ordinary workers at the base of society. Except in times of crisis, they are invisible to the middle class. Unemployed women are even harder to see. One of Le Sueur's achievements is to focus on these women at the bottom, not at a distance from them but as one of them. As a participant observer, her narrative stance is close to the women whose situation she shares and whom she sympathetically observes and brings to imaginative life. She uses the resources of her prose rhythms and language not to look down on and separate herself but to give voice and vitality to those she cares about as one of them. She wants us to see them in the fullest sense possible.

From the outset Le Sueur recognizes that protest is necessary but that instead hunger has induced lethargy. She voices her own protest to reanimate a key Marxist value, the "human being" who has been worn down under the grinding pressure of "city hunger" (p. 166). Her "outcry" makes us aware of an unnamed revolutionary option beyond stealing or killing for bread or timidly crawling the streets. In "Women on the Breadlines" Le Sueur implicitly establishes that depression conditions cry out for basic change. But her main concern is to show precisely the way things are for unemployed women. Le Sueur enters into their inner and outer world without falsifying it by attributing to them a revolutionary Marxist or feminist outlook they do not have.

In the process she makes us aware of characters who are ordinarily passed over in literature. Take Bernice. Fat, inarticulate characters like Bernice almost never receive the compassionate, perceptive attention Le Sueur gives her. In her very imagery of embroidery and magic, Le Sueur values Bernice as a woman, a worker, and a displaced peasant (p. 167). Like Ellen, Ellen's friend, and Mrs. Gray, who also come alive in "Women on the Breadlines," Bernice is a worker—"a real peasant," a proletarian—but particularized, humanized, not an abstraction. Equally important, she is a woman. As a woman and a worker, her hard labor, her struggles, what is really her exploitation and her survival in the face of it—all emerge. Bernice is also a concrete, human example of the immense displacement from Old World to New World, from country to city.

Bernice's situation as a woman without children intensifies a theme at the heart of "Women on the Breadlines," since Bernice will never realize her dream "of having a little house or a houseboat perhaps with a spot of ground for a few chickens." The breakdown of the whole social-economic system has made realizing her dream impossible, just as it has made it impossible for her to have a family. Instead, she sits "bewildered," "hungry"—even Bernice, with her great folds of flesh. "She has been living on crackers. Sometimes a box lasts a week. She has a friend who's a baker and he sometimes steals the stale loaves and brings them to her" (p. 167). Bernice's hunger is profound and goes beyond the painful lack of food to include the immense void, the immense need for nourishment the American system fails to satisfy. Beyond food itself Bernice is starved for community, for a husband and children, for work and security.

As a Marxist artist one of Le Sueur's major achievements is to convey a sense of human dignity, the threats to it, and the unsuspected ways ordinary people sustain a sense of self-worth. As a woman writer, moreover, she has an unusual feel for the delight clothes give. In the face of middle-class disapproval—why can't these improvident people save when they have a little money?—Le Sueur shows that when you get a bit of money "you buy something to dress up in. An excitement takes hold of you. You know it is suicide but you can't help it. You must have food, dainty, splendid food, and a bright hat so once again you feel blithe, rid of that ratty, gnawing shame" (p. 168).

For a woman the ultimate shame is prostitution. Le Sueur discriminates exactly between prudery, the degradation of prostitution, and the life-affirming desire her young girls have for a bit of fun. To forget their hunger in the afternoon they like to go to movies with the men they get to pick them up in the park. The men are willing to pay ten cents to have the company of a girl for the afternoon. And that's it (pp. 169–70). One of the girls "is unbelievably jaunty." She is unemployed and thin—her shoulder blades stick out—but her youth burns brightly and "she runs wild as a colt hunting pleasure, hunting sustenance" (p. 169). Her life energy, her vital sexuality, her concern with the way she looks all give her a sense of personal worth. But under the pressure of hunger, a woman can easily lose her dignity. For a bit of food, the girl's friend Ellen shows her legs in the alley in back of a downtown café. The threat of prostitution is in the background.

Le Sueur stresses that the body is a commodity, "and like every commodity now the body is difficult to sell and the girls say you're lucky if you get fifty cents." Marx demystifies the commodity as the unit containing the basic contradictions of capitalism. For her part Le Sueur focuses on the issues of dignity, of self-esteem: "it's very difficult and humiliating to sell one's body." In a passage reminiscent of

Marx at his best, she then develops a telling analogy whose understatement and intellectual force make us see that a woman trying to sell her body reveals the basic conflicts of contemporary capitalism. "Imagine," she says,

> having to go out on the street to sell, say, one's overcoat. Suppose you have to sell your coat so you can have breakfast and a place to sleep, say, for fifty cents. You decide to sell your only coat. You take it off and put it on your arm. The street, that has before been just a street, now becomes a mart, something entirely different. You must approach someone now and admit you are destitute and are now selling your clothes, your most intimate possessions. Everyone will watch you talking to the stranger showing him your overcoat, what a good coat it is. People will stop and watch curiously. You will be quite naked on the street. It is even harder to try to sell one's self, more humiliating. It is even humiliating to try to sell one's labor. When there is no buyer. (pp. 168–69)

Le Sueur avoids the obvious temptations of sentimentality, sensationalism, or moralism. Instead, she charges her analogy with a core of Marxist terms and concepts and places her women at the center of the contemporary crisis.

In her version of Marx on the working day, in her ending Le Sueur brings alive the conditions of contemporary labor from her special vantage point as a woman, a writer, and a worker unable to find work. She drives home the hard labor her women have done and the terrible insecurity that is their reward. In the process she undercuts the chronic middle-class complaint about the unemployed—that they are lazy, that they do not want to work. "It is appalling," she stresses, "to think that these women sitting so listless in the room may work as hard as it is possible for a human being to work, may labor night and day, like Mrs. Gray wash street-cars from midnight to dawn and offices in the early evening, scrub for fourteen and fifteen hours a day, sleep only five hours or so, do this their whole lives, and never earn one day of security, having always before them the pit of the future. The endless labor, the bending back, the water-soaked hands, earning never more than a week's wages, never having in their hands more life than that" (p. 171).

Le Sueur herself is not listless or passive. For her women the present is bleak and the future is dead. Le Sueur, however, sides with the young who reject "not the suffering of birth, death, love" but "the suffering of endless labor without dream, eating the spare bread in bitterness, being a slave without the security of a slave" (p. 171). This ending is charged with critical, revolutionary implications. By quoting Marx's famous characterization of the worker under capitalism—a slave without the security of a slave—Le Sueur connects her grim portrait with Marx's. She also aligns the future, the young, with the Marxist dream that by implication will replace the failed American dream. Her emphasis, though, is on the bleak ravages of the present.

Throughout "Women on the Breadlines" Le Sueur assumes that her readers will respond actively to her allusions and will have their imaginations quickened and their politics animated by her poetically heightened language and precisely rendered details. As an avant-garde Marxist writer, Le Sueur assumes a fully human audience willing and able to be engaged by her politics, her passions, and the prose-poetry of her reportage. In "Women on the Breadlines," in this version of her avant-garde political art Le Sueur is a pioneering radical critic, an explorer of those the middle class and canonical American literature typically ignore.

Her approach, moreover, was also apparently too strong for the men who decided what constituted acceptably left literature in 1940, when the party published *Salute to Spring.* "I Was Marching" appropriately concludes the collection but "Women on the Breadlines" was excluded. The collection with "Women on the Breadlines" would have been stronger, deeper, and more fully Marxist than without it. At the end of the decade perhaps the residual Popular Front outlook of the party reinforced the reservations Whittaker Chambers had originally expressed. In any case, the exclusion of "Women on the Breadlines" has contributed to the party's reputation as a cultural censor. But the party also supported Le Sueur, published her only book during the decade, and commanded her full allegiance.

"The Fetish of Being Outside"

An example of that allegiance emerges in a *New Masses* debate with Horace Gregory. Gregory touched an exposed nerve in a thoughtful essay he wrote explaining why, despite his long-standing commitment to the victory of the party, he needed to stay outside. In one of the exchanges that distinguish left cultural dialogue during the thirties, Gregory stimulated Meridel Le Sueur to respond in "The Fetish of Being Outside." Because she is even farther than Gregory from involvement in the New York literary wars, in her response Le Sueur passed over these important surfaces and goes to the living center of his position and hers. With the authority that comes from her own artistic independence, she turns Gregory's issue of individualism against him. "For myself," she affirms, "I do not feel any subtle equivocation between the individual and the new disciplined groups of the Communist Party. I do not care for the bourgeois individual that I am. I never have cared for it. I want to be integrated in a new and different way as an individual and this I feel can come only from a communal participation which reverses the feeling of a bourgeois writer. What will happen to him will not be special and precious, but will be the communal happening."[9] Her passion for communal living is equaled only by her revulsion against the rot of a decayed competitive individualism. "I can no longer live without communal sensibility," Le Sueur stresses. "I can no longer breathe in this maggoty individualism of a merchant society. I have never been able to breathe in it. That is why I hope to 'belong' to a communal society, to be a cellular part of that and able to grow and function with others in a living whole" (p. 22).

Her emphasis on living, on the immediate human experience of the communal, goes to the heart of Marxist theory. Her language is also based on the organic processes of life: breathing, growing as an individual and "a cellular part" of "a living whole." For her the "living whole" is inseparable from birth. She celebrates giving birth in a passional heat that fuses thought and action and that creates new works, a new world, and new selves. Le Sueur thus counters what she sees as Gregory's detached objectivity, the fetishized individualism of a middle class that made artists understandably withdraw to preserve their integrity. She simultaneously places the feminist experience of giving birth at the center of her radical politics, an implicit challenge within the predominantly male ethos of the party.

Le Sueur's version of Marxist individualism emerges from deep American and feminist sources. In the vital dialectics of the new individualism, for Le Sueur in 1935 the party plays an explicit and valued role. For her as for Marx, the individual comes into the fullness of his or her potentiality not at odds with but as part of a community, which for Le Sueur centers on the party. For her the party is not a bureaucracy but is integral to "an organic growth pertaining to growth of a new nucleus of society. . . . You belong to that growth or you do not" (p. 22). Le Sueur's special synthesis brings together Marxism, American organicism, feminism, and a Lawrencian commitment to the dark and passional, the latter especially telling in the controversy with Gregory, the author of a book on Lawrence.

Le Sueur knows the transformation she wants is difficult. "It is difficult because you are stepping into a dark chaotic passional world of another class, the proletariat, which is still perhaps unconscious of itself like a great body sleeping, stirring, strange and outside the calculated, expedient world of the bourgeoisie. It is a hard road to leave your own class," Le Sueur realizes, "and you cannot leave it by pieces or parts; it is a birth and you have to be born whole out of it. In a complete new body. None of the old ideology is any good in it. The creative artist will create no new forms of art or literature for that new hour out of that darkness unless he is willing to go all the way, with full belief, into that darkness" (p. 23). Underlying her belief in the either/or nature of the process is her own involvement in the process of birth and also in the conversion process she had traced a year earlier in "I Was Marching." In the background is the ancient Christian imagery of the new birth into the body of Christ. In this emotionally charged imagery, Le Sueur transforms that part of her heritage stemming from the revivals of her Kansas youth and especially from her severe grandmother, a woman whose Puritanical orthodoxy relaxed only in her religion, which "was her theater, her dance, her wine, her song."[10] Le Sueur openly celebrates the faith and passion that are basic to Marxism but which often get lost in left discourse. "The darkness" she has entered is threatening and vitalizing. When she specifies it, as she does with the dark interior and the dark people in "I Was Marching," she minimizes the dangers of irrationalism. Her detailed knowledge of working people, moreover, keeps her treatment of the proletariat from becoming abstract and sentimental, a kind of fetish in its own right—or left.

In the actual practice of her political art, Le Sueur is often more nuanced and modulated than she is in "The Fetish of Being Outside." In this essay her either/or alternatives express Le Sueur's sense of her profound reaction, not against individualism but against competitive individualism and her corresponding sense of the desirability and difficulties involved in a full commitment to the party and the proletariat. Le Sueur is speaking from the depth and immediacy of her own feelings, hopes, and ideas in the context of the depression and the imminent American Writers' Congress; she is not laying down the final law for her own creative practice or providing a guide to theory and action for the 2000s. Le Sueur instead gives an exemplary version of 1930s Marxism-feminism under the pressures, stimulus, and restraints of the party, her historical period, and her powerful personality.

"The Girl"

The next year in "The Girl" (1936)—quite different from, and not to be confused with, Le Sueur's novel, *The Girl*—she tested her position fictionally in a story that is the dialectical opposite of one of her most celebrated works, "Annunciation." As a pair, at the center of *Salute to Spring* "The Girl" and "Annunciation" deepen our insight into Le Sueur as a complex Marxist artist. Through the schoolteacher of "The Girl" Le Sueur extends her treatment of the emotionally tight people of "Corn Village," men and women out of touch with their bodies and at odds with the body of the land. In the middle of the depression Le Sueur has a schoolteacher decide to drive "her neat fine-looking little roadster" through the Tehachapi Mountains, through Indian country, to San Francisco (p. 64). Everything about her is trim, neat, orderly. She teaches history, that key Marxist subject, but unlike a Marxist for her nothing changes—the course is always the same. As opposed to Le Sueur's Marxist stress on the communal, moreover, the teacher is alone and likes it.

Le Sueur arranges the story so that in the course of the drive the teacher is challenged to change, to relate to the sensuous power of the mountains, and to come together with a man—to come out of her isolation by relating to the sensuous land and the sensuous man connected with the curve of the mountains. Perhaps the teacher can be taught. Instead of getting abstract information from books about the tribes and the geological formations, she is challenged to experience them directly, sensuously. This play on natural history as opposed to abstract, intellectualized history is complicated because, as a tight middle-class person, for Le Sueur the teacher represents the history and sensibility of a class. Her preoccupation with her keys, with her coin purse, with her possessions, and above all her work ethic preoccupation with making time—all are challenged by the sensuous, timeless heat and an interlude in the cool shadows, in the earth, with a sensuous man who thinks she is pretty. Because of Le Sueur's commitment to poetic language and Lawrencian experience, in her Marxism she is as opposed to a dry, analytical Marxism as she is to the middle-class denial of the flesh, imagination, and community. In exposing the difference between "information" and sensuous experience, she hits more than one target and gives an unexpected sexual dimension to Marx's concern with sensuous human experience.

To complicate the story's Marxism, in "The Girl" Le Sueur plays variations on the themes and imagery of "The Fetish of Being Outside" and "Corn Village." The man in "The Girl" has been darkened by the sun. He is an unemployed worker associated with the relaxed power of sleep, sex, the unconscious, and elemental nature. For the teacher the combination is frightening and attractive. In "Fetish" the sleeping body of the proletariat is associated with a darkness the middle class also finds frightening and attractive. In her essay, for the middle class Le Sueur poses the challenge of a basic change, a new birth from a risky immersion in this unknown region. In "The Girl" the teacher's difficult move from the middle class into the darkness of the proletariat is complicated by sexual politics and a Lawrencian feeling for the land and the unconscious.

The sexual politics include the teacher's sudden realization "that she despised men and always had," that they want something from her, and that "men hate women with brains." In another context we might well side with her—contemporary feminism makes a strong case for women with brains staying alone and rejecting male demands. But Le Sueur shows the teacher as abstractly cerebral. The teacher, moreover, "always wanted to help men, do something for them, and then really underneath she could hate them" (p. 71). Later, as she begins to respond to the man's sensuality, she protects herself by thinking "she was their equal in every way, she knew that" (p. 74). In deliberately giving the teacher feminist lines, Le Sueur is not so much antifeminist as anti one style of feminism and pro another. She exposes the way feminism can be used as a shield against sensuous experience with men and as a mask for hatred of men. For some contemporary readers "The Girl" generates strong feelings of resistance, of rejection. We do not want our grandmothers, our feminist forebears, writing about women in precisely the way Le Sueur does, acknowledging the hate and exposing instead of endorsing its basis. Le Sueur, that is, refuses to celebrate a cerebral woman and instead criticizes the teacher's view that "men hate women with brains" as a rationalization of her own alienation from her sexual depths. Under the surface Le Sueur is also perhaps undercutting those feminists in the party who had criticized her for having children instead of giving herself entirely to the cause.[11]

Le Sueur is at her best probing, specifying, opening up commonplace moments and scenes that she reveals as full of human significance, as in the exchanges with the men in the lunchroom. In "The Girl" she is equally good on the fierce sun and primitive mountain landscape that progressively impinge on the teacher's consciousness and threaten the security of her habits. The dark man who needs a ride is aligned with what Le Sueur describes as the "curves" and "flesh" of the earth and the darkness and light of the sun, itself "a golden body." The man "looked as if he had been roasted, slowly turned on a spit until he seemed glowing, like phosphorous, as if the sun were in him, and his black eyes were a little bloodshot as if the whites had been burned," and then in the more familiar idiom of the 1930s, "his broad chest fell down easily to his hips as he ground out a cigarette with his heel" (p. 68). He later has "a great odor of milk and hay" (p. 70), so that in his figure Le Sueur combines the innocence of left American pastoral with sexually charged myth and the sexual byplay between a working-class man and a middle-class woman.

In "The Girl" the third-person point of view is basically the teacher's. The teacher is not fully conscious of the implications of her responses but they establish her needs, her possibilities, and her limits. One game in the story is thus the conflict between the point of view of two women, the teacher and Le Sueur, viewing a sexually charged man who is making advances. This game is complicated by the sexual politics of the present. Our willingness or unwillingness to value the way Le Sueur combines myth and the more down-to-earth sexuality between a man and woman also conditions our response, as does our willingness or unwillingness to credit Le Sueur for focusing on sexuality, in contrast to the more customary avoidance in left literature.[12]

For all her resistance to the power of the sun and mountains, the teacher repeatedly responds to them as elemental, sensuous bodies. For her the man in his heat and physical immediacy merges with these elemental presences. Like the man, for her the mountain is sometimes fiercely threatening, sometimes warmly seductive, as when "the great body of the earth seemed to touch her, and she began looking where the shadows were beginning to stroke down the sides of the mounds as if she might sleep there for a while. An awful desire to sleep drugged her, as if she hadn't slept for years and years. She felt warm and furred and dangerously drugged" (p. 75). However desirable, we know it is not easy to relax conscious restraints and slip into the unconscious, into the elemental body of the earth, into the sexual body of another.

As the story unfolds the teacher reveals that she has poetic as well as sexual capacities she has suppressed. A key instance of her sensitivity to the importance of metaphor is that she reverses her earlier stress on abstract book knowledge and, close to conversion, "felt suddenly as if she had missed everything. She should say something more to her classes. Suppose she should say—'The Tehachapi Mountains have warmed and bloomed for a thousand years.' After all, why not? This was the true information" (p. 77).

Le Sueur arranges the story so that the teacher's consciousness has already been deeply stirred by the primitive earth and sun before she meets the man in the lunchroom. When he propositions her in the car—"I could go on to San Francisco with you" (p. 73)—the proposal is mediated by the context, by our sense that "it isn't so hot going alone," in the deepest sense of "alone," and by our awareness that the teacher is stirred and that an organic change would be good. The man's proposal is not based on mutual respect for the full range of her possibilities. She is there, she is pretty, they are both alone, the moment is special, and he knows she is aware of him. The atmosphere is charged with elemental sexuality. The man repeats his offer more than once—"you know I like you, I like you. You're pretty" (p. 74). We know what he wants and we see that he stays with it, insistently but not brutally. For contemporary readers the situation has threatening undertones of rape, but Le Sueur does not support this possibility.

Instead, as she arranges the story, far from taking advantage of the teacher, the man provides an occasion for her to take advantage of. He becomes a focus for her need for renewal at the elemental sexual and natural sources of life. The sensuous landscape he invites her to enter is for her both feminine and masculine, and she responds deeply. Le Sueur's heightened language does full justice to the sexualized body of the earth, to the teacher's feeling of her own body, and to the intensity of her sexuality, "an ache, like lightning piercing stone, . . . between the breasts." But instead of completing this sexually charged moment with the man, like the stone she stays hard, refuses to change, and experiences "a canker of self-loathing" either because of her powerful, unacceptable feelings or because she denies them (p. 79). The emphasis is on the personal and sexual but the episode resonates with the "Corn Village" critique of an entire culture afflicted with holding back. The change she refuses, moreover, has undertones of the organic political-revolutionary change Le Sueur affirms in "The Fetish of Being Outside."

Le Sueur organizes the denouement of "The Girl" around a series of reversals and a celebration of ripeness. The teacher plans to tell the man good-bye by saying "casually—Well, good luck." And she is going to buy him a melon. She can control the situation and maintain her sense of self-esteem by using words and money. Instead, the man gives her a ripe melon and wishes her good luck (pp. 79–80). The golden, sun-ripened melon he offers is a final version of the sexualized body at the center of the story. The gift is at odds with her middle-class world of money, time, and tight restraints. The teacher does not change, does not enter the ripe, sometimes fierce natural world the unemployed worker has been offering her. Instead, she airs out "the smell of buttermilk and hay, started the car and drove to San Francisco because that was where she was going" (p. 80). As in the best of American literature, Le Sueur's concluding drama of the melon, the purse, and the car continues to endow ordinary details with a suggestive charge of meaning. In a canonical literature noted for its sexual avoidances, Le Sueur's treatment of sexuality also gives depth to the traditional opposition between city and country, an opposition that for Le Sueur is strongly anticapitalistic.

"Annunciation"

In "Annunciation" (1935), at the heart and center of *Salute to Spring* Le Sueur uses a contrasting poetic style and a contrasting first-person narrator to highlight differences with "The Girl." In "Annunciation" she perfects a curving, spiraling, nonlinear form that fuses her feminism, Marxism, and poetic sensibility. The form is as sensitive a statement as her organic imagery, her personal, idiomatic language, and her often slightly wrenched syntax. The combination endows her writing with a quality of the everyday slightly estranged, heightened, and revealed as special. This poetic heightening of the ordinary celebrates the beauty and vitality of the everyday material world and is another instance of Le Sueur's Marxism. It is also an implicit criticism of the bourgeois and Marxist values and practices at odds with her deepest commitments.

The form speaks for the value of the spontaneous and improvisatory. Creating it allows Le Sueur to focus on nuances of feeling and perception, to celebrate the stirring within, and to establish deep connections between the ripening, blossoming pear tree, the child ripening within her, and ordinary people, blossoms on the great tree of life, all inseparable from writing as central to her own creativity. Combined with her language, syntax, and concerns, the form affirms a feminist, antipatriarchal, anticapitalistic mode of writing and responding. For Le Sueur, patriarchal capitalism favors the linear and logical. She is also at odds with those versions of Marxism that share the qualities she rejects.

Without at all ignoring the outside world of decaying houses, sickness, and poverty, in "Annunciation" she probes her personal responses to the innermost meaning of the ripening pear tree and her own inner ripening as her child stirs to life within her. What she discovers is her capacity to feel alive and related to the blossoming growth of the tree. The decaying rooming house is connected with sickness, hunger, and worries about money. Its deadening influence epitomizes the impact of a failed capitalism. Repeatedly in *Salute to Spring* the failed economic system penetrates into the innermost recesses of personal and domestic life. In "Annunciation" Le Sueur and her husband can no longer talk to each other. Her husband is chronically enraged at her for not having an abortion. They have no money. Even when they have a little food, she cannot hold it down. She is often sick and hungry, physical realities that in her work also have powerful social-political implications. Deadened and estranged, she discovers life-giving possibilities within herself and in the growing world outside the world of the house, money, and sickness.

Inexplicably, under the influence of the pear tree and the new life within her she feels healthy, not sick, and she experiences herself and the entire world as alive, opening up, quickening with birth. "This time has come without warning. How can it be explained? Everything is dead and closed, the world a stone, and then suddenly everything comes alive as it has for me, like an anemone on a rock, opening itself, disclosing itself, and the very stones themselves break open like bread. It has all got something to do with the pear tree too. It has come about some way as I have sat here with this child so many afternoons, with the pear tree murmuring in the air" (p. 90). Unlike the teacher in "The Girl," the "I" of "Annunciation" welcomes change and the new birth that stirs her body into relation with the body of the world.

It is not only physical. Because Le Sueur's imagination is quickened, her mind helps create the bonds that connect her to the "ripe curves" of the pears within their "scimitar leaves." "The pears are all gone from the tree but I imagine them hanging there." As opposed to the earlier hunger, she imagines a feast of curves and sheltered ripeness, the fruit within the protected curve of leaves like the child within her. The feast extends to those who ordinarily see the world as a stone but who may possibly also feel "round and full" (p. 90). In emphasizing that "I imagine them," Le Sueur calls attention to the creative role of the mind, so that she reinforces her concern with writing as a basic form of creativity, inseparable from pears and children ripening. Le Sueur's project counters both capitalistic aliena- tion and the stereotypical view of left writing as reductive and hostile to the imagination.

Le Sueur precisely renders the intimate experience of the new life stirring within her, "an almost unbearable sense of sprouting, of bursting encasements, of moving kernels, expanding flesh!" (p. 91). The imagery connects her with the life of the fertile corn and wheat fields. The experience is also the basis for her sense of a revolutionary "movement" and the possibility of "making a new world" (pp. 91, 94). In this mood, she transforms the decayed "wooden houses" into "husks . . . swarming with living seed" (p. 91). She later deliberately rejects houses altogether and affirms instead "a deep rebellion" centered on a connection between the seeds of the trees and "my child too from a far seed blowing from last year's rich and revolutionary dead" (pp. 94, 95). In "Annunciation" childbirth is the biological basis for Le Sueur's faith in a revolutionary new world.

In meditating on a revolutionary change of consciousness, Le Sueur recognizes that under present conditions the issue is hardly certain. "You can tell by looking at most people that the world remains a stone to them and a closed door. I'm afraid it will become like that to me again" (p. 90). Although for Le Sueur the elemental process of childbirth does not guarantee victory, the birth process does constitute the material basis within which the new consciousness may emerge.

In the meantime for Le Sueur writing is important, partly because she is a writer, partly because writing itself can provide a matrix and model. It is no acci- dent, then, that at the end of "Annunciation" she explicates her spiraling form and celebrates another set of relations, this time between writing, birth, the sex act, and the speech of the pear tree. "Far inside the vertical stem," she writes, "there must be a movement, a river of sap rising from below and radiating outward in many directions clear to the tips of the leaves" (p. 96). In this image of the sap rising from below, Le Sueur is beginning to bring together the genesis of writing, sex, the revolution, and the growth of the tree. As she continues she discovers that "the leaves are the lips of the tree speaking in the wind or they move like many tongues.

The fruit of the tree you can see has been a round speech, speaking in full tongue on the tree hanging in ripe body, the fat curves hung within the small curves of the leaves." This Emersonian, Thoreauvian vision of the origin of speech has a sensuous, feminist charge to it—the full tongue, the ripe body, and again the womb-shelter of "fat curves within the small curves of the leaves." At the end, "I imagine them there. The tree has shot up like a rocket, then stops in mid air and its leaves flow out gently in a long slow curve. All is gentle on the pear tree after its strong upward shooting movement" (p. 96). In this version the tree reenacts the male sex act in "its strong upward shooting movement," "quick, sudden and rocketing," and then the "leaves flow out gently" and curving birth begins, so that round speech, male and female sex, and birth all flow into each other. Although through the sweep of "Annunciation" the feminine imagery of round, curving speech and womb predominates, at key moments Le Sueur's imagery fuses male and female sexuality so that she counters another form of hierarchy and alienation.

The form of "Annunciation" answers to this vision. Instead of linear progression, we have spirals and round curves, a form that allows for repetition, doubling back, sudden breakthroughs, slow accretions, and meaningful juxtapositions. Take one developing drama in "Annunciation," the contrast between Karl and the ripe pear tree. Our sense of the two emerges through a series of episodes and juxtapositions. By the end we know that Le Sueur cannot speak to Karl whereas the tree has a round speech she feels close to. The tree "has become more familiar to me than Karl. It seems a strange thing that a tree might come to mean more to one than one's husband. It seems a shameful thing even. I am ashamed to think of it but it is so" (p. 96). The problem originates in depression poverty. Karl wants an abortion. " 'Everybody does it,' he kept telling me. 'It's nothing, then it's all over.' I stopped talking to him much. Everything I said only made him angry. So writing was a kind of conversation I carried on with myself and with the child" (p. 87).

For the "I" of "Annunciation" writing is not a monologue but a conversation, a Bakhtinian dialogue. This dialogue emerges partly from her poverty and socially and politically generated separation. The dialogue fuses the personal and the social-political in the interests of preserving for the future the pain and loveliness of the everyday present. At the end Le Sueur deliberately foregrounds herself writing, because in this self-conscious narrative writing is as important as birth and revolution. "I am writing on a piece of wrapping paper now," she emphasizes (p. 97). Karl has not come home again. The writing is partly a response to their poverty and their socially and politically rooted estrangement. Both the writing and the pear tree promise an alternative. The final words thus invoke the central presence in "Annunciation," "the pear tree standing motionless, its leaves curled in the dark, its radiating body falling darkly, like a stream far below into the earth" (p. 97). Unlike Whitman's live oak, we know this dark tree is not alone. It participates in the strong, gentle, curving ripeness of human birth and perhaps of revolutionary change. In this version the sources of change go far down into the earth and into the processes of birth. In emphasizing the dark, Le Sueur again recognizes the mystery and danger involved.[13]

"Tonight Is Part of the Struggle"

In "Annunciation" Le Sueur gives her most sensitive and comprehensive treatment to concerns and situations that recur in *Salute to Spring*, particularly the connection between birth and revolution and the strained relation between young, pregnant women and their husbands. In a recurring, symbolic situation in *Salute to Spring*, a young wife, pregnant or with an infant, is at odds with her husband. Their poverty is the reason. They are hungry in the full sense we have come to understand. In "Tonight Is Part of the Struggle" (1935), the couple bicker angrily about not having enough food for themselves, about not having enough to make milk for the baby, about the husband's hanging around because he is out of work. Again the collapse of the economic system deranges the most intimate personal relations and endangers the continuance of life itself in the image of the watery milk for the baby.

The wife, Leah, wants a little fun. To relieve the monotony, the husband, Jock, suggests going "to that mass meeting at the auditorium" (p. 135). Unlike the organizers and activists of Le Sueur's "Biography of My Daughter," "Dead in Steel," and "Farewell My Wife and Child and All My Friends," Leah is politically innocent. " 'I don't know what a mass meeting is,' she said." In going to the auditorium these two representative, ordinary people join "a vast ocean of dark people, . . . people pouring in swift black rivulets" (p. 136). This torrent invokes the revolutionary power that the unorganized have when they come together. Jock, though, is part of the old consciousness. Le Sueur treats him comically, as a foil for Leah's change: " 'Jeez,' Jock said, this is going to be a lousy show' " (p. 136).

A pregnant woman in the audience, and finally Leah with her infant, are the unofficial protagonists of the show. In contrast to Jock's crude speech, Le Sueur's language becomes supple and complex in dealing with "a heavy woman. . . . She was pregnant, her slow feet, searching only for food and shelter, broken on the loom of childbed, at stove, at work. Below the dark clothes the veins were burst, erupted like the earth's skin, split by the terrible axe of birth" (p. 136). The official protagonist of the show, Tiala, the Communist Party organizer, uses a more abstract language that emerges from suffering like the woman's and carries beyond it to the command, "'Listen,' . . . 'Tonight is part of the struggle'" (p. 137). Most of the rest of his speech comes through indirect discourse, mediated by Leah who testifies that Tiala is in touch with her reality. "He began to tell about things she knew about," specifically about "how they were hungry, how they could not get jobs, how they must fight together" (p. 137).

Originally published in 1935, part of what keeps "Tonight Is Part of the Struggle" from being simple propaganda is the tension between the Third Period revolutionary imperative to "fight together" and the emerging Popular Front deemphasis on militant change. Tiala voices both positions and the implied narrator goes even further. The story is energized by the conflict. "'Two years ago,'" Tiala says, referring to the period of Third Phase militancy, "'we had hunger marches, the seed we planted two years ago takes root now.' He talked in terms of growing, of yeast in bread, she could understand yeast and seed, it excited her." Le Sueur is also at home with this domestic imagery of growth, of nourishing. Le Sueur then approvingly has Tiala use the party's slogans: "'The rank and file,' he said, 'the masses.'" For Le Sueur, these words are compatible with the imagery of growing yeast. Entering into the young wife's consciousness, the implied narrator then goes beyond Tiala on yeast and the masses to a poetic, organic language that brings alive "the great black sea of bodies, heads like black wheat growing in the same soil, the same wind." This imagery extends and deepens the official slogans.

Le Sueur then renders another of the conversions that distinguish her work. Under the pressure of need and the stimulus of the crowd, Tiala's words, and her own sensibility, the young wife experiences a revolutionary change of consciousness. The drama is at once political, psychological, and linguistic. In the drama of languages, of words, the personal, poetic language renders the wife's sudden experience of connection, after which "something seemed to enter her and congeal. I am part, she wanted to say" (p. 138).

What follows is a dialogue of languages and responses. Tiala uses the language of orthodox Marxism: "You are producers, wealth is produced by hand and brain." Leah immediately translates this language into a version of feminism: "I am a producer, she thought with her hand on the protruding belly of the baby, but not from hand and brain." Le Sueur uses the exchange to affirm birth as production, to give women as the producers of children a status equal to the men who, on the orthodox party view, produce wealth through the labor of hand and brain. To emphasize words, another product of "hand and brain," Le Sueur continues to use Leah to underscore their importance. In this case Leah "heard only some of the words," significantly "the ones that her body's experience repeated to her." They are not, it is worth stressing, the words of the moderate Popular Front but rather "the class struggle, militant workers, the broad masses. They were like words in the first primer, gigantic, meaningless, but she leaned over with the others, to see, to hear, to touch, to make real, make the lips form on them" (p. 138). Le Sueur is giving the party a lesson in how to transform the "gigantic, meaningless" words and to make them real through touch and the physical immediacy of the senses, to combine "hand and brain" in a new way that reanimates these basic Marxist values.

At the center is the physical immediacy of birth. "Without warning," the mass of people, "the great body moved" and enacts a cataclysmic process of birth. "Hands lifted, mouths opened together and rising suddenly, lifted by storm and cataclysm, the black body rose, lifted high, a black tide crest of hands, faces, shoulders, like erupted tree roots, black labor root erupted, rising black tide of labor bodies in a thick volcanic tide and there was a roar of flesh, roar of hands of a high key like a body of water on cliff sides" (p. 139). This storm is the "black labor" of birth, work, and the aroused masses. From this "black labor," "the new flesh between her hands jerked as if lassoed, the breath caught in the thin ribs, the baby's face got red as when he was born, the nostrils shot open as if the noisy air was too much to breathe. At the last AYE, it lifted its head, struggled and let out a bawl of rebellion, wonder, amazement" (p. 139).

Under the pressure of hunger and unemployment, the revolution and the new consciousness emerge from organized protest, from the turmoil and struggle of people acting together. For Le Sueur, the woman's experience of giving birth is not only a metaphor of the process but also a necessary corrective aimed at the male theorists who, from her point of view, fail to see the crucial role of women. Through her repeated use of the symbolism of birth, Le Sueur places the deep biological and social power of women at the very heart of the revolution. As in "Annunciation" the example of her own poetically enlivened language shows that Le Sueur values the productions of mind and imagination just as she values the Marxist fusion of "hand and brain." She is not relegating women to the status of mindless breeders but, in the face of official marginalizing, she is instead emphasizing the central importance of women and birth.

In "Tonight Is Part of the Struggle," after the reenactment of birth, Leah thus holds the infant on her shoulder, "the tiny white head like a dandelion top in spring sprouting there amongst the black froth of men from the tool and dye, carpenters' unions, truck drivers, tobacco workers, stockyard workers, and there the dandelion-top new bright head as if just emerged" (p. 139). The child and the spring aligned with the workers assure us that the future is with the unionized workers, who are not bureaucratized but rather participate in the vitality and innocence of the new life of the season and the child. The cohesive renewal even extends to Jock, who "laughed and his ears were red and he put his big hand that was good on the Ford factory belt on the bright tiny head and his eyes said Leah, like when he wooed her" (p. 140).

Through her ending Le Sueur both reinforces and challenges the beliefs of her left audience. She gives hope and insight to her readers through the ritual naming of the unions and even more the ritual reenactment of the birth of a new revolutionary consciousness. She forecasts a new world to emerge for the organized, protesting workers. But Le Sueur complicates the drama. The basic imagery of birth places women at center stage. She also has Tiala urge everyone "to march to the capital to demand security for the workers. Bring your children" (p. 140). Tiala thus fuses the old Third Phase militancy of marches and demands with the emerging Popular Front position on security, not on revolutionary change. The story concludes, however, with Tiala's final words, "'*fellow workers, remember, don't forget. Every hour, every night and tonight is part of the struggle*'" (p. 140). At the end, Tiala invokes a sense of class struggle.

Immediately before Tiala's closing lines, Le Sueur gives an even stronger sense of militant struggle in the voice of her implied narrator. She enters Leah's new consciousness and focuses on the snow and darkness, emblematic of the revolutionary situation Leah is involved in. Leah stresses that with the march coming, now they had something to do, "as if they were all moving forward together . . . and the thick mass would move and spread, explode like black projectiles from their strength" (p. 140). The militant power of that exploding projectile is at odds with the feminist and Popular Front imagery of yeast and security. The destructive, creative power of the exploding projectile also complicates the feminist insight into the violence of the birth process by reversing the emphasis of the birth imagery. The projectile (masculine?) foregrounds the destruction inseparable from the revolutionary militancy of exploding shells. Far from being a simple, one-dimensional story, "Tonight Is Part of the Struggle" emerges from and expresses the complexity of Le Sueur's struggle with the conflicting party and feminist languages and positions that compelled her.

"Salute to Spring"

In "Salute to Spring," the title story of the collection, Le Sueur again explores the central role of women, the birth of a revolutionary consciousness, and the grim strains hunger causes between wives and husbands. The conflicts within the story and the dialectical relation between "Salute to Spring" and "I Was Marching" reveal that Le Sueur's struggle was not confined to a single work. Her imagination returns again and again to variations on a set of themes and images. In "Salute to Spring," she invokes the landlocked, winter America of "Corn Village," a nation and sensibility longing for change or, as the wife of the story says, the battery running down on her squeaking radio, "I want different news, I want to hear it, Lord, different news" (p. 159). In March, at the turning point of the seasons, she tears up a calendar picture of a fat, naked baby. Her own baby is dying of malnutrition. She resents her husband for sitting around, unable to plant the seeds their livelihood depends on. They have no money and no food, the winter hills close in around them, the baby is sick. In the midst of this charged, familiar iconography, instead of giving in to despair, the wife draws on her inner resources and resolves to find something to eat. This elemental affirmation reinforces and is reinforced by her "passion for her children, for having them, for giving them birth" (p. 161). Their hunger is at the center of the story. Mary—her name is not casually chosen— manages to satisfy some but not all of their need for nourishment. Beyond the food itself are the unnamed needs and hungers the remainder of the story addresses.

First, though, Le Sueur again brings alive the way depression poverty cuts into the most intimate relations, turning husbands and wives into knives, so that "every move he made was like a knife cutting her. She felt him so keenly, shut in the house so long together, since harvest, his long thin body, his dark burnt face, both winter pallor and sunburn still on neck and jowls. He was like a knife and every move cut her" (p. 162). The move he makes, however, is toward the movement, and it brings husband and wife together. Their privatized life in the house invokes both the depression and the isolated family under capitalism. The story enacts the healing, cohesive power of cooperative action and promises that a new consciousness and a new, cooperative society can emerge from depression-generated resentments and needs. The beneficiary is not only society but also families and individuals like Mary and Jim. Their representative energy and needs are the source of action, but the action also quickens their energy. Immediately after they decide to break out of the confinement of the house and go to the protest meeting in town, Jim becomes aware of Mary, "ready to fly at him like a black hen, her eyes snapping, her thin nervous body sharp standing against the wind, full of that energy and zip that always pleased him" (p. 163). After Mary comes into her own at the meeting "she felt herself full of the energy of the finest kind" (p. 173). On the way home she sits "close to Jim's long flank" and the overt political message of the story is articulated in the midst of Jim and Mary's renewed sexual interest in each other (p. 173). Le Sueur's commitments are valuable but even Le Sueur cannot consistently overcome the inhibitions of left pastoral, which make it extremely difficult for her to endow Jim with the kind of sexual sensitivity she achieves in "The Girl."

Like marches and strikes, the protest meeting is central to the iconography of the 1930s left. Radical writers focused on these events, party because they were happening, partly because they epitomize the militant, cooperative action that could bring the new socialist world to life from the womb of the old capitalism. In "Salute to Spring," the protest is that of the Popular Front, which for Le Sueur does not include devitalized professors who "don't believe in anything" and who give "sad" counsel of despair to the farmers (pp. 167–68). Instead, Le Sueur has Jim strongly argue a Popular Front position based on respect for America, the Constitution, and paying your debts, hardly an assault on the theory of private property (p. 168). Jim outlines the predicament of farmers who have worked hard, had crop failures, and are now faced with the dilemma of having to lose their farms to get the money for seed or to renege on their debts. He argues "we got to do something. We got to begin to go forward. These things got to be known" (p. 170). The story itself is part of the process of making things known. The "something" Jim advocates doing, however, consists merely of forming a committee to bring the situation to the attention of the authorities. In the story this cooperative enterprise gets results—Mary uses the threat of committee action to get food for her family, so that Le Sueur projects an aura of effective demands. The militancy, however, is very muted, a shadow of "I Was Marching" or "Tonight Is Part of the Struggle."

The explicit sexual politics in "Salute to Spring" are tamer and more one-dimensional than in "Tonight Is Part of the Struggle" or "Annunciation." Mary overcomes her nervousness and speaks at the meeting on the importance of having women represented. Ole Hanson, the chairman, reinforces her message, so that the unity he speaks for includes men and women acting together (p. 171). In counterpoint to the primer quality of the story is the emphasis on renewed energy and reawakened sexuality. Surprisingly, then, Le Sueur does not conclude as we would expect, on an upbeat note to round out her lesson on the value of Popular Front protest, food in the car, energy going, men and women together. The seasonal and human renewal the story turns on leads us to expect the life, not the death of the infant. Le Sueur effectively subverts these expectations. When they return home, Jim and Mary find the baby has died. In stressing the death of the baby and the fatal effects of hunger, Le Sueur powerfully reasserts the claims of the unmet needs that radical change must still address.

The subverted pattern of renewal, however, also includes the reawakened sexuality of Jim and Mary, which continues in a touching form into the conclusion. In contrast to their earlier knifelike opposition, now "she got into bed beside him. He turned the strong scythe of his legs, the thrust and cleft of his breast, and she turned into him, crying" (p. 176). This humanly credible mixture of sexual communion and grief sets up a tension that supplies a context for "I Was Marching," the piece that immediately follows and concludes *Salute to Spring*.

As for "Salute to Spring," the story suggests some of the pressures Le Sueur as a committed party writer was under. Official party positions and the incentive to be positive and affirmative conflict with other phases of Le Sueur's Marxism: with her sense of the role of women in the party, her sense of sexuality, and, even more deeply, her sense of the profound hunger that genuine revolution must address. A common view is that party pressures repeatedly corrupted the quality of the art of the 1930s left.[14] In "Salute to Spring" and "Tonight Is Part of the Struggle," however, Le Sueur shows that engaging official party positions could animate rather than weaken the work of the activist writer.

"I Was Marching"

The conflicts that energize these stories are not at issue in "I Was Marching," which gains strength from Le Sueur's positive involvement in left discourse. To appreciate Le Sueur's radical achievement in "I Was Marching," her conclusion to *Salute to Spring*, we must recall that Le Sueur was working within the genre of 1930s left reportage, so that her personal voice amplified and was amplified by countless others. Because of their role in revolutionary theory and practice, strikes and mass protest meetings were recurring objects of attention in left reportage and fiction. Le Sueur worked within this tradition and transformed its iconography, especially that of the march. In most left reportage the first-person narrator has a personal voice but also subordinates him or herself to the immediacy of the dust-blown farm or the Chevy plant during a sit-down strike. What distinguishes "I Was Marching" from almost every other piece of reportage is the way Le Sueur integrates a narrative of personal conversion with a precise rendering of the strike and all this movement comes to stand for. Only Agee in *Let Us Now Praise Famous Men* handles the "I" with anything like Le Sueur's depth. If John Reed and James Agee are the Tolstoys of left reportage, Le Sueur is the Chekhov of the form.

Beyond "I Was Marching," in her other reportage Le Sueur concentrates on American hunger, literal and symbolic, especially the hunger of unemployed urban women and women on ravaged dust bowl farms.[15] These women are starved for food and also for the fulfillment of jobs, families, and community, all threatened by the pressures of depression capitalism. In "I Was Marching" Le Sueur stresses community but her focus is not on hunger and women. Instead, she turns to a major dilemma for 1930s middle-class radicals, the contradiction between their middle-class origins and its deep impact on consciousness and their allegiance to a new cohesive way of life embodied in the proletariat.[16] During the depression one of the appeals of Marxism was that it offered a communal alternative to the privatized, competitive individualism of a market society that had broken down. Le Sueur goes to the heart of these contradictions in "I Was Marching."

The immediate occasion for "I Was Marching" was the 1934 truckers' strike in Minneapolis. Le Sueur does more than report on the strike. She creates a first-person narrator—call her Meridel Le Sueur. This "I" is an authentic, believable creation, "fictional" in the same sense that the narrator of a good autobiography is fictional. When I refer to the Le Sueur of "I Was Marching," I am pointing to the created "I" of the essay, a creation related to but not the same as the biographical Meridel Le Sueur. The narrator of "I Was Marching," for example, does not tell us about her radical parents. Instead, Le Sueur concentrates on the middle-class sides of her identity, so that she can go deep into her own divided feelings and can trace her own gradual involvement in the strike. Because of her handling of point of view, Le Sueur can be precise about her own fears and hopes and she can do detailed justice to what she sees and feels during the strike. Without making an issue of it, Le Sueur thus succeeds in fusing inner and outer, private and public, the individual and the social. This formal achievement is also a substantive triumph. She faces and resolves the widely shared middle-class fear that if we give ourselves over to a community we will lose our own individuality, that society will dominate and subdue what we find most precious in ourselves.

Through the drama of "I Was Marching," Le Sueur brings alive a version of Marxism in which the middle-class individual acts cooperatively with striking workers. Through this action the Le Sueur of "I Was Marching" changes and in the process strengthens the community she is helping to create, even as the community helps constitute her as an individual. On this view the individual develops fully through meaningful action as part of an evolving community, but not at the expense of his or her individuality. Le Sueur thus makes her own personal transformation a particular instance of a general possibility. The tensions and movements of this particular strike also suggest the prospect of a much more widespread process of cooperative, rebellious action and of a new society emerging from this movement.

Here is a genuine Marxism. Everything is solidly grounded in particulars, in the material processes of the factory, in the precise look and feel of movements that culminate in the rhythm of men and women marching. Far from being obliterated, Le Sueur experiences an intensified vitality. "I feel most alive and yet for the first time in my life I do not feel myself as separate. I realize then that all my previous feelings have been based on feeling myself separate and distinct from others and now I sense sharply faces, bodies, closeness, and my own fear is not my own, nor my hope" (p. 187). The cadence of that final phrase, its placement and formality, give a concluding dignity and emphasis to a discourse that unites and precisely discriminates the physical look and feel of faces and bodies and the more intangible realities of shared fear and hope. At the end, "I felt my legs straighten. I felt my feet join in that strange shuffle of thousands of bodies moving with direction, of thousands of feet, and my own breath with the gigantic breath. As if an electric charge had passed through me, my hair stood on end. I was marching" (p. 191).

This ending is also a beginning. The active image, "I was marching," reconciles without eliminating differences and simultaneously invokes a future beyond the barricades the strikers have erected, a future beyond the blood from police bullets, a future beyond the dead bodies the marchers are commemorating. The future society is grounded in the rhythms of dedicated, cooperative action in the present. The entire movement of "I Was Marching" acts out a vital dialectical rhythm that connects present and future, individual and community, middle and working class, fear and hope.

Le Sueur succeeds in inspiring us not by minimizing difficulties but by showing how she herself overcame her own fears and in the process energized the hope her work affirms. Le Sueur has not written a treatise on the new society or how to achieve it. But she does offer what she shows in the present as an earnest of the future. In the context of the labor militancy of the depression, Le Sueur gives an immediate, tangible example of successful, ongoing struggle. The struggle is not only between classes but within individuals. And Le Sueur's style, her voice, emerges as a model.

As a Marxist artist Le Sueur focuses on change, process, and conflict. The drama of her own personal change reinforces and is reinforced by the larger social-political conflict she participates in. The unity of her work emerges from the clash of personal and social-political conflicts and the accumulation of details whose particularity she respects even as she endows them with a charge of heightened significance. Far from being didactic or one-dimensional, Le Sueur shows a Marxist art responsive to change, implication, and variety. Equally important, her personal integrity—the honesty, concern, and precision of her voice and observation—guarantee that the individual is valued. Le Sueur succeeds in sustaining the individual as integral within the cohesive whole she also values. At the end "*I* was marching," not some faceless, mindless abstraction.

For Constance Coiner, on the other hand, Le Sueur's reportage and especially "I Was Marching" are suspect because Le Sueur is wrong on ideology—according to Coiner, in "I Was Marching" Le Sueur promotes a base-superstructure view that "dangerously underestimates the all-pervasiveness of ideology."[17] For Coiner the issue of ideology is central, but for Le Sueur in "I Was Marching" the conversion process is basic and ideology is a peripheral concern. In the quotation Coiner uses to support her view about base and superstructure, Le Sueur writes, "Our merchant society has been built upon a huge hypocrisy, a cut-throat competition which sets one man against another and at the same time an ideology mouthing such words as 'Humanity,' 'Truth,' the 'Golden Rule,' and such. Now in a crisis the word falls away and the skeleton of that action shows in terrific movement."

As I read this suggestive, elliptical passage, Le Sueur is rendering the sense that the strike, the depression, and the worldwide crisis of capitalism expose the ideological mystifications encoded in "such words as 'Humanity,' 'Truth,' and the 'Golden Rule.'" Le Sueur's emphasis here and throughout "I Was Marching" is on movement, on process, not on a static theory of base-superstructure. The "action" of "the skeleton of that action" refers partly to "the word falls away"—to the demystifying process of seeing that the crisis makes possible. The phrase "shows in terrific movement" looks ahead to the multiple movements Le Sueur renders in "I Was Marching" and back to underscore the powerful dislocations inseparable from "the word falls away." The "skeleton" endows the process with a threatening and ominous sense of death as well as referring to the essentials "of that action." Coiner sees Le Sueur as "redundant" and "didactic" (p. 98) but for me the quoted passage has a challenging, metaphoric openness not easy to pin down. I am skeptical about attributing a simple base-superstructure view to Le Sueur on the evidence of this partly enigmatic and metaphorically compressed passage.

As Le Sueur proceeds her words themselves are simple enough but as they combine in metaphors they resonate and become complex and deep and urgent. Le Sueur's Marxist discourse is rooted in direct statements of physical acts and personal feelings. She varies simple sentences and phrases with longer ones that precisely describe people and emotions and scenes, all based on the integrity of her own seeing and feeling. Le Sueur's personal integrity emerges from the accumulation of hundreds of precise acknowledgments. She keeps us in touch, and, on my experience as a teacher, most readers come to respect her and to respect the accuracy and precision of what she sees and the varied, incanatory rhythms of her way of presenting it.

"For two days I heard of the strike. I went by their headquarters. I walked by on the opposite side of the street and saw the dark old building that had been a garage and lean, dark young faces leaning from the upstairs windows. I had to go down there often. I looked in. I saw the huge black interior and live coals of living men moving restlessly and orderly, their eyes gleaming from their sweaty faces" (p. 178). "The dark old building" and the lean "dark" faces recur again and again. "The huge black interior and live coals of living men" suggest the depths, danger, and vitality of the mines, of the interior regions of self and society. The lower depths and the unconscious are both threatening and fecund. New life comes from these dark sources. The dark unknown is simultaneously the building that houses the strikers and the entire new world the strike foretells. The threat of the unknown is more than balanced by the recognition of "*live* coals" of living men in what Le Sueur later calls "that dark and lively building, massed with men" (p. 179).

Le Sueur reverses the respectable white middle-class view. She invokes images that have powerful, conventionally negative associations. The "dark," "black" interior associated with the "sweaty faces" of striking workers could easily yield a sense of demonic chaos. Instead, Le Sueur responds to the restless vitality and order, the exact reverse of the usual charge against strikers. She amplifies this reversal when she later connects her own middle-class resistance to joining the strike with the very feelings of "disruption, chaos, and disintegration" that are typically held against the workers. In contrast, she sees them as "drawing into a close and glowing cohesion like a powerful conflagration in the midst of the city" (p. 179). This fire destroys, animates, and unifies. It appropriately inspires feelings of awe and hope. "I knew this action to be prophetic and indicative of future actions and I wanted to be part of it" (p. 179).

First, however, Le Sueur has to work through her central fear. "The truth is," she writes, "I was afraid. Not of the physical danger at all, but an awful fright of mixing, of losing myself, of being unknown and lost. I felt inferior. I felt no one would know me there, that all I had been trained to excel in would go unnoticed. I can't describe what I felt, but perhaps it will come near it to say that I felt I excelled in competing with others and I knew instantly that these people were not competing at all, that they were acting in a strange, powerful trance of movement together. And I was filled with longing to act with them and with fear that I could not. I felt I was born out of every kind of life, thrown up alone, looking at other lonely people, a condition I had been in the habit of defending with various attitudes of cynicism, preciosity, defiance, and hatred" (pp. 178–79).

These realizations are at the heart of the Marxist conversion process Le Sueur records. In her narrative even before she joins the strikers Le Sueur vividly shows the massacre that precipitates the concluding march of protest, cohesion, and power. At the outset the strike thus has overtones of a revolutionary action of workers against official force or, rather, of an action that becomes insurrectionary because of the bullets used to stop it. The killed and maimed strikers make readers aware of the real dangers involved. Even more, however, in Le Sueur's text the murders function to inspire readers to act to bring about the future the strike is "prophetic and indicative of" (p. 179).

In practice these acts are often routine but not trivial. In the process of reporting on her increasing involvement with the strikers, Le Sueur gives a sense of what it was like inside strike headquarters on a hot July day in Minneapolis. Until her concluding sentence she also sustains her personal drama of discovery and conversion. In her later work Le Sueur will challenge it but now she accepts the conventional sex roles: a man is in charge; the women serve coffee and sandwiches and wash cups; the men picket. For now what is important is that Le Sueur is involved in a meaningful process—the task at hand, the strike, the new society the strike is helping to create. Significantly, her labor is no longer alienated. "Hours go by, the heat is terrific. I am not tired. I am not hot. I am pouring coffee. I am swung into the most intense and natural organization I have ever felt. I know everything that is going on" (p. 164).

Here is another in a series of episodes that serve as models, that make the new society as alive and immediate as the person speaking to us of what she truly feels and knows. The episode convincingly establishes that in a cohesive society where labor is not alienated, people experience a heightened sense of self and community, of intensified awareness and physical vitality. Factory organization becomes natural, not mechanical. Participants are not mindless cogs in a machine but as unalienated workers "know everything that is going on." The act of pouring coffee is valued, is precisely recorded, and is related to the most general movements in the new society this act is helping to create. In Le Sueur's Marxist aesthetics, the personal and particular receive the same careful, life-giving attention as the large processes they shape and are shaped by.[18]

Another dialectic gives urgency to the remainder of Le Sueur's reportage. She develops a contrast between feeding and fighting. The strikers care for each other, serve coffee and food in counterpoint to the growing apprehension that " 'something awful is going to happen' " (p. 185). It is more than a simple dialectic of cohesive nurturing arising in opposition to and opposed by police bullets. Within the building "a terrible communal excitement ran through the hall like a fire through a forest," so that Le Sueur continues to stress the destructive and creative power of revolutionary activity (p. 184). Liberal discourse tends simply to show the oppressed as victims of brutal power, to appeal to the readers' sympathies for the underdog. In her report on Spain, Dorothy Parker, for example, centers repeatedly on women and children killed by fascist bombs. Dorothy Parker leaves it at that.[19] In Le Sueur's radical discourse, in contrast, working people suffer at the hands of officials, but the people fight back with an energy that promises to destroy the old and to create an entirely new society.

Brought to life through action, the new self moves into unexplored territory. References to movement propel the narrative ahead, just as the movement of masses of men and women in the present foretell and give body to "a future vitality." To commemorate the dead, ten thousand closely packed participants wait silently in front of the flatbed of the afternoon's bullet-ridden truck. "The silence seems terrific like a great form moving of itself. This is real movement issuing from the close reality of mass feeling. This is the first real rhythmic movement I have ever seen. My heart hammers terrifically. My hands are swollen and hot. No one is producing this movement. It's a movement upon which all are moving softly, rhythmically, terribly" (p. 188). Within this rhythm Le Sueur continues to make new discoveries, to record sudden breakthroughs, and thereby to affirm novelty and freedom. She is at odds with those who stress the theory of a Leninist vanguard directing the movement. In Le Sueur's model of the revolutionary new society, action arises spontaneously from below without the need of a leader or leadership cadre. The rhythm of action is not predetermined and it enhances, it does not eliminate the humanity of the participants. This movement is Le Sueur's independent Marxist alternative to the restless, aimless movement she had exposed in "Corn Village." Embodied in the physical movement and rhythms of the march, the Marxist conversion process Le Sueur sustains throughout "I Was Marching" undogmatically shows that we change consciousness through acts that change the material conditions that shape consciousness. And she shows that we can do it.

The rhythms, repetitions, and stresses of Le Sueur's imaginatively charged prose give body to her vision until the very end. In a context of barricades and the power of marching men and women, Le Sueur overcomes her final sense of exclusion and joins in the rhythm of the march. Her vision is grounded in vital material processes. Like Marx, she knows "the philosophers have only interpreted the world; the point, however, is to *change* it." Her achievement is that she records the felt reality of a present moment, embodies the living dialectics of a changed individual and a transformed society, and inspires her readers to struggle toward a communal future. Without falsifying the difficulties, her work makes that future seem real, achievable, and worthwhile. In "I Was Marching" Le Sueur speaks for a precious moment in American history when, poised between present and future, these possibilities were a living part of a national dialogue.

The Girl

In the version of *The Girl* she published in 1978, Le Sueur shifts her emphasis to sexual politics from the Marxist politics that predominate in *Salute to Spring* and in the powerful sections of *The Girl* she published in the *Anvil* in 1935 and in *New Masses* in 1939 and 1940. The two politics are of course intertwined. In *Salute to Spring*, especially in "Corn Village," "Annunciation," and "I Was Marching," Le Sueur draws on her own experience to create an "I" and a resonant, poetically and politically charged discourse. At the other extreme are the first-person narratives that emerge from Le Sueur's immersion in the experiences of other people. Her commitment to people's culture impelled her to listen to countless stories and to turn them into art. Her lyric novel, *The Girl*, which she worked on throughout the middle and late 1930s and returned to in the 1970s, is the most sustained result.

The point-of-view character is the girl, who has no other name, an index of her representative quality. She is young, poor, and inexperienced. We gradually learn that she has come from a small place two hours away from St. Paul, that she is frightened and attracted by what she experiences, and that her sensibility allows us to see and feel the underside of city life. During the depression she is working at the German Village, a bootleg liquor joint that also serves great steaming bowls of stew. The girl comes from an ethnic, working-class background but Le Sueur does not make an issue of ethnicity. Instead, the ethnicity of the characters pervades the novel as an integral component of the people's culture Le Sueur brings to life. The girl is human, vulnerable, and appealing. She reports what she sees and hears, accepts most of it unprotestingly, and, with justification, is often afraid. Because she is not intellectually or socially sophisticated, she does not generate long paragraphs of logically developed ideas. Instead, the paragraphs are short, the personal observations focus on her feelings of fear, hunger, or attraction, and the slightly refracted idiom and syntax frequently convey the unpretentious poetry of the ordinary.

As readers, we play an active role, filling in and making explicit judgments and connections. Le Sueur has an underlying confidence in and affection for both the girl and the reader. She assumes that finally we will respond to the human qualities of the girl and the frequently inhuman conditions she experiences. Le Sueur assumes that as ordinary readers we are able to make connections for ourselves and to respond to what is implied rather than explicitly stated. Part of what is at issue with the girl, the style, and the reader is the question of "the people." For all their shortcomings, Le Sueur has an underlying confidence in the humanity and intelligence of the people—in the girl and in those who read her story. This radical faith in the people animated Le Sueur's political art throughout her long, productive lifetime.

Her faith in the people is basic to Le Sueur's radical discourse, to her Marxism, feminism, and sense of ethnicity, all of which pervade the allusive, idiomatic style of *The Girl*, including the social class, speech, and concerns of its characters. The style of the novel, that is, expresses Le Sueur's Marxism, feminism, and sense of ethnicity in a deep way but in a way that conflicts with pressures within the party for doctrinal orthodoxy and explicit statement. Le Sueur is especially independent in the way she deals extensively and sympathetically with dispossessed people who do not have a working-class consciousness and whose activities are basically counterrevolutionary. The official Marxist view is that in the German Village she is dealing with "the dangerous class, the social scum, that passively rotting mass thrown off by the lowest layers of the old society." In *The Communist Manifesto* Marx and Engels go on to say that this class "may, here and there, be swept into the movement by a proletarian revolution; its conditions of life, however, prepare it far more for the part of a bribed tool of reactionary intrigue."[20] Butch's strikebreaking confirms this view and the robbery does too in a modified way, but Le Sueur's view of her people is much more accepting than the official class analysis.

In her sensitivity to feeling and her avoidance of abstractions, in her concern for oppressed women and her celebration of their suffering and strength, in her belief in the value of American speech and people's culture, Le Sueur is also at odds with the Marxism of European-oriented intellectuals like Rahv and Phillips. Le Sueur recognizes that the people are often brutal and warped, that they often accept false values and live in a hell partly of their own making. But through characters like the girl, Belle, and Amelia, Le Sueur also affirms the underlying vitality, decency, and strength of ordinary people, particularly women, and of a people's culture struggling for expression among those whom the dominant class and even dissident intellectuals typically ignore or despise.

At the Village the German band is Irish, the Booya—the stew—is abundant, but we soon learn that in this marginal world, instability, hunger, and death are even deeper realities than the bootleg booze and the cat having kittens for the men to bet on. Economically, within two or three short, packed chapters, Le Sueur gets us inside the girl's consciousness and inside this vital, precarious world. In contrast to the male-dominated WASP milieu of most canonical American fiction, Le Sueur's world has powerful women as well as men, and the people have names like Hoinck, Stasia, and Ganz. They are only a generation or two removed from the Old World and, though they have inevitably been affected by American attitudes toward success and failure, they have not succumbed to the decorum of what John Murray

Cuddihy calls "the Protestant Etiquette," that discipline in repression and restraint that constitutes respectability for the dominant class.[21]

The girl, for example, is in love with Butch. She loves his "black sleek head," his "long face lean like a fox," and "the way his back was so smooth and silky going to his very small hips."[22] Even at first, as "a virgin from the country scared of her shadow," as Clara describes her, the girl responds to Butch's dangerous sensuality (p. 2). The girl's language brings out the poetry implicit in the idiom and rhythms of ordinary speech.[23] Le Sueur uses the girl as a vehicle of discovery and affirmation. She endows the girl with an unpretentious humanity and inner life and then allows her to respond not according to formula but according to the inner imperatives of her nature in the difficult situations in which she finds herself. Her language is full of independent turns of phrase and perception.

Butch, on the other hand, is a compendium of stock responses. His language seems to emerge from books like *Studs Lonigan* and *U.S.A.*, not from Le Sueur's transformation of ordinary speech. Unlike the girl's language, which is still fresh and compelling, Butch is made to use language that is noticeably dated. He uses expressions like "show the white feather" for being yellow. He monotonously begins sentences, "Gee, baby," and then follows it up with further tough guy clichés. In two pages of free-flowing reminiscence before he dies, however, Butch comes into his own as a fictional voice. In outline, even before this scene Butch is nonetheless a promising but imperfectly realized character whose possibilities and limits are revealing.

A worker conceived within the conventions of the radical fiction of the 1930s, under the pressure of the depression Butch emerges as a displaced American worker who loves machines and the unalienated labor of fixing them and playing ball. Like many others, however, far from being a model proletarian hero he totally lacks a sense of class consciousness. Instead of responding to the depression with revolutionary activity, he gets a job as a scab strikebreaker and later, fatally, he becomes involved in a bank robbery to get the money for the service station he dreams of owning. To his disadvantage, Butch actively accepts the dominant class views about success, about winning. After Butch has been fatally wounded, he learns that Standard Oil makes it impossible for the small owner to survive. The big corporation turns out to be a legal robber. Unlike Standard Oil, however, the little robbers get shot or shoot each other. Through implication Le Sueur exposes the bank robbery as a false alternative to revolution, an attack on a basic capitalistic institution but an attack that affirms rather than subverts the system. In multiple ways the robbery confirms Hoinck's view that everyone steals (p. 74).

Le Sueur repeatedly uses contrasts between Butch and the girl to emphasize the difference between his male-capitalistic outlook and the girl's feminine-cooperative one. Butch lives in a society that systematically produces desires that leave people dissatisfied because they can never have enough, a tendency intensified by the breakdown of the depression. When the girl asks Butch what he wants, he reveals that, against his real interests, he has interiorized the dominant class emphasis on "winning all the time and the good feel it gives you," a "good feel" Butch is unlikely to have very often, since he cannot really win very often. His death after the robbery underscores the point. Butch also wants to be "doing things, you know with the English on it, know what I mean?" (p. 15). The girl is almost never inarticulate about her feelings and desires. As a doer, Butch presumably must also be clumsy with words. But he has been deeply affected by words. His consciousness shows the impact of American advertising and movies, which during the 1920s and 1930s invested heavily in images of fast cars and sexy women. "And driving a fast car," Butch says about what he wants. "And having a girl who likes it and knows how to do it," a desire that brings into the open what the ads and movies keep somewhat implicit. Butch concludes with the working-class version of the dominant class ideology of competitive individualism. "It takes guts, he said, that's what it is, to go through the night. You got to be tough and strong and alone" (p. 15), an outlook that continues to influence American domestic and foreign affairs.

In contrast to Butch's stress on doing, on winning, and on being tough and alone, the girl says "I don't like it alone. . . . I don't want to be alone. I want to be with others" and, even more simply and to the point, "I like to be. I like to feel good, that's what I like" (pp. 15, 24). In typical male fashion Butch puts her down by asserting "Women are dunces. They never say anything definite," so that his failure to understand her noncompetitive view translates into an indictment of women's intelligence (p. 24). Butch has company in believing that people who do not use the official language and categories "never say anything definite" and are therefore mentally inferior.

Butch's charge and its unmasking also bear on the style of *The Girl*. The novel has underlying patterns but Le Sueur deliberately, on principle, does not develop the book in a conventional, discursive, linear way. Like the consciousness of the girl, the novel moves rapidly, focusing now on the girl's concerns, now on the panorama of surrounding people and events. Connections are usually made intuitively, allusively, or through the indirection of racy idioms and metaphors, not by way of formally articulated concepts. The girl is not a master of technical dialectics; she does not deal in abstractions. But she is alert to contradictions and to the flow of feelings and significant happenings. Like the girl, Le Sueur's avoidance of official conventions should not be turned into a complaint that she "never says anything definite."

In the early stages of her relationship with Butch, for all the unconventional language and milieu of the German Village sections, the literary and social conventions are nonetheless the familiar ones of a girl with a man at the center of her life. The move toward birth and female solidarity comes later. In conventional fiction the action typically builds toward marriage. In Le Sueur's feminist-Marxist-ethnic discourse, the action builds toward birth and the rebellious community of women. In the early episodes featuring the girl, however, interest centers around her feelings for Butch. While it is true that this focus is in some ways conventional, presenting it from the girl's point of view results in unconventional and welcome shifts. As a matter of course the girl preempts the typical male role and actively looks for Butch. Instead of men looking at women's bodies, moreover, the girl is open about the way she likes his looks and sensuality.

A certain comedy emerges from Butch's blindness, because from the start he has what he wants without knowing it. His approaches to the girl are clumsy; she worries that her show of feelings will put him off. Instead of a sexually charged dialogue between the girl and Butch, she feels a promising sexual attraction for him and Butch responds with programmatic statements about robbing people of faith or of treating her like a sister and "you runs like a harlot" (p. 24). Through most of the early sections Butch is made to speak and act like a mechanical puppet repeating male chauvinist stock responses to contrast with the girl's vulnerability and vitality.

The contrast between Le Sueur's handling of Butch before and after the robbery reveals something significant about the practice of political art. Le Sueur's underlying respect for and knowledge of ordinary people do not sufficiently enliven her conception of Butch until near his end. Instead of giving Butch an independent language and a free form of expression, Le Sueur succumbs to tough-guy stereotypes, which mandate that lower class American men should be crude, insensitive, and inarticulate, lacking in emotional and linguistic complexity. From a Marxist point of view, Butch is put down as an instance of what the American worker should not be. From a feminist point of view, Butch is a straw man spokesman for male dominance. In contrast to her success with the girl, however, until after the robbery Le Sueur has not managed to do what she does best as a political artist—to use personal language and a liberated form, to get inside Butch, and to bring alive in an independent way his shortcomings, contradictions, and appeal.

As he is dying, however, Le Sueur finds a language and form that do justice to

Butch's possibilities as a proletarian character, which for her includes his working-class and Irish American origins. Freed from the demands of programmatic statements, Le Sueur allows Butch to range freely over the suggestive episodes of his past. As an example of what not to be, Butch was earlier an almost total captive of Marxist and feminist ideologies. At the end he raises radical issues but he does so in a much freer and less constrained way. Butch's fever justifies the kind of mental leaps and fusions that bring out Le Sueur at her idiomatic best, in touch with three-fingered Charlie "from New York came from Miami by freight" and the steelworker who symbolically falls to his death putting up the Empire State Building (p. 91). In these vignettes of his America, Butch comes through as experienced and compassionate. Of the steelworker he says, "I had a pretty big funeral. All the gang. I felt terrible" (p. 91). Butch himself is dying, so that the twist in idiom drives home his own impending death, and his humanity is doubly enforced by his feelings for the dead man he couldn't save. Through these flashes of reminiscence, Le Sueur not only characterizes Butch but also conveys a sense of his ethnic, working-class America, an America of jobs, unemployment, bars, street talk, and hitting the rails. Her two or three pages leave as strong an impression of this side of America as the massive accumulations of *Studs Lonigan* and *U.S.A.*.

Butch's memories are interspersed with a reconstruction of what actually happened at the robbery. The girl has previously repeated time and again the sequence they were to follow. During the robbery she has given a precise account of the way it looked and sounded to her from the getaway car she is driving. She reports the robbery in a detached way, experiencing it "like it was something in a story, something I was reading" (p. 86). Le Sueur gradually builds on the fictional, legendary possibilities of the holdup. In the girl's report of the robbery itself, because she functions like a camera, the holdup reminds us of a film as well as a story, "like a movie when you run it fast and then slow, or run it backwards" (p. 77). Throughout, Le Sueur has played off her unglamorized characters against the Hollywood version. Ganz in particular has none of the sinister charm of a movie criminal. His vicious assault on the girl is especially degraded. The German Village is not picturesque or seedy; it is a place for ethnic working people, some engaged in petty crime, to eat and bet and get drunk and try to forget the depression. An even more important difference with Hollywood is that the entire robbery is charged with feminist and Marxist undertones. Along with the narrative tension it creates, the robbery exposes the way men dominate women and the way people on the margins of society use petty crime to get something, as opposed to trying for real change.

As Butch's memories weave in and out, we learn from him the inside details of what went on in the bank: of Ganz's double cross, the way he shot Hoinck in the back after Butch has given Ganz the money satchel, the way Butch got Ganz and then got it himself. The repetition of the story and film of the robbery gives the holdup a legendary dimension befitting a story told over and over again and important in the lives of the characters and their culture. Le Sueur undermines the glamor of the Hollywood gangster and subverts Hollywood's covert message that crime does pay. The squalid quality of the robbery, the realization that everybody steals, from Ganz to Standard Oil, and especially the fatal betrayals all underscore the holdup as a false solution. Le Sueur's version of the robbery takes its place on the radical left in the ideological discourse of the 1930s. It is easy to miss the ideological implications, however, because Le Sueur has built them into the narrative form and pattern and has relied more on indirection than on explicit statement.

Near his end, though, Butch is accorded the dignity of partial awareness and the resonant language appropriate to it. "Sleep, he said, I been sleeping all my life. My God, do we belong to the human race or don't we?" (p. 94). His language is politically charged, although Le Sueur avoids the obvious slogans. In contrast to sleep and Butch's bleak understanding that "we're trapped honey," at the end of the novel the girl fully joins the human race in the fusion of birth and Workers Alliance protest. With Butch, Le Sueur fuses her left critique with a strong personal accent on the earth and "the sweet marrow of your body" as she has Butch ask, "what are they doing to you now honey? They own the town. They own the earth and the sweet marrow of your body. Watch out! They'll shoot at you from all the windows and blow up the town!" (p. 95). His impending death adds urgency to this warning against the ownership of the ruling class and its form of class conflict—as in the Minneapolis truckers' strike, violence used to suppress the dispossessed but, unlike "I Was Marching," not the workers rising in revolt against the owners.

With increasing desperation Butch concludes,

what was it who made it what got us we come to this bad end?
Be quiet, I said.
We didn't mean any of this we didn't think of any of this, he screamed.
I couldn't make him be quiet now.
He talked about other things, some he had told me, and some of it he hadn't. He thought of all the people he knew ending up with me and then he died. (p. 95)

At the end Butch emerges as human in his combination of partial awareness, energy, and vulnerability. Butch's criticisms are telling, his consciousness has deepened, but he is still understandably negative, because he is not in a position to act on his changing perceptions. In the organizing rhythm of the novel, the girl provides a significant alternative to Butch. In its full personal and social-political meaning and close to the center of the novel, Butch's death is a pivotal event. Playing off against and interweaving with the death are the girl's first experience of sex, her decision to have the child, her conflict with the authorities about sterilization, and the birth that concludes the novel. This organization around the basic human realities of sexuality, death, and birth illuminates the girl's sensibility, the American social world she emerges from, and hope of a new world the birth hints at.

The organizing rhythm of life emerging from death begins early in the novel. The death of the girl's domineering, abusive father—he himself is a victim of an inexorable market society—allows the girl to identify with her mother (p. 39). Liberated by the death of her coercive father and by her mother's revelations about the elementally female, the girl almost immediately experiences "the secret" of sex and later of birth. The intertwining of death, sex, and birth follows first from the death of the father and later from Butch's death, sequences that establish the patriarchal barriers women have to overcome and that establish the conditions for the community of women and the new birth that give the ending of *The Girl* its sense of revolutionary possibility.

The robbery is the male-capitalistic antithesis of the cohesive world of the women and the principled radicalism Amelia speaks for. Through most of the novel Butch speaks for the insatiable desires of capitalism. In counterpoint with the plans for the robbery, Le Sueur gives the girl a vital language to celebrate the contrasting desires she has after sleeping with Butch. These desires, the girl says, "all broke on my tongue like some wild sweet fruit. As if my bark was breaking in spring, or mama rising in me telling me how the flesh can die, be beaten, and lost. I felt a great root springing down and a great green blossom springing up, like my hair sprang up out of my green skull, or a terrible root went in the dark with a hundred mouths looking for food" (p. 53). In contrast to the artificial, divisive desires of capitalism, the girl's desires are as natural as "wild sweet fruit." They relate her to all of life, including the death associated with the "green skull." From deep down, however, the root of sexualized desire animates the green blossom "like my hair sprang out of my green skull," so that the girl is connected to, not separated from, the dark powers of sexualized growth and death. For her death is not final but is rather part of a vital process. She is part of the same process. She sees her bark breaking in spring, so that she sees herself as integral to the trees and the rhythms of the seasons, just as she has her mother "rising in me" and paradoxically telling her the flesh can die. A little later when she runs away from the squalid abortionist, the girl does not explain why she has suddenly decided to have her baby, but in her celebration of desire she has already given her underlying reasons.

Her interludes of compressed poetry bring into the open what is important to the girl. They characterize her, deepen the narrative, alter the rapid pace of the narrative, and establish underground connections Le Sueur usually does not have the girl make explicit. The girl emerges as intuitive, complex, but not cerebral. The reader has to make connections and to respond to the demands of the heightened language. To the extent that we expect left formulas and explicit connections, we are thrown slightly off balance. In *The Girl* Le Sueur gives Amelia a dignified language that makes left slogans a genuine part of the narrative. The girl, however, often uses a more compressed, poetically charged language rooted in American idiom and the speech of ethnic, uneducated people, which is to say the speech of those outside the respectable middle class. The social strata is familiar in left fiction but in Le Sueur's discourse the sparing use of explicit ideological statements goes against the grain of conventional expectation. Le Sueur's language and sequences are simple in some ways but complex and demanding in others. We cannot read *The Girl* casually, as an exercise in skipping, any more than we can *A Portrait of a Lady* or *The Sound and the Fury*.

By the midpoint in the novel the girl has come to realize her need for others, the importance of women, and to understand that having the baby is her alternative to the robbery. These insights, however, are held in suspension, not built on stone by stone. Developments in *The Girl* answer to the rhythms and epistemology of ordinary life in which people do not behave in a linear, logically articulated way but rather act, often without saying why and often against their own best insights. They then surprisingly show they knew better all along. Le Sueur's epistemology gives primacy to feelings, intuitions, emotions, and to the basic experiences of sex, death, hunger, fear, joy, and poverty. In her discourse, conscious reasoning and abstract thought are secondary to the power of metaphor. The girl does not control events but she is not a passive receiver, either. Cumulatively, the girl deepens and develops but, because she does not minutely examine her own thought processes, does not usually supply abstract connectives, and because events carry her along—or she allows herself to go along—the process is discontinuous. Our attention shifts from the girl to those she is living with, which furthers the sense of interruption. As an organizing center, Le Sueur does not want the girl to be either too forceful or too passive. In the practice of Le Sueur's political art the challenge is to show the girl as a representative of the resilience and depth of ordinary people, so that she will have a recognizable individuality that is also compatible with, contributes to, and emerges from a community. Her ethnic and social class is oppressed and fragmented but she has an underlying humanity that survives oppression, draws energy from the vitality around and within her, and intuitively seeks cohesive, life-affirming bonds. As her response to Butch and her mother reveals, the power of sex is crucial.

Her friend Clara is a counterinstance. Clara supports herself as a prostitute and uses the ads in women's magazines to fantasize about furnishing a respectable two-bedroom house in Florida. She also worries that she is going to hell. She and the girl care for each other. "You are so pretty you are so good," the girl tells her, "you won't burn in hell and she gave out a cry and fell to the bed and I just held her" (p. 49). But her uprooted childhood, her vulnerability to conventional social and religious values, and above all the sex-for-pay and its attendant physical and psychological diseases drain Clara of vitality. She becomes increasingly ill and finally, after hell-like shock treatment, dies. Clara's life is an indictment of conventional society. She lives in a social and institutional hell different from the one that obsesses her. Le Sueur structures the novel so that Clara's death coincides with the birth of the girl's child. The girl deliberately names her daughter after Clara to affirm the new light and life that the ending of *The Girl* celebrates.

First, however, Le Sueur has the girl experience a period of transiency. Le Sueur organizes the final sections of the novel around three temporary homes the girl lives in. One is a dark, condemned building whose owner winters in Mexico on the money relief pays her. "The halls were dark and full of rubbish, apple cores, papers, cigarette butts, crusts of bread, old shoes, and once I saw some pancakes that had fallen out of somebody's garbage" (p. 103). In this embodiment of a decayed capitalism, the conversation is dominated by explicit and implicit protest.

In the next house she finds herself in, the girl learns more about the need, to use Amelia's words, to "stand up and fight with the others" (p. 111). This house is the relief maternity home she has been punitively sent to. From Amelia and her own experience she knows "the dicks follow you and the policematrons are trying to get some dirt on you. This woman, I found out later her name was Bradley, would be following me like a shadow. I would buy groceries for Belle, and I would turn my head, and my blood would stop right in my skin, there she would be standing looking at me. She's a stool and why should she be following me around?" (p. 112). The spy system is ostensibly to make sure that women on relief stay away from men. Le Sueur exposes the conventional morality of officialdom and the way the social work bureaucracy uses human values and appeals to friendship to penalize the people they are supposedly helping.

Using what she is really committed to, the language of official discourse, Miss Rice, the social worker, interprets the girl's wariness, energy, and independence as signs of psychiatric maladjustment. The girl certainly needs "a change of environment," because the old environment has hurt her, but the radically new world Le Sueur favors is satirically at odds with the social worker's solution of "casework followup, to inspire poise" and "referral to a psychiatric clinic" if she continues to be upset and rebellious. The sterilization Miss Rice recommends, moreover, is a denial of everything Le Sueur values and is the ultimate betrayal of the appeal to a warm friendship between two women (p. 114). In *The Girl* established institutions, their discourse, and their officials emerge as serious obstacles to the well-being of their clients and the basic changes they need.

After she manages to see Miss Rice's report, the girl has an understandable emotional outburst and is forcibly taken to the maternity home. Although they have been abused and are at the bottom of the social scale, the girl and her cohorts are not passive victims. At the home, Le Sueur brings out the vital, irreverent humor and resourcefulness of the inmates, who keep their spirits up and stay in touch despite the penal inspections. Their solidarity emerges in the touching exchange the girl has with a deaf-mute who befriends and educates her. Their notes to each other articulate the sensitivity of the oppressed to one another's needs, the importance of Workers' Alliance organizing and demands, and the girl's sudden awareness that she is a worker. Through the device of the deaf-mute and the notes, Le Sueur gives voice to those who are ordinarily dumb. The human feelings that flow between the two women give a special warmth and intensity to the Marxist slogans, which come alive and give meaning to the girl's experience. Before they go to sleep the girl's friend "wrote in a bold hand and turned the tiny light on it. *Wake tomorrow!*" (p. 118).

The image of light, the resistance to authority, and the injunctions to organize, demand, and awake all frame and interweave through the conclusion of *The Girl*. The politics of the ending are partly those of the Workers' Alliance protest march Amelia organizes to demand milk for the girl and the dying Clara. But in contrast to "I Was Marching," the march takes place in the muted background of the central action. The demand, moreover, is symbolic, since on the day of the march Clara dies and the girl has the baby the milk is to give her the strength to have.

More important is the militant, precarious solidarity of the women who have occupied an abandoned house and who, in contrast to their earlier talk about not having children, help the girl give birth. They are painfully poor, their situation is marginal, but they have powerful human, maternal resources. Without help from the institutions that fail even to send a taxi, they bring the new life into the new world their community of women exemplifies. The emphasis is on "the new woman" who has been born, on her name, which means "light"—"Clara, Clara"—

and on "a kind of woman's humming . . . all around me. I saw mama in them all," the girl goes on, "the bearing the suffering in us all, their seized bodies, bent bellies hanging, and the ferocity of their guarding. I felt fierce and she seemed to burrow to the nipple as I saw Amelia take the knife she had soaking in alcohol in a beer bottle and cut the cord" (p. 131).

In the strong feminist and Marxist ending of *The Girl* Le Sueur once again uses the reality of birth to establish that a new world can fiercely emerge from the womb of the old.

CHAPTER 4

THE DIALECTICAL IMAGINATION OF JOSEPHINE HERBST
THE TREXLER TRILOGY

As early as 1935 Josephine Herbst's novels had helped expand the theory of radical fiction beyond a narrow insistence on a proletarian setting.[1] As an observer at the 1930 Kharkov conference on revolutionary literature, Herbst had made a liberating discovery. "To me it was new to learn," she stressed, "that subject matter, to be valuable, need not even deal with actual workers, so long as the writer is cognizant of the Marxian theory of class."[2] This revelation focused her thinking about her own family history, which she had planned to use as the basis of an ambitious trilogy. Using the lens of an intuitively dialectical "Marxian theory of class," Herbst views the extended Trexler family and their diverse languages to bring alive the sweep and conflicts of American history and to give a personal, inward dimension to her probing of class, money, and gender. These concerns emerge undogmatically from the network of lives, from the web of languages, from Herbst's distinctive intertwining of past and present, personal and public, feeling and intellect.

By the time of *Rope of Gold* (1939), the concluding novel of her trilogy, Herbst had mastered an approach that allowed her to tap into personal and family experiences and to connect them with a revealing range of ideological conflicts. Her people care intensely about public issues. Their active intellectual debates and principled actions emerge from the core of their being. Or, in the case of Lester Tolman, one of her most imaginatively realized characters is fictionally successful because he is caught so precisely in the act of pretending. Against the great odds of such nineteenth- and twentieth-century American realities as recurring farm depressions, the American preoccupation with money, and the breakdown of personal relations, Herbst's characters struggle to live meaningful, unalienated lives.

The range of characters and Herbst's fluid handling of point of view, her ability to enter into opposing outlooks, allow her to test her doubts and commitments to a left view of America from the 1870s through the 1930s. Her version of Marxism stresses personal as well as class struggle. Issues are tested, not programmatically asserted. Herbst's sense of process, of intertwining, of contradictions not easy to resolve, animate her novelistic form. An unpretentious dialectics characterizes the relation between episodes and sustains vitality as Herbst moves into the final scenes of each of the novels. She gradually works toward the Haymarket anarchists and all they embody about radical protest and revolutionary possibility at the end of *Pity Is Not Enough* (1933). She builds toward the workers' protest march and David Trexler's exclusion at the grave, the burial of the old order—"*Don't mourn, Organize*"—in *The Executioner Waits* (1934). And she concludes the trilogy with the Cuban episode and the final strike scene in *Rope of Gold*, all hard-won affirmations within the iconography of the thirties left, with its emphasis on strikes, protest marches, and international workers' rebellion.

At the end of the trilogy, in counterpoint with her torment over the breakup of her marriage, Vicky Chance sees possibilities in the rebellion of dignified Cuban sugar workers. Anticipating Castro and the Sandinistas, their fire in the mountains compels Vicky Chance's energies and holds out the prospect of a painfully won victory of ordinary workers even in the face of Batista's repression and the acutely rendered role of American absentee owners and official American policy. The concluding episode of the trilogy significantly moves beyond the Trexlers and Chances to a forecast of brotherhood at home as a new force, Steve Carson, affirms his "whole life" in the class war of a sit-down strike.[3]

In the subtlety, honesty, and intensity of Herbst's political art, the concerns of radical politics permeate the narrative from the lively overt discourse of the characters to the deep structure of their personalities and the form of Herbst's fiction. As befits the complexities of her subject matter, Herbst illuminates but does not explain everything. She demystifies without implying that there are final answers. She confronts personal and ideological despair and wins through to precariously sustained affirmations. As a resource against the tyranny of abstractions and as a counter to drawing-room Marxism and to the losses on the left, from Spain to the Moscow Purge Trials, Herbst knows and continues to respect individual, ordinary people, actual men and women, even as she despises the systems they contribute to. "Why blame little men who knew nothing but selling and buying and would pick the fillings from their grandmother's teeth. Even as [Steve Carson] thought this savage notion, he saw the kindly face of Henry Whittle, the grain and feed man, who could not understand why there was no money anymore" (pp. 381–82).

Money, the pursuit of money, the need for "a little more capital" pervade the lives of Herbst's characters. Herbst shows in complex detail the impact on personal and family life of the conflicting beliefs, events, and practices of what she leaves it up to the reader to call American capitalism. If she has a dominant interpretation, it emerges gradually and more by implication than by overt statement. In the web of stories and characters, public and private concerns nonetheless intertwine in ways that cumulatively illuminate the relation of past and present and the results of that American "drive for life" which for Herbst "laid waste as much as it created. A world quite different from any that most men would want rose on the slogan of 'opportunity for all.' "[4]

Pity Is Not Enough

In *Pity Is Not Enough* Herbst begins her own nuanced, evolving interpretation of an America she knows is "open to many interpretations."[5] She uses the Oxtail interludes as one interpretative vantage point. In these interpellated sections Herbst breaks the narrative flow, raises questions, and from the outset introduces a complicating modern perspective on the characters and events of the historical past. In opening the novel and trilogy with "Oxtail, 1905," Herbst foregrounds her fascination with time, not as a philosophical abstraction but as a web of personal, aesthetic, and political energy. For her, history is fluid and open to interpretation; meaning is not fixed and absolute but is constructed. Herbst has her family's letters, diaries, and stories to make sense of, to figure out, to use imaginatively. By interrupting the chronological narrative, by giving the authority of the opening to "Oxtail, 1905," and by posing a series of questions, Herbst immediately confronts us with the challenge of seeing ourselves in the present engaging a novel published in 1933 and ranging from the Midwest of 1905 to the earlier episodes evoked in "Oxtail, 1905."

Precisely because they are disruptive, the interchapters fit in with Herbst's pervasively nonlinear narrative style. In these chapters she gives her personal accent to a formal device Dos Passos and in a modified way Farrell were already putting to their own uses, so that she is working within and contributing to a developing left literary tradition that also includes Brecht's theory and practice of the alienation effect in epic theater. As the Brecht-Lukács dispute reminds us, at issue is the contested terrain of the avant-garde—what form of revolutionary literature quali-fies as avant-garde? In Herbst's case, this issue intersects with questions about the form of women's writing, as in Meridel Le Sueur's views about circular narrative. Cumulatively, Le Sueur and Herbst are among the exploratory, radical writers of the 1930s who, often within the realist-naturalist tradition, combined modernist and other formal innovations with a vanguard critique of the middle class to create in America a vital left avant-garde. Herbst explicitly encodes a dialogue on realism, modernism, and the avant-garde in *The Executioner Waits*.

By the end of *Pity Is Not Enough*, in "Seattle, 1918," Herbst has begun to charac-terize Vicky and Rosamund Wendel, two of the unnamed little girls who with their mother and two older sisters go into the cellar for protection against the cyclone that appropriately opens the trilogy in "Oxtail, 1905." We later learn that Victoria is named after her mother's favorite brother, Victor Dorne, who was forced to change his name from Joe Trexler. By the end of the novel, Joe Trexler's identity has been made thoroughly problematical. The issue of his and Victoria's name is an index of Herbst's concern with questions of identity and relation within the family and the cyclone of the nation.

Speaking communally as "we," for herself and her sisters, Vicky's voice com-ments and questions in the first of the interpellated Oxtail sections, which allow Herbst to express her own memories and concerns before her surrogate, Victoria, enters the narrative as a central character in *The Executioner Waits* and *Rope of Gold*. By opening with "Oxtail, 1905," Herbst in an important sense makes the trilogy Vicky's. Technically, Victoria is the shaping, interpreting imagination that creates the Trexler trilogy but Victoria Wendel, later Victoria Chance, is close to Josephine Herbst. Through Victoria, Herbst's sensibility and voice inform the entire trilogy. Especially in the Oxtail interchapters, Herbst speaks with the insight, eloquence, and authority that will later distinguish her memoirs. In the trilogy the perspective of the Oxtail sections gives a complicating density and intensity to the web of history that emerges from the nonlinear narrative.

Herbst deeply believes that the crucial matters of death and life are insepara-ble from the social-political web from which, she shows, the existential realities emerge. She also deeply believes that such central mysteries as the death by "brain fever" of Catherine Trexler or the insanity and death of Joseph Trexler, the two most powerful organizing centers of *Pity Is Not Enough*, are open to interpretation. "The meaning of these deaths," she has Victoria write in an Oxtail interchapter, "had to wait. Later to all four children it had a different meaning, dependent each upon our different ways of living."[6] Herbst does justice to divergent interpretations by entering into conflicting points of view, a distinguishing formal feature of her political art. But Victoria's background presence gives her interpretation and selection of events a special authority.

From the outset the as-yet-unnamed Vicky sets up an intricate web of characters and relations: the storm, the mother, Anne Wendel, the stories Anne tells in the recesses of the cellar, underground, as the cottonwoods bend and the roof crashes in. The stories focus on Anne's brother, "poor Joe," who had set out to make his fortune and ends up insane, not as Joe Trexler but as Victor Dorne. For the girls, the story of Joe, "the most generous brother," has a compelling, mysterious quality, partly because of their mother's admiration and avoidances, partly because Joe's story taps into the depths of the American mythic, hegemonic belief in financial success, in "equal opportunity for all," in immense fortunes to be made. Through Victoria, Herbst shows that an impelling motive for writing her version, her story—*Pity Is Not Enough*—is to penetrate beyond the romanticized aura her own mother has created around Joseph Frey, the original for Joseph Trexler.

In "Oxtail, 1905," intertwined with the ambiguities and adventure of Joe's story are the failure of Amos Wendel's farm machinery business, debt, injunctions against poverty, and Anne Wendel's high-minded regard for Emerson—"Whosoever owneth the land, the horizon belonged to that one with the soul to see it" (p. 4). The questions that compel the girls—why was he poor Joe? why did he run away?—merge with reminiscences of lightning splitting the willow tree, of drought and failed crops, of the difficulty of raising flowers, and of a wild bird beating its wings in the attic while the storm rages outside. "A wild bird in the house means death," Vicky recalls, but Anne Wendell, energetic and optimistic, disagrees: "it's only a poor bird looking for a place to rest. Poor bird" (p. 2). This response is human and touching but we are implicitly reminded that "pity is not enough."

At her best, as in the Oxtail sections, Herbst fuses the domestic language of flowers and birds with the public language of money, business failure, and the American dream. In *Pity Is Not Enough* she also begins to explore the impact on women of their involvement with men engaged in the quest for "a little more capital." Because Anne Wendel like her brothers is compelled by this slogan and all it stands for, Herbst does not imply a simple set of contrasts. Instead, she shows how deeply nineteenth-century women and "the woman's sphere" are affected by and help perpetuate as well as subvert the man's world of acquisitive capitalism. Mem, Anne and Joe's mother, is especially important in this regard, since she repeatedly sacrifices for the boys at the expense of her daughters. In *Pity Is Not Enough*, through characters like Mrs. Ferrol and Anne's sister, Catherine, and through two pairs of sisters, Lucy and Lenore Blondell and Anne and Hortense,

Herbst further complicates our sense of what it meant to be a woman in late-nineteenth- and early-twentieth-century America. In *The Executioner Waits* and *Rope of Gold*, through Rosamund and Vicky, Herbst goes on to the complexities of the new women of the next generation.

Reconstructing and interpreting Joe's story are thus not the only concerns in *Pity Is Not Enough* but they do command our interest through key sections of the novel. As she begins to focus on Joe in the body of *Pity Is Not Enough*, Herbst starts with him as a young man leaving to make his fortune in the South. In her characteristically nonlinear narrative style, she establishes at the outset the contours, implications, and some of the details of Joe's career. Herbst then turns to what Joe inherited from his father, Joshua, who died respected but in debt in 1859. His legacy is not the substantial estate his character and efforts warrant because in the shifting sands and winds of American capitalism "he put his foot into new ventures too soon and died too soon" (p. 12). In Herbst's vision of America, debt, speculation, prosperity and failure, the familiar ups and downs of American capitalism are there from the start. Encoded in the Trexler family history is a revealing American dynamic. Besides his debts, what Joshua Trexler leaves to all of his six children is the impelling "memory of importance lost" (p. 6).

Joe, in particular, is susceptible. He expects and is expected to raise the family to its earlier prosperity, to take care of his sisters and to make it easy for his mother, Mem, who has returned to sewing button holes to support her children. Partly from Joe's point of view, partly from the implied narrator's, Herbst conveys a sense of hard times, of days without enough food to go around, of Mem doing grinding hard work in the attic and Joe sweating it out in a cellar as an apprentice to a baker and candy maker. Even as a boy Joe rejects the work ethic piety that gives meaning to his mother's life (pp. 18–19). He is attracted instead to the symbols of class, to good clothes, the talk of easy money from rising in politics, to the need for good wine and cigars, "the best that money can buy." "With everybody talking easy money, money that came hard and slow made him feel behind the times" (p. 21). Joe senses opportunities for a bright northerner in Georgia after the Civil War. He will be an early bird. In the world of the work ethic, the early bird gets the worm. To highlight and evaluate the new ethic, Herbst deals with the start of Joe's career in a chapter neatly entitled "The Early Worm." Herbst's understated play with words and values keeps the issues focused and gives her narrative an unpretentious sophistication at odds with the stereotypes about tractor realism.

Similarly, the play on the early bird extends the meaning of "the wild bird beating," images that reappear in the guise of poor Joe's caged mockingbird, an instrument of his downfall and an unobtrusive symbol of his entrapment by the ethos of easy money and gentility. The bird passes on to Joe's sisters, first to Catherine and then to Hortense. The caged bird intensifies the connection between Joe's fraud and Catherine's death. Later the death of the stuffed mockingbird comments quietly on Hortense's marriage, which she has entered into so that she and not Anne will be the first to marry. As Herbst constructs and deconstructs the Trexler's involvement in the American dream and the dynamics of patriarchy, she creates a web of reinforcing low-keyed symbols like the early bird, the wild bird beating, and the stuffed mockingbird, whose status as symbols we can easily miss in the flow of realistic details.

For a book published in 1933, moreover, the similarities between the easy-money syndrome of the Gilded Age and of the 1920s repeatedly give a contemporary resonance to this historical novel, a resonance that continues into and beyond the 1980s decade of junk bonds, insider trading, and multibillion dollar savings and loan frauds. A challenge for Herbst is how to convey Joe's deepening involvement in railroad fraud. She succeeds in capturing his blend of ambition, naiveté, and opportunism, a cluster quite different both from Joe's view of himself and of his mother's and sisters' adulation. In his own voice and from his point of view, Joe never acknowledges the extent of his complicity in milking the railroad—charging for cars that never existed, asking for gifts and kickbacks, participating in a web of politics and finance extending from the governor to bought senators to the exploiting of black voters in Reconstruction Georgia. As a greenhorn and a northerner, Joe wants to fit in and to get ahead; he does not want to appear inexperienced and out of touch with the southern way of doing business. In accepting Blake Fawcett as his standard and model, Joe reveals his susceptibility to a show of good manners and "generosity," a code word for a network of theft, lax accounting, and expensive gifts as the customary way of operating. In suitably updated ways these practices continue to define southern politics, and not southern politics alone.

Herbst economically establishes a cast of insiders who expose the behind-the-scenes workings of American finance and politics. By implication, the venality of Reconstruction Georgia is not so much an aberration as a historically specific and vivid instance of relations, values, and practices that are ordinarily either concealed or modulated. One of Herbst's most successful minor characters is Ton Ferris, a three hundred pound political operator from Ohio. Playing off against Fawcett's sanctimony, Ferris shows the way Bullock, the northern governor, "don't give a little finger for the black man, but he wants his vote and he's cute enough to see if he can get business going with Yankee money, he'll keep his power. And Yankee money won't invest unless it sees the South humbled, humbled low, with nigger votes choked down its throat" (p. 26). In the theater of politics and finance, through his bulk, words, and acts, Ferris confirms the southern view of northern carpetbaggers even as he contributes to a radical exposure of the workings of power, money, and race. Through Ferris's idiomatic irreverence and intelligence, Herbst reanimates for her own uses the stock figure of the hard-boiled political manager.

Ferris loves food, horses, and especially the theater. With Joe as audience, Ferris and Fawcett argue about actors and establish a muted theme of theatricality, with Fawcett playing a role Joe is too impressionable to see as a role (pp. 26–27). When he later uses his profits to buy a showy house in Philadelphia for Mem and the family, the faded actor, Edwin Forrest, is a neighbor, reinforcing the motif of pretense, show, acting, and concealment. These issues come to an intense focus in Catherine's response to Joe's indictment and the death of Mrs. Ferrol, a former actress and the unacknowledged mistress of Aaron Trexler.

Through characters like Ton Ferris, Blake Fawcett and his son, George, and K. I. Trimbel, "the brains of the Fawcett crowd" (p. 39), Herbst not only fleshes out the workings of power, money, and deceit but also brings alive the political drama of Reconstruction Georgia. With all of these characters Herbst successfully transforms originals who played important roles in Georgia politics. She turns Hannibal I. Kimball into T. I. Trimble who, like Kimball, is a wealthy northerner who uses his money and connections with the governor to run the show to his own advantage.[7] Herbst perceptively shows that like many of his successors, Trimble combines an unscrupulous drive for money and power with a facade of religious belief and a rhetoric of religiously tinged civic uplift (p. 42). Herbst's Trimble is a revealing political type, a ruthlessly intelligent behind-the-scenes manager. The contrast between Trimble's cool manipulation of power and Joe's vacillation is especially telling.

With Bullock, the carpetbag governor of Georgia, Herbst keeps the name and follows the career of the historical Rufus Bullock, who came to Georgia from New York in 1859, was elected governor in 1868, and fled to Canada in 1871. Herbst models Ton Ferris on A. L. "Fatty" Harris, "a nonofficeholding carpetbagger" who is Bullock and Kimball's man in the legislature. In a lively scene told idiomatically from the point of view of a firsthand observer, Herbst closely follows the printed record of a crucial legislative session. Harris-Ferris takes the chair, coolly ignores calls for adjournment, orders the sergeant at arms to arrest Bullock's rival, J. E. Bryant, watches while a Negro threatens Bryant and is disarmed, and temporarily carries the day in the key organizing session of the 1870 legislature.[8] To give texture and substance to her political art, Herbst focuses knowledgeably on the manipulation of the political process by insiders who have money, connections, and the support of the power of office, however precarious. In the sequel she similarly cuts through official pieties and shows that the big offenders, Bullock and Fawcett, are pardoned, while the scapegoat, Joe, suffers life-long consequences.

The original for Blake Fawcett, Foster Blodgett, a key member of the Augusta ring, used his influence on Bullock to become superintendent of the state-owned Western and Atlantic Railroad. As superintendent he improved his fortunes and his chances for another run at the U.S. Senate after he was defeated in the legislature the first time. As in the novel, the road was a major source of personal and party funding. In the Fawcett figure, Herbst downplays Blodgett's heavy drinking. Instead, she turns Blodgett-Fawcett into a consummate patrician snake-oil man, suave, deceptive, and unscrupulous.

Political art is often direct and explicit. One of Herbst's achievements is that because she enters into and intertwines divergent points of view, she allows us to figure out and evaluate what Joe Trexler is doing and what his world is like. She rarely makes overt judgments. Instead, the discrepancy between Joe's responses and what we gradually see involves us in a process of discovery about Joe and his tangled American world. Herbst does guide our interpretation. In a cumulative, nonsequential way she uses a combination of telling chapter headings ("The Early Worm," "Bitch Goddess, Success," "Fall Guy"), the irreverent montage of newspaper headlines, and especially Catherine's demoralizing reconstruction from the court depositions. Joe emerges as the sacrificial fall guy. As an unconnected northerner, Joe, Herbst makes us see, is set up by Blake Fawcett to take the blame for the looting of the state road. Joe, for his part, repeatedly makes understandable but questionable decisions. Even after Fawcett is unmasked, Joe never forcefully or effectively figures out how to deal with the situation.

Herbst's characterization of Joe implicitly poses the question of agency. Joe acts and chooses but in ways that expose him as gullible, imperceptive, and outwitted. For better or worse, for all his good looks and ambition, Joe is not ruthless enough to take care of himself. To his disadvantage he has accepted a code of gentility that at a key moment inhibits him from acting decisively against Fawcett. Unlike Trimble, who exploits the contradictions to his own advantage, Joe is caught in the crosscurrents of business and genteel standards. Herbst uses Joe to throw a critical light on the conflicting American hegemonic values and practices that have shaped him.

The danger, however, is that in using him to expose the limitations of his society, Herbst may cause us to find Joe too limited to be challenging. Why doesn't he see clearly and act effectively? Why does he keep his word to Grandma Fawcett when everyone else is breaking theirs and he has earlier been none-too-scrupulous? Why all the shilly-shallying, fighting and then not fighting, running away and coming back after the indictment and then running away again, in the dark of night and on Fawcett's advice? Joe can make us impatient, partly because he is not larger than life but is rather a recognizable American caught up in a mess he has helped create and cannot control. Joe is a little too trusting and optimistic, a little too isolated and too enmeshed in the new American ethic of easy money and good clothes. As we see Joe make a series of questionable choices, at best Herbst generates a tension that connects the fallible reader, character, and culture. In the process she gives another detailed anatomy of the American dynamics of what she unapologetically calls "the bitch goddess, success" (p. 48).

Joe's relation to Lucy and Lenore Blondell opens up further possibilities of development, discovery, and critical exposure. Herbst has Joe characteristically fall in love with Lucy Blondell, a southern beauty whose family has lost its wealth and who appeals to Joe mainly because of her looks. This doomed romance has contributed to the aura Anne Wendel has built up around her brother. Through the Lucy-Joe relation, Herbst shows that romantic love thrives on loss and unattainability. Herbst understands that romantic love is also driven by scarcity as well as unattainability: the loved one becomes even more desirable when he or she is perceived to be a scarce commodity sought by others and likely to escape (p. 217). In keeping with her perceptive anatomy of the dynamics and consequences of romantic love, Herbst further shows that Lucy wants someone to dominate and control her, to "order her to do something it didn't matter what" (p. 217).

At the same time, within the limits set by her patriarchal society, Lucy wants to exercise her power and express her bottled up sexuality. Herbst acutely shows that, partly because Lucy is not conscious of her desires, she suffers painfully. Separated from Joe, "she went around feeling as if something was bottled up in her and it gave her face a curious sly secret look that actually frightened the family" (p. 215). She behaves eccentrically with the suitors who come to the house, affirming her power in ways that make people question her sanity. Lucy, who in part of her mind values power and independence, reacts against the sympathy and "soft compassionate faces" of her family. Lucy wants to dominate and to be dominated. She satisfies both needs in a vivid episode, her assault on "that cat . . . with his meek forgiving nature" (p. 216). She attacks the cat not only as an external representative of a meekness she despises but also as an embodiment of one side of her own socialized self. Herbst perceptively and economically uses the episode with the cat and the sharpened fingernails to reveal the dynamics of Lucy's sexually charged hysteria, a syndrome Herbst characteristically relates not only to Lucy's inner life but also to her society. In a further development of Lucy's low-keyed hysteria, Herbst, who understands nineteenth-century culture, has Lucy turn for solace to religion. Through Lucy's suggestively sublimated response, Herbst captures and exposes the sentimental religiosity of an entire milieu (pp. 216–17).

Herbst uses Lucy's sister, Lenore—the plain, sensible one—to highlight the conventional nature of the Lucy-Joe relation, to open up an alternative, equally unrealizable because of Joe's values and Lenore's looks, and unsentimentally to get inside the relation between the two sisters.[9] Leonore is made to act out the role of self-sacrificing, unrequited love. In a recognizable nineteenth-century pattern, because of her looks and Joe's conventional values, Lenore as a woman devotes herself to a man who is unable to reciprocate. After years of correspondence and separation, before Joe's fatal marriage to Agnes, Joe and Lenore finally meet again. A proposal is in order and would probably have saved Joe, but he is still compelled by the show and glitter Agnes represents. Lenore's late marriage to a kind, widowed minister of modest means is a touching coda to a life spent reading Joe's high-flown, genteel fictions, his made-up accounts ostensibly written from Pompeii and Teneriffe, whereas in reality he is suffering frostbite in a mining camp in the Black Hills.

Herbst reveals the extent to which Lenore has been subordinated not only to Joe's attraction to the conventional beauty of women like Lucy and Agnes but also to his quest for "a little more capital," since during the long period of their separation "Joe was following the rumors of money to be made. As the months went by he was impatient of patient schemes; he had magnetized himself with money and followed money and the news of wealth" (p. 143). For Herbst, the nineteenth-century "woman's sphere" of love and the man's world of money and power are not impermeable. As with Lenore, Herbst repeatedly shows the impact on women of their involvement with men compelled by the acquisition of capital. In a related sense, the Herbst who knows about the politics of Ton Ferris and Blake Fawcett also knows about the nuanced politics of sexuality and gender. In dealing with Lucy and Lenore Blondell and the other women characters in *Pity Is Not Enough*, Herbst anticipates the feminist insight that the personal is political and she does so in a way compatible with bell hooks's view of "the personal that is political, the politics of society as a whole, and global revolutionary politics."[10]

In *Pity Is Not Enough* Catherine's sickness and death are the most powerful instances of the effect on women of the man's world of money, politics, fraud, and dominance. Herbst contrives it so that Catherine makes interrelated discoveries about Mrs. Ferrol's death and Joe's involvement in the railroad fraud. Catherine learns that Mrs. Ferrol, a model of intelligence and independence, has died giving birth to Aaron Trexler's child. Aaron, the oldest in the family, has forced Mrs. Ferrol to leave because, after Joe's failure, the family is returning to Grapeville and Aaron cannot stand the prospect of his mother and mistress in the same vicinity. When she discovers what has happened, Catherine is demoralized. The foundations of her world are further shaken, first by what she sees as the injustice done to Joe and later by her deepening realization of the extent of his complicity. As a sensitive woman she has shouldered "the moral burden" of the family (p. 144), a burden that becomes insupportable under the weight of the documents she finds in Joe's trunk.

Herbst is at her best as she moves in and out of Catherine's consciousness and juxtaposes and intertwines the contrasting languages of domesticity and financial fraud. Catherine learns about Joe's involvement as she reads the impersonal language of the court depositions and newspaper articles about the affair. She is alone in the attic and, in a deeper sense, is isolated: her discoveries have cut her off from her moral and religious supports. The buzzing of the wasps in the attic weaves through the scene, merging with Catherine's awareness of Pony munching grass far outside and, inside, her intensified awareness of what Aaron and Joe have done. In her dream Joe digs for gold and finds Mrs. Ferrol's dead baby, a grim fusion of the preoccupations that are devastating Catherine. Awake, she questions the men she has admired and feels that, unlike them, as a woman she has been sequestered "like a nun" (p. 148). Under the pressure of Aaron's and Joe's deceit and worse, she asks "were men a different race, callous, or did they only hide their feelings and if so why? . . . Her ears buzzed and she felt caught in a trap of questions she could not answer. Trust in the Lord, but her own prayers slid over her like water. Nothing seemed to penetrate her heart anymore. She was all alone" (p. 151).

Catherine's discoveries are powerful but negative, exposing the vulnerability and limitations of nineteenth-century women and the woman's sphere of morality, religion, and sensitivity. Refracted and intensified through the lens of her consciousness, moreover, the full meaning of what Joe and Aaron have done emerges, or, rather, the extent to which what they have done undermines meaning on the old, conventional standards. The experience of finding the destabilizing truth about Joe and Aaron affects Catherine's entire way of seeing, so that "everything looked slightly bloated to her as if warped with a kind of mist that floated between her eyes and the things she looked at" (p. 162). Catherine's sickness, her profound nausea, is not existential but has intertwined social, sexual-gender, and political sources and results. At the end "her body felt cold as ice, as if it did not belong to her head, that was hot and seemed apart from the rest of her, like a balloon that would cut itself loose from the earth and rise and rise. But the bed was rising instead, it seemed to waft them gently up and then to fall like a wave. She was scared and did not dare call out, she prayed again and blamed herself for her little faith" (p. 164). As in feminist fiction from *The Coquette* on, Herbst exposes the extent to which Catherine accepts personal responsibility for a socially constructed situation, even as Herbst brings alive the personal suffering.

Catherine's sickness and death contribute memorably to a central motif in the Trexler trilogy. Throughout the trilogy Herbst has a special sensitivity to and insight into the pain, sickness, and energy of her women characters.[11] In a work distinguished by an affirmative drive, eloquence, and sense of possibility, the sickness and death of women and the death of stillborn babies nonetheless recur, not with a single but with multiple implications. Catherine's nausea and death and their feminist connotations, for example, play off against Vicky Chance's fever and recovery at the end of the trilogy. Vicky is sickened by the breakup of her marriage but, unlike Catherine, she is able to go on to the curative, concluding sense of workers fighting with dignity for a new world. In a convincing, undoctrinaire way, Herbst's version of feminism merges with the possibilities of, in hooks's words, "global revolutionary politics."

Herbst's dramatized emphasis, however, is on the deadly effects of the old order more than on the prospects of the new. Through Joe, Herbst probes the consequences of and thus challenges his influential, widely shared view that "money was power and power was freedom" (p. 175). Joe has gone west in search of the capital he believes will allow him to buy his way out of the Atlanta mess, reclaim his property, and redeem himself. Still compelled by the dream of money and success, still out to make his fortune, Joe experiences the humiliation of a fall in position. He has not been able to use his real name out of fear that the authorities will discover him because of the Atlanta indictment. Even in Grapeville, where he has run the family poultry business under a disguise, "he was not himself, Joseph Trexler, but a Hired Man" (p. 174). Throughout the last half of the novel, Joe's involvement in the pursuit of money and power erodes his sense of identity and culminates in his painful, revealing breakdown.

Joe is deprived of his real name and is unable to trade on the asset of his appearance, particularly after he gets in another jam in Indianapolis and has to borrow money from the family to buy his way out. Deprived of capital, Joe falls back on his only other asset: in accord with classic Marxist analysis, he has to sell his labor. The Grapeville fiction that he is a hired man is no longer a fiction. Instead of his easy job as an insider on the state road, Joe then does grueling physical work as an anonymous railroad laborer. Appropriately enough for a trilogy that culminates in *Rope of Gold*, Joe goes on to the gold fields of Colorado and later the Black Hills. Throughout, Herbst stresses versions of money, power, and labor by intertwining Joe's story at one of the symbolic centers of capitalism with the struggles of Mem and the girls in Grapeville.

Like the other members of the family, David, the youngest, focuses on money but he manages to avoid the hard labor that pervades the lives of his mother, sisters, and brother. As part of her project of demystifying America, Herbst plays off her version of Joe in the gold fields against more glamorized, romanticized accounts. Joe suffers frostbite, he needs to drink to relax from the punishing physical labor, and a quartz crystal damages his eye so that he is forced to have it replaced with an unblinking glass eye. In the fullest sense, Joe's vision is impaired.

In the Black Hills Joe is again an early bird but for him and most of the others the promise of America is not fulfilled. "Money" and "a little more capital" recur in the early sections of *Pity Is Not Enough*. As Joe and the boys "all talked of getting rich" in Deadwood (p. 226), a new language now enters the narrative: "big capital" and for the first time, explicitly, "capitalists" (pp. 226–27). The new vocabulary helps Herbst bring alive both the look and feel of life in the mining camps and the underlying dynamics as the men stake out claims, do cruel, hard labor, and then pool their resources "to be tempting to capital," because individually most of them "had barely made a living" (p. 225). Almost immediately the big eastern "capitalists straggled in and business began to hum." In a miniature of and implicit commentary on the disruptive dynamics of capitalism, in a racy, idiomatic language as far removed from the stereotypes about socialist realism as from those of the popular culture West, Herbst catches the move from individual labor and ownership to capitalist hiring and large-scale ownership (p. 227). In dealing with Joe, Herbst brings alive a key instance of the "civil wars of incorporation" Richard M. Brown sees as basic to the post–Civil War history of the American West.[12]

In this process Joe, as he repeatedly does, "had a panicky feeling that he was being left behind" (p. 227). Instead of a claim to the Homestake Mine, he had staked out a share in the much less lucrative Escondito a few hundred feet away. Speculation in town lots in Rapid City does not work out for Joe. Still without enough capital to make a difference, he becomes an employee. He is superintendent but his position is insecure because as an old-time miner he does not have the will to drive the men as the new ethos demands.

Even more tellingly than with his relation to Lucy Blondell, Herbst opens up the way Joe's involvement in the market world of power, success, and failure permeates and comes to a focus in his love life, so that the market world penetrates to the most private recesses of the self. Joe is attracted to Agnes Mason because "the Mason family were a big bunch of New York promoters with their fingers in a dozen parts of the world and a hard and knowing way of disposing of peoples and fates with a flick of the thumb. They were what Joe wanted to be if he was to get ahead and he knew it and he took a final flying jump at that kind of thing before going down. He never had it in him to be a topnotch successful man, but he liked the shine of it and the spectacle and he couldn't separate himself from it" (pp. 243–44). Agnes Mason, Herbst stresses, "was the fly paper that trapped him even in his inner secret life that should have belonged to himself" (p. 244).

Herbst develops this insight in powerful scenes that do for the last part of the novel what those on Catherine's nausea and death do for the first part. After his eye operation Joe is trapped in a prison of darkness. "He was almost glad of his burning eye to be in the dark. Agnes had no pity for his eye, she was so on fire with pity for herself." This lack of feeling is important but pity is not enough. The larger implications emerge cumulatively, first as Joe exposes Agnes as vindictively self-centered when he tells her "about Lucy and Lenore and his relation to them and made the fatal blunder of making them lovable and loving women." Joe is in the dark but he now paradoxically sees too late that he is married to a loveless embodiment of the market system. Herbst conveys these insights not through abstractions but through the suggestive physical sensations of blindness and disorientation—inside Joe's head "red rings spun and whirled in the darkness" (p. 273)—and through the simple, suggestive details of Joe's response to his marriage. "At last he gave up trying to explain his life. Why should he? What new jailer did he have over him? Could he never be free? She would never call him Joe, always Victor, insisting sometimes to his own face that that was his real name. If she had her way he would never be able to go back to himself and become Joe Trexler once more. Her voice calling him Victor, as he sat in the darkness, sometimes made him dizzy as if he were not sure himself who he was" (p. 271). Herbst uses the double name—the ironic "Victor"—and the symptomatic darkness, burning eye, and vertigo to underscore the impact on identity of Joe's involvement in the market world. "His inner secret life that should have belonged to himself" is thoroughly infiltrated. He wants "to go back to himself" but "Joe Trexler" is no sure alternative. No wonder that Joe's involvement in the hegemonic process results in dizziness and a problematic sense of self.

Another symptom and result of this involvement is that Joe's vision is ruined and he is alone, cut off from sustaining ties (pp. 272, 279). Herbst perceptively and undogmatically has Joe embody the inner isolation that haunts American capitalism. She does not moralize or generalize but rather leaves the conclusion up to the reader. She accumulates the suggestive particulars. Joe stops writing to the family when it ignores his advice and "now that all of the family were getting along without him, he felt cut off from them and everyone" (p. 279). Agnes compounds the isolation. She keeps Joe from his old friends and family. Although he is disenchanted, Joe is also married to her, a relation that highlights the strains and values of the market system. Agnes carps at Joe to make more money, to behave like a man and to drive the men harder. "He had the mine and his wife to contend with and the two were splitting him wide open" (pp. 284–85).

Joe is divided internally and he is alone, separated from his family and basically estranged from his wife. The pressures build. "The business at the mine was making him frantic with worry, he again faced the future stripped of every cent, and to begin over again seemed to crack his skull." The troubles come to a focus on his eye, which Joe feels "had receded back into his head, sometimes he felt that the empty socket was a bright bulb pressing somewhere on his brain" (p. 279). Before Joe cracks, Herbst has him respond sympathetically to a new voice and language, the radical alternative to the discourse of capitalism that has been tearing him to pieces. Herbst has earlier freely incorporated the public documents of the court depositions and newspaper accounts of Joe's indictment. She now has Joe read a contrasting document, the speech of one of the recently executed Haymarket anarchists. "I believe," Joe reads, "that the state of caste and classes, the state where one class dominates over and lives upon the labor of another, and calls this order, yes, I believe this barbaric form of social organization with its legalized plunder and murder, is doomed to die and make room for a freer society." In contrast to the death in life Joe has been leading, "the second he read those words he felt in his bones they were true, but the next he was saying it was idealism, you couldn't take a lot of rattlesnakes and expect them to coo in a bird's nest. But the words seemed to stick in his very skin" (pp. 285–86). They lead Joe to remember his early days in the bakery and to think "it would be better not to try to rise, to stay down in one's beginnings, where there was company and kindness" (p. 286). This momentary acceptance and affirmation of a proletarian point of view is touchingly at odds with Joe's own restless striving to rise.

Joe realizes that the Haymarket anarchists did not believe in God but that "when he thought of the world without God he was very lonely." Through the Trexlers, Herbst shows that the old Christian faith is gradually losing its power to give genuine meaning to life. At the same time, the new communal faith associated with Haymarket is not available to Joe, and his belief in the capitalistic ethos of money and power is shaken. Herbst returns to this theme in the unfinished sermon she places in the context of revolutionary change at the end of the trilogy, a sequence that dramatizes the old faith in the process of being replaced by the new. In *Pity*, no wonder Joe suffers a serious, revealing breakdown. With "the dignity of the dead men's words . . . still ringing in his head," Joe thinks that "he had been on top of the heap, in Atlanta, only it had turned out a dungheap, God damn their souls. He carefully took out his glass eye, it burned him like a glowing ball. But the heat was still in his head. As he tried to move to cool his head near the window, all the blood in his body seemed to rush to his empty socket and he stumbled and fell" (p. 287). Even more than Catherine's, Joe's sickness, which culminates in his insanity, originates in and powerfully evaluates his involvement in the political psychology of American capitalism, which for him centers on the American dream of success and the belief that "money was power and power was freedom." Herbst uses the words and vision of the Haymarket anarchists to suggest an affirmative alternative, so that in the dialectics of the novel they have a resonance that goes beyond their brief appearance.

As she nears the end of the first volume of her trilogy, Herbst looks ahead to the future. She juxtaposes Joe's stroke with an interchapter, "Seattle, 1918," in which Rosamond and Victoria at the start of their adult lives read the words of "the Haymarket Rioters" and find them "alive" in contrast to the "dead" wartime city around them. They wish to be but are not part of the Seattle General Strike that carries the Haymarket outlook into action and into the post–World War I world. But they do reject the lives of their Uncle Joe and his financially successful brother, David. Herbst does not falsify by making Ros and Vicky programmatically militant but, through the responses of these two vital young women, she does associate the vision of the Haymarket radicals with the vitality of the future in contrast to the climactic insanity and death of Joe Trexler and all he represents.

Through the narrative of the concluding stages of Joe's career, Herbst also intersperses sections on the youngest brother, David, who rises as Joe falls, so that as an integral part of her political art Herbst weaves David Trexler into both *Pity Is Not Enough* and *The Executioner Waits*. At the end of *The Executioner Waits* she reinforces the implications of Joe's death by showing David at a funeral, a militant protest march forecasting his own impending death and that of the old order he has come to represent. In *Pity Is Not Enough* and *The Executioner Waits*, through David Trexler Herbst extends her range into the moral and political economy of achieved conventional success. As a novelist, Herbst is at her best with characters who, like David Trexler, challenge her ideologically and personally. Central to her political art is Herbst's ability to get inside conflicting languages, characters, and points of view, particularly those she disapproves of.

From the start David Trexler has a heightened sense of his own importance and a capacity to take for granted the sacrifices his mother and sisters make to send him away to school. In *Pity Is Not Enough* Herbst uses an Oxtail interchapter to stress that when in their turn Vicky and Ros needed money for college, David Trexler sent them nothing, although that was the year he "bought the big Cadillac and took a trip to Death Valley" (p. 264). The destination is a quietly ironic commentary on David's habit of talking big but of spending on himself and not on others. In his will David characteristically leaves an endowment for education "too small to do much more than perpetuate his name." Throughout, David wants to be known for his generosity, he talks family values, and he freely gives advice but not money.

Without demonizing him, in the narrative sections of *Pity Is Not Enough* Herbst catches David's mixture of youth, pomposity, and his shrewd eye for the main chance. She uses the interchapters in *Pity Is Not Enough* to present a David Trexler who is already rich. In the narrative sections, through the counterpoint of her treatment of David Trexler's success and Joe's failure, Herbst convincingly destabilizes both concepts, so that she again calls into question the capitalistic ideology and practices underlying these central values and the characters who embody them.

The Executioner Waits

In *The Executioner Waits* (1934), Herbst continues to use David Trexler to give substance and detail to her demystifying portrayal of respectability and business success. As she does throughout the trilogy, Herbst uses the extended Trexler family as the focus for probing representative American conflicts and contradictions. Herbst is especially good at bringing into the open the contrast between David's recognizably American view that what he is doing is for his children and his underlying contempt for and domination of his son and daughter. Without being dogmatic or preachy, Herbst shows how deeply the ideology of money and property as the basis of self-respect has infiltrated and perverted the ties of affection within the early-twentieth-century middle-class family. Although Mr. and Mrs. Chance are her major examples, she also shows that David Trexler uses this ideology as a screen to cover and justify his own egotism and lack of real affection and generosity, at the same time that he wants to be recognized as a benefactor to his family and community. In contrast to the warmth and support that characterize relations within Anne Wendel's family, Herbst passes an implicit judgment by showing that within David Trexler's family the children's growth is blighted by David's values and control.

Throughout the trilogy, without being doctrinaire or obtrusive, Herbst repeatedly connects the public positions of her characters with their inner, sexual lives, as she does with Lucy Blondell's involvement in the ideology of romantic love. David

Trexler, who began his career with amorous flirtations he hides from his family, spends the years of his greatest prosperity "empty at heart" because, without acknowledging it, he is in love with Millie, his sister-in-law.[13] Herbst does an exemplary job revealing the silences of this relation, the decorum and the unspoken, unreciprocated feelings she makes us aware of through David's outbursts of anger and frustration. Herbst shows that this outrage is fed from personal sources compounded by an ideology of work and financial discipline, an ideology she takes pleasure in undermining.

In dealing with David's branch of the Trexler family, through Sue, Dave Jr. and his wife, and especially David's relation to Minnie, Herbst reveals that a certain unsatisfied sexuality is partly caused by and calls into question the surface respectability David embodies. Although she values his energy and his delight in his acquisitions, Herbst also implies that David's egotism and business values thwart the kind of spontaneity and pleasure she associates with Minnie and the man she finally leaves David's household to marry. Herbst simultaneously suggests a contrast between David's established order and the emerging ethos she connects with Minnie's railroad worker husband and, at the conclusion of the novel, the militant protest demonstration David witnesses at his rival's grave. As she typically does, however, Herbst hints at the revolutionary new world and concentrates on deconstructing David Trexler as an epitome of the growth, energy, and shortcomings of a twentieth-century capitalism shaken to its foundations by the crash of 1929.

Alert to the centralizing tendencies of late capitalism, during the course of *The Executioner Waits* Herbst shows that like the system he illuminates, David Trexler plans to expand his pharmacy business into a chain that will control the best locations in Oregon, Washington, and Idaho, with further growth in the offing. David buys shrewdly and, like others who profited from the war, he makes a fortune during World War I. As representative as David is, however, Herbst refuses to make him into a stereotype. Because of the family's German origins, David is not enthusiastic about the war and he has to be coerced by a vigilante delegation into kissing and displaying the American flag. Even a citizen as respectable as David is not immune from the wartime pressures of patriotism, a motif Herbst returns to with Victoria in Berkeley. For David the resulting humiliation motivates him to fight back, amass a fortune, run the bank, and own much of the town.

During the boom years David invests in Bethlehem Steel and other high-yield stocks. He gains a reputation as a financial advisor and shifts his energy from his drugstores to finance. Integral to her political art, Herbst has David become a spokesman for an influential set of 1920s beliefs that contrast with the International Workers of the World's (IWW or Wobblies) views about class conflict, a radical reading of America at the center of Herbst's vision. She has David become president of the bank and a speaker in demand at business luncheons, purveying homilies about "strict honesty, a fair profit to capital, and equitable wages for labor" (p. 144). David, however, maintains control by encouraging his clerks "to buy homes, with himself as mortgage holder. 'Give your employee a stake in your business,' " he tells his fellow businessmen, " 'make him realize he is your partner, just as you are the co-partner of every business interest in this country, and you guarantee for yourself a safe and happy landing.' " Herbst leaves it up to us to see through David's Chamber of Commerce rhetoric of equality, a "co-partnership" in which the employee is subordinated like Dave Jr.

"The safe and happy landing," moreover, comes to seem problematic as stock prices fall, as investments David has recommended fail, and as David's glowing good health is shaken along with the economy. Herbst concisely renders the sense of developing panic, of David's solid prosperity threatened, making it unlikely that he will be able to leave the carefully calculated bequests he has counted on to perpetuate his memory. In this context of a collapsing economy and depleted health, the concluding scene at the grave assumes a heightened resonance. In a novel that deals at length with the deaths of the older generation of Trexler's, especially of Aaron and Anne, Herbst treats David's death with a commendable in-direction. She simultaneously implies his death and that of the class he represents.

For Herbst, Aaron's illness and death bring into the open long-standing strains within the Trexler family. The infighting between Anne Wendell and her sister, Hortense, over property and unfulfilled family obligations gives a convincing human resonance to Herbst's political art. Grounded in the family drama, the political implications continue to emerge as Herbst both reveals and subverts Anne Wendel's attainment of "a little capital," a dream Anne realizes when she auctions off the lots that comprise the family's share of Aaron's estate. For all her sympathy with Anne's vitality, Herbst passes an implied judgment by having Anne suffer her version of Joe's lost eye. In getting the land ready for auction, Anne has a painful, crippling accident that leaves one of her legs permanently damaged.

At the end of her life, hastening Anne's death is another bitter dispute with Hortense. The resulting pain accelerates Anne's illness and death. Playing off against these intense conflicts and fractures within the Trexler family are the underlying affection between Vicky and her mother, the ties between Anne and her husband, Amos, and the tenacious will to live Anne displays until the end. This dialogue of conflicting qualities, relations, and feelings contributes to Herbst's rendering of the political psychology of the extended Trexler family.

Like the Haymarket anarchists of *Pity Is Not Enough*, in *The Executioner Waits* for Herbst the grass-roots radicalism of the IWW represents for Herbst the militant alternative to the established order David Trexler and the Chances embody. At the center of the novel Big Bill Haywood, the legendary leader of the IWW, and Ed Bates, a rank-and-file Wobbly, bring into focus an energizing sense of the workers' struggle from Kansas to Colorado in the years before and during World War I. Ed's songs embody a defiant workers' culture that inspires Rosamond and Vicky and plays off against the middle-class views of their brother-in-law, Donald Monroe, and the power of the leading citizens of Oxtail.

For the early twentieth century, through a controversial IWW convention in Oxtail, Herbst gives us an anatomy of the middle-American power structure and its conflict with the radicalism she values. She uses two interchapters, "Iowa Farm, 1932" and "Detroit, 1932," to highlight the connection with the novel's present. Integral to her political art, Herbst repeatedly shows her insight into conflicting American values and symbols. As opposed to Ed's radical imagery, she has the reformer, Mayor Handy, invoke the basic American secular and religious values of "the soul" and "honesty," of "order and constitutional methods in human society" as he warns the men "to rid yourself of the idea you can take the world by violence. For you can never do it. It is just a matter of plain common sense to cut that out, because it won't go." Mayor Handy is a well-realized American political type, a former Harvard-educated preacher turned reformer. He is close to David Trexler in the rendered ideological spectrum Herbst brings alive through lively public speeches in *The Executioner Waits*. He and David differ, however, in that Mayor Handy is at odds with the Oxtail business interests he crosses by supporting the IWW meeting but not the IWW. Herbst does justice to Mayor Handy's outlook even as she undercuts it, partly through a certain inflation of his rhetoric, partly by showing the political pressure Mayor Handy succumbs to. Herbst knows that dominant groups are not monolithic.

In the dynamics of this model episode, Herbst goes behind the scenes and enters into the language and politics of the radical IWW, the reform Mayor Handy, and the business powers of Oxtail. Herbst, who has a grasp of American idiom and the political power of capital, outlines the deal the business leaders work out to get rid of the IWW and to save face for the Mayor. Despite his views about violence and constitutional order, Mayor Handy reluctantly agrees to keep the police on the side and to let the American Legion break up the IWW meeting so that "eastern capital" will not be put off but will continue investing in "the dozen different enterprises . . . we've been angling for" (p. 120). For Herbst, reform suffers from a certain religiosity, a selective misreading of the role of violence in American politics, and a vulnerability to political pressure. The integrity, commitment, and esprit of the IWW are at the heart of Herbst's radical politics. Although the IWW is run out of town and by 1934 is no longer a force, Herbst establishes a continuity of radical protest by juxtaposing the episode on the World War I era Wobblies with two depression scenes. In the interchapter, "Iowa Farm, 1932," in the face of another double-crossing Oxtail mayor, farmers defiantly resist a farm foreclosure. In a parallel interchapter, "Detroit, 1932," Herbst moves beyond the Wobblies, enters the consciousness of a young militant, and for the first time invokes Lenin and the Communist Party presidential slate of Foster and Ford. Herbst is less concerned with doctrinal orthodoxy than she is with a continuing line of radical challenge.

In *Pity Is Not Enough* Herbst moves behind the scenes of political and financial maneuvering in Reconstruction Georgia. In *The Executioner Waits* she does the same using Oxtail and the IWW as her focus. She recognizes the power of the owners and the losses of the workers at the same time that she uses the radicals' irreverent, defiant energy to look ahead to the future. In contrast to the stereotypes about socialist realism, Herbst thus avoids making things prettier for workers and farmers than experience warrants but she also sustains a hopeful sense of possibility. As in the ending of the trilogy, the 1932 interchapters, and the IWW-Oxtail sections, a defining trait of Herbst's political art is her sensitivity to loss, injustice, and the dynamics of power balanced against a sense of revolutionary possibility grounded in events and values.

Another feature of Herbst's political art is her fusion of the personal and public, of family history and national history, so that the big public issues have the immediacy of personal and family matters and domestic concerns have a public resonance. Formally Herbst achieves this fusion by intertwining narrative strands and by using the interchapters to highlight continuities between past and present. In the IWW-Oxtail sections, for example, Herbst frames the narrative sequences with "Iowa Farm, 1932" and "Detroit, 1932." Under the chapter heading "Martyrs to a Cause," moreover, Herbst recalls Anne's difficulties with Aaron's estate, including her crippling accident juxtaposed with the drama of the Wobblies in Oxtail as Vicky, Rosamond, and Amos gradually find out what is happening. The incongruous "martyrs," Anne and Big Bill Haywood and his crew, mutually reflect on one another.

For all her affection for Anne Wendel, Herbst deconstructs Anne's commitment to "a little more capital" by having Big Bill Haywood compellingly identify the IWW's anticapitalism with the patriots of the American Revolution, an identification Herbst also uses with the defiant farmers of the Iowa interchapters. She has Haywood tap into the symbolism of the rebellious, liberty-loving, and shoeless troops at Valley Forge. In this context his forceful statement of the revolutionary position—"we are dissatisfied, completely dissatisfied with the existing order of things" (p. 129)—has the authority of Valley Forge and an "existing order" represented by the Trexlers and the Oxtail power structure. No wonder Vicky responds. Although she is not politically committed "she really believed that she was very fitted for a kind of exciting existence that had its base in something besides the usual things people lived for. . . . She even thought she was making things easy for herself by not . . . caring for property or silver tea sets. She really believed that she was pretty well stripped for action and would make a fine soldier in the struggle for a decent world" (p. 141). In the meantime, Vicky gropes.

Her eloquent realization occurs in a chapter, "Behind the Scenes," which further illustrates Herbst's fusion of the personal and public, of past and present as part of a vital political art. In this chapter Herbst contrasts Vicky's view of success with Joe and David Trexler's, goes behind the scenes of the Oxtail business elite's actions versus the IWW and behind the scenes of David Trexler's expansion plans, his emptiness because of Milly, and his feelings about "shiftlessness" as a reason for refusing loans to his neighbors, all in a context of IWW protest, the revolution in Russia, and the round of strikes at the end of World War I. In the framing interchapter, "Detroit, 1932," Herbst reinforces the sense that revolutionary forces in the present are threatening the world of David Trexler and the Oxtail business leaders.

As in "Behind the Scenes," Herbst's radical view of twentieth-century American history is another feature of her political art. She counters the widely shared interpretation of discontinuity between the 1920s as prosperous and apolitical and the 1930s as depressed and politicized. Using the modernist techniques of a montage of newspaper headlines, abrupt cuts to contemporary interchapters, and narrative sections on the strikes, militant protest, and hard times of the immediate post–World War I period, Herbst deemphasizes the Jazz Age 1920s and renders a radical sense of underlying continuity. Rosamond and Vicky, the new women of the younger generation, are the focus for this view of America, or, rather, Rosamond and her husband Jerry Stauffer and Vicky and Jonathan Chance. Like Catherine's and Joe's deaths in *Pity Is Not Enough*, Rosamond's death is one of the organizing centers of *The Executioner Waits*. As she builds toward this tragic loss, Herbst again makes family and American history intertwine.

At the deepest level, when Rosamond becomes pregnant soon after Jerry's return from World War I, the young couple are torn to pieces by their inability to afford a child. The outer world of low-paying jobs and dim prospects has penetrated to their most intimate reality. In contrast to "the existing order of things," Herbst has Rosamond articulate that "what she and Jerry needed was work that used what brains and energy they had, if such things mattered. Were they just fodder, waiting to be chewed up by their own mechanical processes of keeping alive?" (p. 188). In conventional fiction, an episode of personal breakdown as intense as Rosamond's would not undogmatically suggest an alternative world of use value and productive, unalienated labor. In the moments before her death, Rosamond explicitly connects Ed Bates and the IWW with a way out of "the trap" (p. 195), an image that recurs as frequently as her sense of being lost.

In both of these powerful images and throughout the episode, the politics of class and the feminist politics of the body merge as Rosamond faces an anguished dilemma about an abortion she does not want but feels she needs because they cannot afford to support a child. Herbst acutely establishes that upper-class women like Mrs. Troy "went through it again and again" whereas Rosamond "made the rounds of doctors but no one wanted to touch it. Only the poor get the cold shoulder, she told Jerry, feeling as if she were in a fever" as she jumps rope like a girl to bring on a miscarriage. Herbst vividly brings to a focus the days "when a doctor of rather shady reputation finally agreed to do the job" and Rosamond gets cold feet remembering "with terrible clearness the poor women brought into the clinic, their insides poisoned forever, their wombs spoiled for all time, never to bear again. Life wasn't always going to be like this," Rosamond affirms. "Better times would come. . . . To be free, that was all that she wanted. To be well again. To have her body to herself" (p. 193).

Herbst intertwines Rosamond's deep personal sense of the body with an equally deep sense of the body of the land itself, of America as a fertile, pastoral land. Unintentionally looking ahead to her fatal drive, Rosamond thinks about driving across Nebraska "to the Black Hills where Uncle Joe had lived and had gone mad without finding gold." Herbst continues to foreshadow Rosamond's death by having her recall a dreamlike childhood experience that juxtaposes Joe's fatal myth of success with the inverted pastoral imagery of America as a mythic, fertile land. As children Rosamond and Vicky are lost in a cornfield, "in all that green, green, reaching to left and right, in front and back, nothing but the rustle of green and overhead a blue staring eye of sky." The green land, however, is not associated with life but with death, with the fear that they would fall and be lost "until they starved to death in the ripening corn and crows came to pick their white bones or the farmer cut the corn and the shocks would topple around their skeletons, bleached and clean" (p. 191). Just as in Rosamond's mind the fertile land brings forth a crop of death, her own fertile body does the same. Herbst drives home this intensifying association by having Rosamond feel that "her body was as relentless as death," a terrifying, understandable view for a pregnant woman in her circumstances to have.

At the end of the episode, Herbst again renders Rosamond's sense of being trapped, of a need for air that impels her to speed alone at night through the fertile land whose associations deepen and complicate the implications of her death. As opposed to the commodity aesthetics of the dominant culture, Rosamond responds to the beauty and abundance of the land unrelated to the wealth the middlemen of the towns drain from the fields of ripening corn. Herbst charges the episode with a radical questioning of an existing order in which people like Rosamond and her family "feel squeezed and beaten" despite the fact that the rich land "could support all the children anyone wanted" (p. 195). Rosamond's fatal car crash comments powerfully on a society that produces poverty and scarcity in the midst of plenty and that impels her toward a deadly wreck instead of birth and a new life.

The possibility of renewal does emerge from the juxtaposed interchapter, "Summer in Many States 1934." It is a mark of Herbst's political art and a sign of the times that in her fiction she responds to deep personal loss by dramatizing a radical challenge to the prevailing system. In the subtext of this response to the preceding narrative, Herbst implies that personal lives are inseparable from a public world that needs to be radically changed. In "Summer in Many States 1934," instead of using a militant spokesman to present the radical position, Herbst is particularly effective in doing it indirectly through a moderate government expert. He reluctantly and undogmatically makes explicit what needs to be done. The violence usually attributed to the radicals is also shifted to the night riders who support the status quo. At key moments in her trilogy Herbst periodically brings into the open a vision of an alternative to a system that is fatal to individuals like Rosamond and to antagonistic groups like the farmers and storekeepers who are urged to unite in "Summer in Many States 1934."

In the narrative present, the meat-packing strike she has Jerry Stauffer become involved in gives further insight into the workings of the old order and the prospects for the new. Chronologically the time is 1920, so that the similarities with 1934 are reinforced by the "Oxtail 1934" interchapter. In contrast to the received version of the 1920s, Herbst gives us strikes, owner violence, and the abuse of police power. Together with the unemployment and hard times, they are a backdrop to, not in counterpoint with 1934. In contrast to the end of the trilogy, however, the police prevail in this early battle of the class war. Unlike his successor, Steve Carson in *Rope of Gold*, moreover, Jerry is acted on more than he acts. In the strike that concludes the trilogy, Herbst renders a contrasting sense of the workers' developing power. In *The Executioner Waits*, her strategy is instead to develop sympathy for the workers through her vivid description of the power used against them, with Jerry as the focus.

Hit from the rear, Jerry "tripped, fell, was lifted, flung, hit, kicked, raised himself painfully on all fours, and found himself on the floor of the patrol bumping over the narrow streets leading from the packing house district." In a recognizable version of the left conversion process, Jerry is radicalized by the experience, or, rather, the experience of basic injustice and inequality comes home to him with the immediacy of the blows and kicks. They accelerate the conversion process. At this stage, as with Vicky and Rosamond and the IWW, songs are the key. "Jerry wished he knew the words. If he wasn't kicked to death, he'd learn them" (p. 221).

Jerry is a transitional figure in the trilogy, a preliminary version of the more fully developed young radical of *Rope of Gold*, Steve Carson. Before she leaves Jerry Stauffer, however, Herbst has him return to Detroit, get a job at Ford, and develop an articulate sense of class consciousness. Jerry is crucial in developing the political vision of *The Executioner Waits* and he is a reminder of how Herbst operates formally. Herbst, that is, has Jerry look back on the strike and bring into the open details and interpretations he had missed at the time. Instead of writing a strictly chronological narrative and treating an episode like the strike as a self-contained unit, Herbst uses this reinforcing, nonlinear technique as a recurring feature of her political art. "I don't understand all the workings of it yet," Jerry concludes to his new friend, Jonathan Chance, "but I know whose side I'm on, from now on" (p. 240).

Herbst contrasts Jerry's deepening political insights and commitments with Jonathan's plan to move with Vicky to the country and write. After working at Ford, Jerry realizes the problems he and Rosamond had were not the fault of Detroit. "It wasn't a city to blame, it was a system" (p. 263). As a young writer, Jonathan, on the other hand, is associated with the *Smart Set*, the Revolution of the Word, and a total unawareness of the deaths of Rosa Luxembourg and Karl Liebknecht, so that through the differences between Jerry and Jonathan, Herbst dramatizes a split between the political twenties and the literary twenties, or at least the early 1920s. By the time of "A Year of Disgrace" Herbst had worked out a more fluid view of the period in which "it was all flux and change with artistic movements evolving into political crises, and where ideas of social service, justice, and religious reaction each had their special spokesman."[14] But in *The Executioner Waits* the boundaries between the literary and political twenties are sharply drawn. Jerry in particular wants to cut his ties with his literary friends. "He had only one consolation in the world," Herbst stresses in the accents of 1934, "and that was finding out more clearly every day where he stood." He feels, accurately as it turns out, that Jonathan and Vicky will someday "have to face the music and decide what side of the fence they were on" (p. 263).

Although she typically avoids explicit political statements, Herbst has Jerry eloquently voice the principled idealism of the thirties left. Jerry is working at Ford and staying with the Schultz's. In a context of nurturing domesticity—he covers a sleeping ten-year old—Herbst has Jerry affirm that "yes, this was the right place for him. He would stay down, he wouldn't be foolish and try to rise on someone else's neck, he'd stay down, right here with his own people, until someday they could all rise together. And let Jonathan go to the country and think he was living if he wanted" (p. 264). The contrast with Joe and the other Trexlers is as marked as it is with the early Jonathan, who reminds Vicky of her namesake.

In his dedication to staying down and working at the grass roots and to the communal ethic of "rising together," not as a competitive individual, Jerry does not go into the details, but the domestic context filters out the prospect of revolutionary violence. As she often does, Herbst connects violence with the established world of rising "on someone else's neck." In the flow of episodes and characters in *The Executioner Waits*, Jerry has an exemplary, affirmative role. His increasing radicalism throws into relief the complex implications of the more fully developed drama of Jonathan and Vicky Chance and The Parents. Like the Haymarket anarchists of *Pity Is Not Enough*, Jerry Stauffer has an importance that goes beyond his relatively brief appearance in *The Executioner Waits*. Like the Haymarket anarchists and like Ed Bates, Big Bill Haywood, and Joe Hill, moreover, Herbst uses Jerry to articulate the explicit politics of the trilogy. Without being doctrinaire, Jerry's position is compatible with the native radicalism of the IWW and the Communist Party in its celebration of workers, "rising together," and developing a sense of working-class consciousness, of knowing where you stand and which side of the fence you are on.

In *The Executioner Waits* Herbst brings alive Jonathan and Vicky's gradual, tentative development in the direction Jerry has charted. In *Rope of Gold*, as she moves from the 1920s into the 1930s, Herbst opens up the results. First, however, in a series of interspersed chapters all entitled "The White-Headed Boy," she places Jonathan from his earliest years in the context of his prosperous family. Herbst is working with highly charged material, because she stays close to the experiences and conflicts her husband, John Herrmann, had with his own family, with her, and with his writing. In doing justice to a family drama that in 1934 was still being played out, Herbst once again shows that personal and family lives are inseparable from the American hegemonic process she sensitively illuminates.

In contrast to Vicky's immediate family, Jonathan Chance allows Herbst to expand her range into the established upper middle class. For Herbst Jonathan's father, the head of a successful Michigan leather-goods firm, epitomizes the regularity, respectability, and limitations of his class. Quality goods are at the center of Abel Chance's business and personal life. Herbst delights in his stock of immaculate white linen, his fine woolen suits, his crystal and silver. Even as his disapproval of his son intensifies, Mr. Chance continues to send Jonathan expensive, well-cut suits. Like others of his generation and background, however, Abel Chance finds it hard to be generous with his emotions or approval. From his point of view his son, the handsome and intelligent "white-headed boy" of the family, has taken a dangerously bad turn. He is living with a woman who is not his wife, he has published a story in an avant-garde magazine that has been confiscated as, in Mr. Chance's words, "smut," and most important, Jonathan has not settled down to an honest career of moneymaking despite his intervals as a talented and successful salesman. Matters come to a head over a loan Mr. Chance has agreed to so that Jonathan and Vicky can buy the old farmhouse they are living in, fix it up for resale, and continue living and writing in the country on the profits. Because it is presented as a practical moneymaking project, Mr. Chance advances the money at interest. His wife, however, is horrified and has the check stopped. After finding one of Vicky's letters to Jonathan, Mrs. Chance has had a private investigator establish that the young couple are living together immorally.

On the one hand, Jonathan and Vicky personify Mr. and Mrs. Chance as The Parents, agents of middle-class respectability bearing down to tame the experimental bohemianism of the younger generation. As Herbst probes this classic version of the transmission of and rebellion against hegemonic values, however, she succeeds in getting under the surface of Mrs. Chance's intense revulsion. Photographs reveal a pretty, eager young girl who over the years of her marriage has gradually assumed a surface of plump, settled dissatisfaction. Herbst's portrait of Abel Chance allows us to make up our own minds and to see that this marriage, ideal on the outside, has left Mrs. Chance emotionally and sexually unfulfilled. The compensating tie with Jonathan is especially important to Mrs. Chance. Herbst implies that, without being conscious of it, Mrs. Chance undermines her son to keep a measure of control over him. An early example is that she hides a whiskey bottle and then uses it to show that Jonathan cannot be trusted, that he lies, a charge she repeatedly uses against him to get her way in family disputes about Jonathan's future. The whiskey bottle has a heightened significance, because, as he moves into his twenties, Jonathan's drinking intensifies. On the night of the shotgun marriage his parents force on Jonathan and Vicky, "they felt defeated and humiliated and Jonathan got tighter than he had ever been before in his life" (p. 298).

Herbst deftly establishes a connection between Mrs. Chance's feelings about Jonathan, about her own marriage, and about her accumulation of consumer goods. Even before Vicky appears "sometimes Mrs. Chance in her room upstairs felt sorry for her boy. But she had only to go into his room and see the big pictures of girls on his dresser to harden and feel that her husband was quite right to insist on discipline" (p. 235). Herbst goes on to fuse insight, exposure, and sympathy as she presents Mrs. Chance not as a reified enemy but as a troubled and troubling woman under the pressure of her social class and her moment in the early decades of the twentieth century. Herbst intertwines the existential realities of Mrs. Chance's life—the death of a daughter, her children becoming adults—with the socially constructed realities of her marriage, particularly Mr. Chance's joy-killing, disapproving stress on money and Mrs. Chance's consumerist response to the sense of emptiness at the center of her life (pp. 235, 261–62).

Into a context of Mrs. Chance's painful sublimations and the demystified religion of consumerism (p. 262), Herbst introduces Jerry Stauffer's critique of "the system" and his growing desire "to know where he stood" (p. 263). Jonathan and Vicky's "plan that would take the two out to the country where they could live as if on an island" (p. 263) is another contrasting alternative to both Jerry's political radicalism and the Chance's hegemonic commitment to "settling down and living steady and getting a decent job like other people" (p. 281). For Herbst these alternatives, neither abstract nor isolated, penetrate into the most intimate recesses of Jonathan and Vicky's lives.

One of Herbst's major concerns in the last half of *The Executioner Waits* and *Rope of Gold* is to probe Jonathan's problems with his writing and drinking and their impact on his relation with Vicky. Herbst shows that even as a boy Jonathan sided with his father's workers and enjoyed sitting in on Sunday afternoons as they smoked, talked of unionizing, and shared a beer with him. A little older, Jonathan spent time with Bert, a bicycle repairman, similarly listening in and having an occasional glass. This association of drinking and rebellion against his parents' "terrible austerity . . . and rigid conduct as to money" (p. 282) intensifies as Jonathan struggles to decide on how he will lead his adult life. His parents "looked so solid and unshakable it was no use bombarding them with words. Words were nothing to them," both as argument and, later, as the tools of the writer's trade. "His father could shake out his paper and hide behind it, his mother could go on counting the pieces in the linen closet. He might as well try to describe a trip to the moon as to make them see what he wanted. He didn't know what he wanted, just so it wasn't what they had" (pp. 204–5). Jonathan nonetheless wants his parents' approval even as he suffers because "all they wanted out of me is to make a respectable organ grinder of me." At Vidisichis's, a warm meeting place for young Detroit writers, no wonder "Jonathan drank more than two people" and "if it hadn't been for Vidisichis' and the Krause family, he would have taken to drink more than he did" (pp. 239, 235).

His tensions increase after he and Vicky move to the country. Although Jonathan has published a story in a magazine also including Gertrude Stein and Joyce, writers he is of course proud to be associated with, Herbst perceptively shows that the internalized parents undermine his sense of self-worth and the value of his work. Either his disapproving father or "his mother standing big and dominating seemed ever behind him. 'Now Jonathan, just stop that and get me those brass nails I spoke to you about' " (p. 283). In an exemplary analysis of writer's block, Herbst observes that "something was plugging up his mind and when he began to write the dollar world of his father dragged its way across the page and poured hatred into every word. You have to believe in something to write, he concluded, feeling shut-in in his little room, tied down, sick of his own efforts." Unlike Herbst, Jonathan finds himself unable to draw energy from what he loves. "He loved Vicky, their house, the long evenings and the farmers leaning over the fence admiring his new garden and examining the fresh turned soil. All these good things found no place when he sat down to write. He couldn't seem to tap them. His fear of being sentimental, of writing dishonest stuff kept him dipping into the past where there was no danger of being anything but bitter."

For Vicky, who wakes in the night "longing to burst into tears," Jonathan's torment is not funny, although she knows they should laugh at what his parents have done. Herbst uses Vicky to express directly and cogently that "Jonathan had been blighted enough by his parents whose notions of success had become part of their boy. She was certain that his battle with his work was due to the parents and it gave her consolation to blame them. Her letters had been opened wilfully, an attorney had been put on their trail like a bloodhound. And what had they done? They had slept together. Why, it was enough to make anyone laugh and they should laugh, not let it gangrene their very vitals with hatred and bitterness." Herbst characteristically does not leave it as a privatized personal or family matter. She sees clearly that Vicky and Jonathan "should hit straight at the real enemy that had made the parents in the popular image." And as she does with Jerry Stauffer, Herbst again views the parents and all they stand for from a radical perspective, this time that of George Gates, a Wobbly who flees to Russia to escape imprisonment during the Red Scare of 1919–20. "Let the parents have their day," Vicky concludes. "It would not last forever. George Gates had said it would not go on forever" (p. 288).

In the meantime, money counts. Unlike Joe and the other Trexlers, Jonathan and Vicky reject the money world of the older generation and of the dominant society. Herbst's treatment of The Parents succeeds in exposing the human cost of the elder Chances' settled, unsettling ethos. As Vicky indicates, however, in a deep part of himself Jonathan both rejects and accepts his parents' views about money and success. He knows that to succeed in his father's eyes he will have to make a lot of money. He can do it on the road as a salesman but the work is alienating and depletes him and separates him from Vicky. He might be able to make money as a writer turning out trash. In a more mundane way, Jonathan and Vicky are as preoccupied with money as their elders because they are worried about it all the time and need it for kerosene and staples. The canceled loan is devastating because the rejection goes to the nerve of Jonathan's feelings about money, writing, and his way of life. With the loan and the sale of the house, he might have been able to satisfy his conflicting needs at least to the extent of providing a cushion for them to live on. Freed of the immediate pressures and in a way making money on his father's standards, Jonathan may have had more energy available to animate his writing. Instead of reinforcing his sense of self-worth, however, his parents' rejection intensifies Jonathan's dilemmas.

For Herbst in her trilogy literature and politics are integrated and reinforce each other. Jonathan, however, begins to resolve his dilemmas by turning from literature to radical politics, although in his case the consequences are more ambiguous than with Jerry Stauffer and Vicky. He locks up his workroom and hides the key. In a classic instance of the hegemonic process, Jonathan's developing counterhegemonic response is grounded not in the depression but in the dynamics of the Chance family. "He was through with his father's world and he made up his mind that that world was dying. Joyce and Proust had said all that could be said for such a world." Herbst stresses that "his mind's eye knew that the cue was buried in the very farms around him. He could realize the pattern, the system that was creating topheavy wealth for the few and misery for the many. It was just a mental conviction in him during the last of that summer and he began hunting for books to substantiate himself." Herbst, who deliberately avoids exact dates, telescopes the 1920s in her handling of the interlude in the country "during the last of that summer." Jonathan epitomizes the shift from the literary to the political twenties, a shift Herbst shows was already under way before the cataclysm of the depression.

In a forecast of the later conflicts between his political and his personal life, from the start Jonathan "got into arguments with Vicky. She was vague in her ideas but strong in her feelings. It was the other way around with him." Without mentioning the Communist Party, Herbst credits Jonathan with engaging in a significant, independent process of political analysis. "The IWW had been licked," Jonathan realizes. "Why? Where was the stream now? It must be there, under the surface. Through what channels was it working?" For Jonathan the stream reaches the surface in *Rope of Gold* when, after a period of effective radical farm activism, he joins the party. In the meantime "he felt cut off, out in the country he began to realize that he really was on an island. The farmers were too patient, they trusted too much" (p. 291). They are, Herbst has Jonathan realize, too deeply affected by the prevailing hegemony. As she does repeatedly, Herbst shows the extent to which the political, public, and family worlds penetrate into the depths of the relation between Jonathan and Vicky. Frustrated by his neighbors and what they reveal about the larger political situation, Jonathan drinks too much and "Vicky had a terrible fear and premonition he would end like Uncle Joe." Herbst goes on to render the tensions, attractions, and conflicts between the two as Jonathan falls, "his face deadly pale, his eyes blank. . . . Then he began to cry, and she felt a kind of terror. What could she do to comfort him?" Vicky's response—"he couldn't love her or he wouldn't feel so terrible"—is deeply disturbing because Herbst reveals that even a woman as perceptive as Vicky accepts personal responsibility for a socially constructed situation, one that threatens her love, the very basis of her tie to Jonathan.

Although Vicky knows that Jonathan's torment originates in his relation to his parents, the forces that shaped them, and the prevailing politics of inequity, Herbst perceptively reveals that for Vicky as for many other women, this knowledge is not enough to make a difference. What takes precedence, Herbst shows, is the conventional construction of the woman as savior of the erring man. In Vicky's version the emphasis shifts to her anxiety that Jonathan doesn't love her but underlying this fear is the unstated premise that it is her fault, that she is somehow responsible and as a result "he couldn't love her or he wouldn't feel so terrible." In 1934, while her own marriage was unraveling, Herbst goes back to the early stages and succeeds in exposing a deadly syndrome neither she nor her fictional surrogate was able to do anything about. The exposure is nonetheless a significant achievement of her political art.

Equally important is her characterization of Vicky as an eager young woman for whom "anything was all right so that they got somewhere, so that they kept a decent purpose in living" (p. 278). Herbst is especially good with Vicky's wry insights into her "romantic," emancipated life in the Greenwich Village of the early twenties, before she meets Jonathan. Vicky emerges as liberated, exploratory, and open to joy, loneliness, and depression. As she develops through the trilogy, she grows into a remarkable woman character, a measure of the success of Herbst's political art. By the time of *Rope of Gold*, not without cost Vicky has moved beyond her earlier reliance on "some man who 'knew something' " to explain things so as to make sense of the present and give promise of a radical future (pp. 254–55).

Beyond what Vicky herself does in Berkeley, Seattle, and the Village, Herbst has Vicky register important, reinforcing emotional and thematic resonances. Through Vicky, Herbst deepens the association of Rosamond's death with the injustice of the present system and the hope for a radical future. For Vicky "her sister's death, all the deaths of the broken and bleeding, of the young who had wanted to live in a fine world, seemed part of herself and she dramatized their suffering and linked it with her own. . . . If she had any pang it was that her sister seemed to have died so futilely." Vicky concludes, significantly, that "it would be a consolation to die for a cause that would go on, forever" (pp. 254–55).

Herbst's opening up of Vicky and Anne Wendel's feelings about "forever" is a revealing instance of the way she subtly intertwines the personal and political, just as she does points of view, narrative strands, and domestic and radical languages. From Anne Wendel's point of view Herbst looks back to the early, difficult days in Grapeville, to Anne's present satisfaction as a woman developing and selling property, and to her basic nurturing values, "sitting at the foot of the table to a real good dinner with the children on either side and Papa at the head carving their own bird that she had fattened and fed." These moving memories merge with her present sense that in laying out the Grapeville development "she could almost see the trees and the houses where people would actually live and breathe and children would be born and life would go on, forever" (p. 252). The pathos is intensified because Herbst does full justice to Anne's decency and her life-affirming commitment to a way of life Herbst shows is unlikely to "go on, forever," certainly not for Vicky.

In Greenwich Village, Herbst has Vicky pick up the refrain word as her friend Cora laments a betrayed relation with a man who, Cora says, "is gone, so far as I am concerned, forever." In this context of painters, designers, and Greenwich Village infidelities, Vicky goes deep into her origins when she asks herself about "forever," "what was it about that word that was so haunting and desirable. It was the word engraved inside of Anne Wendel's wedding ring that came off her hand so seldom, only sometime when she had been kneading dough and took it off. The children had picked up the ring, caked with the white dried dough, to read the initials and the date and word *forever* that was so much more amazing than their father and mother could ever be. What ideas had been given to them that secretly they longed for love that would go on and on like a great stream" (p. 256).

To frame Vicky's meeting with Jonathan, Herbst brings alive the dream world of childhood security and longing for "love that would go on and on like a great stream." The haunting desire for permanence gives an added resonance to the passion and instability of their relation, just as "forever" merges with images of the nurturing life of her parents and the radical cause Vicky longs for to replace the earlier way of life. Herbst also celebrates both the worlds of domestic love and of radical politics by using the image of the animating stream. The conflict between these two reinforcing worlds emerges powerfully in *Rope of Gold*.

Herbst repeatedly fuses feeling and ideas, the personal and public, as she does in her probing of Vicky's feelings about "forever." Integral to her practice of political art, at the center of the trilogy Herbst also challenges still influential views about the separation of politics and literature. She simultaneously brings into the open significant ideas about realism, modernism, and the avant-garde. She does so by dealing with an important side of the literary twenties in counterpoint to the developing political radicalism that concludes *The Executioner Waits* and culminates in *Rope of Gold*. In Detroit during the early twenties Jonathan is part of a group of struggling young writers who want to publish in places like the early *Smart Set* and the avant-garde magazine Jonathan breaks into. They are symptomatically unaware of the murders of the German Marxists, Rosa Luxembourg and Karl Liebknecht, "shot in the back" (p. 164). Instead, they express their rebellion against the prudery and restraints of The Parents through a cult of Rabelais who "had pressed all his hate and love of the lousy world into a book that reeked of the filth and fun of living" (p. 163). Codwollopers and codpieces fill their conversation. To great effect Jonathan also recites the dadaist poetry of Kurt Schwitters, particularly "Momma, the man is standing there." Jonathan is equally good at reciting *The Waste Land* and Gertrude Stein, so that he is aligned with the experimental modernism of dada and the avant-garde poetics of Eliot. Similarly, his allegiance to Rabelais encodes a cultural and sexual rather than overtly political rebellion.

Herbst explicitly raises the issue of a conflict between modernism and realism through Jonathan's friend, Tolman. Tolman has frequented the Paris cafés, he has followed Joyce's lead and applauded at the famous Antheil recital, and although he has not written his book on Balzac, he is adept at making his New York friends envy his European experiences. He may also be a fake, Herbst has Vicky observe, since unlike Jonathan he hasn't written anything. Herbst credits Jonathan with independent principles and ideas and she explores his torment as he moves from literature to radical politics. Tolman, on the other hand, embodies the fashionable expediency, first of the modernist twenties and later of the socially engaged thirties. In *The Executioner Waits* in one of the party scenes she perfects in *Rope of*

Gold, Herbst has Tolman say "the old realism was dead. The old language was dead. The old literature was dead. People like Joyce were creating a new world of language" (p. 312). Tolman goes on "with the air of a priest" to celebrate work that is "all sound, when you listen long enough, a real meaning comes out of it." These promising ideas are undercut by Tolman's pretensions and later by his "contradicting himself. He said words must be rediscovered for their own uses, they must be refound in their native significance. . . . Words should be used with the precision of tools, delicately and surely." The purpose, Tolman says in opposition to the project of *The Executioner Waits*, is "to reveal the inner reality, . . . to unfold the inner consciousness of the mind, that works in the dark and does not know itself" (pp. 313, 314).

Embedded in *The Executioner Waits* is a dialogue on the avant-garde novel. In her practice Herbst uses words "with the precision of tools." Her nonlinear realism, her fluid shifts in point of view, and her handling of the interchapters, moreover, all benefit from the modernism Jonathan and Tolman bring into focus. In Herbst's 1930s version of the avant-garde, the emphasis is nonetheless on her intensifying political radicalism, on the fusion of personal, family, and national destinies, not on "the inner consciousness of the mind, that works in the dark and does not know itself." Herbst writes within and reanimates the realistic tradition. In the process she contributes to the left avant-garde that is one of the significant achievements of the political culture of the 1930s. "The old realism" may be dead but Herbst's practice shows that a new realism is alive, animated from intertwined personal, family, and political sources. As her own example shows, moreover, literature and politics reinforce each other; they are not separate and at odds, as they are for Tolman and Jonathan.

Herbst's affirmation of her version of left avant-garde realism places in perspective her concluding treatment of David Trexler and the older generation of the Trexler family in contrast to the evolving commitments of Jonathan and Vicky Chance. As *The Executioner Waits* circles to a close, Vicky and Jonathan are living in a farmhouse in the same region of Pennsylvania in which the Trexler family originated. Of the older generation, Mem and Joe, Anne and Aaron have already died, Hortense is ill, and David has survived but his death is in the offing. Herbst opens and closes the novel with David Trexler. His visit to the young couple highlights the contrast between old and new, as Herbst indicates in the section heading, "The Future Belongs to Them." Jonathan is living in a world of militant farm protesters and he is more concerned with organizing his neighbors to save a mortgaged farm than he is in Uncle David. The Crash has taken place, David's stock is falling, and his visit to the grave of Millie's husband, a former railroad worker, is alive with the militant threat of men and women marching to protest the killing of a fellow striker. Herbst conveys a concluding sense of revolutionary ferment among farmers and workers who respond to the IWW slogan, "*Don't mourn. Organize*" (p. 340).

At the grave, which might as well be that of David Trexler and all he stands for, "the crowd stood tight, a hard nucleus like a fist that would never open, and he looked toward it appealingly for sympathy for David Trexler, the little orphan, but it was staring at the grave and did not see him" (p. 340). Herbst ends with a memorable version of left iconography: the crowd of mourning workers is "tight," cohesive; they are a "hard nucleus," a vanguard, and "like a fist that would never open" they are militantly implacable. They have been wronged, they have a just cause, and in the new world they forecast, David Trexler is as invisible as they are in the world he has prospered in. "The Future," Herbst emphasizes, "Belongs to Them."

Herbst succeeds in the difficult political art of revealing the inequities of the present and of inspiring hope in a radically altered future without falsifying the actual power relations or turning her characters into the stock figures of polemical discourse. Death and possibility characterize the endings of *Pity Is Not Enough* and *The Executioner Waits*. Herbst has Vicky copy into her notebook the radical slogan from Goethe, "*to suffer or to win, to be a hammer or an anvil*" (p. 23). Although she is attracted to the slogan, Vicky, like her creator, is almost never given to either/or responses. More characteristic of Herbst's political art is her insight that "it was easier to hold off death than to hold off torn tablecloths and worn bedclothes and curtains that had hung in the same place year in and year out." Writing from a deep familiarity with the lives of ordinary women, Herbst knows that "a battered coffeepot is sometimes harder to contend with morning after morning than sickness in the house" (p. 23). Her political art spans the gamut from Goethe's hammer and anvil to the battered coffee pot and torn tablecloths and the sickness and death that in their rendered social-political context are also part of the fabric of the lives she respects and helps us understand.

Rope of Gold

Five years after publishing *The Executioner Waits*, in *Rope of Gold* (1939) Herbst continued to illuminate America by entering into the divergent lives and points of view of a panoramic range of characters. Carrying over from the last third of *The Executioner Waits*, Jonathan and Vicky are central. Herbst draws on immediate, painful personal experience influenced by and contributing to the left politics of the crucial depression years, especially 1933–37. In the process of writing the trilogy, as she shows in the first chapter of *Rope of Gold*, Herbst has fully developed her talent for bringing to a focus conflicting outlooks and a sweep of class and gender positions.

Rope of Gold begins in 1933 with an intense political argument in Mr. Chance's comfortable, upper-middle-class living room. Herbst knows Mr. Chance's territory as well as she does the ambience of radical farm protest and the conflicts between hunted miners and company thugs in Harlan County. As they enter the narrative through the consciousness of Vicky and Jonathan, these radical elements reverberate against the settled ease and rectitude of the elder Mr. Chance. In *Rope of Gold* Herbst avoids reductive stereotypes about depression America as a realm of the unemployed and down-and-out. She also sustains a radical outlook in the organizing form of her fiction, which culminates in a successful sit-down strike. In this embodiment of class war, the factory setting and its central figure, Steve Carson, give promise of a new world at odds with the prosperous family gathered at Mr. Chance's for Mrs. Chance's funeral.

At the outset the family is together but for the last time. The strains within the family, the interwoven recollections of Vicky and Jonathan Chance, and the depth of disagreement between Jonathan and his family—all succeed in conveying the urgency, the dislocations, the personal and public resonances of a charged moment in American history. Herbst's sensitivity to the creative relation between language and audience and to the nature of discourse communities animates the opening scene, in which Jonathan falls flat as he tries unsuccessfully to recreate in his father's living room the vitality of his speech before a radical farm group. Ironically, as a salesman for the party, Jonathan later becomes aware of his glibness as opposed to "the new language" the cause demands at its best (p. 6). Herbst is sensitive to the dilemma of those like Jonathan who are attracted to the party, who are committed to the act, to the primacy of doing, and who also write and love words but deplore glibness and public relations. "Jonathan had always believed that literature was not argument but the history of men's feelings, the search for the hidden springs of men's actions, and if he turned to the farmers now, it was not as a substitute for a job undone" (p. 40). The party, however, takes Jonathan from a life of unalienated action in the country to the drawing rooms of the rich where to further a good cause he accepts party discipline and uses words like "peace" so ambiguously that he loses his own self-respect.

In the opening chapter, through the memorable particulars of a conflict about an inheritance at an earlier funeral, Herbst reveals exactly what Jonathan is up against, not from the party but from his family—which is to say, she reveals from the inside what is important in a system centered on the ownership of property. Aunt Hettie's "little black veil," Jonathan recalls of the earlier time, "had whistled out over her teeth as she gesticulated in her black kid gloves. White wrists, bleached as bone, had shown from between glove and cuff with a morbid threat of the grave. She had begun to cough with a kind of fury, calling names and yelling something about stacked cards and Uncle Ed holding all the aces and their poor father turning in his newmade grave." Jonathan recalls that his "father had shriveled with the disgrace of the quarrel that had threatened to rupture the family forever. He, of all the connection, had acted a noble part. He had resigned his share to be reallotted as thought fit. Aunt Hettie had thereupon grabbed the bank corner and for thanks never spoke to him again" (p. 5). Aunt Hettie, caught in the act, never reappears but like other secondary figures in the feast of Herbst's fiction she contributes to our understanding of the human resonances of the system Jonathan and Vicky are challenging.

As she probes the breakup of Vicky and Jonathan's marriage, now entering into one, now into the other's point of view, Herbst sensitively opens up the politics of gender intertwined with radical politics and the impact of the old patriarchy, in Jonathan's case represented by his father and all he stands for. For Herbst personal relations may be finally private and inscrutable but they are not privatized. From Vicky's point of view, her husband's increasing involvement as a farm organizer leaves her isolated, left out. Jonathan attends meetings, comes home late or not at all, and thrives on the down-to-earth activity. Vicky shares his commitments but resents the neglect. Ironically, an important stage in their separation is Jonathan's decision to join the party and become a section organizer. He takes out his card alone instead of together with Vicky. The crosscurrents of political involvement, its impact on personal relations, and in Jonathan's case his need to act independently, in reaction against the interiorized demands of his father, combine to give the sequence a convincing, low-keyed authority. Herbst does not create either heroic, cardboard organizers or the reductively slanted portraits of Dos Passos's Mary French and Ben Compton. Instead, she gets inside the movement and those compelled by it and does justice to their efforts and to their flawed humanity.

As a historical and human marker, for us what is particularly revealing is that Vicky Chance, one of the new women of the 1920s and 1930s, has to struggle to achieve a measure of control over her own life. She is simultaneously liberated and enmeshed. Her mother actively encouraged her to think of a career as a lawyer, as a legislator like her grandfather. "And she had never breathed such foolishness as that she must choose between 'a career' and marriage. It would have been the last thing on earth for Anne Wendel to suppose that a child of hers should forfeit love and children. Her girl was merely to have everything the world holds" (p. 47). As we know and as Herbst reveals, these demands place an almost unbearable burden on women. To her credit, Vicky responds to the "symbols of some bursting kind of life [her mother] had wanted for her daughter" (p. 48). Vicky has lived independently. She does not accept conventional middle-class views about sexuality, marriage, and money. In the country, however, Jonathan functions in the world of political affairs and she stays home, increasingly lonely and in need of an involvement Jonathan is too preoccupied and too vulnerable to encourage. This neat replication in the lives of radicals of the conventional patterns they reject is not the only element in their lives. But Herbst underscores the emotional impact of Vicky's dependency and Jonathan's activity by departing from the generally autobiographical basis of Vicky's character. While she and John Herrmann were in the country, Josephine Herbst wrote and published two first-rate novels, a creative achievement she deliberately filters out of Vicky's life. Herbst is perceptive and detailed about the dynamics of Jonathan's blocked creativity. In exploring the subtle shifts in power in their relation, however, in her fiction she chooses to remove what in her own life was a source of self-esteem that must have intensified her husband's problems.

Although it does not detract from her as a successfully realized character, moreover, Vicky also emerges as more conventional than her creator, who was involved in an intense relation with Marion Greenwood.[15] In the novel, Vicky is instead attracted to Kurt Becher, a dedicated German radical. Together with Jonathan's jealousy, this relation further undermines the marriage. The tie with Kurt Becher is emotional, not sexual. Kurt satisfies Vicky's need for a sympathetic, intellectual involvement. Herbst thus simplifies and conventionalizes the intensities of her own life. Vicky is still fiery, active, and politically acute. To the extent that Kurt Becher is a shadowy figure, however, to the extent that Vicky's feelings for him are warm and relatively unintense, and to the extent that Jonathan's jealousy is relatively unjustified, to that extent the changes shift the sense of the rights and wrongs of the situation more in her favor than in Jonathan's. Jonathan, moreover, eventually falls in love with another woman and leaves. Vicky is far from a passive victim but for all of her passionate independence she is also made to act out a familiar pattern in which men take the initiative and women suffer the consequences. The sexual politics in the novel are thus more defused and conventional than in Herbst's own life. The intertwining of the personal and the public animates Herbst's political art. Her reticence, her unwillingness to engage the reverberations of her relation with Marion Greenwood, mark a limit in her creation of radical political fiction.

The troubled relation between Vicky and Jonathan and the emotional disturbances it causes are nonetheless central to the organizing rhythms of the novel. In counterpoint with contrasting couples—Steve Carson and Lorraine, Lester Tolman and Elsie, Cliff and Nancy Radford—Herbst enters now into Jonathan's, now into Vicky's point of view. Underlying Vicky's present loneliness and sense of neglect is the loss of a child, a miscarriage that connects Vicky and Rosamond, colors Vicky's feelings about Jonathan, and contributes to the pattern of loss and renewal, although not as powerfully or complexly as with Rosamond. In the ebb and flow of powerful feelings, Vicky understandably withdraws from Jonathan, who has threatened to leave her if she has the child and who, she feels, has never been with her when she needs him. She also sees that Jonathan is destabilized by the slightest criticism. He has a deep need for constant, unquestioned love. His sense of self-esteem is precarious and Vicky's knowledge of his family oddly aligns her with them in his mind.

Despite her insights into Jonathan, his neglect and casual affairs, and her feelings for Kurt Becher, Vicky nonetheless does not sustain her emotional withdrawal. At best, given their political passions and their desire to live worthwhile lives, Vicky and Jonathan try "to make their love extend beyond the room and not become just a shelter" (p. 12). As Herbst perceptively follows Vicky's swings of feeling, she generates insight into the unstable relation between the personal and public, between love and politics. Under the pressure of physical and emotional separation, Vicky tells Jonathan, "It's no good if it always comes back to whether I love you or not. I love you, all right. You might as well ask me if I breathe. Or do I want to live without my liver or lights? The trouble is the earth's shaking and we stand here talking about love" (p. 92). Later, however, "at the dark roots of their lives the very ground fell away" (p. 116), and, in her loneliness, Vicky "suddenly wanted only to love; to sit quietly beside Jonathan, to touch him would be something. Jonathan, Jonathan, oh don't let him stop loving me, she thought" (p. 122).

One of Herbst's achievements is to probe Vicky's intense suffering as her marriage gradually breaks up, not in a linear, logical way but with powerful swings of feeling. Because of her persistence, intensity, and honesty, Herbst cumulatively gives her portrayal of the deteriorating relation between Vicky and Jonathan a larger-than-life status. For a sympathetic reader the precarious love of these two characters finally lives in the imagination with the same kind of energy as the great love stories. Because American literature is notoriously weak in precisely this area, including Herbst's trilogy in the received canon would be a welcome addition.

The pain of Vicky and Jonathan's separation, their displacement from home, the undermining of their house as a physical and emotional structure, and Vicky's gradual recovery reverberate with the successes and failures of radical dairy farm organizers, the structure of dustbowl wheat farming, and the investigation of the sugar industry. Herbst knows milk, wheat, sugar, and cars. She also knows the people and the hard labor that drive these basic systems, which illuminate the larger structure of a late capitalism in crisis. Herbst typically particularizes, so that she conveys a sense of individual people and the larger structures that shape their lives, even as her people make and sometimes try to change these systems radically. The personal feelings and struggles of Vicky and Jonathan Chance thus give an undoctrinaire particularity to this ideologically charged novel.

Herbst similarly enters into the lives and point of view of ordinary people like Tim Robb, a hardworking Pennsylvania dairy farmer. Through Robb she shows the way farmers were encouraged to take out loans during the good years just after World War I. Then "the Bank became a maw to be filled. It was like a bull critter that hasn't got what it takes, but eats its head off just the same, terrifies the herd and lives for himself, strictly speaking, with nothing to offer. The Bank got snacks and it growled. It got a full meal and it purred. The Bank," Herbst goes on, "was always in their thoughts," the interest due taking precedence over toys for the children. "The Bank had its hand on their shoulders, stood beside their bed, pulled their shoelaces from their shoes" (p. 52). Herbst continues to open up the workings of the market system as it affects small farmers like Robb. "Who could blame the clover, or the corn, or the wheat?" she has Robb ask. "It grew well enough. If he filled his barns, the milk still did not overtake the mortgage. It might inch up a little, as if the two were running a race and the milk was riding an ox cart and the mortgage, driven by the crafty Mr. Cream-pie Mullins [the banker], was speeding ever ahead in a fine eight-cylinder car" (p. 53). No wonder Robb, like Jonathan, becomes an activist in the radical farm movement whose dynamic of protest, cooperation, and friction Herbst brings alive.

Through a series of speeches, arguments at parties, and the sermon at Tub's funeral, Herbst also conveys a lively, not always flattering sense of the public discourse of the thirties left. Her own sympathies are with the fallible farmers and workers at the bottom and with those like Jonathan, Robb, and Steve Carson who combine dirt under their fingernails with principles, ideas, and action. She uses Vicky to undercut the well-intentioned radicalism of those who give to the Scottsboro Boys and listen to and then ignore a silicosis victim at a prosperous fundraiser. At the same meeting, with charismatic sincerity Clement Gregory, addressing those who "are not workers," calls for "a bloodless revolution of the white collar class to save the world from the onrush of what had happened in Germany" (p. 120). Herbst previously had Vicky question the "young men and women with good jobs [who] talked glowingly of 'throwing themselves into the class struggle' as if it were a tropical sea" (p. 118). She is equally critical of Gregory, of whom an onlooker says, "my dear lady, sincerity without a program isn't going to make a social revolution. What's he proposing? Another British Labor Party, without Labor, the most bankrupt investment a man could conceive of?" (pp. 121–22).

At another party "a young man with a stern haughty face was trying to impress everyone with the extent of his radicalism. Shakespeare had no message for this age; one man's notion of truth was unimportant and even presumptuous, organization was the only thing that mattered." Unintimidated, Herbst puts this extreme party orthodoxy in its place through Mr. Penner, who "said drily that he hoped the speaker wasn't imagining himself superior in ignoring Shakespeare; the tired businessmen of America had always been of that company" (pp. 397, 398).

As a political novelist, Herbst uses figures like Clement Gregory and the intense young man to fill out the left range in the political-ideological spectrum of the novel. Jonathan and Si Greenough take her into the center of the party. Figures like Tim Robb and especially Steve Carson bring to life a militant, grass-roots left activism. Vicky's acts and responses further characterize the principles, appeals, and abuses of the organized left. Through Tolman, Herbst catches the wavering expediency of intelligent intellectuals who operate within the political culture of the left. At the other extreme is Ed Thompson and the danger of American fascism. In the middle Cliff and Nancy Radford bring the impact of the depression home from the point of view of the decent, ordinary American middle class. Throughout, Herbst has her characters engage representative ideas and critical positions. Sometimes using powerful imagery, urbane satire, or revealing juxtapositions, Herbst tests, evaluates, and probes.

She has Jonathan play an active role in this nuanced process of exploring and demystifying. Jonathan is deeply affected by the old capitalistic patriarchy of his father and by the new movement that may replace it. In *The Executioner Waits* Herbst convincingly showed that Jonathan's family transmits the values and practices of the larger system into the depths of his personality. In *Rope of Gold* he is fulfilled for a time working one-to-one with his neighbors as a radical farm organizer. But the dialectics are not simple or reassuring. "Even if the 'Line' were wrong," Jonathan believes, "this refound potentiality of fellowship of man for man must be real" (p. 240). Although the movement is not discredited and although Jonathan has moments of personal realization as an organizer, Herbst also shows that the party turns him against his basic impulse into an attractive front, into a well-dressed salesman for the cause but as far removed from the work he values as when he was on the road as a moneymaker. In a lovely scene Herbst exposes his contempt for his fund raising at comfortable upper-middle-class gatherings. The scene culminates when he meets a woman who accepts him without reservation, so that his party work and self-contempt make his falling in love seem touchingly understandable. Here is a new world in the making, a new couple and the new ideology, but not without their flaws.

For her part, as Victoria Chance struggles to overcome her feelings of loss and loneliness, she also works with increasing independence as a radical journalist acutely analyzing and bringing alive conditions in the dustbowl and in the sugar industry. As they cross the country on an assignment, Lester Tolman, urbane and well dressed, introduces Vicky as his secretary but she is not really subordinate. In Cuba she begins to recover from the feverish sickness of separation. She succeeds in establishing a deep connection with the Cuban rebels. Their voices gradually prevail over her sense of personal desolation and her own voice begins to answer to theirs. Although Batista breaks their strike, she affirms to the "realistic" Tolman that " 'it's not finished,' she said, pulling on her gloves angrily as if he had insulted her. 'It isn't all over. You'll hear of all this again' " (p. 401). At the end, as she returns home "the road and fields were solid ground and the objects of the earth like sleepy animals were rising to their knees" (p. 406). Intricately, the personal and public intertwine, as do the politics of gender and the revolutionary politics of class.

Herbst further develops these concerns through Steve Carson and Lorraine, who come together as Jonathan and Vicky separate. The Steve Carson figure could easily become a cardboard abstraction of the young militant who points the way to the future. Instead, Herbst endows him with a rendered past and a believable inner life. His father's radicalism centers on Eugene Debs's Socialist Party and its news-paper, *Appeal to Reason*. Steve Carson is grounded in and moves beyond this early-twentieth-century version of American radicalism. For Herbst, his story is also inseparable from that of his stepmother whose touching narrative brings into focus the deprivation, exploited labor, and sexual vulnerability of a young girl struggling into adulthood in the Dakotas of the early twentieth century. As she typically does, Herbst locates her characters in the web of family relations unless, as with Lester Tolman, the absence is itself telling.

As Steve Carson struggles to figure things out, he takes part in the farmers' strike Herbst had dealt with in the interchapters of *The Executioner Waits*, so that this militant activity moves into the main narrative. Steve sees that the farmers' anger peters out, however, and "he raged at his father about the way they had allowed themselves to be sold down the river by Milo Reno with nothing gained" (p. 154). With Steve as with Vicky, Herbst does not overstate the radical possibilities she nonetheless uses Steve to affirm. The section heading is "Now, Not Tomorrow."

For all his reservations, increasingly for Steve "the truth as he saw it was that the damned machinery didn't work anymore. The system was screwy and there was nothing to do with it but hand it to the junk heap the way you would an old car, maybe salvage a few bolts and parts. He got encouragement from the talk that seemed to him to strip the gears bare. Soon people would realize the old contraption would not haul the load" (p. 206).

Intertwined with this idiomatic version of the left celebration of machinery and radical change is Steve's sensitivity to the beauty of the fields, his "tenderness for the world," and his desire to know more (p. 206). As a positive figure in the spectrum of Herbst's political art, Steve Carson gains credibility because Herbst has him combine sensitivity and a questioning, nondoctrinaire militancy. For Herbst, he is an imaginatively realized embodiment of the radical tomorrow he is committed to. Although Herbst arranges it so that Steve is impatient with his father's IWW-Debs version of radicalism, she also carefully omits connecting Steve explicitly with the Communist Party.

Through Steve, Herbst conveys a sense of the way ordinary people struggle to sustain mortgaged farms and to organize and fight back against programs and forces that deplete instead of help them. She also uses Steve to get inside the automobile factories, to render a sense of hard labor on the belt, the impact of this labor on men and their families, and the intensity of the union busting and blacklisting that precede the turn of the tables in the final, symbolic strike. Impelled by his desire to engage in meaningful radical change, Steve moves from country to city and back. His return is motivated by Lorraine's pregnancy. Although Mr. LaRue proposes a shotgun marriage, Steve does not have to be coerced. He does resent working for Lorraine's father, another of the prosperous patriarchs who, like Mr. Chance, David Trexler, and Grandpa Radford, complicate the lives of the younger generation. In a muted way, much less intense than with their contrasting counterparts, Vicky and Jonathan, the marriage and impending birth reinforce the politics of the concluding strike.

At the other extreme from Steve Carson is Jonathan's brother-in-law, Ed Thompson. Through Ed, Herbst takes us behind the scenes of the upper-level management of the automobile industry. Herbst moves knowledgeably from radical unionizers on the belt and militant farm organizers in Pennsylvania and Iowa through the declining middle-class lives of Cliff and Nancy Radford to the inner circles of American industry. In her account, the industrialists have a kind of decadent sophistication, they endure and undercut the right-wing speeches of visiting Englishmen, and they are open to the moves of a strong leader. Ed's family has been eased out but he has survived by combining public relations and public speaking techniques with a grasp of world politics and a ruthless desire to succeed. Through his admiration of Hitler, Father Coughlin, and Huey Long, he is aligned with a developing American fascism. Herbst uses Ed to validate the left view that a segment of American big business is dangerously profascist. Ed's special projects are, appropriately enough, a secret union-breaking industrial police force and his investment in Liberty Laboratories, manufacturer of a tear gas that can be used to put down popular uprisings ranging from Cuba to the sit-down strikes. As part of his job, Ed spies on his workers and connives with the police.[16] Beyond his job he savages Roosevelt and talks up the virtue of an authoritarian leader controlling the slavelike masses.

Perhaps not coincidentally, in his personal life Ed is restless in his marriage and he has a keenly rendered affair that shows his ruthless energy. Even with Ed, who primarily fills a space in the ideological spectrum of *Rope of Gold*, Herbst responds sympathetically to his struggle to survive. Before he becomes a power she illuminates the pain of his situation and grants him an inner life when, at a banquet, "his attention was unnaturally sharpened to stray conversation as if he were pinned beneath a wrecked car waiting for help" (p. 31).

Ed is in charge of the forces that unsuccessfully try to break the final sit-down strike. For the reader the cohesion of the workers and the energy of the strike are reinforced by the affirmation of the concluding chapter heading, "The Earth Does Move." This resonant quotation associates radical change with the scientific validity and martyrdom of Galileo. Herbst also builds toward a sense of future possibility in a moving sermon an old minister preaches at the funeral of Steve Carson's friend, Tub. Tub has been murdered by vigilantes for his part in the radical farm protests in what Herbst nicely highlights as "the Bad Lands." The old man touchingly confuses Tub with his own son, killed in the war, and he merges the powerful imagery of Christianity with an unmistakably left emphasis on cleaning out the temples and doing the work of Christ again. "His followers had perverted His words," the old man concludes. "They had cast their eyes too long at heaven and had scorned earth and mankind whom He had come to save" (p. 381). The minister is grief-stricken and undoctrinaire. For the reader if not the speaker, the sermon implies that the new religion of saving radical change is to replace the outworn religion of orthodoxy, so that Herbst gives the revolutionary new society the authority of both the new Marxist faith and the new science connected with Galileo. Through repeated juxtapositions Herbst has the episodes in Cuba and the Bad Lands mutually reinforce one another. The sermon is one climax. Vicky's sense of promise after her experience with the Cuban revolutionaries is another.

Despite Ed's efforts, Steve Carson and the concluding strike—"the earth does move"—bring this sequence and the trilogy to a powerful, suggestive close.

In dialectical opposition to the energies and values Herbst affirms in her concluding sections, in *Rope of Gold* the threat of dictatorship and big-business contempt for workers and ordinary people are powerful manifestations of a worldwide threat. Although her narrative is centered in America, Herbst effectively intertwines the Cuban and Bad Lands material. Sugar, as Tolman says, nakedly reveals the workings of the entire system. Reverberating through *Rope of Gold*, moreover, is the immediacy of Nazi terror and the trauma of the burning of the Reichstag. Tolman, who has been there, brings his German experience into the center of the novel. His account of the crashing "dome of glass," the burning of the Reichstag, recurs again and again. Herbst simultaneously establishes the importance of the event and subverts Tolman's self-conscious exploitation of the experience. In one particularly effective sequence Herbst juxtaposes Tolman's account of Nazi police tactics with a chapter, "Boy in the Cell," on the police framing and jailing of the rebellious Iowa and Dakota farmers, including Steve Carson. The repressive brutality of the Middle Western cops and owners exposes a disquieting similarity Herbst leaves it up to us to see and judge.

Intertwined with the rendered characters and events of the narrative sections, Herbst uses the interchapters to extend her range and to convey a sense of radical protest and official repression from the Bonus Marchers in Washington, D.C. (1932) through the shoeless Cubans on their march (1935) to the defiant voice of a Lincoln Brigade veteran who in 1938 affirms in the face of the defeat in Spain that "we got the living, they got the dead" (p. 407). In these strategically placed chapters Herbst convincingly enters the language, experience, and values of a series of those at the bottom of society. She gives voice to their ordinarily silenced eloquence. The interchapters are as good as Dos Passos's biographies with the important difference that these first-person prose poems do justice to the voice and outlook of nameless people. Their grievances, dignity, energy, and values contribute to the sense that the old world deserves to and with effort will be changed. With their sensitive invocation of Lincoln, their compassion for the oppressed, and their rebellious affirmations, the interchapters emerge from and validate the frequently maligned values, insights, and choice of subject matter of the Popular Front.

As a radical political artist, Herbst faces the challenge of dealing with losses as well as gains and of nonetheless conveying a sense of affirmative possibility. In the interchapter on the loss of the Spanish Civil War, "If you take me to Kirkwood, I'll get to St. Louis all by myself: Tortosa, Barcelona Road, 1938," she confronts one of the most demoralizing defeats for the thirties left and attempts to go beyond it. In the case of the broken rebellion in Cuba, she relies on Vicky's faith, a convincing one in view of her frequent skepticism about paper revolutionaries who "pushed frantically into picketing, rode cars to hunger marches, sweated at the midnight lamp of Marxist discussion" (p. 40). Integral to the dialectics of the trilogy and particularly of *Rope of Gold* is Herbst's recognition that the farmers are easily co-opted, that it is not simple to balance between day-to-day details, as Si Greenough prefers, or to stress the energizing utopian vision, as Jonathan argues for. The novel is full of debate, questioning, qualification, and satire, particularly of the fashionable, self-interested radicalism of the rich, who see the movement as a train they should have a ticket for, just in case. The cumulative sense of radical possibility is convincing partly because it emerges from a series of telling episodes that do justice to the defeats, abuses, and shortcomings of the organized left.

As a radical political artist, Herbst also recognizes the need for "a new language" to convey her vision (p. 6). In her Trexler trilogy her response is to use, celebrate, and evaluate the old American languages of money, power, and protest and to make them new again. From the start she enters into conflicting points of view and renders the diverse voices of an extended American family. Her fluid, nonlinear narrative method is to intertwine a multiplicity of characters, events, and outlooks, to fuse the personal and public, and to reveal the broadly political implications in the family dramas she brings to imaginative life. Her nondoctrinaire Marxism, her sensitivity to the energy and dilemmas of women, and her feel for the grass roots, for the rebellious potential of farmers and ordinary people, characterize the entire trilogy. As Herbst comes closer to the present in *Rope of Gold*, she also views her American material from the perspective of the international threat of fascism.

In conventional American discourse, love is compartmentalized as private, not public and political. From Joe Trexler, Lucy and Lenore Blondell, and Agnes to Vicky and Jonathan Chance, however, Herbst succeeds in aligning love and politics. She views the glamour, pain, and losses of love as inseparable from the social-political context her love stories emerge from and illuminate. Like the classic European and American realists, Herbst is centrally concerned with love and money. In her trilogy Herbst reanimates the old realism and makes it into a memorable 1930s version of the left avant-garde. We have been trained to identify the avant-garde with the modernism of Eliot and Faulkner or with the disruptive narrative methods and outlook of *U.S.A.* Herbst's nonlinear, fluidly dialectical narrative method and her fusion of political radicalism and artistic experiment and innovation relate her to and help her carry forward a nonmodernist avant-garde tradition we have lost sight of as avant-garde.

Herbst was stimulated by the left discourse of the thirties, with its emphasis on class conflict, the resistance of farmers and workers, and the threat of war and fascism. As a lens on her own life, the life of her family, and the history of America, "the Marxian theory of class" helped her interpret and make sense of her personal, family, and national past and present. Intertwined with the passion of love, the complexities of class, money, and gender are central. In her trilogy Herbst responds to the energy streaming in from events and from the deepest recesses of her imagination she conveys a sense of contradiction, of oppositions, of change and instability leading precariously to a radically altered future. In the form and rhythms of her fiction Herbst is a living embodiment of a dialectical imagination.

Coda: A Note on Criticism

In contrast to the view I have been developing, in *Labor and Desire* for Paula Rabinowitz *Rope of Gold* reveals all of the flawed qualities she sees in the genre of the 1930s revolutionary novel. Rabinowitz accordingly and pejoratively classifies Steve Carson as a "proletarianized farmer."[17] For her the proletariat must always be masculine and in her view Herbst goes beyond the call of duty. "More than metaphorically gendering the proletariat as masculine," Rabinowitz argues, "Herbst describes Steve Carson as the heroic proletarian through a traditional bildungsroman. . . . Carson becomes the model revolutionary at the expense of a series of female characters" (p. 167). On this interpretation, of course, the character and novel are defective, defects compounded by another structural, generic contrast. For Rabinowitz within the proletarian genre the left intellectual is always feminized and is always opposed to the virility of the masculine proletariat, so that 1930s proletarian narrative is also always feminized and suspect. "Within the class and gender configurations of 1930s revolutionary fiction," Rabinowitz insists, "one is always situated in relation to the male worker. His excessive virility marks both the working-class woman and the intellectual man as insufficiently gendered—she as the masculine female, he as the effeminate male" (p. 169).

Steve Carson, however, poses a serious challenge to this model. Herbst has characterized him as in love with ideas. He loves to think, to analyze, to figure out problems ranging from production on LaRue's farm to the reorganization of society. He cares about concepts, about machinery, about the beauty of the land, about Lorraine. Through Steve Carson, Herbst brings alive the possibility of fusing thought and revolutionary action, of doing away with the alienation that has tormented characters like Jonathan and that mark the America she has sensitively rendered in her trilogy. Steve Carson is an exemplary version of Gramsci's organic intellectual and in some ways of Foucault's specific intellectual, a person who works for change in the specific sites of this particular office or factory or farm, except that as a 1930s radical, Steve Carson suggests the possibility of general change. Rabinowitz, however, cannot grant Steve Carson his status as an intellectual because to do so would undercut her prescriptions about the gendering of the entire proletarian genre. In giving a forecast of the possibility of going beyond alienation, moreover, Herbst as a 1930s Marxist may be in advance of a contemporary poststructuralist feminist like Rabinowitz, who is alert to antagonisms but not to their possible resolutions.

Women play a shifting role in the narrative Rabinowitz presents. As victims they highlight and discredit the privileging of the masculine, as in the view that Steve Carson achieves his status as proletarian hero "at the expense of a series of female characters." But why any more at the expense of a series of women than of a series of men—his father, whom he disappoints and disagrees with, for example, or Mr. LaRue? Or why at anyone's expense? Herbst presents an unidealized portrait of American life and American family life. Pain, disappointment, affection, and conflict are all parts of that life. The presumably temporary separation from Lorraine (at Lorraine's expense?) underscores the human cost both characters pay as Steve Carson helps to bring a revolutionary world alive. Similarly, in *The Executioner Waits* Rosamund's decision to return home dramatizes the human cost she and Jerry pay in the old world Steve, Jerry's successor, is seeking to change. The continuity with Jerry Stauffer, the contrast with the fatality of the Rosamund-Jerry relation, and even more the contrast with Jonathan and Vicky all contribute to the resonance of the concluding sections on Lorraine and Steve Carson.

In Rabinowitz's version Steve Carson also achieves his end at the expense of his stepmother, whose story collapses into one of what Rabinowitz calls Herbst's "melodramas of female sacrifice" (p. 167). To reduce Herbst's complex portrayal of strength, exploitation, and love to a one-dimensional melodrama, however, is to make programmatic purity take precedence over all other considerations. The program similarly dominates when mothers inspire rather than deplete the narrative, as in the peculiar claim that Jonathan and Steve both "draw on the memories of their dead mothers as sustenance for their activism" (p. 164). Herbst has gone into detail on the extent to which Mrs. Chance has infiltrated Jonathan's consciousness and is at the center of his writer's block. As an inner force she opposes, she does not sustain either his writing or his activism.

In dealing with Jonathan's troubled character, Rabinowitz stresses the role that the feminization of the intellectual and of narrative must play, so that for her Jonathan's difficulties are grounded in and expose the gender prescriptions of the proletarian genre as Rabinowitz has defined it. As Elinor Langer has established in great detail, however, in deeply probing Jonathan's life Herbst closely follows the life of her husband, John Herrmann, in his relations to his upper-middle-class parents and to her.[18] The script Herbst follows and deconstructs was written by the dominant society of upper-middle-class America, not, as in Rabinowitz's account, by Mike Gold and the genre of 1930s left fiction. Herbst meticulously and sympathetically shows the damage this dominant-society construction did to Jonathan, his mother, and his marriage. One major problem with Rabinowitz's categories is that they leave inadequate room for the deconstructive powers of left writers like Herbst, at the same time that they filter out Marxist insights and hopes or such revealing contrasts as that between two versions of left intellectual, Jonathan and Steve Carson.

Of the most significant female character in *Rope of Gold*, Vicky Chance, we learn that she is silenced and disappears near the end of the novel because "ultimately the proletarian aesthetic, which cannot support the presence of a female body that has not become a maternal body, precludes the possibility of an embodied intellectual and a nonmaternal female" (p. 162). But Vicky's struggle and achievement are not precluded but are realized and valued. Her experience with the militant Cuban workers helps her win through from the demoralization of her broken marriage. As the trilogy moves to its concluding episode, Vicky adds the power of her voice, language, and experience to those which culminate in Steve Carson and the promise of the sit-down strike. It is important for Herbst to conclude the novel with Steve Carson, who moves the narrative beyond the Trexler family. The vision that pervades the concluding sections is equalitarian and revolutionary. Vicky Chance contributes significantly; she is not silenced, she is not disembodied, and she does not disappear.

Another voice that contributes powerfully to the sense that the new Marxist faith will prevail is that of the preacher, whose sermon takes its place along with the best in American fiction. His eloquence and his touching inability to finish suggest strongly that the old religion of Christianity is being replaced by a new system of belief, underwritten by the concluding actions in Cuba, the Bad Lands, and the Flint sit-down strike. Herbst undogmatically combines words and deeds, fuses the international and the local and farmers and auto workers. She reinforces these mutually supporting forces by associating them with the scientific prestige and suffering of Galileo—"the earth does move." Far from confirming the alleged "failure of language" as a defining thematic and formal feature of *Rope of Gold*, the sermon testifies to Herbst's ability to enter divergent languages and to reanimate them for the purposes of her radical political art.

The "failure" Rabinowitz insists on repeatedly is not Herbst's, and it is not that somehow *Rope of Gold*, *The Executioner Waits*, and *Pity Is Not Enough* are the exceptions that prove the genre/gender rules Rabinowitz stipulates. The problem is with Rabinowitz's deterministic structuring of the proletarian genre and her reductive application of "laws" that often seem to exaggerate the power of genre and of her version of Mike Gold's supposedly unnuanced masculinist prescriptions and to minimize the critical, creative, deconstructive power of radical artists like Josephine Herbst.

CHAPTER 5

RICHARD WRIGHT'S *NATIVE SON*
AND THE POLITICAL UNCONSCIOUS

In *Native Son*, Bigger struggles for freedom against the oppressive constraints that bear down on him. The power of the dominant white society keeps him hemmed into a corner of the city. "I reckon we the only things in this city that can't go where we want to go and do what we want to do," Bigger tells his friend Gus.[1] In seeing himself as a "thing," as an African American Bigger in his way shares the insight Wright articulated in dedicating *Black Power* "to the unknown African who, because of his primal and poetic humanity, was regarded by white men as a 'thing' to be bought, sold, and used as an instrument of production."[2] Although Bigger has been made to see himself as a "thing," he nonetheless feels intensely. As an American, he has taken deep into his personality the belief that he has a right "to go where we want to go and do what we want to do." As an African American, he has also taken deep into his personality the fear and hatred of white power. "Where do they live?" Gus asks. "Bigger doubled his fist and struck his solar plexus. 'Right down here in my stomach,' he said" (p. 22). Wright connects the external facts of segregation, poverty, stunted opportunities, and white power with the realities that live deep inside Bigger.

"They don't let us do *nothing*," he tells Gus. Unlike those who bury their resentment and accept the situation, Bigger distinguishes himself as an American because, against great odds, "I just can't get used to it. . . . I swear to God I can't. I know I oughtn't think about it, but I can't help it. Every time I think about it I feel like somebody's poking a red-hot iron down my throat." Wright draws on the conflict between the professed values of the dominant society and Bigger's experience as an African American when he has Bigger go on to drive home the charges, simply and powerfully. "We live here and they live there. We black and they white. They got things and we ain't. They do things and we can't. It's just like living in jail. Half the time I feel like I'm on the outside of the world peeping in through a knot-hole in the fence" (p. 20).

Everything about Bigger is charged with radical political implications. He is not a revolutionary—he is not committed to overthrowing the white society he knows oppresses him—but he is a rebel. From the party perspective his intelligence, rebellious energy, and exposure of oppression are promising but Wright shows that Bigger could easily turn to the right. He is fascinated with militaristic, authoritarian leaders, with the exploits of Mussolini, Hitler, and Japan (p. 130). In his rebellious alienation from the dominant white society, Bigger is open to authoritarian politics because, in contrast to the party position, for him what is primary is race, not the proletarian unity of white and black workers or self-determination for the oppressed Black Belt "nation within a nation."[3] Wright understands that for Bigger, primarily because of the dynamics of race, to destroy whites and unify blacks and his own personality is a project with deep appeal.

For Wright himself as distinct from Bigger, "a Marxist analysis of society . . . creates a picture which, when placed before the eyes of the writer, should unify his personality, organize his emotions, buttress him with a tense and obdurate will to change the world. And, in turn," Wright continues, "this changed world will dialectically change the writer. Hence," Wright affirms, "it is through a Marxist conception of reality and society that the maximum degree of freedom in thought and feeling can be gained for the Negro writer." For Wright, although "Marxism is but the starting point," it was one that sustained him throughout his life.[4] As for the Communist Party's version of Marxism, Wright eventually concluded that his long involvement with the party interfered with the liberating "freedom in thought and feeling" the party had given him.[5]

While he was writing *Native Son*, however, not only in the ambivalence of the concluding sequences but also in the deep structure of characterization and evaluation, Wright's active engagement in 1930s communism permeates and strengthens the novel, validating Wright's view that "I owe my literary development to the Communist Party and its influence, which has shaped my thought and creative growth."[6] Under the pressure of his deepest sense of reality, in *Native Son* Wright was able to test his conflicting allegiances as a writer, as a black man, and as a Communist, culminating in Bigger's rejection of the hope of a Communist conversion. The radical politics of *Native Son* are thus inseparable from but not limited to the concerns of the party.

In my judgment the party stimulated and supported Wright, he took party positions seriously, he criticized as an engaged insider, he did not falsify his own deepest experience to satisfy ideological imperatives, and in testing his commitments he strengthened his art. In literature, moreover, as Barbara Foley has shown, the party line was not fixed or monolithic. Two important, opposing Communist reviews of *Native Son* confirm Foley's view and suggest the extent to which Wright was free to work within, go beyond, and push against Communist positions, or rather the reviews indicate that the way committed intellectuals viewed Communist positions depended significantly on the intellectual.[7]

In *Native Son*, as in his attraction to fascist dictators, race is central to Bigger's political consciousness, but for Wright as for the party race is also intertwined with class, with the rendered material circumstances of Bigger's life. Bigger does not have money, he lives in a mean, one-room apartment, he is always aware that he has nothing and "they got everything. . . . They own the world" (p. 23). Bigger lives in a competitive, capitalistic society where self-worth depends significantly on how much a person owns, with the freedom of movement and choice that go along with money. No wonder Bigger questions whether he and his family are worth anything. Because they have done nothing, he thinks, perhaps they deserve to live the way they do, an appalling infiltration into his feeling-belief system of the prevailing views of the larger society (p. 118). Wright succeeds in making Bigger a compelling character not by airbrushing him but by bringing into the open his complex views and feelings. What emerges from the depths of the political unconscious is unsettling to readers along the entire spectrum, from left to right.

Bigger feels he is living in jail, the place where conventional society places those it punishes for breaking the official rules. Wright, however, turns the sense of confinement into a powerful social-racial-political critique that pervades *Native Son* from Bigger's acts and feelings to the expressionist settings and the very weather of the novel. *Native Son* is dominated by scenes of enclosure, from the tensely confined room of the opening scene through the expressionist buildings where Bigger kills Bessie and hides out like the rat he has earlier beaten to death to the luridly lit basement and the final jail scene.

"Book One: Fear"

In a carefully constructed sequence, Wright moves from the confines of the apartment to the surrounding world of the street and then beyond the limits of the Black Belt into the white territory of the Daltons. Far from opening up vistas, however, the sequence intensifies the sense of confinement. The conversations with Gus and playing white make explicit the extent of the political, economic, and racial pressures that cause Bigger to feel he is living in jail. The first thing Bigger encounters when he enters the street is a picture of the embodiment of the hostile white world, the prosecuting attorney, Buckley, whose eyes relentlessly follow Bigger. Later in the novel even the outdoor scenes have a sense of oppressive enclosure as the white storm cuts off visibility and the white winter cold penetrates to the depths. The settings in *Native Son* encode the power of the white world and the pervasive reality of oppression. Through contrast, the settings also throw into relief the countertheme of freedom.

In *Native Son* Wright penetrates deep into the political unconscious. One of his achievements is that he finds actions and imagery adequate to deal with the highly charged material he engages. Like the settings, almost everything in *Native Son* is open to multiple interpretation because, as in a dream, the powerful surfaces of the novel are inseparable from a complex of underlying concerns. These animating political-racial realities and Wright's way of narrating them make *Native Son* at once literal and expressionist.[8] Wright's political art, his version of realism-naturalism, is another instance of the left avant-garde and another example of how far removed the best left literature of the 1930s is from the reductive "crude naturalism" alleged against this radical tradition.[9]

Throughout *Native Son* Wright enters into Bigger's point of view and, like Le Sueur, Herbst, and many others on the left, he gives voice to the inarticulate, or, rather, to those who use a language different from that of the educated white middle class. One function of the scene with Gus and playing white is to establish that Bigger can articulately express his feelings and ideas. With his family, however, Bigger is curt and abusive, as he is in the poolroom. In the presence of the Daltons, Bigger shuffles and mumbles even beyond his conscious intention to act as he supposes he should around whites. Wright knows that the audience makes a difference and that under the pressures of his life Bigger for the most part expresses himself crudely.

Wright also knows that Bigger's inner life, his inner language, is subtle, deep, and complicated. The contrast between Bigger's inner and outer speech is central to the political art of *Native Son*. In choosing to interpret Bigger's feelings and ideas in the language of the dominant class instead of having Bigger use his own dialect, Wright sides with Frederick Douglass and his literary successors as opposed to Harriet Wilson (*Our Nig*) and those in the blues and jazz traditions who have made black vernacular into unforgettable poetry. Wright himself is deeply rooted in the blues tradition; in his final scene he renders a black and blue response to Bigger's dilemma. In the texture of his interpretative language, however, Wright chooses to create a narrator who eloquently turns the language of the dominant class to his own uses.[10]

Especially in "Book One" and "Book Two," the third-person narrator of *Native Son* stays close to Bigger's inner experience. The narrator, sympathetic, perceptive, but not identical with Bigger, is one of Wright's major creations. But to insist too much on his independence from Bigger distorts the narrator's role and impact. The narrator functions to give us the full range of Bigger's experience, to bring into the open Bigger's inner feelings, ideas, and implications, often to place them in a larger racial-political context, and almost always to play off against and challenge the conventional external view of Bigger. The narrator's interpretations are almost always reliable. They significantly constitute the Bigger Thomas who emerges into the deep, complex central figure of *Native Son*. Readers who make a sharp distinction between the narrator and Bigger and who separate Bigger from the narrator's interpretations end up with a reduced, diminished view of Bigger.[11]

In another sense, the narrator's interpretations are so thorough and compelling they do not seem to leave the reader much to do. Take the passage in which, after the powerful action with the rat, Wright uses the third-person narrator—let's call him Wright—to explain for the first time what has been going on inside Bigger, why he acts as he does toward his family. "He hated his family," Wright says, "because he knew that they were suffering and that he was powerless to help them. He knew that the moment he allowed himself to feel to its fullness how they lived, the shame and misery of their lives, he would be swept out of himself with fear and despair. So he held toward them an attitude of iron reserve; he lived with them, but behind a wall, a curtain. And toward himself he was even more exacting. He knew that the moment he allowed what his life meant to enter fully into his consciousness, he would either kill himself or someone else. So he denied himself and acted tough" (p. 9).

Repeatedly in *Native Son* Wright probes the dynamics of Bigger's hate, a basic emotion whose racial-political-economic sources include the rat-infested apartment, Bigger's sense of powerlessness, and his awareness of his family's suffering. Bigger is not a monster. He does feel for his family but what dominates is a hatred directed not against the underlying causes but against those he cares for but cannot help. This racially-politically-economically constructed hatred is an indictment of the dominant society. At the same time, Bigger is not glamorized and he is not a victim. Wright endows Bigger with unusual energy and depth, so that his feeling of powerlessness testifies to how deeply the restrictions of the white world have penetrated his consciousness.

Power is a key personal and political concern. For Bigger viewed either as an American or an African American man, to have power is crucial to his sense of manhood. The simple ability to provide for his family is involved. "We wouldn't have to live in this garbage dump if you had any manhood in you," his mother tells him (p. 7). The Dalton job is at least a start but the conditions undermine rather than bolster Bigger's sense of manhood and power. Unless he takes the job, they will be evicted and probably starve. Bigger feels he has no choice and choice is important to his sense of self-worth. No wonder "it maddened him to think that he did not have a wider choice of action" (p. 12). In this case his seething anger, another of his recurring emotions, is fed by his sense "that they had tricked him into a cheap surrender" (p. 11). What is at stake is Bigger's sense of possibility, of what he is capable of. He has dreamed of being a pilot but he can't get the training. When he plays white, he imagines being a general. He has a culturally sanctioned desire for a life of courage, skill, adventure, and command. Movies and pulp magazines make him feel good because as escape they feed his imagination and momentarily relieve the tensions of his life. In a passage the Book-of-the Month Club suppressed, Wright evaluates the process by having Bigger and Gus masturbate in a darkened movie theater. Bigger then watches a newsreel that shows Jan pursuing a sexually attractive Mary, who arouses Bigger. His response underscores the sexual dimension of the culminating scene in Mary's bedroom.

Bigger's dreams and especially the movies are driven by and play off against such realities as the rat, the apartment, and the undermining and religion of his mother. As a conservative representative of the dominant society, Bigger's mother attempts to make him accept his lot, to take unprotestingly what is given to him, to run on the tracks that have been laid down, and to thank the Lord for what He provides (pp. 9–10). In the face of Bigger's sullen rebellion her strategy is to denigrate him as worthless, as lacking manhood, as "the most no-countest man I ever seen in all my life" (p. 7). By eroding his sense of self-worth, his mother intensifies Bigger's feeling of powerlessness.

In his first explicit analysis of that feeling, Wright goes on to stress that Bigger "knew that the moment he allowed himself to feel to its fullness how they lived, the shame and misery of their lives, he would be swept out of himself with fear and despair." Because Wright's language is both specific and sweepingly general, it demands complex interpretation. All of the key words have been or soon will be defined through acts and imagery, through the tense particulars of "how they lived" and Bigger's confrontation with "the fear and despair" at the center of his life. Wright's insights and diction, his cadences and repetitions—"he knew," "the moment he allowed"—attribute to Bigger a deep knowledge and a taut, precarious sense of self-control. Bigger has only a groping awareness of what he wants and, as the proposed robbery dramatizes, his fear of whites goes even deeper than his conscious understanding. Bigger nonetheless knows profoundly. He is not ignorant. The issue of knowledge—the impulse to find, feel, and express the meaning of his life—is a defining feature of his character. That knowledge and meaning, central values in Western culture, should for Bigger be inseparable from deadly violence is one of Wright's most disturbing insights. "He knew," Wright understands, "that the moment he allowed what his life meant to enter fully into his consciousness, he would either kill himself or someone else."

Bigger's self-destructive, self-punishing impulse recurs again and again, often intertwined with his desire to obliterate others, particularly white people. When Mary wants to "*see* how your people live, . . . Bigger knew that they were thinking of his life and the life of his people." His response is that "suddenly he wanted to seize some heavy object in his hand and grip it with all the strength of his body and in some strange way rise up and stand in naked space above the speeding car and with one final blow blot it out—with himself and them in it" (pp. 79–80). Through the lift of language, through the image of Bigger "in naked space above the speeding car," Wright invokes the universe even as he connects Bigger's feelings of destructive and self-destructive violence to the environing realities of the Black Belt through which the car is speeding. To "rise up" in this way is not what the party had in mind but it is a crucial dimension of the political psychology Wright probes in complex detail.

Wright continues to probe this disturbing political psychology when, after Jan shakes Bigger's hand in a grip rooted in the left symbolism of black and white hands intertwined, Wright has Bigger deconstruct the symbol.[12] To begin with "he felt foolish sitting behind the steering wheel like this and letting a white man hold his hand." Although he feels that perhaps Mary and Jan "did not despise him," they nonetheless made him feel—and Wright's choice of the words "conscious" and "black skin" is deliberate and reiterated—intensely "conscious of his black skin," to the extent that what he knows is a symbol of shame has become his entire identity, pervading his conscious sense of who he is. "They made him feel his black skin by just standing there looking at him, one holding his hand and the other smiling. He felt he had no physical existence at all right then; he knew he was something he hated, the badge of shame which he knew was attached to a black skin" (p. 76). For Bigger, when "they were thinking of his life and the life of his people," they are thinking of his black skin and the rat and the "shouts and bickering" that make him "sick of his life at home" (p. 12). "The badge of shame" is his black skin, his identity—"he had no physical existence at all right then," Wright stresses. Wright anticipates Helen Lynd's insight that shame as distinct from guilt is closely aligned with identity, that to shame someone goes to the core of a person's identity.[13]

For Bigger "shame and misery" are inseparable. The shame and misery are the stigma of race compounded by the material impoverishment compounded by the awareness that influential white Americans live comfortably and move freely, and that for them both poverty and race are signs of moral worthlessness. Bigger's hatred and self-hatred impel him to want "to blot it out—with himself and them in it." The simple words, "to feel to its fullness how they lived, the shame and misery of their lives," turn out to be disturbingly complex, as are the connections between the socially-racially-politically-economically constructed hatred, self-hatred, anger, fear, despair, shame, misery, and deadly violence.

Bigger lives behind a wall that separates him from his family, his friends, and his deepest feelings. Externally, the wall is constructed by white people who have shaped powerful structures to keep him in his place. Wright sees that in responding to white power, Bigger has taken it deep inside and has walled off a dangerous, vital part of his personality. Bigger accepts and rebels against the white power that oppresses him. Despite his impulse to know, Bigger thus keeps "what his life meant" from entering fully into his consciousness because he cannot live with that meaning. His violent protest—"to blot it out—with himself and them in it," to "either kill himself or someone else"—is also part of the meaning of his life. Violated, Bigger is violent. The defiant energy of his response both affirms his underlying value and expresses his fear and hatred of whites and of himself. Bigger not only fears whites, moreover, but also the violence of his own reaction, partly because of the retribution it will bring, partly because of his underlying humanity.

A significant variant of this complex political psychology emerges in the robbery episode. In the rhythms of his narrative, Wright moves back and forth between intense action and analysis of Bigger's equally intense inner life. As he rings the changes on key words and all they signify, terms like "hate" and "fear" accumulate layers of reinforcing meaning. They are not simple or static and, although we think we understand them, they are usually not self-evident. These internal, personal emotions are always connected to the structures and processes of the world of racial, political, and economic power. In his meticulous probing of Bigger's political psychology, Wright is not repetitious; he reinforces and subtly varies and cumulatively takes us deep into the dynamics of oppression and rebellion. In going as he does into the depths of the political unconscious, Wright prepares for and opens up the full implications of Mary's killing, beheading, and burning and Bigger's conscious acceptance of what he has done. Despite the resonance and insight of particular sequences of action and analysis, however, the persistent accumulation, the subtle shifts of interpretation, and the basic language and complex processes repeatedly, powerfully imply that no single formulation adequately gets at the meaning of what Bigger is and does. Wright suggests that something large is always urging for expression and our response beyond any one articulation or interpretation. The killing and its aftermath are crucial because they are charged with the deepest racial-sexual ambivalences of American culture. But even the killing and Bigger's response, with all of their symbolic resonances, do not tell the whole story, which requires the totality of *Native Son* for its unfolding.

In a typical preparatory passage, this one on the robbery of Blum's store, Wright begins simply and directly by stating that "Bigger was afraid of robbing a white man and he knew that Gus was afraid, too. . . . He had argued all of his pals but one into consenting to the robbery, and toward the lone man who held out he felt a hot hate and fear; he had transferred his fear of the whites to Gus." The two basic emotions of hate and fear come together in Wright's analysis: "He hated Gus because he knew that Gus was afraid, as even he was: and he feared Gus because he felt that Gus would consent and then he would be compelled to go through with the robbery" (p. 27). But why should he hate Gus instead of sympathize with him? The intensity of Bigger's response shows how deeply his sense of self-worth, his sense of manhood, depends on his view of himself as courageous. To admit to a paralyzing fear of whites is intolerable, and he hates Gus for feeling the same unacceptable fear that threatens his own sense of self-worth.

Just as Wright discriminates different versions of the dynamics of hate, he discriminates different forms of fear, some of them feeding Bigger's "hot hate." Earlier, instead of feeling for his family, Bigger hates them because he feels power-less to help them—his manhood is again involved and so is his fear of whites and of his own violence. As Wright shows repeatedly, the internalized power of whites and the intensity of his own responses make it difficult for Bigger to express or feel sympathy. What he does feel pervading his body is hate, of himself and, in this case, of Gus as a surrogate for the whites. He releases "the hysterical tensity of his nerves" in a verbal assault on Gus, then in vivid thoughts of murderous violence, and finally in a hysterical attack with his fists and knife (pp. 28–30, 39–44). Wright patterns the novel so that when Mrs. Dalton appears in Mary's bedroom, the dynamics of Bigger's fear, underlying hatred, and hysterical violence are similar but with the complicating addition of powerful sexual-racial ambivalence. The robbery, the symbolic assault on white property, prepares for the killing of Mary, the assault on a rich, beautiful white woman, a sexually charged symbol of white wealth and capitalistic privilege.

Wright has the challenge of developing Mary just enough to give a sense of her and at the same time of keeping her sketchily outlined so that for Bigger "she was not real to him, not a human being; he had not known her long or well enough for that" (p. 128). We do not know her well enough for her to be a human being, either. The killing of a fully developed Mary would make it exceptionally difficult for readers to accept Bigger. As it stands, Mary has a well-intentioned but insensitive desire "to *know* these people." Operating from an unquestioned position of superiority, she repeatedly discriminates between "them" and "us," as in "*they* live in *our* country" (my italics). For Mary "they" are "your people," a usage that undercuts the universality of her view that "they're *human*" (p. 79). In his sensitivity to the racial politics of the pronoun, Wright contrives it so that Mary's use of pronouns is consistently at odds with her sense of shared humanity.

Mary is often but not always oblivious to the impact on Bigger of her interest in seeing what is to him a source of deep shame. She cries when she realizes that, despite her goodwill, Bigger does not in fact want to eat with her and Jan (p. 82). Her response suggests that Mary has some feeling for the larger dilemmas of the drama of imperfect understanding and partial communication she and Bigger enact. The pressures of race, class, and sex are all involved in this drama, particularly from Bigger's point of view.

From Bigger's point of view, in a scene the Book-of-the-Month Club censored, Wright uses the newsreel to establish that the movies have constructed a Mary who is attractive because she is rich and sexually provocative. She may be "their symbol of beauty" (p. 188) but for the media she is also their symbol of money and sex. The Marxist implications are even more overt in the censored than in the published version. "*Here are the daughters of the rich,*" the commentator intones, "*taking sunbaths in the sands of Florida. This little collection of debutantes represents over four billion dollars of America's wealth and over fifty of America's leading families.*" Later, the camera and commentator focus on Mary and Jan embracing and kissing. The commentator then connects Mary and Jan with Communists, developing the association of sexual freedom and communism. Bigger not surprisingly begins to look forward to his new job "with a sense of excitement," stirred by what he has seen and by Jack's remark that "rich white women'll go to bed with anybody, from a poodle on up. They even have their chauffeurs." Bigger remembers a story about "a Negro chauffeur who had married a rich white girl and the girl's family had shipped the couple out of the country and had supplied them with money." Consciously Bigger stresses the money Mary and the job can lead to but barely below the surface he is is also thinking that "maybe Mary Dalton was a hot kind of girl" (pp. 34–37).

As he builds toward the scene in the bedroom, Wright develops the political psychology of sexual relations between the races. He focuses on the emotions that drive, provide the context for, and finally erupt in murder. Mary's questions about "his life and the life of his people" repeatedly make Bigger hate and want to kill her, as in the powerful passage in the speeding car. When Mary cries, Bigger as a black male withdraws from her "as though she were contaminated with an invisible contagion" (p. 82). Bigger has been conditioned to fear contact with white women. Wright is preparing us for the depth and intensity of Bigger's fear when Mrs. Dalton appears in the bedroom. Bigger withdraws because Mary is threatening and she is threatening because he is attracted to her, deathly afraid of the consequences, and ashamed of his own strongly mixed feelings. Wright is entering dangerous territory, the relatively unchartered territory of the political unconscious in its American racial-sexual form.[14] His expressionist language accurately characterizes this territory as Wright reveals that Bigger "felt ensnared in a tangle of deep shadows, shadows as black as the night that stretched above his head" (p. 82).

The drinking that goes on in the car furthers the sense of entry into a dreamlike state where ordinarily repressed feelings can emerge. Jan is a committed Communist and Mary is about to join the party but they do not conform to the official model of asexual sobriety any more than Wright's political art conforms to the official model of socialist realism. Bigger feels "almost drunk." His lips are numb; "he was floating in the car and Jan and Mary were in back, kissing, spooning" (p. 89). Mary continues to define herself as "a bad girl" (p. 90) by drinking even more than before. She is not only sexually active but she is also very drunk. Wright exploits the drinking to render a series of male–black male fantasies. He presents Mary in sexually provocative poses, "slumped down in the seat . . . her legs sprawled wide apart." Because of the drink but also perhaps because of Mary, "Bigger's head was spinning" (p. 91). When Mary says, "you're very nice, Bigger" and then "leaned her head on his shoulder," Wright keeps the ambiguity perfectly poised (pp. 91–92). Is Mary making advances, is she simply making conversation, is she too drunk to know what she is doing? Wright, for his part, knows that as a result of Mary's questions and laughter, Bigger again "tightened with hate" because "again she was looking inside him and he did not like it" (p. 92). In this highly charged context of hate and attraction, Wright makes it explicit that Bigger is terrified that "a white man would . . . see him here with her like this" (p. 93).

Wright continues to bring out that Bigger's feelings are mixed, "a mingled feeling of helplessness, admiration, and hate." He responds to Mary as "beautiful, slender, with an air that made him feel that she did not hate him with the hate of other white people. But for all of that, she was white and he hated her" (p. 93). Fear is basic to the murder but Wright is clear that racial hatred is also involved. Instead of presenting a sanitized Bigger Thomas, Wright goes on to stress that Bigger does not call for help because "in spite of his hate"—we might say, inseparable from it—"he was excited standing here watching her like this," as he is when "his hand circled her waist and the tips of his fingers felt the soft swelling of her breasts."

Wright is moving progressively deeper into the ordinarily repressed dynamics of the American political-racial-sexual unconscious. He does justice to the ambiguities and ambivalences of this region. As a man and a black man, is Bigger taking sexual advantage of a drunk white girl? Is Mary actively responding or simply drunk when "each second she was leaning more heavily against him"? As the episode develops, Wright continues to raise these and other powerful issues. To what extent do we have the gender politics of a man abusing an intoxicated woman? To what extent do we have an explosive mix of culturally constructed lust and racial and deflected personal hate leading toward rape? To what extent do we have the socially unacceptable revelation of a white woman responding sexually to a black man? To what extent do we have an underlying fear that goes to the center of Bigger's self and to the core of the power relations between whites and blacks in America?

As Wright has Bigger come ever closer to the "white bed" (p. 96), Bigger feels a mounting "excitement and fear" intertwined with a reiterated hatred inseparable from desire (p. 94). As the physical contact increases—"his fingers felt the soft curves of her body"—Bigger has "a sense of physical elation" that he expresses in the demeaning oath, "this little bitch!" (p. 95). The vernacular commonplace converts Mary into a female dog in heat, a culturally constructed object of male lust. The tension increases as Bigger carries Mary's limp body up the stairs and somehow finds her room. "Holding her in his arms, fearful, in doubt, . . . his senses reeled from the scent of her hair and skin." Mary's "face was buried in his shoulder; his arms tightened about her." In another of the consistently ambiguous passages of a kind of tantalizing foreplay, "her face turned slowly and he held his face still, waiting for her face to come round, in front of his. Then her head leaned backward, slowly, gently; it was as though she had given up" (p. 96). What she had given up is left open—her struggle for consciousness, her will in a covert seduction?—or does she give in to desire for Bigger, a socially unacceptable impulse no longer held in check because she has been drinking? Does her head lean backward and "her lips touch his, like something he had imagined" because she is drunk or because she has given in to her desires—or both?

With a sure sense of what was most powerful, suggestive, and threatening to its contemporary American audience, the Book-of-the-Month Club censored the passage in which Bigger's sexual intentions and the possibility of Mary's active response emerge most directly. "He tightened his arms as his lips pressed tightly against hers and he felt her body moving strongly. The thought and conviction that Jan had had her a lot flashed through his mind. He kissed her again and felt the sharp bones of her hips move in a hard and veritable grind. Her mouth was open and her breath came slow and deep" (p. 96). The overt sexuality anticipates the displaced sexuality of the murder as Bigger presses down tightly with the pillow, "Mary's body heaved," and finally "he did not feel her surging and heaving against him" (p. 98).

Before that end, however, Wright has Bigger remain in the room, although he knows he should leave. Bigger is as close to having sex as Wright can arrange it. Bigger "leaned over her, excited. . . . not wanting to take his hands from her breasts. She tossed and mumbled sleepily. He tightened his fingers on her breasts, kissing her again, feeling her move toward him," a move that either reinforces the suggestively "hard and veritable grind" or is simply the sleepy reaction of an intoxicated woman. In either case, Bigger "was aware only of her body; his lips trembled. Then he stiffened," not in sexual consummation, however, but in fear as "the door behind him creaked" (pp. 96–97).

Wright has carefully prepared for the "hysterical terror" and the dream-nightmare aura appropriate to his probing of the political-sexual-racial unconscious. He taps into its depths to show that "a hysterical terror seized [Bigger], as though he were falling from a great height in a dream." Bigger's worst fears are realized in the "ghostlike" form of "a white blur"—Mrs. Dalton. "Fear," "frenzy dominated him" (p. 97). His fear is intensified by his knowledge that he has been about to have sex with a white woman, the ultimate crime for a black man raised as he was in the American South of the early twentieth century. Wright has already aligned the frenzy, the hysterical fear of whites, with a complex racial hatred and sexual desire. He has succeeded in keeping Mary's role ambiguous, an achievement in itself in the context of official attitudes in both the party and the dominant culture of the 1930s.

In a profound insight into the dynamics of the American political unconscious, Wright has Bigger express his deepest feelings in the racially and sexually charged language of violence against a white woman. Recall that Wright has established that, in the depths of his personality, Bigger fears, hates, and has been oppressed by a white, male-dominated, capitalistic society. One symbol of that society is the unsullied virtue of the white woman, a guarantee of the power of her protectors as her purity is a guarantee of the moral superiority of what in other respects looks like the pillaging of a Darwinian jungle. Although Wright uses Mary to undercut elements of this cultural myth, he uses Buckley and the mob to show its continued power. As he has done with his family and Gus, through displacement Bigger expresses his feelings not against white men but, in the logic of the political unconscious, against a symbol of the dominant society, a white woman.

Bigger's violence is at once murderous and self-protective, racially hostile and driven by fear of whites, and it is powerfully inflected with the imagery of sex. Wright is saying that for Bigger and those like him, the consummation of murder is more plausible, more in touch with the underlying realities than the consummation of sex. Wright has also kept alive the possibility that, for Bigger, the sexual consummation itself would have been the violence of rape. At the end, then, using the culturally coded imagery of the sex act, Wright has Bigger complete what he started. "He grew tight and full, as though about to explode." For her part "Mary's body surged upward and he pushed downward . . . with all of his weight." Near the end "Mary's body heaved" and "he felt the sharp pain of her fingernails biting into his wrist." Then "he did not feel her surging and heaving against him. Her body was still" (pp. 97–98). Here is the return of the repressed, with a vengeance.

Wright has Bigger Thomas erupt from the depths of his culture's most powerful myths of racial and sexual relations, those involving black men and white women. These myths function to control both white women and black men, to keep them in their places, and to legitimize the dominance of white men. Through Wright's complex, perceptive treatment, he has Bigger and to a lesser extent Mary challenge this control. Even more deeply than he engages the symbolic status of white women, Wright taps into the myth of the black rapist. As Winthrop Jordan has shown, historically this myth embodies projected white male sexual anxieties and justified the systematic suppression of black men.[15] Wright draws on the threatening energy of the myth even as he deconstructs it by showing Bigger's intrinsic power, the processes of the cultural construction of his dominant emotions of fear and hate and desire, and the nuanced complexities and ambiguities of Bigger's responses. Unresolved ambiguity is the key, as it is in the possibility of Mary's active cooperation, itself an element in the myth of white women attracted by sexually potent black men.

Looking back on what Bigger has done, however, Wright minimizes the ambiguity. In building up to and rendering the murder, to the extent rape is a possibility, Wright keeps open not only Bigger's complex feelings about race but also the sense of rape as violence against a woman. Wright later shifts the emphasis to the racial oppression that drives Bigger. "But rape was not what one did to women," Bigger thinks. "Rape was what one felt when one's back was against a wall and one had to strike out, whether one wanted to not, to keep the pack from killing one." Wright continues to redefine rape by removing women and substituting whites when he recognizes that Bigger "committed rape every time he looked into a white face. He was a long, taut piece of rubber which a thousand white hands had stretched to the breaking point, and when he snapped it was rape" (p. 263). In a general way Wright perceptively recapitulates the extent to which white oppression is involved in constructing "the black rapist." In the process, however, as he typically does in the retrospective sections of "Book Two" and "Book Three"—Max's speech is an example—Wright minimizes the damage to women, filters out Bigger's sexual ambivalence toward Mary, and stresses racial violence directed against blacks and in return against whites.

Wright begins the process in the immediate aftermath in Mary's bedroom when he has Bigger shift from the repressed complexities of sexual attraction, racial hatred, fear and self-protection, and possible rape and murderous violence. Instead, he has Bigger become aware that he is surrounded by "a vast city of white people. . . . She was dead," Bigger understands, "and he had killed her. He was a murderer, a Negro murderer, a black murderer. He had killed a white woman. He had to get away from here" (p. 100). The result of this shift in emphasis to race, murder, and self-protection is that the earlier sexual ambiguities and Bigger's power over Mary are replaced by a much more unequivocal sense of Bigger as a black man confronting the overwhelming odds of hostile white power. Having acted out his deepest fears and desires, moreover, Bigger is now free of his hysterical frenzy. He is lucid and aware, and he acts intelligently, all qualities as valued by the dominant society as his uncontrolled violence and subsequent actions are feared and denigrated. To achieve that degree of freedom, understanding, and control people in the dominant society take as a given, Wright shows the terrible ordeal Bigger has to endure, first at Mary's and then at Bessie's expense.

While he was carrying Mary to her room, Bigger had felt as if he "were acting upon a stage in front of a crowd of people" (p. 95). What he continues to act out is a part in a culturally scripted "nightmare" (p. 102). Although for Bigger "it was unreal," he also "felt he had been dreaming of something like this for a long time, and then, suddenly, it was true" (p. 102). From the innermost reaches of the political unconscious, his own and his culture's, Bigger compounds the previously repressed dream of sexually charged murder by beheading and burning Mary. The basement, underground, and the fire and furnace become central protagonists in an expressionist drama. Bigger, "seared with fire," experiences a "fiery pain" that reverberates through *Native Son*, as does the recurring image of "a huge red bed of coals [that] blazed and quivered with molten fury" (p. 104). The fire and furnace are a powerful image of guilt, retribution, demonic hellfire, the intense destructive and creative energies of the unconscious itself, the very instrument of Bigger's escape and capture.

Bigger is repeatedly unable to save himself by shaking down the furnace, which becomes inseparable from the bones and charred remains of Mary Dalton. The molten coals recur with the persistence of a nightmare that simultaneously establishes Bigger's self-affirming defiance and will to live and also his humanity, his horror at what he has had to do to come into the relative freedom and meaning of his life. Or are these images and Bigger's paralysis in the face of the fire signs that his consciousness has been deeply infiltrated by conventional values that thwart his desire to escape? In any case, to drive home the horror, Wright describes the beheading in precise detail. Dan McCall argues that his description, like that of the murder, is conducted in the language of the sex act. If so, Wright again shows gender and racial violence as the American surrogate for sex.[16]

"Book Two: Flight"

Native Son opens with the clanging of an alarm clock—Bigger is asleep and it takes the alarm to rouse him. At the start of "Book Two: Flight," Bigger is in much closer touch with his own unconscious than he was earlier. "In answer to a foreboding call from a dark part of his mind, he struggled to come fully awake" in every sense of that suggestive phrase. As a commentary on the empowering, liberating effect of his actions, Bigger wakes up on his own; he no longer needs a mechanical aid. In a scene that parallels and contrasts with the opening, Wright then probes Bigger's new consciousness. Instead of experiencing psychic and moral decline after the murder, Bigger becomes aware for the first time that his tone of voice means something and that he has some control over it (pp. 114–15). In a book that stresses awareness, moreover, Bigger looks at his family and surroundings and sees them clearly "for the first time," part of Wright's opening up of the crucial images of seeing and blindness.

As he explores Bigger's emerging black political consciousness, Wright again has Bigger engage the intense oppression his family has endured (pp. 115–16). At the start of the novel Bigger kills the rat. At the start of "Book Two" Bigger looks at his family and sees the same conditions the rat symbolizes, but Bigger now has much greater insight and control, although not as much as in his euphoria he believes he has (p. 120). He nonetheless does not need an alarm to wake him up. At the start of the novel Buckley's eyes follow Bigger inexorably. At the start of "Book Two" Bigger is beginning to see for himself. He is not trapped in the gaze of white power and, although he is deeply affected by that power, in response he is developing a rebellious black political consciousness. In key passages, moreover, Wright succeeds in illuminating the more general political psychology of rebellion.

He does so early in "Book Two" when, in one of the most perceptive and controversial sections of *Native Son*, he establishes that the murder and Bigger's conscious acceptance of what he has done free Bigger's energy and have a liberating, creative power. "The thought of what he had done, the awful horror of it, the daring associated with such actions"—the courage in contrast to the fear that has pervaded his life—"formed for him for the first time in his fear-ridden life a barrier of protection between him and a world he feared. He had murdered and had created a new life for himself" (pp. 118–19). The idea of the creative power of murder offended contemporary reviewers, and no wonder, since in developing the idea Wright uses the cherished values of individualism and autonomy to characterize Bigger and indict the society that has oppressed him and made murder inseparable from the meaning of his life. In acting out his worst fears and desires, Bigger has released energy and given himself choices. The earlier "fear and despair" were inseparable (p. 9). The despair, the burden of hopelessness, was rooted in his sense of the power of white people, his feeling that change was hopeless, and his fear of his own violence and the punitive violence of white people.

Now that he has done the most terrifying acts he can imagine, for a time he does not feel afraid. He has choices and he looks ahead, not in despair but with a measure of "confidence which his gun and knife did not" provide. His "new life," including its terrifying sources in the murder and in Bigger's subsequent choices and acts, "was something that was all his own, and it was the first time in his life he had anything that others could not take from him" (p. 119). In a society of possessive individualism, the ownership and control of property are the preconditions for the ownership of psychic capital, the psychological and personal freedom basic to a sense of self-worth in America. Bigger, who has been deprived of the control of property, has in a sense entered the middle class. The price he has paid is an indictment of the dominant society and a reminder of the extent to which Bigger has accepted as well as rebelled against its values and practices.

To highlight the contrast with the earlier wall of repression and internalized white power, Wright uses the image of "a natural wall from behind which" Bigger can see and act on his own, in touch with his deepest sources of energy, as opposed to the "iron" inner wall of "Book One." Formally, Wright time and again rings the changes on the central images and insights of "Book One." In this case he recognizes that Bigger no longer feels vulnerable to "what his family thought or did." Contributing to Bigger's sense that he is in control of his own life is the exhilaration of knowing that his family was "incapable of even thinking that he had done such a deed. And he had done something which even he had not thought possible" (p. 119). Bigger's fear has consumed his energy. What he has done has released this energy. Although he is still removed from his family and friends, Bigger no longer experiences an inner wall that divides him from his depths and separates him from his family and other black people.

As part of his retrospective probing of Bigger's political psychology, Wright stresses that although in a sense the murder was an accident, "not once did [Bigger] feel the need to tell himself that it had been an accident." Bigger's conscious acceptance of what he has done is crucial psychologically and politically. In developing his insights, however, Wright continues to filter out the full range of Bigger's tangled, ambivalent feelings. "He was black," Bigger thinks, "and he had been alone in a room where a white girl had been killed; therefore he had killed her. That was what everybody would say, anyhow, no matter what he said." But in framing the issue around murder, Wright distracts attention from what in practice everybody does say: Buckley, the newspapers, the white mob all convict Bigger of raping Mary. Part of Wright's achievement is that in rendering the murder in "Book One," he keeps rape in focus as one genuine possibility; he does not sanitize the bedroom scene. But later he does. Wright's language after the murder obscures the ambiguity about rape, just as the focus on killing keeps Bigger's hatred unmentioned.

As he goes on to probe Bigger's rebelliously defiant political psychology, however, Wright almost immediately turns to the racial hatred he has left in the background in his retrospective analysis. In explaining that hatred, Wright presents white people not as human beings but as powerful natural forces. "To Bigger and his kind," he observes, "white people were not really people; they were a sort of great natural force, like a stormy sky looming overhead, or like a great swirling river stretching suddenly at one's feet in the dark." Bigger, that is, reifies white people, a reification that pervades *Native Son* from the freezing white winter landscape to the expressionist buildings of the inner city. Instead of seeing white people as human beings and what they do as shaped by human agency, Bigger turns them into impersonal powers beyond the reach of human control. Without granting legitimacy to this power, Bigger nonetheless reluctantly accepts it. "As long as he and his black folks did not go beyond certain limits, there was no need to fear that white force. . . . As long as they lived here in this prescribed corner of the city, they paid mute tribute to it" (p. 129).

But the force of his rebellious defiance and "his hate toward the whites" (p. 131) lead Bigger in "rare moments" to long "for solidarity with other black people. . . . He would dream of making a stand against that white force" (p. 129). Wright understands, however, that Bigger's passionate black militancy is both driven and thwarted by the power of whites who have infiltrated his consciousness. In a significant advance beyond his fight with Gus in the poolroom, Bigger now realizes that the earlier dynamics of fear and hate keep him and Gus apart. He sees clearly that his fear and hatred of whites should not be displaced in distrust, fear, and hatred onto other blacks. Bigger is beginning to develop an explicitly black political consciousness. His vision, "his hate and hope turned outward from himself and Gus; his hope toward a vague benevolent something that would help and lead him, and his hate toward the whites." This hatred is now based on a profound awareness that the whites "ruled him, even when they were far away and not thinking of him, ruled him by conditioning him in his relations to his own people" (p. 131).

One result of this conditioning is that Bigger despairs of establishing bonds with other black people because "he felt there was too much difference between him and them to allow for a common binding and a common life." The internalized power of whites is such that even as he struggles to develop his political consciousness, Bigger feels that blacks could achieve a sense of a common life and purpose "only when threatened with death; . . . only in fear and shame, with their backs against a wall, could that happen. But never could they sink their differences in hope" (pp. 129–30). Bigger nonetheless does have vague benevolent hopes.

Wright accepts that Bigger's political consciousness is complicated and has contradictory strains, and he gives it to us unsanitized. Specifically, having seen at first hand the way the Daltons live, Bigger now has a standard of comparison that reinforces a recurring strain of black self-hate. On the morning after the murder, when he awakes and looks around at his home "he hated this room and all the people in it, including himself." Despite his awakening and his growing power of vision and in contrast to his earlier powerful criticism of white oppression, what Bigger sees around him reveals that he accepts that perhaps he and his family had to live as they do because they themselves are at fault, "because none of them in all their lives had ever done anything, right or wrong, that mattered much" (p. 118). Bigger, however, has done something "right or wrong, that mattered," and though voicing a charge of previously suppressed feeling has value, Bigger does more than accept white views that blacks are to blame for their own oppression.

If Bigger's self-hatred and his feelings that black people deserve what they get are offensive to African American theorists of black consciousness, his hatred of whites and his authoritarian, fascist tendencies are unsettling to whites in general and thirties white radicals in particular. Tapping into the repressed passions of the political unconscious, Wright has Bigger feel "that one way to end [white-inspired] fear and shame was to make all those black people act together, rule them, tell them what to do, and make them do it" (p. 130). For Wright, Bigger's authoritarianism is inspired by a noble vision and longing for black unity, a longing frustrated by his sense of the realities of American life. "Dimly, he felt that there should be one direction in which he and all other black people could go whole-heartedly; that there should be a way in which gnawing hunger and restless aspiration could be fused; that there should be a manner of acting that caught the mind and body in certainty and faith. But he felt that such would never happen to him and his black people" and, in a recurring impulse and image, "he hated them and wanted to wave his hand and blot them out" (p. 130).

His mother's Christianity and Jan and Mary's communism are two possibilities for resolving his frustrated desire for "a manner of acting that caught the mind and body in certainty and faith." Wright, however, opens up a third alternative that appeals to Bigger's energy, his hatred, his alienation, and his desire for wholeness. "Of late he had liked to hear tell of men who could rule others, for in actions such as these he felt that there was a way to escape from this tight morass of fear and shame that sapped at the base of his life. He liked to hear of how Japan was conquering China; of how Hitler was running the Jews to the ground; of how Mussolini was invading Spain. He was not concerned with whether these acts were right or wrong; they simply appealed to him as possible avenues of escape. He felt that some day there would be a black man who would whip the black people into a tight band and together they would act and end fear and shame" (p. 130).

In this rich brew from the depths of the political unconscious, Wright manages to have Bigger go against the basic positions of the left's principled opposition to war and fascism. He touches the exposed nerves of the fascist assault on loyalist Spain, of Hitler's persecution of the Jews, of Japan's growing militarism. Instead of an image of black and white hands together, he invokes the threat of a powerful black dictator who would unify his people, end their "fear and shame" on the model of the release of energy Bigger experienced after the murder, and by implication wage race war against whites, on the same model. Some of the implications of Bigger's political psychology of rebellion are as threatening to the left as they are revealing of powerful tendencies in the African American political tradition from the early Malcolm X through Louis Farrakhan.

Through his characterization of Bessie and his treatment of Bigger's relation to her, Wright goes on to develop insights into the politics of race, money, and sex. At the outset, Bessie is "blind" (p. 151). Before her death, Wright accords her the dignity of awareness. Bessie sees. What she sees in the beginning is that with Jan and Mary around, as she tells Bigger, "you wouldn't even look at me when I spoke to you" (p. 150). Wright leaves it up to us to see the disruptive impact of race on personal feelings and relations. For Bigger these feelings are commodified. The ransom demands for money and the money Bigger has taken from Mary move to the center of discourse and plot in the scenes with Bessie. Their first meeting is conducted under the aspect of money, of Bessie's questions about buying, of Bigger's use of the money to buy Bessie (pp. 151–52). Bessie uses sex to test her power over Bigger (p. 149). Bigger answers with the lure of money. Wright shows that under the pressures of race and poverty, Bessie and Bigger act out a basic dynamic of the environing white, capitalistic society.

Money is important because Bigger and Bessie have had so little of it. Wright uses Bessie to reinforce the sense of how hard life is for those who live within the white-imposed confines of the Black Belt. Bigger "felt the narrow orbit of her life. . . . Most nights she was too tired to go out; she only wanted to get drunk. She wanted liquor and he wanted her. So he would give her liquor and she would give him herself. . . . He knew why she liked him; he gave her money for drinks" (pp. 157–58). This exchange relation is one of those Wright focuses on as he uses Marxist insights to clarify black experience.

Wright then probes Bigger's political psychology as it emerges in his feelings about power over black women. Wright stubbornly tells the whole unglamorized story, in liberal white eyes an even more unflattering version than his revelations about Bigger and fascism.[17] He reveals that for Bigger "there were two Bessies: one a body that he had just had and wanted badly again; the other was in Bessie's face; it asked questions; it bargained and sold the other Bessie to advantage. He wished he could clench his fist and swing his arm and blot out, kill, sweep away the Bessie on Bessie's face and leave the other helpless and yielding before him." Intensifying the stereotypes about blacks in general, on one cultural construction black women even more than women generally consist of desirable bodies and negligible minds. Bigger accepts this demeaning construction and wants to destroy the thinking, capitalistically bargaining side. Does his fantasy of violence against a black woman underlie the more socially acceptable survival motive that impels Bigger when he actually beats Bessie to death or are the two motives separate?

In any case, Bigger compounds the fantasy with a dream of exclusive possession and dominance that carries to an extreme his society's construction of women as objects to be possessed. Bigger fantasizes about Bessie that "he would then gather her up and put her in his chest, his stomach, some place deep inside him, always keeping her there even when he slept, ate, talked; keeping her there just to feel and know that she was his to have and hold whenever he wanted to" (pp. 159–56). Deprived, Bigger would deprive. Having no possessions, Bigger would possess

Bessie absolutely. Fine for Bigger, not so fine for Bessie. The imagery of the "stomach, some place deep inside" connected with the elemental acts of eating and sleeping and exclusive possession carry us back to a very early stage of child development fused in this case with a very public construction of the ownership of women, as Wright continues to bring into the open the unsettling dynamics of the political unconscious.

As it unfolds, Bigger's relation with Bessie is dominated by his violence against her. To get Bessie to go along, Bigger first threatens to slap her and later "his black open palm swept upward in a narrow arc and smashed solidly against her face" (pp. 205, 210). The killing surfaces early. Bessie realizes that if Bigger has killed Mary, "you'll kill *me*" (p. 204). She wants to back out but she knows too much, and Bigger plans almost from the start to get rid of her (p. 205). Bessie "whimpers" repeatedly. She is lost, she knows, and the way Bigger treats her is simply an extension of the hard life Wright has her invoke. "I ain't done nothing for this to come to me! I ain't had no happiness, no nothing. I just work. I'm black and I work and don't bother nobody" (p. 206). Bessie represents triply exploited labor, as a black, as a woman, and as a low-wage worker. Unlike Bigger, she is a victim, not an agent. To avoid the pathos connected with Bessie, Wright systematically presents Bigger in postures that preclude sympathy for him even as they demand understanding.

Just before her death, Wright has Bessie reinforce the view that "all my life's been full of hard trouble. If I wasn't hungry, I was sick. And if I wasn't sick, I was in trouble." Now, however, Wright credits Bessie with full insight. "I see it now," she says. "I ain't drunk now. I see everything you ever did to me. . . . I see it all now. I been a fool, just a blind dumb black drunk fool" (p. 265). "Not with anger or regret," what Bigger sees is "what he must do to save himself and [he feels] resolved to do it" (pp. 265–66).

Wright then has Bigger reenact the key motifs leading up to Mary's murder. As in "a tortured dream" (p. 229) or "nightmare" (p. 259), the reenactment is recognizable but distorted. Instead of taking place in the Dalton's comfortable white house, the setting is an expressionist variation, one of the freezing, empty buildings that were formerly mansions of the rich. Like the entire region around it, the building, with its dark interior and its black, gaping windows "like the eye-sockets of empty skulls" (p. 266), is part of the scene's nightmare commentary on the meaning and complex sources of Bigger's actions. The nightmare imagery emerges from the depths. Bessie's death is on Bigger's mind fused with his understanding that the building and the rotting core of the city around it are connected with white wealth and power and the impoverishment and containment of blacks. Wright again shows his sensitivity to the workings of the political unconscious. He combines nightmare imagery with Bigger's explicit awareness that the building or ones like it are owned by Mr. Dalton's South Side Realty Company and that Mr. Dalton "would rent houses to Negroes only in this prescribed area, this corner of the city tumbling down in rot" (p. 199).

As an embodiment of the economic and racial process of oppression, in its full symbolic import the building is an appropriate setting for the murder. With its ambience of "empty skulls" and "black windows, like blind eyes" (p. 198), the building also sets the stage for another episode in Wright's drama of seeing and blindness. The expressionist cityscape of which the building is a part similarly combines a sense of white power, money, death, and blindness (pp. 198–99). The immediate death is Bessie's and she moves from blindness to sight. In the language of the political unconscious, the building and cityscape also suggest that in a profound way larger system is pervasively blind and deadly, an accomplice in the rape and murder.

Within the building, as part of the twisted, nightmare reenactment of the scenes with Mary Dalton, instead of carrying Mary inside in a passage full of erotic foreplay, Bigger "dragged [Bessie] across the threshold, and pulled the door after him" (p. 266). As in the earlier episode, they drink, but unlike Mary, Bessie has to be forced to. Bigger experiences sensations from the alcohol similar to the earlier ones. Much more important, unlike the ambiguity of Mary's responses, Bessie repeatedly pleads with Bigger to stop, so that the sex act that precedes the murder is an act of rape. Wright is carefully establishing a basis for Bessie's final exploitation at the trial. There, instead of taking her as valuable in her own right, Buckley uses Bessie simply as a vehicle to convict Bigger of raping Mary, a rape he did not literally commit.

In rendering the one he does commit, Wright again contrasts the inner and outer view of Bigger's acts. From Bessie's viewpoint or that of an ordinary reader, what Bigger does is monstrous. In entering into Bigger's mind and feelings, however, Wright does justice to the tension Bigger experiences and the "desire . . . insistent and demanding" (p. 269) that leads him to ride "roughshod over her whimpering protests."[18] In context the "desire" is sexual, and Bigger dominates Bessie for sexual reasons. In the rape and subsequent murder, there may or may not be a subtext of hatred against and a desire to control, possess, and kill black women. When Wright has Bigger carry out the murder, what is on Bigger's mind is a fierce desire to survive, to escape, "that driving desire to escape the law" as he hesitates and then forces himself to use the brick (p. 273). It is only after he has thrown her bloodied body down the airshaft that Bigger remembers the money in Bessie's pocketbook. Is this crucial Freudian slip a sign of guilt and humanity?

Does Bigger punish himself for the murder by depriving himself of the money he needs to complete the escape he has killed for? On this view, he cannot force himself to retrieve the money, just as he cannot force himself to save himself by shaking down the furnace. Or has Bigger internalized and turned against himself the punitive views of the dominant society?

In the underground scenes in the Dalton basement, Wright continues to probe the underground dynamics of the political unconscious. He uses another symbolic setting, an expressionist one that fuses structures, structures of power, and Bigger's torment and "tortured" responses. The luridly lit basement, its raging beast of a fire, and its cast of white interrogators encode the wealth and power of the white world, the complex meaning of Mary's murder, and, inseparable from it, the full meaning of Bigger's life. Wright frames these underground scenes by having Bigger restate the meaning of his life, not discursively as he does on the morning after the murder but in the language of the unconscious. Bigger dreams that in a lurid red light reminiscent of the glaring furnace he runs and carries a slippery wet package that turns out to be "his *own* head—his own head lying with black face and half-closed eyes and lips parted with white teeth showing and hair wet with blood and the red glare grew brighter." As the dream continues, Bigger runs, sweats, and stumbles over coal from the furnace. Even in the dream he hopelessly tries to find a place to hide because "white people were coming to ask about the head," now his own fused with Mary's. It was "slippery with blood in his naked hands and he gave up and stood in the middle of the street in the red darkness and cursed the booming bell and the white people and felt that he did not give a damn what happened to him and when the people closed in he hurled the bloody head squarely into their faces *dongdongdong . . .*" (pp. 189–90).

One interpretation is that Bigger's guilt at what he has done causes him to identify his own head with the bloody head he has severed from Mary's body. This fusion or exchange is a nightmare version of the exchange relation Wright repeatedly underscores. Consciously, for example, for Bigger "the knowledge that he had killed a white girl they loved and regarded as their symbol of beauty made him feel the equal of them, like a man who had been somehow cheated, but had now evened the score" (p. 188). The exchange here is the death of a beautiful woman for the feeling of equality that should come at a very different price in a system where black people are not systematically cheated. Bigger's sense of what he has had to do to achieve a sense of equality is less a comment on him than on the warped exchange system he participates in. In his dream, the exchange of his bloody head for Mary's suggests the full human cost for the participants in the system.

Consciously, moreover, because he has the choice of staying or leaving, Bigger "felt a certain sense of power, a power born of a latent capacity to live" (p. 188). After the murder and his responses to it, Bigger often experienced a feeling of freedom and power. In his dream, however, what surfaces are Bigger's anxieties about the enormity of what he has done, his apprehension about white power, and his fear that he cannot escape. In accord with this change in his state of mind, the insistently ringing bell, the *dongdongdong* that finally brings him awake, is a reminder that, in significant contrast to the opening of "Book Two," Bigger does not wake up on his own. Even as in the dream "the people closed in" on him, however, Bigger defiantly throws the bloody head in the face of his pursuers. As an image of his life, this culminating act of defiance captures the sense that beginning with the murder and emerging from the depths, Bigger has thrown himself and what he has done in the face of the white world.

Throughout the underground scenes Wright's expressionist language—Bigger's "dread," his paralysis, the pervasive "glare of the furnace"—is powerful and compelling (pp. 212, 228). Wright emphasizes the distortions by having the interviews implausibly take place in the lower regions of the house, in the face of the furnace. Within this expressionist setting Wright effectively uses official languages that complement the more imaginatively charged setting and Bigger's mounting hysteria. In using one of these languages, that of the vocabulary and bullying tactics of the Chicago authorities, Wright exposes the red-baiting and anti-Semitism of Britten, Mr. Dalton's head of security and a representative of the middle levels of Chicago officialdom. Wright similarly brings into the open the way the newspapers construct a story and people it with characters who emerge from unquestioned cultural myths. A mild example is the reporter who says, "say, I'm slanting this to the primitive Negro who doesn't want to be disturbed by white civilization" (p. 247). In subsequent stories about Bigger as a black ape whom southerners know how to control, Wright draws almost verbatim on Chicago *Tribune* stories about the Robert Nixon case. In these stories, which contribute to the lynch mob hysteria surrounding Bigger's trial, Wright continues to expose media constructions. He implicitly contrasts his own complex story and its multiple languages and interpretive possibilities with the newspapers' influential, culturally sanctioned, and much more reductive stories.

Wright has an underlying sympathy for Bigger and he endows him with the larger-than-life qualities of a hero who expresses the complex meaning of his culture. But unlike the one-dimensional characterizations of "the primitive Negro" and "the black ape," for Wright Bigger's stature and meaning are not programmatically positive as the media's are systematically negative. Instead, Wright stresses Bigger's paralysis and hysteria. Bigger is unable to shake down the furnace. He repeatedly responds to "the muffled breathing of the fire and [sees] directly before his eyes Mary's bloody head with its jet-black curly hair, shining and wet with blood" (pp. 223–24). Are these visions and inability to act to save himself signs of Bigger's humanity, a recognition from deep within of the terrible act he has committed? Or are these signs of internalized white power, of punitive white power operating internally to punish and prevent him from completing his escape? In any case, far from presenting Bigger as progressing from sleep to wakefulness, from entrapment and self-hate to freedom, at the moment of discovery Wright invokes "the feeling that [Bigger] had had all his life: he was black and had done wrong; white men were looking at something with which they would soon accuse him" (p. 253).

Even as Bigger struggles to escape, Wright reinforces the sense Bigger has had from the start, that he is trapped, that he is living in jail. As in an expressionist film the police searchlights "circled slowly, hemming him in; bars of light forming a prison, a wall between him and the rest of the world" (p. 299). This wall looks ahead to the prison of "Book Three" and back to the exposure of the oppressive wall of white economic and racial power that Bigger simultaneously takes inside and rebels against. The "natural wall" he has achieved and behind which he is able to act with a measure of freedom turns out to be vulnerable to white power. Bigger knows but cannot accept that blacks are confined to a rotting corner of the city. Within this circumscribed area the police and vigilantes hunt for Bigger to make an intimidating example of him. As they progressively hem him in, their search intensifies the sense of confinement and oppression Bigger struggles against. Like the "natural wall," his earlier feeling of freedom is replaced by his sense that "he was trapped" (p. 284). Wright even contrives it so that Bigger envies a black rat he sees escape safely into a hole (p. 288). Although his actions speak for his will to freedom, not until after his capture is Bigger able to reaffirm consciously his desire to be free and whole and to have ties with other people. Under the pressure of pursuit, however, Wright stresses that Bigger "had an almost mystic feeling that if he were ever cornered something in him would prompt him to act the right way, the right way being the way that would enable him to die without shame" (p. 300).

As the noose tightens, Wright amplifies the political, racial, and economic implications encoded in the main narrative. He has Bigger become an observer as well as a participant. In one of a series of carefully staged episodes, Bigger, hunted, intensely cold and hungry, looks into the unshaded window of a one-room apartment. In a doubling of the theme of sight, Bigger watches the children watching a "familiar" scene of intercourse that reactivates the powerful critique of the early chapters (pp. 285–86). Soon after, Bigger overhears two black men argue about what he has done. The militant one who sides with Bigger says, "they don' care whut black man they git. We's all dogs in they sight! Yuh gotta stan' up 'n' fight these folks." But Wright knows the sense of militant solidarity is far from universal. "'N' git killed?" his friend answers. "Hell, naw! Ah gotta family. Ah gotta wife 'n' baby. Ah ain't startin' no fool fight. Yuh can't git no justice pertectin' men who kill" (pp. 290–91).

In a third view of black life, Wright has Bigger look into a black church. He has Bigger go fully into its appeal and his own deeply secular response. Bigger sees the world of the church as full, rich, and self-contained, "humble, contrite, believing. It had a center, a core, an axis, a heart which he needed but could never have unless he laid his head upon a pillow of humility and gave up his hope of living in the world. And he would never do that" (p. 294). Instead, along with the "something" that "would enable him to die without shame," Bigger has a defiant personal and racial pride and an intense "hope of living in this world." These qualities are integral to the political psychology of rebellion Wright illuminates. Wright has not filtered out the doubts, the hatred of self and other blacks, the authoritarian tendencies and the interiorized white power that are also involved. But in the depths of Bigger's personality Wright finds a complex of rebellious affirmations.

In contrast to this language of rebellion, to show from still another perspective what Bigger and other blacks are up against, Wright intersperses into his series of vignettes of black life a medley of official voices, a series of incendiary, racially pejorative newspaper headlines and stories. Ostensibly about the manhunt for Bigger, already convicted in print as the "Negro rapist and murderer" (p. 284), they provide the ideological justification for invading black homes and ruthlessly intimidating the black population. When Bigger is finally captured and dragged down the stairs, "his head bumping along the steps," the newspaper language recurs in the accompanying cries to "kill that black ape!" At the end, "two men stretched his arms out, as though about to crucify him," so that Wright puts the official language of religion to subversive uses. He elevates Bigger into a crucified recipient of the racial violence Christianity ideally opposes (pp. 313–14).

"Book Three: Fate"

After the intensities of the first two books, the pace changes into the jail and trial scenes of "Book Three: Fate." The opening in jail is a measured, prolonged variation on the scenes of awakening that begin "Book One" and "Book Two." Bigger goes into a deep sleep, a profound, deathlike withdrawal from the restated meaning of all he has done and failed to do. For the first time "the fear of death" enters

Bigger's inner discourse, fused with "the fact that he was black, unequal, and despised" (pp. 316–17). As he goes on to outline a possible dialectic of rebirth, Wright attributes to Bigger a hunger "for another orbit between two poles that would let him live again; for a new mode of life that would catch him up with the tension of hate and love." This new mode of life with its tension of hate and love is a compelling version of the Communist activism whose appeal Wright had rendered in such poems as "A Red Love Note," "Strength," and "Everywhere Burning Waters Rise," an appeal he was to analyze in *American Hunger*.[19] Bigger has previously rejected the universal appeals of Christianity. Now Wright invokes the universal appeal of communism.

Wright understands from the inside that "there would have to hover above [Bigger], like the stars in a full sky, a vast configuration of images and symbols whose magic and power could lift him up and make him live so intensely that the dread of being black and unequal would be forgotten; that even death would not matter, that it would be a victory." This intense, transforming engagement "would have to happen before he could look them in the face again: a new pride and a new humility would have to be born in him, a humility springing from a new identification with some part of the world in which he lived, and this identification forming the basis for a new hope that would function in him as pride and dignity" (p. 317). In beginning with this prospect, Wright looks ahead to the concluding drama of Max's speech and Bigger's final response. As an organizing center for the novel and as the core of Bigger's political consciousness, Wright leaves open the possibility of a Marxist conversion experience, a rebirth in which the Communist images and symbols would lift Bigger above "the dread of being black and unequal" and would give meaning, pride, and dignity to his life.

In the immediate aftermath, however, it is not Communist universalism that prevails but rather Bigger's rebellious assertion of black pride. At the inquest he realizes that the whites "regarded him as a figment of the black world which they feared and were anxious to keep under control. The atmosphere of the crowd told him that they were going to use his death as a bloody symbol of fear to wave before the eyes of that black world. And as he felt it, rebellion rose in him. He had sunk to the lowest point this side of death, but when he felt his life again threatened in a way that meant he was to go down the dark road a helpless spectacle of sport for others, he sprang into action, alive, contending" (pp. 318–19). Throughout "Book Three" Bigger's feelings ebb and flow around the poles of the fear of death, his sense of himself as a black man, his depleting racial fear, hate, and shame, and his need for meaning, pride, and dignity.

These feelings merge and emerge in the tense confines of his jail cell, the less forceful equivalent in "Book Three" of the basement scenes and setting of "Book Two." Through the interviews in the cell Wright conveys a sense of black life and Bigger's responses, as he did in the vignettes of "Book Two" and, most powerfully, in the early chapters of the novel. The exchanges in the cell also establish basic points of reference for the drama of belief that dominates the final pages of *Native Son*. As Bigger's family and friends, the minister and Max, Jan and the Daltons, and Buckley crowd into the cell, Wright again presents Bigger as a character with a deep inner life and a capacity to live from his depths. Particularly relevant to the concluding drama, "from the very depths of his life . . . Bigger felt a wild and outlandish conviction surge in him: *They ought to be glad!* . . . Had he not taken fully upon himself the crime of being black?" (p. 342). In showing Bigger as a kind of reverse Christ, Wright stresses Bigger's defiant black pride, his rebellious affirmation.

This inner force has to struggle with Bigger's continuing feeling of his and his family's "weakness" and "naked shame" under the gaze of the white people. Bigger tries to reassure his family and simultaneously deal with "the hate and shame" he feels because of them and the whites. At the center of the concluding drama, increasingly Bigger feels a need to express himself, to find a language, "to think of words that would defy them, words that would let them know that he had a world and life of his own in spite of them" (p. 342). In contrast to the final scene, Bigger fails. He uses the same words as he does with Max at the end—"I'm all right" (p. 344)—but he immediately feels ashamed that he misled his family by trying "to appear strong and innocent before" them.

The episode with his family is one of several that focus on the drama of Bigger's halting, nonlinear deepening of insight. Instead of rendering the linear development of a model self, Wright arranges almost all of these episodes to show the unresolved flux of Bigger's conflicting feelings, along with a gradual, never fully settled deepening of awareness. Wright has Bigger recognize for the first time, for example, that he is not alone, that he is part of his family (p. 345). This acceptance, however, does not prevent Bigger from feeling a "shame" that "amounted to hate" when his mother prays with him and then crawls to Mrs. Dalton (p. 349).

Basic to the drama of "Book Three," Bigger has a deep need to find a language and to tell, to make known his underlying feelings, particularly the "hate that he had not wanted to have, but could not help having" (p. 356). Impelled by this need to explain the murder, Bigger succumbs to Buckley and confesses. But in the face of the white audience, Bigger is unable to "link up his bare actions with what he had felt; . . . his words came out flat and dull" (p. 358). Bigger fails in his first attempt to find words to "let them know."

A central drama in the concluding section of *Native Son* is nonetheless Bigger's search for a language that will allow him to explain the meaning of his life. After he opens himself to Max, Bigger realizes that, instead of Max, he "wanted to save his *own* life." Although he is still unable to "put his feelings into words," he nonetheless "wondered wistfully if there was a set of words which he had in common with others, words which would evoke in others a sense of the same fire that smoldered in him." As part of the dialectic of his inner life, Bigger is repeatedly pulled between his hate and his longing for a life-giving union with others. In "Book Two" this impulse toward union expresses itself politically in Bigger's attraction to versions of black militancy, to hatred of whites and a vague, benevolent hope of union with other black people. In "Book Three" Wright has Bigger express a desire for a more universal union. This new language, this new hope for "a set of words which he had in common with others" implies the Communist conversion Wright had outlined. Under the threat of death in the electric chair, Bigger is divided between his vision of dying alone and "an image of himself standing amid throngs of men, lost in the welter of their lives with the hope of emerging again, different, unafraid." Torn in opposing directions, Bigger wonders, "was not his old hate a better defense than this agonized uncertainty? Was not an impossible hope betraying him to this end?" (p. 422).

In counterpoint to Bigger's agonized struggle to find a common language that will do justice to his life as he approaches death, Wright includes a range of conflicting languages. In a strong expressionist episode that looks ahead to Ellison's crazy-sane inmates of "The Golden Day," Wright has a university-educated black prisoner translate the language of white sociology into a radical indictment of racial oppression. The man is crazy, or rather what he says is sane and his insanity is a commentary on the conditions he exposes but cannot change (pp. 396–99).

Even more important, the religious language of Bigger's mother and the minister again brings alive the tempting appeal of Christian certainty and resignation (pp. 325–30). Bigger "feared and hated the preacher because the preacher had told him to bow down and ask for a mercy he knew he needed; but his pride would never let him do that, not this side of the grave, not while the sun shone" (pp. 359–60). Wright connects Bigger's refusal and his pride with the ethos of manhood he acquired as a young black man on the streets. In "Book One" Wright illuminates the painful conflicts Bigger experiences because he accepts this code of manhood. In "Book Three" Wright presents "the song of manhood" as integral to Bigger's rebellious assertion of a black pride compatible with his communal hope (p. 359).

The language of Christianity and the street "song of manhood" represent conflicting strains within the black community. At the other extreme from these representative African American languages, from the black prisoner's language of social science, and from Bigger's search for a language to explain the meaning of his life, Wright includes the official language of the white newspapers. This is the language of headlines like *"Negro Rapist Faints at Inquest."* The stories center on reports that " 'he looks exactly like an ape!' exclaimed a terrified white girl. . . . Though the Negro killer's body does not seem compactly built, he gives the impression of abnormal physical strength. He is about five feet, nine inches tall and his skin is exceedingly black. His lower jaw protrudes obnoxiously, reminding one of a jungle beast" (p. 322). Because the stories' overt racism is excessive on current standards—in public speech we express our racism in more subtly coded ways— the stories may allow contemporary readers the luxury of an unearned feeling of progress and superiority. In any case, taken as they are almost without change from the Chicago *Tribune* reports of the Robert Nixon case, the newspaper stories accurately render the prevailing 1930s white discourse on race.[20] The stories are a necessary complement to the more imaginatively powerful sections of *Native Son*.

The same holds for Wright's deconstruction of official languages and attitudes in the ritualized speeches, questions, and answers at the inquest and trial. As the coroner race-baits and red-baits Bigger and Jan, Wright uses the courtroom question-and-answer format and the coroner's unfair rigging of the procedure to build up a sense of urgency. Max correctly establishes that the coroner is attempting to "inflame the public mind," to create a lynch mob hysteria outside the courtroom to pressure the court to convict Bigger (p. 369). In this political trial, the deployment of power and the loading of questions give these episodes a quality of expressionist distortion. The coroner's questioning of Jan, for example, is the verbal equivalent of a scene by Max Beckman or George Gorz (pp. 369–75). Although the political art in these scenes is not as intense as in those leading up to the murder or in the face of the furnace, in his modulated versions of expressionist distortion Wright nonetheless successfully uses exaggeration and an appeal to the reader's violated sense of fair play to expose the illogical linkages of an influential style of official discourse. Throughout the inquest and trial, the obvious injustice of the coroner and Buckley's consistent assertion that, with Jan's "Communist" complicity, Bigger had sex with Mary, that rape is the powerful underlying issue, also serves to distract attention from the tangle of motives Wright probes in "Book One."

At the close of the trial Wright has Buckley juxtapose high-minded phrases about the "safety and sacredness of human life" with his repeated insistence on "the death penalty" (p. 475). For Buckley there is no inconsistency, since for him Bigger is not a human being. As a self-proclaimed dispassionate, impersonal agent of "the holy law," Buckley has a disquieting tendency to use inflammatory, racially biased language that converts Bigger into a "sub-human" animal (p. 477). On this view, Bigger raped and murdered Mary because it is the nature of "black lizards" and "black apes" to rape and kill, just as it is the duty of white law officers to punish and suppress this bestial assault on civilization (pp. 476, 481). To expose further the racially loaded barbarian-civilized binary, Wright enters into Buckley's language and outlook and has him declaim, "every decent white man in America ought to swoon with joy for the opportunity to crush with his heel the wooly head of this black lizard, to keep him from scuttling on his belly farther over the earth and spitting forth his venom of death!" (p. 476). In dealing with Buckley, Wright gives play to his own talent for capturing the contradictions and extreme rhetoric of the racist right in its 1930s version.

The contrast with Boris Max's language and view of the case could not be more sharply drawn. Wright uses the political art of Max's eloquent courtroom speech to restate key insights into Bigger and what he represents. Through Max, Wright complements the inside view he has given along the way with an elevated outside perspective into the historical, economic, and racial forces that shaped Bigger. Max—in his name Wright plays on "Marx," just as his first name, "Boris," has Russian associations—Boris Max is a Jewish Communist lawyer from the International Labor Defense, the same organization that defended the Scottsboro Boys.[21] His speech emerges from and deepens our sense of the tensions, virtues, and limits within the Popular Front, a movement open enough to include the conflicting strains within this much maligned character.

As with much of the discourse of the Popular Front, because of the audiences— particularly the white judge who is hearing the case and the white readers who are reading the book—Wright has Max modulate but not surrender his Marxism. Max's entire strategy is to get us to understand so that words like "crime" will have a new meaning, a deepened political meaning. He hopes and assumes that once we grasp the full complexity of Bigger's situation, including the complicity of white society, the verdict will be life imprisonment, not death (p. 445). Using key Marxist terms like "oppression" and the basically Marxist approach of historical, economic, and political contextualizing, Max plays an important role in Wright's drama of the political unconscious. In the academic criticism of Native Son, however, his powerful speech is typically either neglected or scorned.[22]

Central to his argument is a telling Marxist analysis of the difference between injustice and oppression, an analysis that relates Bigger's way of life to its historical origins in slavery (pp. 452–53). If only a few people for a few years had been involved, Max argues, it would have been unjust. But slavery was not unjust; it was oppression (pp. 454–55). As an integral part of the 1930s Communist discourse on slavery, Max's strategy is to explain Bigger's actions by connecting his way of life and sense of right and wrong with their historical sources.[23] Similarly working within and giving his own emphasis to the party's discourse on "the Negro Question," Max argues that however offensive and controversial, the creation of "their own laws of being" (p. 455) is the historical context for Bigger's act of murder as creation (p. 466).[24] In his strong Marxist analysis of the dynamics of slavery, Max assumes that indirect slavery still exists in the restricted opportunities and the exploitation Bigger experiences. For Max as for many others in the Popular Front, however, the oppression of blacks merges into the more general oppression the successors of the conquerors continue to practice against all workers. Max forcefully brings the oppression into the present and into the courtroom by arguing that Buckley, the other politicians, the owners, and the newspapers created mob hysteria to demand the death penalty, whereas Chicago gangsters have killed and gone free. In the best tradition of Popular Front communism, Max goes behind the facade and into the hardball politics that underlie the creation of the mob to expose what he sees as the economic and political interests racial hysteria serves (pp. 447–49).

He is even more compelling in his analysis of the political psychology of present-day oppression not inside the oppressed but within "the mob and the mob-masters." All of them, Max understands, "know and feel that their lives are built upon a historical deed of wrong against many people, people from whose lives they have bled their leisure and their luxury! Their feeling of guilt is as deep as that of the boy who sits here on trial today. Fear and hate and guilt are the keynotes of this drama!" (p. 449). In a brilliant move, Wright uses Max to apply the key terms of Bigger's political psychology to those who are oppressing him, including the judge and most of his readers. Max sees that the prosecution bases its case on "guilt-fear" so that white people who know they are guilty of a deep wrong they are not going to correct will do what people do—"kill that which evoked in them the condemning sense of guilt" (p. 453). As part of his project of stressing oppression and refusing to use the idea of injustice, moreover, Max perceptively observes that "if I should say that he is a victim of injustice, then I would be asking by implication for sympathy; and if one insists upon looking at this boy in the light of sympathy he will be swamped by a feeling of guilt so strong as to be indistinguishable from hate" (p. 453).

Beginning with the scene with the rat, Wright shows the inner and outer conditions of Bigger's life from Bigger's point of view. He uses Max to reflect analytically on what he presents as "a mode of *life* in our midst, a mode of life stunted and distorted but possessing its own laws and claims, an existence of men growing out of the soil and prepared by the collective but blind will of a hundred million people." The "blind will" takes the form of Mr. and Mrs. Dalton, of Buckley and the coroner, of the conquerors in the historic "struggle for life" Max outlines. His related image of a "stunted and distorted mode of life" has understandably offended African American critics, beginning with Ben Davis Jr. and Ralph Ellison.[25] For his part, Max's strategy is to insist on the complicity of the dominant white society in creating the conditions from which Bigger and his crime emerged. For Max, if we neither understand nor change these conditions, "then we should not pretend horror or surprise when thwarted life expresses itself in fear and hate and crime" (p. 451).

One key difference between Max's language and perspective and those Wright brings alive from Bigger's point of view is the latter's assertion of a rebellious, defiant African American personality proudly unwilling as both an American and a black person to accept the restrictions the dominant society imposes. The phrase "thwarted life" catches only a part of the full reality Wright has focused on, just as it misses the full depth and intensity of Bigger's fear and hatred. Elsewhere, however, Wright has Max make a good faith effort to do justice to these feelings of hate and fear.

Because of his double focus on the dominant white society and on Bigger and what he represents, Max is able to bring out hidden implications in the political psychology of each group. Max anticipates Baldwin's "The Fire Next Time" and looks back to Wright's treatment of the "dynamite" Harlem response to Joe Lewis when he tells the court, "kill him and swell the tide of pent-up lava that will some day break loose, not in a single, blundering, accidental individual crime, but in a wild cataract of emotion that will brook no control" (p. 456).[26] This threat of a volcanic black uprising is a radical version of the white mob scene in *Day of the Locust*. Wright has Max combine the threat with a sophisticated analysis of the role consumerism plays in the politics of violence. He focuses on "the riots" that would follow if the millions stimulated by advertisements and the "dazzling" appeals of the media were like Bigger thoroughly, mockingly frustrated in their desire to partake of the happiness and fulfillments dangled in front of them (pp. 459, 470). In a political trial, Max repeatedly counters the threat of the white mob with the threat of violent uprisings that border on insurrection. At the end of the 1930s "the very atmosphere of our times" is charged with radical possibilities (p. 470). The so-called consumer riots of the 1960s and the assaults on shopping centers in Los Angeles after the 1992 Rodney King verdict are simply examples that confirm Max's diagnosis, if not his implied political hope.

As part of his political strategy Max generalizes Bigger. "Multiply Bigger Thomas twelve million times," Max argues, "allowing for environmental and temperamental variations, and for those Negroes who are completely under the influence of the church, and you have the psychology of the Negro people" (p. 463). This generalizing tactic leads to powerful insights and significant avoidances. It allows Max to present a hard, unsparing portrait of "a separate nation, stunted, stripped, and held captive *within* this nation, devoid of political, social, economic, and property rights." Max is giving his independent version of the party's position that African Americans constitute an oppressed nation within the nation and should have territorial autonomy and the right of self-determination in the Black Belt of the South (see Chapter 1). Max's generalizing tactic, moreover, allows him to threaten and, in the process of arguing for Bigger's life, to make a strong case for basic change. Killing Bigger is foolish, Max says, since "the more you kill, the more you deny and separate, the more will they seek another way of life, however blindly and unconsciously" (p. 463).

Unexpected but equally important, in describing "the way of life" the dominant society has forced on twelve million Biggers, Wright also uses Max to expose and critique the left, to show the extent to which conventional racial stereotypes have penetrated the language and consciousness even of a character as committed to equality as Max. Wright accordingly has Max use the traditional racist language of blacks as predatory animals living in the jungle (pp. 455–56). As John Reilly recognizes, Wright persistently cauterizes racist stereotypes by pushing them to the extremes and forcing readers to confront the results, even when the results are not flattering to his own party.[27]

Wright combines this exposure with positively rendered Marxist categories as he has Max go on to argue that "the relationship between the Thomas family and the Dalton family was that of renter to landlord, customer to merchant, employee to employer. The Thomas family got poor and the Dalton family got rich." In the process, Max tells the grieving Dalton family, "you kept the man who murdered your daughter a stranger to her and you kept your daughter a stranger to him" (p. 457). The threat is that the killing multiplied by twelve million will continue unless basic changes are made.

Intertwined with this recurring threat, Max puts his own independent accent on a language he shares with others in the Popular Front, a patriotic use of the American Revolution and the Declaration of Independence.[28] Working within and deepening the discourse of the Popular Front, Max appeals to a parallel between the revolutionary founders of America who "struck for their freedom" and the twelve million African Americans, "conditioned broadly by our own notions as we were by European ones when we first came here." Max emphasizes that they "are struggling within unbelievably narrow limits to achieve that feeling of at-home-ness for which we once strove so ardently" (pp. 463–64). In appealing to shared values, aspirations, and a shared revolutionary tradition, Max is at once high-minded and implicitly warning that people will fight for their freedom and a sense of "at-home-ness." His attention to the nonmaterial motive of being rooted in the universe is an independent perception that challenges the anti-Communist stereo-types about Popular Front discourse as either vapid or crudely reductive.

Max continues to invoke the American Revolution and to frame his argument with values central to American political culture in general and the Popular Front in particular, the commitment in the Declaration of Independence to the "inalien-able rights" of "life, liberty, and the pursuit of happiness." Wright has Max recog-nize that "we did not pause to define 'happiness.'" Contrary to money-oriented Americans as well as vulgar Marxists, however, Max sees "that happiness comes to men when they are caught up, absorbed in a meaningful task or duty to be done, a task or duty which in turn sheds justification and sanction back down upon their humble labors." Max understands that "men can starve from a lack of self-realization as much as they can from a lack of bread! And they can *murder* for it, too!" As he goes on, he skillfully calls attention to the threat of a revolutionary war driven by desperation and the idealism of "a dream to realize our personalities" implicit in Bigger's situation as a representative African American (pp. 464–65).

As a Popular Front Marxist, however, Max does not stress the racial implications but rather the oppression and rebellious drive to self-realization the Biggers of America share with other oppressed Americans. When he later focuses on "the heart of this moment[,] . . . the question of power which time will unfold," Max conjures up the image of "another civil war." The racial issue is implied but subordinated to the issues of class and property. Max emphasizes that "if the misunderstanding of what this boy's life means is an indication of how men of wealth and property are misreading the consciousness of the submerged millions today, [another civil war] may truly come" (p. 470). As late as 1940, throughout Max's version of Popular Front discourse, the threat of revolution is still alive.

For Max, Bigger is both like and unlike "us," different in that the dominant society has constructed a stunted nation within a nation, similar in that, as Max puts it, again referring to the American Revolution and the American dream of freedom, "do we think that the laws of human nature stopped operating after we had got our feet upon our road?" Max responds to Bigger's revolutionary potential as "part of a furious blaze of liquid life-energy which once blazed and is still blazing in our land. He is a hot jet of life that spattered itself in futility against a cold wall" (p. 465). In this political context, Bigger's furious blaze of life-energy goes back to the origins of the nation; again it is not specifically racial.

Having established a political context, Max can then boldly challenge common sense by asking "but did Bigger Thomas really *murder?*" Max distinguishes between "killing," which Bigger obviously did, and "*living*, only as he knew how, and as we have forced him to live. The actions that resulted in the death of those two women," Max concludes, "were as instinctive and inevitable as breathing or blinking one's eyes. It was an act of *creation*" (pp. 465–66). Unlike the version of these important ideas Wright develops in the first two books, however, he has Max almost totally ignore the sexual complexities and the related fears that drive Bigger's actions. In deemphasizing the complexities and ambiguities of sex and rape, Wright has Max continue a project he himself began in the immediate aftermath of the killing. To the extent that Wright wants Bigger's political psychology to represent twelve million African Americans, to that extent he understandably moderates conceptually what his narrative dramatizes. Similarly, in dealing with Bessie, Wright's dramatized version is more suggestive than the stress on self-preservation he gives both at the time of the murder and rape and in Max's interpretation. In both versions Wright suppresses the possibility of a deep hatred of black women.

In the uncensored text of Max's speech, however, Wright does enter tabooed territory. To discredit Bigger and support the rape charge, Buckley established that Bigger masturbated while watching Mary in the newsreel. Wright has Max turn this charge into an indictment of the entire process that conditioned Bigger's relation to Bessie and the world. "Was not Bigger Thomas' relationship to his girl a masturbatory one?" Max asks. "Was not his relationship to the whole world on the same plane? His entire existence was one long craving for satisfaction, with the objects of satisfaction denied; and we regulated every part of the world he touched. Through the instrument of fear, we determined the mode and quality of his consciousness" (p. 468). In having Max dare to use masturbation as a central political category, Wright challenges deeply held cultural conventions. His Marxist analysis is culturally as well as politically radical.

We need to keep in mind both Wright's uncensored and his dramatized versions of Bigger's relation to Mary and Bessie, moreover, to appreciate fully Max's telling political insight that "every thought [Bigger] thinks is potential murder. Excluded from, and unassimilated in our society, yet longing to gratify impulses akin to our own but denied the objects and channels evolved through long centuries for their socialized expression, every sunrise and sunset makes him guilty of subversive actions. Every movement of his body is an unconscious protest. Every desire, every dream, no matter how intimate or personal, is a plot or conspiracy. Every hope is a plan for insurrection. Every glance of the eye is a threat. *His very existence is a crime against the state!*" (p. 466). In this powerful Marxist interpretation of the significance of Bigger's life, Wright has Max transform Bigger's murders into political crimes. To animate Max's insight, Wright has assimilated and related to the present pioneering Communist scholarship on American slave insurrections and fused the language of this scholarship with the Communist sensitivity to subversive, insurrectionary "crimes against the state."[29] He uses both interrelated languages to convey as political the results of the American mythology of race and sexuality. When Bigger uses his own language, he does not deny Max's view but he does give it a significantly different emphasis. Bigger speaks racially of taking "fully upon himself the crime of being black" (p. 342). Bigger's explicit political consciousness, moreover, centers on black militancy, hatred of whites, and the appeal of fascism, projects that were deeply threatening to the party, so that through Max and Bigger Wright strengthens his novel by carrying on an active dialogue with the party.

In the organizing rhythms of *Native Son*, Wright uses Max's compelling arguments to reanimate near the close of the novel the possibility of a Marxist conversion for Bigger, a prospect Wright had outlined at the start of "Book Three." Wright furthers this possibility by having Bigger respond to Jan and Max as human beings. Significantly, when Bigger thinks of Jan's offer of friendship, for him "a particle of white rock had detached itself from that looming mountain of white hate and had rolled down the slope, stopping still at his feet. The word had become flesh. For the first time in his life a white man became a human being to him; and the reality of Jan's humanity came in a stab of remorse: he had killed what this man loved and had hurt him." Reinforcing the image of the no-longer-reified white mountain, Wright uses the basic image of blindness and sight: Bigger "saw Jan as though someone had performed an operation upon his eyes, or as though someone had snatched a deforming mask from Jan's face" (pp. 333–34).

Wright develops both the images of the white mountain and of blindness and sight in his treatment of Bigger's response to Max. After speaking deeply with Max, "for the first time in his life [Bigger] had gained a pinnacle of feeling upon which he could stand and see vague relations he had never dreamed of." Wright then applies to race his Marxist understanding of the process of reification, the process that attributes larger-than-life, impersonal powers to social forces human beings have constructed. "If that looming white mountain of hate were not a mountain at all," Wright has Bigger think, "but people, people like himself, and like Jan—then he was faced with a high hope the like of which he had never thought could be, and a despair the full depths of which he knew he could not stand to feel. A strong counter-emotion waxed in him, urging him, warning him to leave this newly seen and newly felt thing alone, that it would lead him to but another blind alley, to deeper hate and shame" (p. 418). Wright is probing the conflicts of conversion, the birth of a new consciousness. In the context of the Popular Front and the thirties left, the new consciousness would be revolutionary or proletarian or Marxist/Communist.

Wright develops these possibilities by having Bigger affirm his desire for a wholeness that is universal and does not involve the earlier desire for a union with other black people coupled with hatred of whites. Instead, Bigger longs for the life-giving warmth of simply knowing that outside his prison other human hands and hearts exist and would respond to his hands. They are not the "black hands" of Wright's famous poem but rather a forecast of a Communist conversion, since "in that touch, response of recognition, there would be union, identity; there would be supporting oneness, a wholeness which had been denied him all his life" (p. 420). Wright explicitly underscores the universal implications by having Bigger imagine "a strong blinding sun sending hot rays down and he was standing in the midst of a vast crowd of men, white men and black men and all men, and the sun's rays melted away the many differences, the colors, the clothes, and drew what was common and good upward toward the sun" (p. 420). In the image of the "blind-ing" sun, however, Wright simultaneously affirms and undermines the conversion; or rather, through the image of blindness he keeps alive a strong reservation, as he does in Bigger's fear that "it would lead him to but another blind alley."

Under the influence of Max's words and his recognition of him as a person, Bigger's feelings oscillate. As he does repeatedly, he struggles to find a language that will express the full meaning of his life. Max's Communist language of wholeness, of identity and union, has a powerful appeal. But Bigger is also depressed to the point of longing for death when he "felt that he was sitting and holding his life helplessly in his hands, waiting for Max to tell him what to do with it; and it made him hate himself. An organic wish to cease to be, to stop living, seized him" (p. 399), the powerful recurrence of the same feeling he had after his capture. The earlier rebellious assertion of his pride in himself as a person and as an African American reasserts itself in the form of Bigger's desire to "save his own life" and to find for himself "a set of words which he had in common with others" (p. 422). As an integral part of the concluding drama of belief, Wright keeps open the extent to which these words coincide with Max's.

He has Bigger repeatedly want Max to explain even as Bigger himself has a driving impulse to talk. In the latter mood Bigger "was trusting the sound of his voice rather than the sense of his words to carry his meaning" (p. 492). Wright carefully locates Bigger in the center of an African American discourse Frederick Douglass first analyzed in his discussion of the sorrow songs, which communicate "if not in the word, in the sound;—and as frequently in the one as in the other."[30] The words Bigger does use—"I'm all right"—gain force as the final episode develops. In a drama of perception and belief in which Bigger again and again "looked at Max's gray eyes" (p. 492), Wright plays off the personal and African American implications of Bigger's developing consciousness with his attraction to Max's language and the Popular Front faith "Max had given him [,] the faith that at bottom all men lived as he lived and felt as he felt" (p. 493).

The contest is intense. At a key moment, as Bigger is explaining himself to Max "Bigger was on the verge of believing that Max knew, understood; but Max's next words showed him that the white man was still trying to comfort him in the face of death" (p. 495). As the phrase "the white man" indicates, the racial issue is central for Bigger. Almost immediately, though, in another of the recurring shifts, Wright has Bigger think, "yes, Max knew now." As Max fastens his eyes upon Bigger's face, Bigger wants Max to give him the "knowledge of how to die," which Bigger realizes is inseparable from the "knowledge of how to live" (p. 495).

First, however, Bigger again asserts himself. Using the basic imagery of sight, he tells Max that "I sort of saw myself after that night. And I sort of saw other people, too." What Bigger sees in the present anticipates Max's final reaction: Bigger "saw amazement and horror on Max's face." Perhaps in response, Bigger temporarily pulls back from the implications of what he has said. He tells Max that "I didn't mean to do what I did. I was trying to do something else. But it seems like I never could." What Bigger says rings true as far as it goes but it is radically different from his concluding insights and from the tangled complexities at the time of the murder. In the meantime, in imagery Wright has consistently developed, as Bigger faces death he explains that "I'll be feeling and thinking that they didn't see me and I didn't see them." Bigger then articulates a version of Max's own position when he asks, "b-b-but you reckon th-they was like m-me, trying to g-get something like I was, and when I'm dead and gone they'll be saying like I'm saying now that they didn't mean to hurt nobody . . . th-that they was t-trying to get something, too?" (pp. 496–97).

Because Bigger is essentially using Max's own language, why, then, does "a look of indecision and wonder come into the old man's eyes" (p. 497)? This look is different from the earlier "horror" or the "terror" to come. Does this "look of indecision and wonder" have to do with the immanence of Bigger's death, wonder that Bigger is groping toward conversion, indecision about what role to play? In any case, Wright has Max answer with a moderate version of the Popular Front faith whose militant version animated his courtroom speech. Wright has previously used expressionist buildings to dramatize the structures of racial, economic, and political power. He now has Max use the buildings of the sun-drenched Chicago Loop to illustrate the power of belief and the structures of power. Max argues that what holds up these immense structures is "the belief of men. If men stopped believing, stopped having faith, they'd come tumbling down." In his courtroom speech, Max repeatedly invoked the threat of violent revolution but as he talks to Bigger and the reader, in the accents of the moderate Popular Front he instead stresses a change of mind leading to the nonviolent "tumbling down" of the existing structures of authority and privilege.

As a Communist, however, Max wants Bigger to know that "those buildings sprang up out of the hearts of men, Bigger. Men like you. Men kept hungry, kept needing, and those buildings kept growing and unfolding" (p. 498). Max is giving a lesson in the way capitalists exploit the labor of oppressed working men like Bigger so that the wealth ordinary workers produce goes into the growing, unfolding buildings while the workers who produce the wealth stay hungry and needy. Max also wants Bigger to see that as an empowered but exploited worker he is one of a class; that race is secondary to class. The rich owners who control things say "that black people are inferior. But, Bigger," Max stresses, "they say that *all* people who work are inferior" (p. 500).

As part of his project of aligning Bigger's aspirations with those of millions of other workers, Max varies his image of the growth of the buildings. Simplifying and sanitizing the full range of what Bigger felt, Max tells Bigger that "what you felt, what you wanted, is what keeps those buildings standing there. When millions of men are desiring and longing, those buildings grow and unfold." The buildings are now an image of the material and spiritual creativity of an American civilization enlivened by democratic millions. In the midst of the depression, however, "those buildings aren't growing any more." Because of the failures and inequities of capitalism, "a few men are squeezing those buildings tightly in their hands. The buildings can't unfold, can't feed the dreams men have, men like you." Max not only connects Bigger to the exploited workers who make the buildings but also to the owners, those "inside the buildings" whose belief has been shaken, who are "restless, like you, Bigger" (p. 498).

To explain why they nonetheless hate Bigger, Max ignores the historical and economic perspective of his courtroom speech, a perspective that would have allowed him to place racial hatred in historical, economic, and political context. Instead, Max uses the language of vulgar Marxism, a language he had previously avoided. Max now focuses exclusively on greed and fear. He stresses that "the men who own those buildings are afraid. They want to keep what they own, even if it makes others suffer. In order to keep it, they push men down in the mud and tell them that they are beasts. But men, men like you, get angry and fight to re-enter those buildings, to live again." In his moderate Popular Front parable, Max has again reached the key point of violent revolution and again, as with the buildings nonviolently "tumbling down," he is at pains to mute those possibilities of volcanic insurrection he had stressed in his courtroom speech. He tells Bigger, "you killed. That was wrong. That was not the way to do it." The right way, "too late for you now," is the moderate Popular Front approach, "to . . . work with others who are t-trying to . . . believe and make the world live again" (p. 499).

Max concludes that "on both sides men want to live; men are fighting for life. Who will win? Well, the side that feels life most, the side with the most humanity and the most men. That's why . . . y-you've got to believe in yourself, Bigger" (p. 500). Max emphasizes life, humanity, and the democratic triumph of numbers and avoids the tangled realities of revolutionary class conflict. At the end, he is speaking the language of Popular Front moderation. The Max of the final pages of Native Son is significantly different from the Max of the courtroom speech. We need to recognize and stress this difference instead of treating Max as a unified figure. Through the two Maxes, Wright brings alive conflicting strains within the discourse and political culture of the Popular Front. In contrast to his handling of race as a powerful, polarizing issue, however, Wright does not bring the conflict about volcanic revolution and peaceful change into direct opposition. These divisions within Max nonetheless contribute significantly to the drama of belief that animates the ending of Native Son. Beyond the divisions within Max, the Popular Front commitment to the black culture of the blues also comes alive at the end of Native Son.

First, however, in the concluding exchanges between Bigger and Max, Wright enacts a drama of belief and conversion that has been building throughout "Book Three." In my judgment the formulations at the start of "Book Three" and in Max's courtroom speech represent more compelling versions of Popular Front discourse than Max's reductive last words. There is a contest between these conflicting strains. At the end the even more important contest is between Max's Popular Front outlook and the Popular Front involvement in a blues and black-consciousness view of Bigger. Within Wright and within the Popular Front there were conflicts about the relative importance of the party's commitment to the blues and black cultural tradition, as distinct from the party's political stress on class and worker solidarity. As these issues emerge in the novel itself, something large is at stake centering on Bigger's view of himself.

To open up these issues Wright has Bigger put Max's ideas to his own uses. "When I think about what you say I kind of feel what I wanted," Bigger tells Max. Bigger then goes on to contradict Max, who has said that what Bigger did was wrong. Instead, "it makes me feel," Bigger affirms, "I was kind of right." Although Max urges Bigger "to believe in yourself," when Bigger reiterates that "I'm all right" and tells Max he can go home, something unexpected and powerful is happening within Bigger. Recognizing the change, Max "backs away from [Bigger] with compressed lips" when Bigger asserts that "when I think of why all the killing was, I begin to feel what I wanted, what I am" (pp. 500–501).

In one of the novel's central passages Bigger then goes on to clarify and redefine his identity. " 'I didn't want to kill!' Bigger shouted. 'But what I killed for, I *am*! It must've been pretty deep in me to make me kill! I must have felt it awful hard to murder' " (p. 501). Wright has shown that Bigger has killed for freedom, to be whole, to choose, and to express the full meaning of his life. This meaning includes a complex of racial hate, fear, self-hate, sexual attraction, violence, and misogyny as well as Bigger's defiant unwillingness to accept the restrictions the dominant white society has imposed on him. After Bigger rapes and murders Bessie, Wright has him ask, "what was he after? What did he want? What did he love and hate? He did not know. There was something he *knew* and something he *felt*; something the *world* gave him and something he *himself* had; something spread out in *front* of him and something spread out in *back*; and never in all his life, with this black skin of his, had the two worlds, thought and feeling, will and mind, aspiration and satisfaction, been together; never had he felt a sense of wholeness" (pp. 277–78). Bigger has earlier felt that his entire identity was embodied in his black skin. After the rape and murders, he feels there was "something the *world* gave him and something he *himself* had," a view that may or may not contradict his earlier sense of identity depending on the extent to which the self he affirms is black. At the end he says "what I killed for, I *am*!"

Wright has shown that Bigger is in part socially and racially constructed. At the end Bigger achieves a black and blue sense of self different from his affirmation of himself as opposed to "the world." At the end Bigger moves beyond the binary oppositions the conventional social-racial constructions generate, as in his earlier series of polarized alternatives. Bigger fully accepts "what I killed for" and in so doing he fuses what "the world gave him" with the self he affirms. This black and blue self is not universal or color blind. No wonder Max recoils as he does again when Bigger, who has earlier said "I'm all right," now makes a powerful ethical claim: "what I killed for must've been good!" In his drama of sight and blindness, Wright has Bigger say "I feel all right when I look at it that way." Then two final images of Max, whose "eyes were full of terror" and who "groped for his hat like a blind man" (p. 501).

The terror is understandable. Bigger has rejected Max's moderate Popular Front view that the killing was wrong and that class takes precedence over race. For a political person like Max, Bigger's affirmation of himself as an individual and as a black person contains the latent threat of intense racial conflict. The changes required to avoid that terrifying conflict, moreover, are significantly different if race, not class, is basic. As a man of the Popular Front and as a white man, Max has good reason to feel terror. Wright does not end with what for Max would have been a reassuring Communist conversion. Such a conversion would imply that militant, oppressed blacks are a cooperative part of the larger working class, all struggling together to change exploitative conditions. Bigger would gain his identity and become whole as a self not in isolation or as part of the black community but as a member of the working class. The Communist symbology Wright had outlined at the start of "Book Three" would be reaffirmed at the climax of the novel.

Instead, in the face of death Wright has Bigger experience the painful, exhilarating birth of a new consciousness but not one fully in line with party—or any other—orthodoxy. Before he says good-bye to Max, Bigger's last words are, "tell Jan hello" but he is accepting Jan as a person, not as "Comrade Jan," as a party member. Bigger has developed beyond his earlier hatred of whites and his fascination with a black dictator who might unify his people and make him whole, beyond shame and fear. Bigger repeatedly says that he did not want to hate or kill but that he accepts and values what he did. In the last act of a tense drama of belief and conversion, before Bigger dies Wright has him find his own language. Bigger's last dialogue with Max and his final "faint, wry, bitter smile" imply a black and blue sensibility: a full acceptance of the political, economic, and racial forces that have shaped him and an equally powerful affirmation of his inner creative and destructive energies and value. Bigger's complex personality can be neither reduced to nor separated from the racial, political, and economic powers that, along with Bigger's own power, are crucial to both his consciousness and his society. Through Bigger, Wright affirms a deep politics inseparable from the black and blue language and style at the heart of African American culture. In the process of exploring the depths, contradictions, and complexities of the American political unconscious, in his final scene Wright renders a precarious moment of birth before death. The scene and novel draw energy from and contribute to the cultural dialogue of the Popular Front, even as Wright as an African American and a participant in the Popular Front reanimates the "wry, bitter smile" of the blues through Bigger's complex affirmations in the face of death.

CHAPTER 8

MURIEL RUKEYSER'S *THE BOOK OF THE DEAD*
THE MODERNIST POEM AS RADICAL DOCUMENTARY

During the thirties American writers went to Harlan County to support unionizing miners in their fierce battle with the big coal companies, and some were arrested on picket lines in front of Ohrbachs. They witnessed the trials of the Scottsboro Boys—"witnessed" in the full sense of the word. They went to Spain, some to fight, some to report. And they went to unlikely places like Gauley, West Virginia. As a young poet who combined political passion with a modernist sensibility, Muriel Rukeyser was there at the second Scottsboro trial; she went to Spain; and she and a documentary photographer friend, Nancy Naumburg, went to Gauley, West Virginia, to see for themselves what Union Carbide had done to the black and white workers who were dying by the thousands of silicosis, an incurable lung disease they contracted from breathing glass dust while they were drilling the Gauley Tunnel. One result of Rukeyser's trip is *The Book of the Dead*, the long poem she uses to begin her 1938 collection, *U.S. 1*.[1]

Albert Maltz had used his own trip to the Gauley Tunnel as the basis for his short story, "Man on a Road," which appeared first in the January 8, 1935, issue of *New Masses*, then later that year in the anthology, *Proletarian Literature in the United States*, and in 1938 as part of Maltz's collection, *The Way Things Are*. In the January 15 and January 22, 1935, issues of *New Masses*, Bernard Allen filled in the background behind Maltz's story in a long article, "Two Thousand Dying on a Job." These stories, for all their differences with Rukeyser's version, are part of the left dialogue her work emerges from and contributes to. In addition to them and her own observation, Rukeyser also used the 1936 printed record of the hearings before a House subcommittee investigating the Gauley tragedy, particularly the

testimony of Philippa Allen, an articulate New York social worker intimately familiar with what went on. The year before she testified, Allen had presented her
findings in the *New Masses* articles she published under the pseudonym, Bernard
Allen. In a further connection with the left, the subcommittee hearings were
prompted by Congressman Vito Marcantonio's bill to correct conditions and
compensate the silicosis victims. A year after *New Masses* had begun exposing the
Gauley situation, the congressional hearings and the influential dominant-class
media widely reported the story, so that Rukeyser could assume an audience
familiar with the details of this well-publicized example of what for the left was
corporate capitalism at work.[2]

In noting her sources, Rukeyser mentions "other documents, including the
Egyptian *Book of the Dead* (in various translations), magazine and newspaper
articles on Gauley Bridge, letters and photographs" (p. 147). Her understatement
conceals a complex of bold literary and political commitments. Rukeyser fuses the
immediacy of the Gauley dead with the timelessness of the Egyptian *Book of the
Dead* and that in turn with the documentary language of congressional hearings
and "magazine and newspaper articles on Gauley Bridge, letters and photographs."
She has assimilated, subverted, and turned to her own politically radical uses the
modernist techniques of poems like Eliot's *The Waste Land*.

In place of Eliot's use of *The Golden Bough* and *From Ritual to Romance*, Rukeyser uses *The Book of the Dead*. At key points she identifies with the mother, Isis,
not with either Osiris or with Eliot's Tiresias.[3] The title and periodic quotations
from the Egyptian *Book of the Dead* reinforce the implication of death and rebirth
as both religiously timeless and politically timely. The road, U.S. 1, is both an
American highway and, as Philip Blair Rice indicates, "the Osiris Way described in
the Egyptian *Book of the Dead*. The tunnel is the underworld, the mountain stream
is the life-giving river, the Congressional inquiry is the judgment in the Hall of
Truth. And the whole tale, of course, is an emblem of rebirth: the dead, in the
fullness of time, shall rise to shape a new world. This scheme is suggested rather
than presented."[4] Rukeyser puts this scheme and her sources to her own radical
uses: she passes her own radical judgment on the congressional inquiry, for example, which in her version is not an authoritative final tribunal of Truth. The road,
river, and congressional inquiry, the deaths and their causes, moreover—all are
intensely American. In contrast to Eliot's studied avoidance of American references and locales, Rukeyser frames her *Book of the Dead* with a detailed sense of
region and the sweep of American history, commitments she has in common with
other left writers of the 1930s.

The title, *U.S. 1*, and the introductory poem, "The Road," both show her sensitivity to imagery and concerns she shares with these radical artists. Rukeyser's U.S. 1, the highway through the heart of America's historic Atlantic coast, is associated with the Osiris Way but, even more, it is part of a system of roads that crisscross the literary map of the thirties left—Dos Passos's Vag and his American journey at the start of *U.S.A.*; Maltz's "Man on a Road"; Richard Wright's "Transcontinental," with its locomotives and speeding cars and panorama of the nation; Le Sueur's "The Girl" and her vision of America in "Corn Village"; Algren's *Somebody with Boots*, on the road and down-and-out. During the 1930s the journey as a basic motif in American literature receives a powerful political accent—or accents, since these writers are not uniform.

In *U.S. 1* and *The Book of the Dead*, Rukeyser also shares with other left artists a concern with the documentary. Among the achievements of Popular Front culture is the documentary, in film, photography, and reportage. In *The Book of the Dead* Rukeyser takes her place along with Joris Ivens and Leo Hurwitz, Meridel Le Sueur and Josephine Herbst. As Rukeyser puts it in *The Life of Poetry*, "the work of Joris Ivens, Paul Rotha, Grierson, Legge, Lerner, Steiner, Van Dyke, Strand, Hurwitz, Ferno, Kline, Flaherty, and the groups that formed behind such productions as *Spanish Earth*, *Crisis*, *Native Land*, *The City*, and *Heart of Spain* sent an impulse through the other arts."[5] Rukeyser responded to that impulse. In *U.S. 1* and especially in *The Book of the Dead*, she shows her belief that "poetry can extend the document" (*U.S. 1*, p. 146). Like others in the tradition she emerges from and contributes to, Rukeyser says of her intentions that "I wish to make my poems exist in the quick images that arrive crowding on us now (most familiarly from the screen), in the lives of Americans who are unpraised and vivid and indicative, in my own 'documents.'"[6]

Beyond the films, *The Book of the Dead* also needs to be seen as one in a series of works by 1930s documentary photographers, collections of photographs with accompanying text: Margaret Bourke-White and Erskine Caldwell's *You Have Seen Their Faces* (1937), Archibald MacLeish's *Land of the Free* (1938), Walker Evan's *American Photographs* (1938), Dorothea Lange and Paul Schuster Taylor's *An American Exodus* (1939), Berenice Abbott's *Changing New York* (1939), Richard Wright and Edwin Rosskam's *12 Million Black Voices* (1941), and Walker Evans and James Agee's *Let Us Now Praise Famous Men* (1941). These collections are closely related to the large, ongoing Farm Security Administration (FSA) photography project.

Formally, *The Book of the Dead* can be seen as a series of documentary photographs framed by "The Road" and "West Virginia" at the start and concluding with the powerful sequence from "Alloy" through "The Book of the Dead." "In writing for sequences of stills," Rukeyser observes, "the motion of the sequence is a primary consideration. The editing and arrangement of the photographs will determine the flow of the text."[7] Both in the sequence and within poems, Rukeyser uses quick cuts, montage, and personally charged images as well as a range of public languages, including carefully edited and well-paced versions of the congressional hearings. Rukeyser does not spell things out. Meaning accumulates; it is not neatly packaged. Even the basic facts connected with the Gauley Tunnel emerge gradually; like an epic poet dealing with traditional material, Rukeyser can play on her audience's familiarity with the Gauley Tunnel. The individual poems in their arrangement and internal discontinuities not only suggest a collection of vital documentary photographs but they also answer to the gnomic quality of the spells and chants in the Egyptian *Book of the Dead*. The organizing pattern of death and renewal from the Egyptian *Book of the Dead*, moreover, is implied and is open to varying interpretations. In Rukeyser's modernist and politically radical version of the documentary, the reader is an active participant, not a passive observer, so that not all readers will agree and different readers will inevitably respond to some poems, sequences, and implications more fully than to others.

Rukeyser's approach is nonlinear and avant-garde. Her prosody is subtle, accomplished, and powerful. She is committed to explore the resources of language and to "*extend* the documentary" (emphasis added). Her aesthetics have significant political implications, just as her politics influences her poetics. Rukeyser assumes a fully human audience, an audience as responsive to imaginative leaps as it is to the dignity of women like Mrs. Jones or to African American workers like George Robinson "who holds all their strength together" (p. 22). She does not talk down to her readers. She assumes a degree of literacy and imaginative curiosity that implies a politically as well as poetically engaged and empowered audience.

Within the poem she conveys the company's knowledge that the men were drilling through almost pure silica; that Union Carbide, through its subsidiary, Rinehart and Dennis, deliberately decided not to drill wet to cut down the dust because wet drilling cost more; that the company did not warn the men to wear masks because, as one foreman said, the black workers were not worth the $2.50. Rukeyser establishes that Union Carbide deliberately altered the course of the tunnel so that it could drill through the richest vein of silica, a product it then diverted to its steel-making plant at Alloy, West Virginia. Although the stated purpose was to drill a tunnel for generating electricity for public sale, the real purpose was to sell all the power to a Union Carbide subsidiary and, after its discovery, to supply the silica used in steel production.

Within the poem the workers and their families emerge not as one-dimensional victims but as dignified people who are suffering because they needed jobs and were taken advantage of. The congressional committee reveals what happened, and Rukeyser reveals the committee's failure to do any more. Because even a liberal Congress is not about to address what is in effect deliberate murder, Rukeyser leaves it up to us to draw the radical conclusion that fundamental change is necessary. In left reportage the writer typically leaves the call to action implicit in the iconography and details of the report. In Rukeyser's avant-garde version of the report or documentary, the reader who has actively participated in the poem has an intensified sense that something is terribly wrong with prevailing conditions.

In the context of the 1930s, however, Rukeyser seemed to John Wheelwright to be insufficiently Marxist because she focuses on shockingly bad conditions, "the excrescences of capitalism," and "makes no root attack upon everyday exploitation." We can defer for a moment considering the extent to which such "excrescences" are themselves representative. Wheelwright also hit hard against Rukeyser because she is "obscure" and lacks "clarity." According to Wheelwright, "revolutionary writing in the snob style does not reach a proper audience."[8] What constitutes a "proper" audience, however, is not easy to determine. From the perspective of the present, what is impressive is that Rukeyser's "snob style" combines with a politically charged content in ways that continue to make us see and feel. Rukeyser does so as a writer committed to the Popular Front, because, it bears repeating, she is grounded in the concerns of this movement. In her fusion of high art, left politics, and the innovative documentary, she reminds us that the Popular Front had a high culture dimension that has faded from our memories.

For current readers, another value of *The Book of the Dead* is that in her intensity and urgency Rukeyser brings alive the view that, far from being an "excrescence" of capitalism, the Gauley tragedy, including Union Carbide's New Kanawha Power Company, is part of a continuum that goes back to the England of Marx's "The Working Day" and Engels's *The Condition of the Working Class* and that goes on through Union Carbide's Bhopal catastrophe to its Kanawha Valley plant at Institute, West Virginia, and whatever the latest "excrescence" turns out to be. On August 12, 1985, the West Virginia twin of the Union Carbide Bhopal, India, chemical plant sent out a cloud of toxic fumes that hospitalized 135 people suffering from breathing problems, burning eyes, nausea, and dizziness. Like the one in Bhopal, India, but on a smaller scale, the explosion was caused by substandard safety equipment and human error, despite a $5 million investment after Bhopal. The West Virginia plant, like the one in India, was located next to a residential area for workers.

By the 1980s the twenty-mile Kanawha Valley had become the center of a major chemical industry. Not far from the site of the Gauley tragedy, Union Carbide,

Dupont, Olin, FMC, and Diamond Shamrock all contributed to the prosperity of the region and to high rates of birth defects and cancer, the 1980s successors of silicosis. Cancer, for example, was 21 percent above the national average. Beyond the "acceptable," routine leaks from valves and gaskets, the Union Carbide plant at Institute had sixty-one leaks or spills in the five years preceding the 1985 explosion. Headaches and hacking coughs were common. From the Institute plant alone "the 1981 emissions included nearly 146 tons of butadiene, 11 tons of ethylene oxide, 50 tons of chloroform, 17 tons of propylene oxide, 10 tons of benzene, and, although it was not reported then, a harmless whiff of methyl isocyanate, or MIC—the lethal stuff of Bhopal."[9]

In the spirit of *The Book of the Dead*, we can test the view that, from New Kanawha Power and Gauley Bridge in 1935 to Kanawha Valley and Institute in 1985, Union Carbide is a convenient focus for the tendency of American corporations to present a benign front, to put profits first, to treat workers as commodities, to scuttle health and environmental laws and precautions, and, when they can, to treat America as a Third World country. For us Rukeyser in *The Book of the Dead* provides a point of reference to gauge the extent to which the basic tendencies of corporate capitalism have changed since the 1930s, public relations aside. The same applies to the other writers of the thirties left as they bear on the present. Rukeyser shares with the other radical writers of the 1930s a principled hope that basic change is possible. One change between then and now, of course, is the loss of this hope.

"The Road"

Rukeyser's *U.S. 1* appeared in the same year as the Federal Writers's Project guidebook, *U.S. 1*. In "The Road" (pp. 9–10) Rukeyser introduces us to her world, which is our ordinary world slightly heightened. She establishes a direct connection with us, gets us with her from the start on "these roads" as if we know them, too, and have been thinking about them with her. "These are roads to take when you think of your country," she begins. Revelations follow about "your country" as she gets us past the "well-travelled six-lane highway planned for safety," "past your tall central city's influence" to "centers removed and strong, fighting for good reason." In a recognizably American way she values these "centers" away from the city as a center. How and why these "strong" centers are "fighting for good reason" will emerge in the remainder of *The Book of the Dead*. For now "your country" has become not only the United States but also the country as opposed to the city when Rukeyser repeats, "these roads will take you into your country." To the extent that the Osiris Way is in the background of "these roads," it is a distant background.

In the foreground Rukeyser has us "select the mountains, follow rivers back, / travel the passes." As she has us move ourselves deep into West Virginia, she uses place names lovingly—"the Midland Trail," "iron Clifton Forge"—and she critically evokes the contrast between the working places and "the wealthy valley, resorts, the chalk hotel. / Pillars and fairway; spa; White Sulphur Springs. / Airport. Gay blank rich faces wishing to add / history to ballrooms, tradition to the first tee." Another contrast is with the landscape around her destination, New River Gorge: "the land is fierce here, steep, braced against snow, / rivers and spring." Documentary language and photography are basic to Rukeyser's organization and approach. Appropriately, the photographer and her "inverted image" appear for the first time, initiating the images of seeing Rukeyser deliberately uses in subsequent poems. The "inverted image" the photographer views also prepares us for a complex series of "inverted images" of America. In Rukeyser's America the present of Union Carbide and Gauley Tunnel emerges from and sometimes clashes with the history and natural history of the country, a connection Rukeyser begins to establish by cutting immediately to John Marshall who in 1812 "named the rock" first called Marshall's Pillar "but later Hawk's Nest," the site of the fatal tunnel.

"Here is your road," Rukeyser says again at the end of "The Road," "tying you to its meanings." She then specifies the meanings: "gorge, boulder, precipice." The meanings are as immediate as the fierce land "braced against snow, river and spring." The precipice, boulder, and gorge accumulate their fierce meanings as Rukeyser progresses through *The Book of the Dead*. Then a phrase concluding "The Road": "Telescoped down, the hard and stone-green river / cutting fast and direct into the town." To underscore an ending that is not an ending, Rukeyser avoids a rhetorical climax and uses the understatement of a sentence fragment. She also uses the slight heightening of internal rhyme (down/town) to introduce the river, another of her protagonists, and to come to a temporary close at the end of her introductory poem.

"West Virginia"

In "West Virginia" (pp. 11–12) Rukeyser takes the river and locale back to their colonial sources. This abrupt imaginative leap begins to fill in the history she started with John Marshall. At the start "they saw rivers flow west and hoped again." At first we do not know who "they" are but we soon understand that this hope for the sea is disappointed. The powerful rivers flowing west are nonetheless connected with the vital promise of America, an organizing motif Rukeyser reemphasizes at the end of "West Virginia" and at the end of *The Book of the Dead*. The "they" of the opening are "1671—Thomas Batts, Robert Fallam / Thomas Wood, the Indian Perecute, / and an unnamed indentured English servant." As part of her concern with the documentary, Rukeyser incorporates direct quotations from their journal to establish that they are mistaken in their belief that "WATERS, DESCENDING NATURALLY, DOE ALWAIES RESORT / UNTO THE SEAS INVIRONING THOSE LANDS."

Inseparable from this public language is the leap of personal association Rukeyser has with the "spilled water which the still pools fed. / Kanawha Falls, the rapids of the mind, / fast waters spilling west." Kanawha Falls is not only "the rapids of the mind" but also the site of the "New Kanawha Power Company, subsidiary of the Union Carbide and Carbon Company," the company responsible for those who "have from time to time died from silicosis contracted while employed in digging out a tunnel at Gauley Bridge, West Virginia."[10] For Rukeyser, the rapids of the mind, the as-yet-unmentioned New Kanawha Power Company, and the history she immediately returns to are all interconnected. Her version of the documentary, that is, includes the poet's mind as well as "the battle at Point Pleasant, Cornstalk's tribes, / last stand, Fort Henry, a revolution won."

As she moves from the American Revolution to the Civil War, in her version of the documentary Rukeyser also experiments with verbal montage:

> the granite SITE OF THE precursor EXECUTION
> sabres, apostles OF JOHN BROWN LEADER OF THE
> War's brilliant cloudy RAID AT HARPERS FERRY.

Instead of a linear quotation of the inscription on the granite monument to John Brown, Rukeyser breaks up the inscription and intersperses notation words that signal the coming of the Civil War ("precursor," "sabres"), so that John Brown and his sabres emerge as precursors and apostles of the war, even as the "brilliant cloudy RAID" merges with the "brilliant cloudy" war. The symbolic weather of the raid and war merge with "floods, heavy wind this spring," perhaps the present of the poem merging with the immediacy of the past as Rukeyser sketches the separation of West Virginia from Virginia in the Civil War and then "troops / here in Gauley Bridge, Union headquarters, lines / bring in the military telegraph. / Wires over the gash of gorge and height of pine." In a context filled with merging and principled conflict, for Rukeyser John Brown deserves the special attention her montage encourages the reader to give him. As a militant rebel John Brown is a historical precursor not only of the war but also of a radical response to the deaths at Gauley Bridge. In *The Book of the Dead* Rukeyser returns to John Brown to body forth her revolutionary affirmation at the climax of "The Bill" (p. 65) and later in her 1940 poem, "The Soul and Body of John Brown."

In "West Virginia" Rukeyser shifts back to her protagonist, "the water / the power flying deep / green rivers cut the rock / rapids boiled down, / a scene of power." This boiling natural power looks ahead to the electric, corporate, governmental, and radical power Rukeyser deals with later in *The Book of the Dead*. A forecast is the enigmatic stanza,

Done by the dead.
Discovery learned it.
And the living?

The phrase "done by the dead" may complete the immediately preceding "a scene of power," referring elliptically to the workers who drilled the power tunnel.

In response to the question "and the living?" Rukeyser concludes "West Virginia" with another of her quiet, understated, suggestive endings:

Live country filling west,
knotted the glassy rivers;
like valleys, opening mines,
coming to life.

In the phrase "live country filling west," Rukeyser plays off the living and the living country against the dead and reinforces her opening imagery of rivers flowing west, of simultaneous disappointment and the American Dream, the hope connected with the power of life-giving water "filling west." The "live country" "knotted," perhaps dammed, "the glassy rivers," which are "glassy" because of the silica that will cause painful deaths. In her elliptical style Rukeyser sketches a West Virginia, valleys, opening mines, "coming to life." The affirmation of life is inseparable from the recognition of death, not as a metaphysical or religious abstraction but as a result of a misuse of the "power" of the "glassy rivers."

"Statement: Phillipa Allen"

Rukeyser makes these political implications explicit in "Statement: Phillipa Allen" (pp. 13–15), the poem she juxtaposes with the ending of "West Virginia." In contrast to the suggestive, elliptical style of "West Virginia," in "Statement" Rukeyser uses the congressional transcript and records the exact words of the questions and testimony of Phillipa Allen. Rukeyser edits the order of the testimony and gives it the dramatic form of question and answer—in the original, Phillipa Allen testifies at length and the congressmen only occasionally raise questions. Throughout, Rukeyser selects and arranges Allen's words so as to highlight the political poetry latent in ordinary speech. This documentary impulse is at once bold, radical, and restrained.

Rukeyser uses Phillipa Allen to establish basic information about "the Gauley tunnel tragedy, which involves about 2,000 men." She juxtaposes the quoted lines from page 2 of the *Investigation* with the information from page 25 that their salary "started at 40¢ and dropped to 25¢ an hour." Rukeyser leaves it up to us to make judgments about the price of labor, the extent of need, the degree of exploitation, and the exact value of 2,000 human lives at 25¢ an hour. Then, instead of commentary, Rukeyser takes an exchange from page 25:

—You have met these people personally?
—I have talked to these people, yes.

She juxtaposes these lines with her rearrangement on the page of bald data from page 3 of the *Investigation*, vouched for by Allen's personal knowledge of "these people":

According to estimates of contractors
2,000 men were
    employed there
    period, about 2 years
    drilling, 3.75 miles of tunnel,
    To divert water (from New River)
    to a hydroelectric plant (at Gauley Junction).
The rock through which they were boring was of a high silica content.
In tunnel No. 1 it ran 97.99% pure silica content.

The placement of the words on the page slows us down and emphasizes what we might skip over in prose. Throughout "Statement" part of the effect comes from our understanding that Allen's words are taken directly from the printed transcript of the congressional investigation but are rearranged on the page to reveal unsuspected cadences combined with the restrained presentation of details whose shocking implications gradually emerge. The significance of the understated recital about 97.99 percent pure silica emerges in what follows.

Rukeyser moves to page 20 of the transcript and interrupts the logical, linear flow of Allen's testimony just enough to underscore the emotionally disturbing revelation that

The contractors
    knowing pure silica
      30 years' experience
      must have known danger for every man
  neglected to provide the workmen with any safety device

To place this indictment in its political and corporate context, Rukeyser then returns to page 3 of Allen's testimony:

The tunnel is part of a huge water-power project
    begun, latter part of 1929
    direction: New Kanawha Power Co.
      subsidiary of Union Carbide & Carbon Co.
    That company—licensed:
    to develop power for public sale.
    Ostensibly it was to do that; but
    (in reality) it was formed to sell all the power to
      the Electro-Metallurgical Co.
      subsidiary of Union Carbide & Carbon Co.
        which by an act of the State legislature
        was allowed to buy up
    New Kanawha Power Co. in 1933.

Rukeyser slightly varies the punctuation of the transcript to heighten the dry, factual quality ("begun, latter part of 1929 / direction: New Kanawha Power Co."), as distinct from the more lyrical, personal style of other sections of *The Book of the Dead*. People from Bhopal, India, to Institute, West Virginia, can testify as to whether this spare lesson in corporate subterfuge and the use of corporate power has or has not dated.

Rukeyser continues to focus on the contradictions of power as a central concern by moving to a new context Congressman Griswald's statement (p. 27 of the *Investigation*),

—They were developing the power. What I am trying to get at, Miss Allen, is, did they use this silica from the tunnel; did they afterward sell it and use it in commerce?

Rukeyser has previously established that the company "enlarged the size of the tunnel, due to the fact that they discovered silica and wanted to get it out." Phillipa Allen does not explicitly support the charge that the company intended to sell the silica but rather that the interlocking corporations "used it in the electro-processing of steel," so that we can draw our own conclusions. To help in the process Rukeyser's poetics allow her to include chemical formulas as an almost lyric refrain along with folk song echoes ("Shipped on the C & O down to Alloy") and revelations of corporate maneuvering:

SiO_2 SiO_2
The richest deposit.
Shipped on the C & O down to Alloy.
It was so pure that
                              SiO_2
they used it without refining.

In her testimony Allen has brought out that geologists from Union Carbide's subsidiary "knew that the tunnel was to go through pure silica and then they enlarged the tunnel of project no. 2 from 32 feet to 46 feet at the location of the richest silica deposit." In two sentences Rukeyser uses, Allen goes on to say, "this was to enable them to take out more valuable silica rock, which was loaded on cars at the tunnel mouth and shipped on the C. & O. tracks down to the Alloy, W. Va., plant of the Electro Metallurgical Co., where it was stored in the yard. It was so pure it was used without refining" (*Investigation*, p. 20). Through her handling of the refrain, her placement of Allen's words on the page, and a slight compression and rearrangement, Rukeyser again brings into the open the political poetry of ordinary speech.

From pages 11 and 12 of Allen's testimony Rukeyser quotes directly that "All were bewildered. Again at Vanetta they are asking, / "What can be done about this?" Before Phillipa Allen leaves, Rukeyser has her address the issue by saying

I feel that this investigation may help in some manner.
I do hope it may.

As much as she values Allen, Rukeyser also uses the genteel formality of Allen's speech to stress her distance from the workers and to cast doubt on how much good the investigation will do.

At the end of "Statement" Rukeyser returns to the beginning of Allen's testimony:

I am now making a very general statement as a beginning.
    There are many points that I should like to develop
    later, but I shall try to give you a general history of
    this condition first. . . .

For Allen and Rukeyser "this condition" refers not only to men "dying like flies" from silicosis (*Investigation*, p. 3) but also to corporate power, exploitation, and domination, political diseases inseparable from the lung disease. Rukeyser ends in a way that invites us to fill in, that conveys a sense of an uncompleted process, and that allows her to go into "this condition" not in general but in the specifics of "Gauley Bridge" and subsequent poems. Within the poems that compose the long poem, *The Book of the Dead*, Rukeyser has several strategies that allow her at once to avoid rhetorical climaxes and to convey a sense of tentative closure combined with a move to the poems that follow.

"Gauley Bridge"

At the beginning of "Gauley Bridge" (pp. 16–17), by viewing the city from the point of view of the camera—"camera at the crossing sees the city"—Rukeyser reinforces the organizing idea of a series of documentary photographs. The scene is a familiar one from thirties documentaries,

> a street of wooden walls and empty windows,
> the doors shut handless in the empty street,
> and the deserted Negro standing on the corner.

Rukeyser uses a stripped down style to focus on the harsh, empty details, emphasized by the twist of "deserted Negro," not "deserted corner" but doubly deserted, both as part of a desolate urban scene and as a black man in a West Virginia town.

Rukeyser meticulously uses the vantage point of the camera "fixed on the street" at the railway crossing to record what comes into view:

> The little boy runs with his dog
> up the street to the bridge over the river where
> nine men are mending road for the government.
> He blurs the camera-glass fixed on the street.

Rukeyser then turns the camera inside, to the hotel owner "keeping his books behind the public glass" and, behind the postoffice window,

> a hive of private boxes,
> the hand of the man who withdraws, the woman who reaches her hand
> and the tall coughing man stamping an envelope.

To reinforce the sense of meticulous documentary notation, Rukeyser records the details inside the post office and bus station in a series of incomplete sentences. In this randomly observed scene a man coughing, the symptom of the fatal silicosis, is simply taken for granted as part of the flow of routine details.

After "the yellow-aproned waitress" in the bus station, in the next frame Rukeyser gives us

> The man on the street and the camera eye;
> he leaves the doctor's office, slammed door, doom,
> any town looks like this one-street town.

In her self-reflexive use of documentary, for Rukeyser the camera eye, like the earlier rapids of the mind, is as much a part of the scene as the man on the street. In a context of precise physical notation, the phrase "the man on the street" records a physical presence but in a way that generalizes him into the representative "man on the street," a connotation that contributes to the irony of "any town looks like this one-street town." "Any town" may look like this town but this town is also special because of "the tall coughing man" and this "man on the street" who leaves the doctor's office, the "slammed door" and "doom" conveying a sense of emotional disturbance and finality, presumably for the same reason the man in the post office is coughing. Everything about the town of Gauley Bridge is ordinary and recognizable but slightly heightened because, whereas people everywhere get sick and die, in Gauley Bridge some of them suffer and die from silicosis.

Rukeyser continues to develop the simultaneously special and representative quality of Gauley Bridge by accumulating the common objects that, along with the coughing man and the man on the street, give this American place its precisely rendered look and meaning. "The naked eye" and the "camera" are again part of a scene that includes

> Glass, wood, and naked eye: the movie-house
> closed for the afternoon frames posters streaked with rain,
> advertise "Racing Luck" and "Hitch-Hike Lady."

The figures who have peopled the earlier part of the poem or photograph reappear, familiar now as

> Whistling, the train comes from a long way away,
> slow, and the Negro watches it grow in the grey air,
> the hotel man makes a note behind his potted palm.

The rain, the wish fulfillment movies, the "grey air" and the approaching train

And in the beerplace on the other sidewalk
always one's harsh eyes over the beerglass
follow the waitress and the yellow apron—

"the yellow-aproned waitress" noted earlier in the bus station—these unglamorous, commonplace details are the backdrop for Rukeyser's concluding stanza:

What do you want—a cliff over a city?
A foreland, sloped to sea and overgrown with roses?
These people live here.

Abruptly, "what do you want"—the picturesque details of the conventional guidebook or landscape painting, a pretty, comforting scene, "a foreland, sloped to sea and overgrown with roses?" Instead, "the empty street, / and the deserted Negro," the "posters streaked with rain," the "red-and-white filling station" and, unremarkably, the coughing man and the man on the street: "these people live here," in a place that has value and a claim on our attention because of them.

In "Gauley Bridge" Rukeyser brings alive a documentary aesthetics of precise observation and self-reflexive involvement. The language is stripped down, the sharply focused details are noted, and the reader or viewer is invited to fill in, as with the elliptical scene of the man on the street leaving the doctor's office. Rukeyser uses this aesthetic to render an American subject matter of the ordinary made luminous through accurate recording, understated revelation, and implied protest. The deserted Negro, the yellow-aproned waitress, the bus station, the "Racing Luck" and "Hitch-Hike Lady," the men dying of silicosis, the "one-street town," the railroad tracks and the whistling train, the "grey air" and the red-and-white filling station, the "beerplace" and the underpass—all are familiar objects and characters in the iconography of the Popular Front, with its special attention to blacks, ordinary workers, and the abuses of capitalism. As she does throughout *The Book of the Dead*, in the political art of "Gauley Bridge" Rukeyser draws energy from, works within, and contributes to the political culture of the Popular Front.

Like the long poem it is an integral part of, "Gauley Bridge" derives part of its meaning from this cultural context. When the poem appeared in the April 1, 1939, issue of *Scholastic*, this context of Popular Front political culture did not have to be supplied but was alive as part of the general culture a magazine like *Scholastic* emerged from and transmitted. What is problematic, however, is how the poem fared removed from the context of *The Book of the Dead*. Dorothy Emerson, the editor of *Scholastic*'s "Poetry Corner," intelligently addressed the problem any anthologist faces, how to make one or two poems from a long work accessible. She tactfully established that "Gauley Bridge" was part of *The Book of the Dead*, "a group of poems dealing with 'the Gauley tragedy,' in which several thousand workers toiled under such bad conditions that they died from having breathed in silica, fatal as fine glass-particles." She states that as one of these workers "the man leaving the doctor's office will die here, in Gauley Bridge, West Virginia." She also introduces the poem by way of "The Road," the camera, and the gaze of the tourist.[11] But even with her helpful, sympathetic commentary, does "Gauley Bridge" by itself really convey the full implications of Rukeyser's documentary aesthetic and the organizing role of documentary photography as a vehicle of witnessing and of political exposure and protest? These questions also bear on the issue of the role of anthologies in making poems from the past available to contemporary readers. "Gauley Bridge" gains its full meaning and impact as part of a larger composition but *The Book of the Dead* is not a candidate for anthologizing. A group of representative poems—Rukeyser's for her *Selected Poems* or summaries like Dorothy Emerson's—can nonetheless make a difference. To her credit, in her Rukeyser selection, *Out of Silence: Selected Poems*, Kate Daniels faces up to the problem by reprinting the entire *Book of the Dead*.[12]

"The Face of the Dam: Vivian Jones"

The next poem in Rukeyser's accumulating collection of documentary images and insights, "The Face of the Dam: Vivian Jones" (pp. 18–19), is not likely to be singled out for anthologizing but in the poem Rukeyser achieves an elegiac tone, a sense of loss and quiet protest, and a fusion of Marx, modernism, and the first direct echo of the Egyptian *Book of the Dead*, so that "The Face of the Dam" makes its contribution to the total effect of *The Book of the Dead*. Vivian Jones is the engineer of the now unused locomotive that carried silica on the C & O from the Gauley Tunnel to Alloy. Instead of the camera, Rukeyser uses the movement of the clock to organize the poem and convey a sense of time passing. As the clock moves from the hour to the quarter and then to the half, the movement in the present parallels the move of Jones's memory into the past and that in turn underscores the sense of death and how it happened and who is responsible:

> On the quarter he remembers how they enlarged
> the tunnel and the crews, finding the silica,
> how the men came riding freights, got jobs here
> and went into the tunnel-mouth to stay.

Rukeyser has prepared for this quiet, deadly revelation by situating Jones "on the hour" at the gorge where "he sits and sees the river at his knee":

> There, where the men crawl, landscaping the grounds
> at the power-plant, he saw the blasts explode
> the mouth of the tunnel that opened wider
> when precious in the rock the white glass showed.

Rukeyser exposes the landscaping as a form of public relations concealment even as she reveals the contrasting violence of the blast.

> Jones then returns to what is on his mind:
> Never to be used, he thinks, never to spread its power,
> jinx on the rock, curse on the power plant,
> hundreds breathed value, filled their lungs full of glass
> (O the gay wind the clouds the many men).

"Value" picks up the earlier use of "precious" ("when precious in the rock the white glass showed"). The "value" the men breathe is literally the pure silicon, the glass, but the term is from Marxist discourse—as part of a system of commodity exchange the glass has value and the men breathe the profit, the surplus value the company gains from the rock and from them. Through this Marxist usage Rukeyser gives a compressed, idiomatic indictment of capitalistic greed and indifference to the workers' lives: "jinx on the rock, curse on the power plant." She juxtaposes the Marxist language of "value" and protest with the parenthetical echo of phrases modeled on the Egyptian *Book of the Dead*.[13] This use of contrasting languages from traditional sources is a modernist device, as in Eliot's

> O City, city, I can sometimes hear
> Beside a public bar in Lower Thames Street

or

> O Lord Thou pluckest me out
> O Lord Thou pluckest

or

> O you who turn the wheel and look to windward.

In her refrain line Rukeyser mourns for "the many men." It is worth stressing that as a left writer she values them. Unlike Eliot in *The Waste Land*, she does not diminish them through contrast to the dignity of the tradition or the indignity of their own actions.

Rukeyser goes on to convey a sense of the grandeur of the dam, "the great wall-face," and the power of the water, "immense and pouring power, the mist of snow, / the fallen mist, the slope of water, glass." The powerful, life-giving water is now inseparable from glass, visually and because of the silica. As a result, the water is now connected with death:

> O the gay snow the white dropped water, down,
> all day the water rushes down its river,
> unused, has done its death-work in the country,
> proud gorge and festive water.

The variation of the ritualistic refrain from the Egyptian *Book of the Dead* ("O the gay snow") intensifies the sense of the perversion of festive life and power by the "death-work in the country."

At the end, Rukeyser gathers together her refrain words and uses them and the clearing, "gay" weather to record a contrasting, haunting sense of loss:

> And the snow clears and the dam stands in the gay weather,
> O proud O white O water rolling down,
> he turns and stamps this off his mind again
> and on the hour walks again through town.

"Praise of the Committee"

In the sequences of *The Book of the Dead* Rukeyser sensitively varies the pace and language of the poems, just as she focuses, sometimes on a single person, sometimes on a more general revelation of the human cost of capitalistic values and practices. She uses Vivian Jones and the sensuous details and elegiac tone of "The Face of the Dam," for example, to play off against the more impersonal documentary style of "Praise of the Committee" (pp. 20–23). As in "Statement: Phillipa Allen," in "Praise of the Committee" she again rearranges direct quotations from Allen's testimony to present information, some of it new, some of it already rendered in more lyric or elliptical language, so that Rukeyser achieves the power of an incremental layering effect. We already know that

> Almost as soon as work was begun in the tunnel
> men began to die among the dry drills. No masks.
> Most of them were not from this valley.

The freights brought many every day from States
all up and down the Atlantic seaboard
and as far inland as Kentucky, Ohio.

Now we learn for the first time that

After the work the camps were closed or burned.
The ambulance was going day and night,
White's undertaking business thriving and
his mother's cornfield put to a new use.

These spare, declaratory sentences have an incantory effect. Rukeyser tells enough
to let us know that something is terribly amiss and she appeals to our imaginations
for the rest: to figure out why "the camps were closed or burned" and to realize
that the cornfield has been turned into a graveyard. In compressing Allen's testimony, Rukeyser chooses to eliminate the fact that the company "had torn [the
camps] down to get rid of the workmen who were suing" (*Investigation*, p. 11).

Instead, she cuts to direct quotations about lawsuits and liability from Phillipa
Allen's discussion with a company lawyer at the Union Carbide's stockholders'
meeting (*Investigation*, pp. 12–13). The quotations are jumbled to dramatize that
the corporation has manipulated the men, the language, and the legal process to
avoid lawsuits and its responsibilities to its workers. Rukeyser conveys this idea in
fragments that express how emotionally disturbing the revelations are:

" 'Terms of the contract. Master liable.'
"No reply. Great corporation disowning men who made. . . ."
After the lawsuit had been instituted. . . .

Then she uses the first of a series of Brechtian interpolations like those in a
Living Newspaper: "*The Committee is a true reflection of the will of the people.*" The
sharp contrast between the committee and the corporation may also be setting up
the congressional committee, which may not be "a true reflection of the will of the
people." The beleaguered defense committee of a subsequent scene and identifying
line seems closer to "the will of the people" than the official committee is. The
congressional committee, for example, hears from the local doctors. We later learn
that far from being "a true reflection of the will of the people," most of the doctors
are either indebted to or pressured by Union Carbide. At this stage, however,
Rukeyser simply has them report,

Every man is ill. The women are not affected.
This is not a contagious disease.

But in ways the doctors do not intend, the women are affected and, as Rukeyser dramatizes in "The Doctors" (pp. 37–41), so is the credibility of the physicians, especially Dr. Harless. Is the committee's credibility called into question through association, the deadpan presentation, and the use of the interpellated sentence?

The next interpellation, moreover, *"The Committee meets regularly, wherever it can,"* introduces not the congressional committee but rather the grass-roots defense committee, women and men we become familiar with as the speakers of the dramatic monologues of subsequent poems:

> Here are Mrs. Jones, three lost sons, husband sick,
> Mrs. Leek, cook for the bus cafeteria,
> the men: George Robinson, leader and voice,
> four other Negroes (three drills, one camp-boy)
> Blankenship, the thin friendly man, Peyton the engineer,
> Juanita absent, the one outsider member.

Instead of the elevated setting of a Washington hearing room,

> Here in the noise, loud belts of the shoe-repair shop,
> meeting around the stove beneath the one bulb hanging.
> They come late in the day. Many come with them
> who pack the hall, wait in the thorough dark.

Rukeyser was there, in a scene that recurs in the literature of the thirties left.

In "extending the documentary," Rukeyser continues to fuse material, language, and sympathies ordinarily excluded from canonical poetry. Anticipating later revelations, she invokes "the crooked lawyers" and turns against them their economic argument that

> If the men had worn masks, their use would have involved
> time every hour to wash the sponge at mouth.
> Tunnel, 3⅛ miles long. Much larger than
> the Holland Tunnel or Pittsburgh's Liberty Tubes.
> Total cost, say, $16,000,000.

As the details and revelations about the masks gradually accumulate, we become increasingly aware of the extent to which, for a representative capitalistic institution, the value of economic gain combines with indifference to human beings. Rukeyser leaves the judgments up to us. Part of the effect comes from her spare use of figures—"3⅛ miles"; "total cost, $16,000,000." It goes against the decorum of most anthologized American poetry to turn against capitalism the raw economic details, the crass dollar amounts, the crooked lawyers, the shoe-repair shop, or the political justice implicit in "WEST VIRGINIA RELIEF ADMINISTRATION, #22991." Number 22991 is part of a system in which we learn of the defense committee that

> Active members may be cut off relief,
> 16-mile walk to Fayetteville for cheque—
> WEST VIRGINIA RELIEF ADMINISTRATION, #22991,
> TO JOE HENIGAN, GAULEY BRIDGE, ONE AND $^{50}/_{100}$,
> WINONA NATIONAL BANK, PAID FROM STATE FUNDS.

The figures speak for themselves in a drama of implied protest that gains energy and urgency from the way Rukeyser engages us, gets us to fill in details and judgments she has eliminated as she strips away transitions and includes just enough of the damaging or inspiring revelations to bring alive what the company and legislature have done and the response of the Defense Committee, of people like George Robinson, who

> holds all their strength together.
> To fight the companies   to make somehow a future.

The fight is first against Union Carbide and its subsidiaries but the grammar enlarges the statement to include an imperative to the general class war "to make somehow a future." At the outset, Rukeyser had referred to the unnamed inland centers "removed and strong, fighting for good reason." As she moves into *The Book of the Dead*, Rukeyser progressively opens up the meaning of this "fighting for good reason."

Rukeyser varies styles not only between poems but within them. She throws into relief the documentary language and protest of "Praise of the Committee," for example, by interjecting a line that lyrically recalls the fatal beauty of the dam and river juxtaposed with a contrasting scene of a defense committee meeting in a dark hall, men coughing, we now know, from the "pure crystal" they have breathed:

> The dam's pure crystal slants upon the river.
> A dark and noisy room, frozen two feet from stove.
> the cough of habit. The sound of men in the hall
> waiting for word.

Rukeyser then focuses on their breathing:

> These men breathe hard
> but the committee has a voice of steel.

One climbs the hill on canes.
They have broken the hills and cracked the riches wide.

She records a double protest, that of the collective "steel" voice of the committee that makes up for the damaged individual voices and her own revelation of the impaired breath of men crippled at work. The men are physically but not morally "broken," imagery Rukeyser applies to the hills in her compressed indictment, "they have broken the hills and cracked the riches wide."

Not only the breath but also the eyes of those in the room compel Rukeyser, who sees

In this man's face
family leans out from two worlds of graves—
here is a room of eyes,
a single force looks out, reading our life.

In the eyes, "the two worlds of graves," the family resemblance fuses with, again, the death that pervades *The Book of the Dead*. Rukeyser then turns the imagery of eyes on us. Far from being depleted, those in the room are a united force. And in a reversal of what we are doing, reading about them, they are "reading our life," bringing us to the test.

In the final two stanzas Rukeyser uses still another style, a series of questions that imply the Egyptian dead of the original *The Book of the Dead* merged with the Gauley dead who pervade "the river" and the "rigid hills," who "warn the night" and "waken our eyes," who run "through electric wires" and "speak down every road." At the end

Their hands touched mastery; now they
demand an answer.

The "mastery" may refer to the power of the tunnel or the skill of their work and, in any case, looks ahead to quotations from the Egyptian *Book of the Dead* in "Absalom" (p. 29). Equally important, in the accents of the thirties left "they *demand* an answer."

"Mearl Blankenship"

The voice that articulates this demand is the poet's, the same voice that sets the scene in "Mearl Blankenship" (pp. 24–26) for the touching monologue of this "thin friendly man." Rukeyser places him near the stove and the "loud machines" of the shoe-repair shop and establishes that like many others, he has been "voted relief, / wished money mailed." Then she goes on, using quotation marks to emphasize that the words are his. Rukeyser has waited until well into *The Book of the Dead* before she has one of the workers tell his story for himself. She has prepared us and now Mearl Blankenship says simply,

> "I wake up choking, and my wife
> "rolls me over on my left side;
> "then I'm asleep in the dream I always see:
> "the tunnel choked
> "the dark wall coughing dust.

In this deadly nightmare the "choked" tunnel "coughing dust" merges with the painful results, the "choking," coughing man. Then the letter Mearl Blankenship has written to send to "the city, / maybe to a paper":

> Dear Sir, my name is Mearl Blankenship.
> I have worked for the Rinehart & Dennis Co
> Many days & many nights
> & it was so dusty you couldn't hardly see the lights.

Rukeyser uses rhyme to heighten slightly the ordinary language Blankenship uses to show us the silicon dust pervading the night of the tunnel. As he continues, without condescension or fuss Rukeyser perfectly captures the language of work, the unsubordinated syntax (& . . . & . . . &), and the matter-of-fact rendering and acceptance of the fatal power relations in the tunnel:

> I helped nip steel for the drills
> & helped lay the track in the tunnel
> & done lots of drilling near the mouth of the tunnel
> & when the shots went off the boss said
> If you are going to work Venture back
> & the boss was Mr. Andrews
> & now he is dead and gone
> But I am still here
> a lingering along.

Culminating in the last two lines, the speech rhythms, the idiom, the off-rhyme (gone/along), and the shift from "&" to "but" emphasize the dying fall of Blankenship's life.

Rukeyser interrupts Blankenship to place him in a new setting, this time near the river against the rock, a setting that allows her to reinforce his nightmare fusion of man and tunnel, here as "grey river grey face / the rock mottled behind him / like X-ray plate enlarged." The grey, mottled face and the X-ray, reminders of the lung disease, lead into Blankenship's restrained, powerful account of his condition:

> J C Dunbar said that I was the very picture of health
> when I went to Work at that tunnel.
> I have lost eighteen lbs on that Reinhart ground
> and expecting to loose my life
> & no settlement yet & I have sued the Co. twice
> But when the lawyers got a settlement
> they didn't want to talk to me
> But I didn't know whether they were sleepy or not.

Rukeyser waits until "The Dam" (p. 57) to bring out that some of the lawyers are secretly agents of the company. In "Mearl Blankenship" she makes us feel that on a bare outline of the situation, the lawyers and the company are not really sleepy. As for Blankenship,

> I am a Married Man and have a family. God
> knows if they can do anything for me
> it will be appreciated
> if you can do anything for me
> let me know soon

The last word resonates because, we know, Blankenship and his family are in need and he will be gone—soon.

Beyond the telling revelations about the lawsuits, Blankenship's health, and conditions in the tunnel, in "Mearl Blankenship" Rukeyser's fidelity to his language and sensibility conveys her respect for him as a working man. Her tribute to workers like Mearl Blankenship and George Robinson and to women like Mrs. Jones emerges in the subtlety, accuracy, and moving power of their speech rendered into poetry. In this political poetry the politics are deeply encoded in the language itself, so that Rukeyser does not need slogans about workers to celebrate their dignity, importance, and humanity. She has the committee speak in a voice of steel, but in *The Book of the Dead* individual workers like Blankenship are not militant members of the vanguard. They are decent men and women who needed work, were lied to and exploited by the company, and are now saying modestly, "it will be appreciated / if you can do anything for me." Like the speakers who follow, however, Mearl Blankenship is a member of the defense committee, so that he is doing more than politely asking.

"Absalom"

In the next in a series of poems in which the workers and their families speak in their own words, in "Absalom" (pp. 27–30) the speaker is Mrs. Jones, another member of the defense committee and the mother not of one but of three sons who have died of silicosis. Her husband is dying and unable to work. Her language is straightforward and affecting:

Shirley was my youngest son; the boy.
He went into the tunnel.
   My heart   my mother   my heart   my mother
   My heart   my coming into being.

Rukeyser juxtaposes the mother's words with what becomes a lamentation as she moves to her poem Spell B of the Egyptian *Book of the Dead*. Rukeyser focuses on the heart and the mother as integral to her political art. She also elides the promise of life ("my coming into being") with the mother's revelations about sickness and death, first of her three sons, culminating in Shirley, the Absalom of the poem, and then of her husband, in the immediately following line, "my husband is not able to work." This simple statement gains force from its juxtaposition and contrast of styles with the suggestive lamentation from the Egyptian *Book of the Dead*. Is Shirley the lamenting voice of "*my heart my mother*"? Does he merge with the dead Egyptian whose heart "is weighed in the scales of the balance against the feather of righteousness"?[14] For him is there a promise of life or an exposure of the suffering and death the company has caused—or both? Or are the "my" of "my heart" and "my husband" the same? Does the dead Egyptian merge with Mrs. Jones and compound the sense of social, economic, and political wrong? Or are we to keep all of these possibilities in mind? In any case, in the remainder of the poem Rukeyser continues to juxtapose Mrs. Charles Jones's testimony (*Investigation*, pp. 37–40) with fragments from the Egyptian *Book of the Dead*. This opening up of possibilities and a denial of closure is basic to Rukeyser's avant-garde political art in which she fuses documentary precision, powerful feeling, and a range of languages.

In the fullest sense Mrs. Jones cares for her son:

Shirley was sick about three months.
I would carry him from his bed to the table,
from his bed to the porch, in my arms.

   My heart is mine in the place of hearts,
   They gave me back my heart, it lies in me.

The quotations from the Egyptian *The Book of the Dead* center on the heart, the seat of feeling, humanity, and life.[15] These connotations reinforce Mrs. Jones's humanity, intensify her sense of loss and, as she continues, expose what the doctors lack. Dr. Harless in particular refuses to X-ray the boys because "he did not know where his money was coming from." Mrs. Jones goes on,

I promised him half if he'd work to get compensation,
but even then he would not do anything.
I went on the road and begged the X-ray money,
the Charleston hospital made the lung pictures,
he took the case after the pictures were made.

Mrs. Jones adds Shirley's words and feelings to the account. When he dies he wants his mother to have him opened up to

"see if that dust killed me.
"Try to get compensation,
"you will not have any way of making your living
"when we are gone,
"and the rest are going too."

   I have gained mastery over my heart
   I have gained mastery over my two hands
   I have gained mastery over the waters
   I have gained mastery over the river.

The chant from *The Book of the Dead* amplifies and gives urgency to this narrative of suffering and loss. The positive note of "mastery over my heart," the sense of renewal, and the invocation of "the waters" and "the river," with their reference both to the river at Gauley Bridge and the waters and river of life—these positive associations also throw into ironic relief Mrs. Jones's narrative of legal manipulation, company power, and government hostility:

The case of my son was the first of the line of lawsuits.
They sent the lawyers down and the doctors down;
they closed the electric sockets in the camps.

As she continues the names of the dead resonate, as do the place names—"the whole valley is witness." In a compressed style Rukeyser has Mrs. Jones establish the role of the relief officials who refuse to mail checks so that

> I hitchhike eighteen miles, they make checks out.
> They asked me how I keep the cow on $2.
> I said one week, feed for the cow, one week, the children's flour.

What gradually emerges is that after the doctors first called what the boys had pneumonia or "would pronounce it fever,"

> Shirley asked that we try to find out.
> That's how they learned what the trouble was.

From Shirley, who has opened out a way into the tragedy, Rukeyser segues to the last of the quotations from *The Book of the Dead*,

> *I open out a way, they have covered my sky with crystal*
> *I come forth by day, I am born a second time,*
> *I force a way through, and I know the gate*
> *I shall journey over the earth among the living.*

Rukeyser has previously associated crystal with the deadly silica, one of the multiple ironies her montage generates. In particular, in the context of Rukeyser's poem the traditional affirmation of rebirth has a specifically human and implicitly radical connotation, reinforced by the mother's concluding declaration:

> He shall not be diminished, never;
> I shall give a mouth to my son.

"The Disease"

Mrs. Jones speaks as a mother. Like Rukeyser, she does not proceed in a linear way and, though the word is not hers, the heart is alive throughout her account. Her words, her voice, constitute a discourse with values, accents, and insights significantly different from those of the impersonal doctor who testifies in "The Disease" (pp. 31–32). In juxtaposing "Absalom" and "The Disease," Rukeyser highlights some of the differences Carol Gilligan discusses in *In a Different Voice*. These differences between masculine and feminine discourses animate and complicate the political art of *The Book of the Dead*.

The doctor who is testifying as an expert gives a scientific, detached account that Rukeyser periodically interrupts to highlight the facts and to undercut the impersonality of the lecture. In his way the doctor, too, is interested in the heart, although for him it takes the form of describing the heart in a series of X-rays that illustrate the stages of silicosis. In the second stage, for example, "here is the heart. / More numerous nodules, thicker, see, in the upper lobes." As he continues into the third stage, the doctor says,

> And now this year—short breathing, solid scars
> even over the ribs, thick on both sides.
> Blood vessels shut. Model conglomeration.

Then an abrupt interruption in another voice, another discourse, the words of one of the men who restates the doctor's facts:

> "It is growing worse every day. At night
> "I get up to catch my breath. If I remained
> "flat on my back I believe I would die."

In the counterpoint of the poem the questions of a congressman and the words of the dying man both expose the way the doctor avoids direct, human statements at the same time that all three discourses drive home the fatality of a disease that "gradually chokes off the air cells in the lungs," causes "difficulty in breathing . . . and a painful cough," and, finally,

> Does silicosis cause death?
> Yes, sir.

"George Robinson: Blues"

Although Rukeyser undercuts it, the doctor's scientific voice predominates in "The Disease." After this interlude, Rukeyser shifts back again to the voice and point of view of the men in the tunnel in the contrasting language of "George Robinson: Blues" (pp. 33–34). In this poem Rukeyser does full justice to a form as highly valued in Popular Front circles as the black worker who begins,

> Gauley Bridge is a good town for Negroes, they let us stand around, they let us stand
> around on the sidewalks if we're black or brown.
> Vanetta's over the trestle, and that's our town.

Through Robinson's subdued irony and awareness, Rukeyser has him quietly expose this "good town." She has him continue to affirm his own blues sensibility even as he returns to locales and conditions we have been prepared for in earlier poems:

> The hill makes breathing slow, slow breathing after you row the river,
> and the graveyard's on the hill, cold in the springtime blow,
> the graveyard's up on high, and the town is down below.

The hill and the slow breathing, the river and the graveyard are by now familiar but that the graveyard is on the hill looking down on the town below is new and so are the suggestions of a mythic crossing to death. Rukeyser is equally effective with the slow beat, the repetitions, and the internal rhymes.

As this blues song unfolds, Robinson looks at the ways men died,

> thirty-five tunnel workers the doctors didn't attend,
> died in the tunnel camps, under rocks, everywhere, world without end.
>
> . . . .
>
> When the blast went off the boss would call out, Come, let's go back,
> when that heavy loaded blast went white, Come, let's go back,
> telling us hurry, hurry, into the falling rocks and muck.

Vivian Jones and Mearl Blankenship have prepared us for the blast and the dust but Robinson drives home the immediacy of "falling rocks and muck" and he begins associating the explosions and dust with race, with the white that covers everything. The drinking water, "the camps and their groves were colored with the dust,"

> it stayed and the rain couldn't wash it away and it twinkled
> that white dust really looked pretty down around our
>   ankles.

The white dust is the great equalizer:

> As dark as I am, when I came out at morning after the tunnel at night,
> with a white man, nobody could have told which man was white.
> The dust had covered us both, and the dust was white.

Ashes to ashes, black to white—but not as part of a natural, ageless process but as a result of the silica dust, the blasts, and all the racial and economic forces that drive them, forces Robinson implies and Rukeyser suggests elsewhere in *The Book of the Dead*.

Rukeyser gets inside and celebrates George Robinson as much through the form of the blues as through the compelling explicit content. In the range of languages and forms in *The Book of the Dead*, "George Robinson: Blues" is memorable for its restrained revelations about race, working conditions, and the way men died; for Rukeyser's unself-conscious mastery of the blues; and for the ironic protest of the black speaker.

"Juanita Tinsley"

In moving from George Robinson's sensibility to that of another member of the defense committee, Juanita Tinsley, "the one outsider member" (p. 21), Rukeyser speaks in the voice and from the point of view of a dedicated woman from a more privileged social class than the others (pp. 35–36). "I know in America there are songs," Juanita Tinsley says,

> forgetful ballads to be sung,
> but at home I see this wrong.

We understand that along with illuminating Juanita Tinsley's conscience and commitment and her attraction to the "forgetful ballads," Rukeyser is also reminding us that songs like "George Robinson: Blues" or the balladlike "Mearl Blankenship" are not at all "forgetful."

Rukeyser deftly sketches Juanita Tinsley's circumstances, "my family house, / the gay gorge, the picture books" and then the association of "the face of General Wise / aged by enemies, like faces the stranger showed me in the town." As another motive for action, she connects the patrician general suffering from his enemies and the "faces . . . in the town," also "aged by enemies": "I saw that plain, and saw my place." Reversing Eliot, Juanita Tinsley associates April with the hope ahead,

> and next month with a softer wind,
> maybe they'll rest upon the land,
> and then maybe the happy song, and love,
> a tall boy who was never in a tunnel.

The pathos emerges from the contrast between "the happy song, and love"—"the forgetful ballads"—and the grim world of the tall boy in the tunnel.

"The Doctors"

This principled, "feminine" discourse highlights the contrasting documentary style of "The Doctors" (pp. 37–41), which begins with direct quotations from the court record of Mr. Bacon's examination of Dr. Hayhurst. The abrupt change from "Juanita Tinsley" and the stark differences with the language of the conventional "happy song" give added interest to the accumulating list of Dr. Hayhurst's scientific credentials, replete with dates, figures, and names that ordinarily do not appear in canonical poetry:

> director of clinic 2½ years.
> Ph.D. Chicago 1916
> Ohio Dept. of Health, 20 years as
> consultant in occupational diseases.
> Hygienist, U.S. Public Health Service
> and Bureau of Mines
> and Bureau of Standards.

The last two lines give a quiet emphasis to a stanza that has its own integrity and appeal, not the least of which is the authority it gives to Dr. Hayhurst's succeeding testimony. As she does with Dr. Hayhurst's credentials, Rukeyser compresses and rearranges his words for emphasis and to heighten the sense of ordinary speech. As he reveals,

> Danger begins at 25%
> here was pure danger
> Dept. of Mines
> came in, was kept away.

After we realize the full significance of this recurring feature of the labor history of West Virginia, Rukeyser has Dr. Hayhurst give a list of the names silicosis used to be called—"miner's phthisis, fibroid phithisis, / grinder's rot, potter's rot"—ending with the simple judgment, "These men did not need to die."

Without mentioning his name or the fact that he is the newspaperman who investigated Gauley Bridge for the *Pittsburgh Press*, Rukeyser then moves to the testimony of Gilbert Love, who establishes that Dr. Harless, the company doctor, had backed down under pressure, or as Love discreetly puts it, "I cannot say that / he has retracted what he told me, but possibly he had been / thrust into the limelight so much that he is more conservative / now than when the matter was simply something of local interest." Dr. Harless refuses to appear before the Committee—"Dear Sir: Due to illness of my wife and urgent professional / duties, I am unable to appear as per your telegram." But he does argue, "situation exaggerated" and that, although "I am sure that many of these suits were based on / meritorious grounds, I am also convinced that many others / took advantage of this situation and made out of it nothing less than a racket."

The charge that the victims are somehow taking advantage, are involved in a racket, has a long history continuing into the present discourse on welfare and poverty. In the case of Dr. Harless—we recall him from Mrs. Jones's poem—the prose form itself, set off on the page from, for example, Dr. Hayhurst's lines, further undermines his credibility. Even within the baldly documentary poems, Rukeyser varies and plays off against the form.

Another interest in this documentary poem is the drama Rukeyser creates: without speaking in her own voice she uses the testimony of Dr. Hayhurst and Gilbert Love to frame Dr. Harless's conventional minimizing of the problem and then she has Congressman Marcantonio expose the contradictions in Dr. Harless's position. Under the shadow of men dying of acute silicosis, Rukeyser also uses exchanges between Dr. Goldwater and Congressman Griswold about the causes of the disease to satirize the doctors' practice of qualifying their statements. She juxtaposes a long-winded speech dodging the issue of causes with a simple, idiomatic line: "Mr. Griswold. Best doctor I ever knew said 'no' and 'yes.'"

In keeping with an aesthetic that values diverse languages, montage, and reader involvement, Rukeyser interrupts the documentary language of the hearing with a sphinxlike commentary:

The man in the white coat is the man on the hill,
the man with the clean hands is the man with the drill,
the man who answers "yes" lies still.

And then a final series from the trial court record to establish over the company's objections—"objection overruled"—that the lungs in question were silicotic. At the end Rukeyser stages a quiet drama in which truth wins out over the corporate lawyers at the same time that she shows the fatality of the disease as a medical illness with origins in a network of power and profit.

"The Cornfield"

Not quite by accident Rukeyser then slips in another take on Gauley Bridge. In "The Cornfield" (pp. 42–44) she returns us from the courtroom, the hearing, and the language of experts and brings into focus, from the inside, the graveyard cornfield, the H. C. White Funeral Services, and White's activities as integral to *The Book of the Dead*, both to her poem and its Egyptian namesake. "Error, disease, snow, sudden weather" Rukeyser begins, without preamble and in the notation form she favors. We have seen the weather from the beginning and the error and disease have accumulated. They gain added meaning as Rukeyser takes us into White's "good car," the one he used to transport corpses to the cornfield.

They say blind corpses rode
with him in front, knees broken into angles,
head clamped ahead.

White has falsified death certificates to name pneumonia, pleurisy, and tuber-
culosis as the causes of death, instead of silicosis. A good old southern boy, he

tells about Negroes who got wet at work,
shot craps, drank and took cold, pneumonia, died.
Shows the sworn papers. Swear by the corn.
Pneumonia, pneumonia, pleurisy, t.b.

At the start of the stanza, juxtaposed with the "blind corpses," Rukeyser has
prepared for the interjected refrain line, "swear by the corn":

Swear by the corn,
the found-land corn, those who like ritual.

This swearing is the reverse of White's "sworn papers." The refrain has a strong,
ironic charge. Rukeyser invokes the ritual world of the Egyptian *Book of the Dead*,
the ancient world of death and renewal, of the slain and resurrected corn and other
fertility gods from Isis and Demeter to Christ. These ritual associations with "the
corn" merge with the Gauley Bridge cornfield, with the slain, blind corpses and the
falsified affidavits, with "the cornfield, white and wired by thorns, / old cornstalks,
snow, the planted home." The thorns are both literal and suggestive of Christ; "the
planted home" is both "this house . . . sealed with clay" of the first stanza and the
dead White has planted. Through association with the slain corn gods, the corpses
buried beneath the corn assume the status of martyred divinities. Rukeyser holds
in suspension the issue of their resurrection.

That it will take the form of a radical political renewal is implicit in her indictment of the racism, the lying, and the Union Carbide contractor, "Rinehart &
Dennis, [who] paid him $55 / a head for burying these men in plain pine boxes."
She calls on George Robinson to expose how fast the men were buried to prevent
investigation:

I knew a man
who died at four in the morning at the camp.
At seven his wife took clothes to dress her dead
husband, and at the undertaker's
they told her the husband was already buried.

In "The Cornfield" Rukeyser has something for everyone: "For those given to contemplation: this house" we have visited. For "those who like ritual . . . Swear by the corn." And

> For those who like voyages: these roads
> discover gullies, invade, Where does it go now?
> Now turn upstream twenty-five yards. Now road again.
> Ask the man on the road. Saying, That cornfield?

From the opening "The Road" Rukeyser takes us to "these roads" and "that cornfield." For connoisseurs of cornfields,

> For those given to keeping their own garden:
> Here is the cornfield, white and wired by thorns

Eliot's Hieronymo never sprouted in a garden so charged with implied radical political protest.

Rukeyser opens up these implications. She gives a meticulous rendering of the unmarked graves,

> unmarked except for wood stakes, charred at tip,
> few scratched and named (pencil or nail).
> Washed-off. Under the mounds,
> all the anonymous.

Then, in a different voice, partly her own, partly one of the Egyptian dead, partly the Gauley dead, she turns to

> Abel America, calling from under the corn,
> Earth, uncover my blood!
> Did the undertaker know the man was married?
> Uncover.
> Do they seem to fear death?
> Contemplate.
> Does Mellon's ghost walk, povertied at last,
> walking in furrows of corn, still sowing,
> do apparitions come?

The fractured, discontinuous verse, the allusions, and the command of the Egyptian dead and those buried in the cornfield, "Earth, uncover my blood!" combine to generate a sense of passionate urgency. Rukeyser intensifies the command by repetition: "Uncover" and later, "Contemplate," a new application of this word first introduced in the opening stanza. Through the compression of "Abel America" all of America is now identified with the Gauley dead calling for a full uncovering. These dead, moreover, are identified both with the ancient Egyptians and with Abel slain by a Cain Rukeyser points to through the spectacle of "Mellon's ghost" incongruously "walking in furrows of corn, still sowing."

Mellon, the millionaire banker, one of the three richest and most powerful Americans, was of special interest to Rukeyser because he was, among other positions, head of the aluminum monopoly, the Aluminum Company of America, which kept up the price of aluminum ware, controlled the aluminum wire needed for long-distance electrical transmission, and kept down the production of the metal used in manufacturing airplanes. Mellon's fortune and business practices had been in the news throughout 1935 because the government was prosecuting him for income tax evasion and two years earlier he had been the subject of Harvey O'Connor's hard-hitting *Mellon's Millions: The Biography of a Fortune*, with chapter titles like "The Perfect Monopoly—Aluminum," "Petroleum Diplomacy," "Miners and Machine Guns," "The Mellon Machine in Politics," and "The Fortune Goes Marching On." Mellon, hardly "povertied at last," is from a left perspective the very embodiment of American capitalism. Rukeyser ironically merges him with both Cain and the world of fertility and resurrection. What is he "still sowing" and what of the "apparitions" that haunt the land, his "ghost" and the apparitions of the corpses beneath the corn?

As for the line "do they fear death?" it echoes an earlier question about "the men who have this disease":

—Do they seem to be living in fear
or do they wish to die?

Rukeyser holds this question in reserve. First she returns to the garden, engaging us as she has throughout by direct address:

Think of your gardens. But here is corn to keep.
Marked pointed sticks to name the crop beneath.
Sowing is over, harvest is coming ripe.

To reinforce the affirmation of the revolutionary harvest that will avenge and reap "the crop beneath," the dead inseparable from their slayers, Rukeyser supplies the answer to the question that has been posed twice and that she has held in suspension:

—No, sir; they want to go on.
They want to live as long as they can.

More fully than in any of the preceding poems, in "The Cornfield," another of her politically radical variations on modernist themes and techniques, Rukeyser brings together the Egyptian, the revolutionary, and the documentary languages that compel her imagination.

"Arthur Peyton"

In "Arthur Peyton" (pp. 45–46), the next poem, the affirmative, revolutionary note of "The Cornfield" is subordinated to Rukeyser's rendering of the personal cost Peyton has paid and the $21.59 he has received. Rukeyser includes the lawyer's letter

> enclosing herewith our check . . .
> payable to you, for $21.59
>   being one-half of the residue which
>   we were able to collect in your behalf
>   in regard to the above case.
> In winding up the various suits,
>   after collecting all we could,
>   we find this balance due you.

The verse format emphasizes the lawyers' banal stock phrases and underlying fraud by highlighting them and implicitly contrasting them with more customary poetic language and sentiments. Rukeyser juxtaposes this document with the contrasting series of words and phrases that open the poem:

> Consumed. Eaten away. And love across the street.

In contrast to the deadly, coherent logic of the letter, Peyton's personal tragedy comes through in the fragments that render his disturbed emotional state, consumed, eaten away by the disease, and as a result, as we discover, unable to marry his "love across the street."

In the remainder of "Arthur Peyton" Rukeyser uses montage to engage us, to make us feel, and to open up the human and inhuman implications of the Gauley situation. She brings together and strikes sparks from the two languages she has started with, the personal language of love, distress, and disease and the public language of the lawyer, the doctor, and of Peyton in his role as engineer as distinct from lover and victim. Take the sequence

> After collecting
>   the dust   the failure   the engineering corps

> O love   consumed   eaten away   the foreman laughed
> they wet the drills when the inspector came
> the moon blows glassy over our native river.

"After collecting the dust"? The $21.59 as dust? The dust, the failure, the engineering corps: the failure to inspect or to allow inspections, the signals the laughing foremen used to warn the men to wet drill, but only when the inspector came—this indictment and these "failures" elide with the resulting "dust" and with the lawyer's swindle of $21.59 and all it represents about the failure to protect and compensate the men. The interspersed repetition, "O love   consumed   eaten away" now has a fuller context so that the lament of "O love" resonates and merges not only with the failures (the foreman's laugh, the failure to inspect, the dry drilling, the fatal dust, and the resulting failure of love) but also with the ironically romantic moon "glassy"—the silica again—"over our native river." At the end, Rukeyser returns to and varies the image of the glass and "our native river."

First, however, she continues to merge public and private languages, as in the touching

> O love tell the committee that I know:
> never repeat you mean to marry me.
> In mines, the fans are large (2,000 men unmasked)
>   before his verdict the doctor asked me How long

What Peyton knows is that his disease and his love impel him to say "never repeat you mean to marry me." As a mining engineer he also knows that in mines but not in the tunnel "the fans are large" and that the 2,000 unmasked men are sick and dying. And he knows that in his exchanges with the doctor not only did the doctor ask him questions but he himself also asked, "How long":

> I said, Dr. Harless, tell me how long?
> —Only never again tell me you'll marry me.

The pathos of Peyton's situation, its causes, and the pain of his concern emerge gradually through his repeated plea and its varied contexts. Rukeyser suggests but does not spell out Peyton's story. She uses montage and central details to get us to fill in.

We gradually learn, for example, that Peyton not only cares for his love but also for his region, for the beauty of

> the sky birds who crown the trees
> the white white hills standing upon Alloy

Without a pause, Rukeyser uses Peyton's sensitivity, involvement, and his own situation to intensify his juxtaposed charge:

—I charge negligence, all companies concerned—
two years O love two years he said he gave.

The beauty of "the white white hills," moreover, is inseparable from the deadly silica that constitutes this "hill of glass" (p. 47) and contributes to Peyton's indictment. However forceful she is, throughout "Arthur Peyton" and *The Book of the Dead*, Rukeyser understates the charges against the companies, their racism, and the system of corporate capitalism they represent, as she does in Peyton's simple statement, "I saw the Negroes driven with pick handles." Rukeyser refrains from opening up the spectacle of the white foremen driving black workers back into the tunnel after the blasting.

At the end, Rukeyser has Peyton gather together into a powerful new configuration details, images, and preoccupations that have been on his mind throughout his poem:

the long glass street   two years, my death to yours
my death upon your lips
my face becoming glass

Instead of "my lips to yours," it is "my death to yours / my death upon your lips," so that the unnamed reality, death, becomes explicit for the first time fused with, also for the first time, the sexual intimacy of his love. Not only in Peyton's "glassy" moon but also throughout *The Book of the Dead*, glass has figured, as it does increasingly in the surreal images that drive "Arthur Peyton" to its close. Peyton's face becomes the glass that is killing him and, in a variation on the image, their thwarted love turns into

a mirror of our valley
our street   our river   a deadly glass to hold.

"Our native river," "our valley," "our street"—Peyton is rooted in this communal world now mirrored in a deadly glass. Peyton's representative agony emerges in his final cry,

Now they are feeding me into a steel mill furnace
O love the stream of glass a stream of living fire.

Phillipa Allen revealed that, in Peyton's words, "all companies concerned" knew the value of the silica to be used by Electro-Metallurgical to make steel. Through

Arthur Peyton, Rukeyser reveals the human cost, the human agony, of using human beings to make steel.

"Alloy"

"Arthur Peyton" is the last of the dramatic monologues in *The Book of the Dead*. In "Alloy" (pp. 47–48) Rukeyser immediately reinforces what she has rendered in Peyton's voice. "This is the most audacious landscape," she begins, referring to the brilliant white hills around the town of Alloy. Then she seizes on the 1930s popular culture image of the audacious gangster to drive home the radical political insight that

> The gangster's
> stance with his gun smoking and out is not so
> vicious as this commercial field, its hill of glass.

To develop the image of the smoke generated by this vicious, more-than-criminal commercial field, Rukeyser, as she did with "the sky birds" and "the white white hills" in "Arthur Peyton," juxtaposes the beauty and "the stored destruction" of the landscape as the smoke rises to form clouds over the hills of Alloy:

> Sloping as gracefully as thighs, the foothills
> narrow to this, clouds over every town
> finally indicate the stored destruction.
> . . . .
> And down the track, the overhead conveyor
> slides on its cable to the feet of chimneys.
> Smoke rises, not white enough, not so barbaric.

In stanzas like

> Hottest for silicon, blast furnaces raise flames,
> spill fire, spill steel, quench the new shape to freeze,
> tempering it to perfected metal

Rukeyser continues to develop a sense of the actual steel-making process. The intense heat of "the electric furnaces produce this precious, this clean, / annealing the crystals, fusing at last alloys." What they also produce are the dead workers who, like Arthur Peyton, are fed into the living fire of the furnace. In "Alloy" it is not one but "a million men . . . forced through this crucible." Then,

Above this pasture, the highway passes those
who curse the air, breathing their fear again.

Does Rukeyser ironically imply that those on the road, like the reader and the poet, are "above" the suffering below? In any case, Rukeyser juxtaposes the machine and the garden to convey the "curse," the protest of the men. Using "breathing" in a double sense, she simultaneously fuses their breathing of the poisoned air with "breathing their fear"—their fear of death, their fear that instead of air they are breathing dust and death.

This compression of the physical reality and the moral and political response prepares for the even more powerful ending:

The roaring flowers of the chimney-stacks
less poison, at their lips in fire, than this
dust that is blown from off the field of glass;
blows and will blow, rising over the mills,
crystallized and beyond the fierce corrosion
disintegrated angel on these hills.

The dark, satanic mills are reconstituted on American soil in an intense reversal of the promise of the American Dream Rukeyser had invoked in "West Virginia." The fatal, poisoned dust "blows and will blow." Just as the deadly glass becomes Arthur Peyton's face, the crystallized dust endures "beyond the fierce corrosion" and becomes the "disintegrated angel," the symbol of white, heavenly perfection turned into gleaming crystals the very opposite of angelic.

"Power"

As she gathers momentum, Rukeyser amplifies the religious and political implications of "Alloy" in the crucial sequence, "Power" and "The Dam." Before she moves into the depths, first of the powerhouse, then of the dam, in "Power" (pp. 49–53) Rukeyser draws on the resources of classical poetic forms and language to bring alive the setting: "the quick sun," the warm mountains, a vital, sexualized landscape that answers to the love and sexualized body of the poet who "sees perfect cliffs ranging until the river / cuts sheer, mapped far below in delicate track, / surprise of grace . . . as lovers who look too long on the desired face / startle to find the remote flesh so warm." The heat of the day is life-giving, not the terrifying, deadly heat of "Alloy" and "Arthur Peyton." Rukeyser begins and ends the first stanza of "Power" with images of the life-giving sun in what could be a marvelously sensual love poem paying tribute to

A day of heat shed on the gorge, a brilliant
day when love sees the sun behind its man
and the disguised marvel under familiar skin.

By the poem's final line, "this is the end," "the suns declare midnight."

Before she can move into the depths to face death and night, however, Rukeyser must first enter the powerhouse. From above her eye follows the power lines' "narrow-waisted towers" until she reaches the powerhouse standing

skin-white at the transmitters' side
over the rapids   the brilliance   the blind foam.

Answering to her own ambivalence about the power she is dealing with, Rukeyser's verse form becomes more irregular, more agitated than in the first stanza as she gives us once more "the rapids   the brilliance   the blind foam" that drive the turbines.

The powerhouse we are entering is "midway between water and flame," midway between the water of the dam and the flame of the furnace. The elemental language also suggests the ritualistic water and flame of the Egyptian *Book of the Dead*. The powerhouse is transitional, a stage not only in the transmission of electricity but also in a process of death and renewal, a renewal Rukeyser has prepared for in the sensuous celebration of the opening stanza. Having raised these expectations, however, Rukeyser immediately qualifies them by applying the grim and, as it turns out, revolutionary word "terminal" to the powerhouse and all it stands for. "Terminal" also casts its shadow and hope on the reiterated refrain line from the opening poem, "this is the road to take when you think of your country," a line that renews our sense of the promise and betrayal of America fused with the journey on the Osiris Way, a journey that has political as well as religious implications.

Inside the powerhouse Rukeyser responds to the colors, "the effective green, grey-toned and shining," to the "tall immense chamber of cylinders" and the play of light and color as "the rich paint catches light from three-story windows, / arches of light vibrate erratic panels on / sides of curved steel." As Rukeyser moves into the depths of the powerhouse, the light becomes increasingly symbolic but at first it has a precise, visual, documentary existence. Rukeyser similarly focuses on the "wheels, control panels, dials, the vassal instruments" of a technology she both values and connects with death, "terminal." In this setting she gives us the creator and presiding spirit of the powerhouse, "the engineer Jones, the blueprint man, / loving the place he designed, visiting it alone." His identifying line is "This is the place."

As they descend the stairs, Jones, ignoring or unaware of the men killed building the tunnel, announces that "they said I built the floor like the tiles of a bank, / I wanted the men who work here to be happy." His intentions, including the probably unflattering reference to the bank, are still bathed in "light laughing on steel, the gay, the tall sun / given away." In her next line, "the iron steps go down as roads go down," Rukeyser continues to keep alive the sense of the journey on the road with its American and Egyptian connotations.

Now in "the second circle, world of inner shade," Rukeyser precisely records the "hidden bulk of generators, governor shaft, / round gap of turbine pit" and further down, "here are the outlets, butterfly valves / open from here, the tail-race, vault of steel, the spiral staircase ending, last light in shaft." This technological world is also a "world of inner shade" whose relation to the Egyptian *Book of the Dead* is reinforced by saying explicitly of the entire region, particularly the wire flooring of the turbine pit, "this is the scroll, the volute case of night, / quick shadow and the empty galleries." "Inner shade," "night," and "last light in shaft" mark the change from the sunlit world of the opening, a change Jones underscores with the single word, "gone."

In the midst of this dark, powerfully suggestive setting, Rukeyser abruptly intrudes a contrasting voice, language, and tradition, Miltonic and Old Testament:

" 'Hail, holy light, offspring of Heav'n first-born,
'Or of th' Eternal Coeternal beam
'May I express thee unblamed?' "

Rukeyser has already established the blame. From the vantage point of Milton's religiously charged language and the central symbol of light (*Paradise Lost*, 3.1–3), the corporate and technological world of the powerhouse emerges as a blasphemous bringer of light. What is at issue is a primal violation of the West's most basic divine and secular principles.

Moving still further into the underworld, Rukeyser records the fear that accompanies both a descent into darkness on the "uncertain rungs" of a steep ladder and the fear that accompanies entry into a region associated with death. In this suggestive setting, Jones amplifies his identification with the place he has created:

"This is the place. Away from this my life
I am indeed Adam unparadiz'd.

Some fools call this the Black Hole of Calcutta,
I don't know how they ever get to Congress."

Rukeyser mixes high and low languages to endow Jones with a sense of humor and to develop the themes of death and Paradise Lost. Jones speaks about his "life" in a place of death. And, although he does not realize it, it is precisely *in* his place that he is "indeed Adam unparadiz'd," an identification that resonates with the quotation from *Paradise Lost* and with the underlying theme of the lost American Dream, or, rather, with the accumulating sense that the technological and economic power associated with the Gauley Tunnel are inseparable from the loss of the promise of America.

Spiraling downward on "the drunken ladder," in contrast to the earlier play of light and color Rukeyser now stresses that "a naked bulb / makes glare, turns paler, burns to dark again. Brilliance begins, stutters." In this uncertain light, or dark, she leaves Jones, "the tall abstract," and encounters "the ill, the unmasked men" of the Gauley Tunnel. These dead enter through association with the mask of the welder who says directly,

"A little down,
five men were killed in widening the tunnel."

Rukeyser herself now enters the tunnel,

Shell of bent metal; walking along an arc
the tube rounds up about your shoulders, black
circle, great circle, down infinite mountain rides,
echoes words, footsteps, testimonies.

Beneath "the second circle," in the tunnel, the "black circle, great circle," "words, footsteps, testimonies" echo:

"One said the air was thin, Fifth Avenue clean."

But despite this testimony before the subcommittee, the air was not clean. As Rukeyser penetrates further "along created gorges" she deepens the contrast with the earlier sunlit, heat-warmed gorge. Suddenly,

all the light burns out.
Down the reverberate channels of the hills
the suns declare midnight, go down, cannot ascend,
no ladder back; see this, your eyes can ride through steel,
this is the river Death, diversion of power,

the root of the tower and the tunnel's core,
this is the end.

The tunnel merges with the Egyptian underworld, the fear of being trapped merges with the fear of death without renewal, the reverse of the ritual drama enacted again and again in the Egyptian *Book of the Dead*. The river in West Virginia merges with the river Death, not, however, mechanically but to emphasize the connection with, in the fullest sense, the "diversion of power, / the root of the tower and the tunnel's core."

Within the political culture of the thirties left as well as within mainstream American culture, the dynamo and the triumphs of technology had an honored place. In "Power" Rukeyser counters this tendency with an intense, nuanced critique that draws energy from the Egyptian, Miltonic, and Marxist traditions. She goes into the depths, confronts death, the men killed in the widening of the tunnel, and, the light burned out, goes to the root and the core, the technology and the corporate capitalism, the diversion of power, and announces, "this is the end." Rukeyser is recording a moral and political judgment on the world of the powerhouse, on the diversion of power. Her concluding line has the force of "this should be and will be the end—a new, revolutionary world should follow." The religious and metaphysical associations of the Egyptian underworld and the Miltonic allusions deepen the moral and political implications but the sense of the "terminal," of "the end" is not in my judgment a pessimistic or despairing assertion of the finality of death.

"The Dam"

Rukeyser immediately emphasizes her political, aesthetic, and religious view of process, of endings leading to new beginnings. In the context of the water spilling over the great dam, she begins "The Dam" (pp. 54–58) by playing off against and opening up the underlying implications of "this is the end":

All power is saved, having no end. Rises
in the green season, in the sudden season
the white the budded
                    and the lost.

Rukeyser celebrates the natural process of the water rising in the spring, "the green season," itself part of the process of "the white the budded" merging with "the lost" that, however, is also "saved, having no end." "The white the budded" suggests flowers and, in Rukeyser's continuing iconography, the silica white of the water, an association that gives a political dimension to the elliptical "the lost." In the context of "The Dam" and the whole of *The Book of the Dead*, moreover, the rising in the green season also has a compressed, radical implication that Rukeyser develops later in the poem. In her poetics, Rukeyser favors elliptical, compressed mergings that bring together ordinarily separated areas of feeling and thought. At the start of "The Dam" she brings together the ongoing natural power of the water and the seasons in a way that connects them with the silica white of the tunnel, the power of the dam, and the politics of the entire of the Gauley project. These associations with radical politics and natural processes are themselves intertwined with the religious rhythm of death and renewal connected with the Egyptian *Book of the Dead*, which Rukeyser soon quotes.

She first celebrates the beauty of the water falling over the dam, "yielding continually / sheeted and fast in its overfall, . . . falling, the water sheet / spouts, and the mind dances, excess of white," so that the mind, too, is involved. The "excess of white" is both a sign of beauty and disease, "white brilliant function of the land's disease." Rukeyser has already presented "the land's disease" in all of its dimensions: as silicosis, as the company's exploitation of the men, with "the land" generalizing out to America.

Before she develops these implications, Rukeyser again pays documentary tribute to the energy of the dam,

> Many-spanned, lighted, the crest leans under
> concrete arches and the channeled hills,
> turns in the gorge toward its release;
> kinetic and controlled, the sluice
> urging the hollow, the thunder,
> the major climax
> > energy
> total and open watercourse
> praising the spillway, the fiery glaze,
> crackle of light, cleanest velocity
> flooding, the moulded force.

Immediately after this rush of language, the perfect placement of "energy," and the concluding "crackle of light" and "moulded force," Rukeyser cuts to another language, a passage from the Egyptian *Book of the Dead*:

I open out a way over the water
I form a path between the Combatants:
Grant that I sail down like a living bird,
power over the fields and Pool of Fire.
Phoenix, I sail over the phoenix world.

The water, the Pool of Fire, and the power of the god pick up images and themes Rukeyser has been developing. The religious promise of renewal and eternal life puts in perspective the land's disease, the thunder and the fiery glaze, even as the phoenix and the phoenix world look ahead to the revolutionary implications Rukeyser invokes at the end of "The Dam."

She also looks back, not only to the end of "Power" but also to "West Virginia." In "West Virginia" she had evoked the early explorers who "saw rivers flow west and hoped again." She connected this version of the American Dream with its denial, Kanawha Falls and all it signifies, and that in turn with "spilled water which the still pools fed. / Kanawha Falls, the rapids of the mind, / fast waters spilling west." In "The Dam" Rukeyser again evokes "the white surf filling west, / the hope, fast water spilled where still pools fed." This sense of American possibility and its denial merges with the rendered particulars of this specific site "between the rock and the sunset, / the caretaker's house and the steep abutment, / . . . Steep gorge, the wedge of crystal in the sky." The dam, "the wedge of crystal in the sky," is again associated with the deadly, beautiful crystal. And the "fast water spilled where still pools fed" now has a much fuller resonance than when Rukeyser first used this language in "West Virginia."

After this complex fusion of personal and political languages, Rukeyser immediately adds a contrasting language, another discourse, to her accumulating flow of associations with the dam and the entire Gauley project. She raises the technical questions

How many feet of whirlpools?
What is a year in terms of falling water?
Cylinders; kilowatts; capacities.

Her response is the scientific language of equations, of

Continuity: $\Sigma Q = 0$
Equations for falling water.

This scientific "balance sheet of energy that flows / passing along its infinite barrier" reinforces the sense of infinite power "having no end." But in *The Book of the Dead* the scientific discourse itself is subordinated to Rukeyser's political, personal, documentary, and religious concerns.

In "The Dam," for example, Rukeyser converts her own work into a document and then, as she does with the congressional hearings, she subtly reworks her own words as she has earlier done with Philippa Allen's and Mrs. Jones's and as she will soon do again with the congressmen. She brings together in a new way revised lines from "Praise of the Committee" (p. 23). There, referring to the corporations who have broken the men and the hills, she had acutely written, "they have broken the hills and cracked the riches wide." In "Praise of the Committee" she had given us the unified defense committee: "here is a room of eyes, / a single force looks out, reading our lives." And in a series of questions she had merged the Egyptian and the Gauley dead, "running in these rigid hills," "warning the night, / shouting and young to waken our eyes." They also run "through electric wires." At the end, militantly, "their hands touched mastery; now they / demand an answer."

The corporation, the defense committee, and the Gauley and Egyptian dead are the referents of the "they" and "who" of the lines from "Praise of the Committee." In "The Dam" Rukeyser changes "they" to "it" and goes on to characterize the energy of the falling water:

It breaks the hills, cracking the riches wide,
runs through electric wires;
it comes, warning the night,
running among these rigid hills,
a single force to waken our eyes.

Instead of a scientifically neutral "balance-sheet of energy," the power of the dam and water is now associated with corporate exploitation, with "cracking the riches wide" and the accompanying agony Rukeyser has repeatedly shown. Now "it comes, warning the night." The energy running through the electric wires is now inseparable from the dead who have made the electricity possible. At the end of the stanza, merged with the united front of the defense committee, the energy of water and dam becomes "a single force to waken our eyes."

Rukeyser moves from this compressed, subtle warning to a much more explicit political critique, one of the most overt and hard-hitting in *The Book of the Dead*:

They poured the concrete and the columns stood,
laid bare the bedrock, set the cells of steel,
a dam for monument was what they hammered home.

Blasted, and stocks went up;
insured the base,
and limousines
wrote their own graphs upon
roadbed and lifeline.

Through her play of mind and language, Rukeyser drives home that stock profits and a kind of monumental pride are responsible for the blasting and construction of the dam. She neatly reifies the privileged corporate owners who instead of people become "limousines." Through compression and her play of language, Rukeyser continues to pass judgment on an entire system in which stock profit graphs leave their imprint on "road bed and lifeline," on the physical world of the dam and on the lives—and deaths—of those who built it.

In this new context she then repeats

Their hands touched mastery:
wait for defense, solid across the world.

Associated as it is with the defense committee, the line now strongly suggests that the workers have "touched mastery," that after the abuse and domination she has recorded, in the class conflict they have allies: they "wait for defense, solid across the world."

The defense immediately begins at home with a series of quotations from the congressmen on the committee: "Mr. Griswold: 'A corporation is a body without a soul.'" Mr. Dunn and Mr. Marcantonio confirm their colleague by establishing that, far from the workers' perpetrating a racket, in Mr. Marcantonio's words,

I agree that a racket has been practised, but the most damnable racketeering that I have known is the paying of a fee to the very attorney who represented these victims. That is the most outrageous racket that has ever come within my knowledge.

Letting the juxtaposition speak for itself, Rukeyser then quotes Philippa Allen's testimony that "Mr. Jesse J. Ricks, the president of the Union Carbide & Carbon Corporation, / suggested that the stockholder / had better take this question up in a private conference."

In one sense "the dam is safe. A scene of power." The power is both corporate and physical but "the scene of power" also includes those whose "hands touched mastery," so that as a product of corporate capitalism, the dam is not safe. Rukeyser emphasizes the role of the system of investment and profit by including a facsimile of a newspaper stock and dividend quotation for Union Carbide (p. 57).

In the long, suggestive closing stanza of "The Dam" Rukeyser subtly merges the discourses she has brought to life in the poem. The effect is complex, as if she has superimposed layers of photographic images, now one of them becoming sharply visible and taking precedence, now another, but all of them simultaneously reinforcing the others. Abruptly juxtaposed with the immediately preceding discourse of capitalism and Marxist exposure, "this is a perfect fluid," Rukeyser begins, so that the water is her text. From the start, however, as she follows the course of this "perfect fluid" Rukeyser suggests several subtexts. The water may be "perfect,"

surviving scarless, unaltered, loving rest,
willing to run forever to find its peace
in equal seas in currents of still glass.

But this "perfect," timeless, "scarless" embodiment of natural vitality and eternal life highlights the contrast with the uses it has been put to. As Rukeyser has shown again and again, the "scarless" water is quite different from the scarred landscape and the scarred lungs and lives of the workers. The "peace" and the "currents of still glass" in particular recall Arthur Peyton's contrasting, agonized cry,

Now they are feeding me into a steel mill furnace
O love the stream of glass a stream of living fire.

Rukeyser goes on to fuse her earlier scientific discourse with a powerful political language. At first the elliptical phrase, "effects of friction," seems to come from the same world of technical discourse as "$\Sigma Q = 0$ / Equations for falling water." But as she specifies the "effects of friction," Rukeyser also develops an implied drama of class conflict:

Effects of friction: to fight and pass again,
learning its power, conquering boundaries,
able to rise blind in revolts of tide,
broken and sacrificed to flow resumed.

As she describes the water on its way to the dam, Rukeyser uses the language of political revolt, of the vicissitudes of fighting, "learning its power," "conquering boundaries," "rising blind in revolts," being "broken and sacrificed" to a "flow" that nonetheless continues. Because she withholds the subjects of her series of active infinitive and participial phrases, we are invited to fill in as Rukeyser strongly suggests an affinity between the power of the water and a struggling working class.

As her recognition of the "broken and sacrificed" indicates, Rukeyser knows about losses in the process of struggle and "blind" revolt. But even more she responds to the never-ending power the water both embodies and symbolizes. She immediately stresses this ongoing energy, though her word, "power," gives it a suggestive political resonance:

> Collecting eternally power. Spender of power,
> torn, never can be killed, speeded in filaments,
> million, its power can rest and rise forever,
> wait and be flexible. Be born again.

Beyond its association with the phoenix world of resurrection and the natural world of renewal, the "power" that in her opening "rises in the green season" now has an intensified radical connotation. Rukeyser continues to use the vitality of the water to affirm the rise of a new class and a new world not, perhaps, today but "its power can rest and rise forever, / wait and be flexible. Be born again."

At the end, Rukeyser returns to her beginning, characterizes the present of war and "confusion of force," and reaffirms her faith in a radical future:

> Nothing is lost, even among the wars,
> imperfect flow, confusion of force.
> It will rise. There are the phases of its face.
> It knows its seasons, the waiting, the sudden.
> It changes. It does not die.

Rukeyser again leaves open the "it" that "will rise," that "changes," and that "knows its seasons." The multiple implications of her ending that is also a beginning include the power of the natural world, the power of the phoenix of resurrection, and the power of revolutionary change. In the face of the wars and confusion of her period, Rukeyser affirms a radical faith that encompasses politics, religion, and nature.

"The Disease: After-Effects" and "The Bill"

Rukeyser juxtaposes this radical, modernist affirmation with two documentary poems. In "The Disease: After-Effects" (pp. 59–61) and "The Bill" (pp. 62–65) Rukeyser reanimates our sense of the full impact of silicosis, the inability of a liberal Congress to do any more than "recommend," and the corresponding need for a militant, radical response. At the start of "The Disease: After-Effects" Rukeyser has the unnamed radical congressman, Vito Marcantonio, propose a series of measures that bring alive the political climate of 1936. He proposes an "embargo on munitions / to Germany and Italy / as states at war with Spain." Complementing this Popular Front position, he supports the movement to "free Tom Moody," the radical questionably jailed for twenty years and repeatedly the subject of appeals to the governor of California. The congressman's last two proposals are "A bill for a TVA at Fort Peck dam. / A bill to prevent industrial silicosis."

Rukeyser then shifts to "the gentleman from Montana," the unnamed Congressman Jerry O'Connell. She has him go inside and into the past to place his current politics in the context of his own life and that of his working-class father. Through a series of personal, childhood memories, he recalls that as a five-year-old he clipped tea roses as "remembrance for strikers," including his father. As a striker "at the Anaconda mine" his father is connected with "the Socialist mayor we had in Butte"—"they broke" him, "shot father. He died: wounds and his disease. / My father had silicosis." Through O'Connell, Rukeyser develops the political etiology of "the disease." For us this congressional voice from the past is a reminder of what during the 1930s was acceptable public discourse.

Rukeyser then draws on Congressman Griswold's speech in the *Congressional Record*[16] to remind us that silicosis is, in her earlier phrase, "the land's disease": "widespread in trade, widespread in space! / Butte, Montana; Joplin, Missouri; the New York tunnels, / the Catskill Aqueduct. In over thirty States. / A disease worse than consumption." But "only eleven States have laws. / There are today one million potential victims. / 500,000 Americans have silicosis now. / These are the proportions of a war." Rukeyser develops the sense of war through personal images of "foreign parades, the living faces, / Asturian miners with my father's face, / wounded and fighting, the men at Gauley Bridge, / my father's face enlarged." She fuses the Spanish Asturian miners "wounded and fighting" Franco with her "father's face," just as she identifies "the men at Gauley Bridge" with "my father's face enlarged."

This personal and public identification of her wealthy father at one with the Spanish workers and the Gauley dead reemerges as a grim internationalist vision: "always now the map and X-ray seem / resemblent pictures of one living breath / one country marked by error / and one air." The X-ray and the "living breath," powerful emblems of silicosis, merge with the map of the "forgetful countries" suggestive of the "embargo on munitions" and the other "forgetful" policies toward Spain, Germany, and Italy that link them with Gauley Bridge as "one country marked by error and one air." No wonder that for Rukeyser the defense "committee and its armies" are oppositional "sources of anger" and "meaning":

and all our meaning lies in this
signature: power on a hill
centered in its committee and its armies
sources of anger, the mine of emphasis.

Rukeyser includes a strong stanza bringing into focus the physiology of silicosis, "a gradual scar formation; / this increases, blocking all drainage from the lung, / eventually scars, blocking the blood supply, / and then they block the air passage-ways. / Shortness of breath, / pains around the chest, / he notices lack of vigor." In a crucial passage she juxtaposes this "blocking" with another, the political: "Bill blocked; investigation blocked." For the defense committee "all our meaning lies in this signature" now "blocked" like the lungs of the 500,000 men who pass judgment on and pose a militant threat to the congressmen who have ignored them as they metaphorically look down from the galleries, to the congressmen "a row of empty seats, mask over a dead voice." The mask at once emphasizes the muting of their voices in Congress and embodies the masks the company failed to provide and the "dead voice" that literally resulted.

In "The Bill" Rukeyser makes these implications vivid and specific. She economically gathers together what the subcommittee has learned about Union Carbide and its subsidiaries and the Hawk's Nest tunnel where the "drilled rock contained / 90—even 99 percent pure silica." Rukeyser gives a bare recital of the "facts that were known" about silicosis and how to prevent it through wet drilling, respirators, and proper ventilation. Then a staccato account of the company's action and inaction. She uses colons and sentence fragments to convey the sense of notes, to break up the normal flow of conversational syntax, to strip down the sentences and get us to fill in. Combined with the details of what the company did and failed to do, the effect of this form is a powerful, restrained indictment "of negligence. Wilful or inexcusable."

Rukeyser juxtaposes the subcommittee's concise, detached language with a more urgent, contrasting sequence in which the men indicate what drove them to Hawk's Nest,

Depression; and, driven deeper in,
by hunger, pistols, and despair,
they took the tunnel.

The economic forces of depression and hunger merge with the actual physical force the company used to drive the men back into the tunnel. Through her abrupt cut to "P. H. Faulconer, Pres." of the contracting firm and "E. J. Perkins, Vice-

Pres.," who "have declined to appear," Rukeyser exposes the weakness of the sub-committee and the venality of the company and its officials. They assert "they have no knowledge of deaths from silicosis," although "their firm paid claims." Compounding the injustice, "under the statute $500 or / $1,000, but no more, may be recovered."

The subcommittee knows the price that has been paid for electric power and knows the men need "to be vindicated" but aside from recommending more investigations and requiring the company to bring "their books and records," in its view the subcommittee "can do no more." In opposition to this well-intentioned liberal response, Rukeyser concludes with a powerful radical vision. She reinvokes John Brown, explicitly at the end and implicitly at the beginning of the stanza, where she refers elliptically to "words on a monument," the words on the monument to John Brown she stressed in "West Virginia" (p. 12). Rukeyser merges John Brown's militant rebellion and assertion of principle with the rebellious storms connected with the "Capitoline thunder" of ancient Rome. Unlike the subcommittee, for Rukeyser "it cannot be enough." Instead, she affirms the radical view that

> The origin of storms is not in clouds,
> our lightning strikes when the earth rises,
> spillways free authentic power;
> dead John Brown's body walking from a tunnel
> to break the armored and concluded mind.

In "our lightning strikes when the earth rises," Rukeyser fuses revolutionary, communal action with the primal power of nature itself. The "power" the spillways "free" is now fully political. At the end, John Brown and all he stands for merge with the Hawk's Nest Tunnel and the Gauley dead. For her, the lightning of militant action is important, but even more Rukeyser emphasizes the impact on the mind of the genuinely revolutionary power John Brown embodies. Far from being rigidly dogmatic, in what could stand as an epigraph to her own poetics, Rukeyser has the radical, John Brown, open up the fortress of "the armored and concluded mind."

"The Book of the Dead"

In her culminating poem, "The Book of the Dead" (pp. 66–72), as she does with John Brown, Rukeyser continues to reenliven the images and concerns of her opening poems. At the start and throughout her concluding poem, it is worth stressing, Rukeyser circles back to earlier poems, so that she uses the form of her work to reinforce her vision of process and renewal, of rebirth in religion and in revolutionary politics. Now that we have traveled them with her, Rukeyser tells us again, "these roads will take you into your own country," "into a landscape mirrored in these men." It is our own country in ways we prefer to ignore but also in its rebellious energy. The Gauley dead represent both the country's need and capacity for rebellion, even as they indict the country, the landscape, which is "mirrored in these men" through the image of the silica, the glass, made into a powerful metaphor of their representative quality.

In a sequence of questions, Rukeyser opens up the meaning of these men who embody the answer to the first question,

> What one word must never be said?
> Dead, and these men fight off our dying,
> cough in the theatres of the war.

For Rukeyser, as a way of stressing our identification with the Gauley dead, as they resist death "they fight off our dying." They also function as protective deities in a scheme of death and renewal, and as a political warning "they fight off our dying." In 1938 "the theatres of the war" again brings the class war in West Virginia into relation with the war in Spain and the approaching World War II.

"This is a nation's scene," Rukeyser reiterates, and then asks and answers her third question:

> What three things can never be done?
> Forget. Keep silent. Stand alone.
> The hills of glass, the fatal brilliant plain.

Rukeyser underscores the radical credo—never forget, keep silent, or stand alone—with a symbol of what makes the credo necessary, the fatal "hills of glass."

She then returns to the multiple wars—"the facts of war forced into actual grace"—and moves beyond "seasons and modern glory" to bring alive the American past as she had earlier in "The Road" and "West Virginia." Using the image of "thirteen clouds / lining the west horizon with their white / shining haliations," Rukeyser gives a compressed history of American conquest, "throwing off impossible Europe." After recapitulating her earlier treatment of westward expansion and the American Dream, she leads us "to windows, seeing America / lie in a photograph of power, widened before our forehead." Rukeyser associates this image of glory with a modern one never far from her thoughts or feelings, the struggle in Spain,

flashing new signals from the hero hills
near Barcelona, monuments and powers, parent defenses.

Rukeyser then returns to merge the West Virginia river and the green world of the American West, "green ripened field, frontier pushed back like the river / controlled and dammed." After what she has shown throughout *The Book of the Dead*, the image of the dammed river effectively undercuts the promise of the virgin land. As she continues, Rukeyser combines the traditional imagery of American possibility, of "the flashing wheatfields" and "the flourished land," with a deconstructive language of sterility and death, of "lunar plains / grey in Nevada," of "a world of desert, / the dead, the lava" inseparable from "the extreme arisen / fountains of life." For Rukeyser, who expresses an understandable ambivalence about America, "this fact and this disease" are at the root of her negative feelings.

For her

> our ritual world
> carries its history in familiar eyes,
> planted in flesh it signifies its music
> in minds which turn to sleep and memory,
> in music knowing all the shimmering names,
> the spear, the castle, and the rose.

Rukeyser sees our shared "ritual world" of American and Egyptian myth alive in the "familiar eyes" and "flesh" of the men and women of Gauley Bridge. "Knowing all the shimmering names, / the spear, the castle, and the rose," the traditional music of the hill country is a link to the ancient past.

Far from being an escape into a timeless realm remote from the present, however, Rukeyser again insists that all of us are one with the victims of Gauley Bridge, that

> planted in our flesh these valleys stand,
> everywhere we begin to know the illness,
> are forced up, and our times confirm us all.

Again moving from present to mythic past, Rukeyser calls up from "the museum life . . . a fertilizing image" of Isis, her wings protecting us from death, "in her two hands the book and cradled dove," further symbols of eternal life. Rukeyser then once again fuses past and present, the worlds of resurrection and of radical politics. For her

This valley is given to us like a glory.
To friends in the old world, and their lifting hands
that call for intercession. Blow falling full in the face.

Gauley Bridge is a gift, a call to the inspired action and state of being Rukeyser connects with "glory" in the sense of "adoration and praise offered in worship." In the same spirit she continues to associate Gauley Bridge with the Spanish Loyalists, with "friends in the old world, and their lifting hands / that call for intercession." In both Spain and West Virginia, Rukeyser feels personally "blow falling full in the face." A defining feature of Rukeyser's radical politics is that she is sensitive to oppression not in the abstract but as an immediate physical reality. Reinforcing and inseparable from her politics, a defining feature of her poetics is her practice of stripping down the sentence, cutting out transitions, and using fragments without a definite subject, a practice that allows her economically to suggest a range of possibilities, to fuse the personal and public, and to engage the reader as an active participant in the process of her political art.

Rukeyser typically generates an emotional intensity that communicates even when the reader has trouble following her conceptually. The obscurity John Wheelwright complained about often results from a poetic compression that can give the impression of a private language strongly inflected with personal associations, as in the stanza,

All those whose childhood made learn skill to meet,
and art to see after the change of heart;
all the belligerents who know the world.

Rukeyser immediately returns to a much more public language. In the accents of a modernist Whitman committed to the language and values of the Popular Front, she addresses as "you" a panorama of figures at home in her work and in the iconography of the Popular Front. As a supporter of the proletariat, Rukeyser turns the imagery of the gorge, the dam, and the flowing river away from their destructive connotations and celebrates the power, not of "countries" but of "you workers." Her emphasis on peace is her version of a widely shared Popular Front commitment, infused for Rukeyser with the value of love. Rukeyser then addresses "the young . . . finishing the poem"—her poem as it draws to a close. These are the young who "wish new perfection." In a tradition going back to Whitman, for Rukeyser reading the poem releases an idealism and energy that inevitably impels the reader to "begin to make," an injunction that in 1938 not only applies to incipient personal creativity but also resonates with the left slogan, "change the world."

Also like Whitman, Rukeyser is at one not only with the poetically and politically inspired young but also with "you men of fact," the scientists and technicians she urges to "measure our times again," so that she enlists the "men of fact" in the enterprise of judging a present in need of radical renewal. The scientists, the young, the workers, and the "surveyors and planners"—

These are our strength, who strike against history.

Rukeyser moves from this militant affirmation of rebellious strength to the Gauley dead "whose corrupt cells owe their new styles of weakness / to our diseases." In one of her most telling political insights, Rukeyser inverts conventional etiology and exposes silicosis as a corrupt illness originating in a contagious disease, the sickness of the body politic.

As she continues, Rukeyser makes us see and feel the full significance of the work these men did. Ironically, they carried "light for safety on their foreheads" as they "descended deeper for richer faults of ore, / drilling their death." They are not "drilling a tunnel" or "drilling ore"—they are "drilling their death," which is to say that through the power of compression Rukeyser brings alive the political, moral, and physical reality involved in "descending deeper for richer faults of ore."

The Gauley dead merge with others "across the world" in a surreal vision of "avoidable death" that at once warns against the system of exploitative profit and war and forecasts its doom. At the end of *The Book of the Dead* death is not an abstraction but a tangible reality inseparable from physical agony and its sources in capitalistic exploitation, symbolized not only by the Gauley dead but also by "the luminous poison" of those who, "touching radium," "carried their death on their lips and with their warning / glow in their graves." To even more powerful effect,

These weave and their eyes water and rust away,
these stand at wheels until their brains corrode, these farm and starve

These representative figures are not passive victims but, in a further although less compelling catalog of Popular Front heroes,

Are known as strikers, soldiers, pioneers,
fight on all new frontiers, are set in solid lines of defense.

As she typically does, Rukeyser then opens up the poetic, visual, and intellectual implications of this Popular Front position. For her

Defense is sight; widen the lens and see
standing over the land myths of identity, new signals, processes

They are, to begin with, the "new signals, processes" of metallurgy, of "alloys" and "certain dominant metals" which involve "new qualities, / sums of new uses." As Rukeyser widens her lens near the end of *The Book of the Dead*, she brings together in her vision of a radically new America "myths of identity" and the materialist processes of science and technology. The "new processes, new signals" elide with "new possession," with radical political and social change. For Rukeyser the revolutionary new world is grounded in and symbolized by the processes of science and technology,

A name for all the conquests, prediction of victory deep in these powers.

As she moves toward the end of *The Book of the Dead*, Rukeyser self-reflexively describes her political art. Speaking as much to and about herself and her project as to the activist reader, she says,

Carry abroad the urgent need, the scene,
to photograph and to extend the voice, to speak this meaning.

She conveys the sense of urgency through the form as well as the substance of her utterances, through the elliptical fragments that generate energy and involve the reader as an active participant in the process of her modernist political poetry. Her next line, "Voices to speak to us directly," for example, characterizes precisely what Rukeyser has attempted and achieved in poems like "Statement: Philippa Allen," "Mearl Blankenship," and "George Robinson: Blues," just as these and the other poems in *The Book of the Dead* use the photograph, extend the voice, render the scene, and "speak this meaning" it takes all of her ambitious poem to communicate.

Relying on sentence fragments, active clauses and participial phrases we complete, Rukeyser reinvokes the journey she began with us in "The Road." She gathers together what we have accomplished together

As we move,
As we enrich, growing in larger motion, this word, this power.

"Power" now gains another connotation to go along with those of the river and dam and the revolution, a sense connected with the word, the poem, the mind—with "this meaning" and "this word." Then Rukeyser puts to new uses the myth of discovery and conquest she had drawn on earlier in "The Book of the Dead" and in poems like "West Virginia." Now, with the "fanatic cruel legend at our back," she looks ahead hopefully and taps into the positive energy of the American myth of the virgin land, of westward expansion. She aligns the energy of this basic American myth with the "red" future, with "speeding ahead" to the red revolution, "the red and open west, / and this our region, / desire, field, beginning." Just as it is grounded in the processes of science and technology, for Rukeyser the new, emerging America has the best qualities of the "open west." At the end, moreover, Rukeyser reinforces her vision of beginning.

In her final lines, referring for the last time to the men she has presented to us throughout *The Book of the Dead*, Rukeyser celebrates

communication to these many men,
as epilogue, seeds of unending love.

Her poetics and her radical politics come together in this concluding affirmation of organic growth and "unending love."

Coda: A Note on Criticism

In his wide-ranging, suggestive *American Culture between the Wars*, Walter Kalaidjian argues for a feminist center as basic to *The Book of the Dead*. The interpretation is appealing because it makes the poem relevant to vital contemporary concerns and recovers the Rukeyser of the 1930s for current readers. Kalaidjian bases his interpretation, first of all on what he believes "stands out as the poem's at once most desperate and heroic portrait[,] . . . the mother's compassionate narrative in the 'Absalom' section that augurs women's revisionary authority in 'Power' and in the long poem's final title piece 'The Book of the Dead.' "[17] Without taking anything away from the moving voice of Mrs. Jones, however, is it really true that she stands out over all the other characters Rukeyser brings to life—over Arthur Peyton and his anguish, pain, and protest, for example, or over the beauty, suffering, and blues sensibility of one of the many African Americans in the poem, George Robinson, who "holds all their strength together" (*Book*, p. 22), or over the simple, deadly revelations of Mearl Blankenship? In privileging Mrs. Jones as mother, Kalaidjian in effect sets up a competition in victimage and heroism, playing one character and group off against another. In placing Mrs. Jones as woman and mother on a pedestal at the center of the poem, Kalaidjian recovers the poem for liberal contemporary readers at the expense, I believe, of Rukeyser's 1930s, Popular Front commitment to equality, to celebrating the achievements and suffering of common people. As I read *The Book of the Dead*, Rukeyser tries and succeeds in doing justice to each of her characters as an individual, as a member of the committee of workers fighting back against corporate, capitalistic exploitation and injustice, and as a common person collectively constituting the people. On this view it is a serious mistake to place one person or group over others, apart from their common suffering and protest.

My second reservation is more technical. In the transition from death to life at the end of "Power" and into "The Dam," on Kalaidjian's interpretation "speaking in the persona of the goddess, the poet claims for herself 'power over the fields and Pool of Fire. / Phoenix, I sail over the phoenix world' " ('Book,' 15 [55]—174)." But is the speaker from the Egyptian *Book of the Dead*, the Phoenix, really female? Isn't the Phoenix androgynous and, as a spiritual power, beyond sex and gender? In this documentary poem with its medley of independent voices and points of view, moreover, is it self-evident that Rukeyser is speaking in her own voice rather than giving autonomy to the voice from the Egyptian *Book of the Dead*?

Kalaidjian celebrates "the ecstatic force of the feminine" as the basic, effective redemptive force in the poem (p. 174). For Kalaidjian, this feminist power comes through in lines from the Egyptian *Book of the Dead*, lines Rukeyser uses to complex effect in "Absalom":

I have gained mastery over my heart
I have gained mastery over my two hands
I have gained mastery over the waters
I have gained mastery over the river.

("Book," p. 29)

In context, the passage articulates an ideal that throws into relief the absence of many of these qualities in the lives of Mrs. Jones and those she speaks for, even as the poem speaks for their value and partial realization in Mrs. Jones's life and words. In context, the lines from the Egyptian *Book of the Dead* do not establish the triumphant feminist power Kalaidjian attributes to them, a triumph he would justifiably be the first to criticize as excessive if it took the form of, in his words, "blind faith in the proletariat's imminent triumph over capital" (p. 170). Instead, Rukeyser's hard-earned "prediction of victory / deep in these powers" (*Book*, p. 71) involves her renewed affirmation of the power of science and technology, of the red revolution, of the fighters in Spain, of the strikers and workers at home, and finally of the power of the word fused with the power of love.

In making the maternal and feminine the central redemptive powers in the poem, Kalaidjian downplays Rukeyser's Marxist, Popular Front forces and values and seriously minimizes her subversive irony and nuanced critique of American corporate capitalism. It is only under the sign of "the feminine" or "feminism" that Kalaidjian allows Rukeyser's "social muse" to speak for change, although not for the red revolution (p. 186). He similarly mutes Rukeyser's excoriating exposure of finance and corporate capitalism in favor of her recording what is much less radical, against "the disturbing signs of the industrial workplace" and for "the heroic figures of the American people" (p. 186).[18] Kalaidjian filters out Rukeyser's political radicalism and in place of her Popular Front Marxism substitutes "Popular Front feminism," a contemporary category that makes acceptable the moderate degree of social, not political, criticism he grants Rukeyser. Kalaidjian has effectively read out Rukeyser's 1930s Marxism, elided it totally with an admirable New Deal moderation, and read in an equally admirable but, in context, out-of-place contemporary feminism.

As we reconsider previously neglected achievements, cultural politics inevitably plays an active role. As a result of the cultural politics of the Cold War, Rukeyser's early poetry was marginalized along with the left movement she belonged to. As Kalaidjian's important work reminds us, in responding to the very different cultural politics of our period, in which feminism has a significant place, there is an analogous danger in imposing current feminist and green values on 1930s literature rather than respecting the historically and politically grounded integrity of the earlier work. However unfashionable some of her commitments are, Rukeyser endows them with an energy and complexity that deserve attention in their own right, which is to say, as part of the cultural politics of the 1930s left in general and of the Popular Front in particular. I agree with Kalaidjian that Rukeyser's "revolutionary mix of verse and reportage still has the potential for doing productive cultural work today" (p. 187). But for me "revolutionary" has Marxist, Popular Front connotations Kalaidjian has minimized. Because the Popular Front was animated from moderate and revolutionary sources, as we recover work from this challenging period it is especially difficult and especially important to do precise justice to the fusion.

For his part David Kadlec believes that Rukeyser was an "essentializing poet" who has "written out" the racial implications of the Gauley Tunnel tragedy in favor of a class-based portrayal that at times also ignores the gendering and class bias of the x-ray evidence she supposedly favors. Rukeyser is "essentializing" because, for many postmodern critics, the Marxist writers of the 1930s are by definition "essentializing." As for the application of this view, "erasing" race seems too strong for the creator of "George Robinson: Blues." Instead, Rukeyser stresses equality, not race or gendering. She places women and African Americans as equals with white men as members of the committee and as exploited workers damaged by Union Carbide and fighting back. The "state mechanisms" Rukeyser exposes, moreover, are not the New Deal photographers Kadlec refers to but, much more politically radical, the Congress's failure to act.[19]

The muting of Rukeyser's radicalism and her supposed failure to live up to current views on race, class, and gender pervade Kadlec and Kalaidjian's treatment of New Deal documentary photography. These critics to the contrary, Rukeyser uses the documentary camera positively to help her structure and record scenes and organize her poem. Following Kalaidjian, Kadlec nonetheless argues that Rukeyser both exposes the complicity of New Deal photographers in the capitalistic abuses of Gauley Tunnel and at the same time shares their complicity. To reach this intellectually attractive conclusion, however, Kadlec has to ignore the obvious reference not to "falsifying" New Deal photography but to Rukeyser's friend Nancy Naumberg and her on-site camera—her "camera at the crossing sees the city" ("Gauley Bridge," p. 16). How do we distinguish between Kadlec's indicted "state documentarian's equipment" and Nancy Naumberg's valued documentary camera?[20]

The indictment of New Deal photography and the complicity of New Deal photographers with the capitalistic abuses of Gauley Tunnel are claims Kadlec and Kalaidjian impose on *The Book of the Dead*. These charges are based on two early references to glass, "the camera-glass fixed on the street" and "viewing on ground-glass an inverted image," allusions that for these critics invoke the deadly silica of Gauley Tunnel. In the sections on "Arthur Peyton" the connection between glass and silica is abundantly, powerfully established in context. At the start of the poem, however, "groundglass" and "camera-glass" do not have negative implications but are simply accurate terms Rukeyser uses, minor instances of her technical knowledge and affection for precise characterizations. The hard, congealed "camera-glass" and "groundglass," moreover, are the exact opposite of the fine particles of "white glass" that kill at Gauley Tunnel.

To cite one more instance, to criticize New Deal documentary photography Kadlec takes the phrase "widen the lens" out of context and uses it to support his view that Rukeyser portrays "the x-ray camera as a medium that was less tainted and more encompassing than the conventional camera."[21] His assertion of the superiority and wider scope of the x-ray camera relative to the conventional documentary camera, however, has no basis either in Rukeyser's text or critical essays and reviews. The words "widen the lens" do not refer to x-ray cameras or x-ray photography but to her own poetry that, like the documentary camera, will now "widen the lens" to deal with "myths of identity" and the "new signals, processes" of metallurgy and the "new possession" of radical political and social change. To my knowledge, moreover, in her essays and reviews Rukeyser never discusses x-rays. She never mentions the x-ray camera in the poem or in her other writing. Rukeyser does, however, write extensively and sympathetically about documentary photography, an interest that pervades and structures *The Book of the Dead*.

Despite Kadlec's implied claim that of course Rukeyser was familiar with the fascinating Foucaultian discourse on x-rays he supplies, he needs to demonstrate that Rukeyser knew this material and, more important, that she shares his views on the centrality of x-ray evidence and its superiority over the conventional documentary. This demonstration needs more than Rukeyser's telling but occasional references to x-ray evidence. Instead, Kadlec attributes to Rukeyser a commitment to x-ray photography and then undercuts her for failing to accept the results of recent scholarship on the gendering, racism, class bias, and uncertainty of interpreting x-ray evidence.[22]

Both Kadlec and Kalaidjian have written substantial, stimulating work. Both of these critics, however, seem to me to have crossed an important line: instead of respecting the integrity of an earlier period, they invoke vital contemporary values and assumptions in a way that distorts rather than clarifies Rukeyser's work.

CHAPTER 7

THE LEFT POETRY OF LANGSTON HUGHES

As a radical poet Langston Hughes was able to draw on his family tradition, the resources of the African American oral, blues, and jazz traditions, his personal experience of racial insult and oppression, and the engaged communism of the 1930s. Taking account of his left political poetry helps restore an important, neglected dimension of Hughes's art, even as his radical work speaks for the 1930s, a decade of struggle and protest that animated his imagination. Because at the high school level Hughes is *the* representative African American poet, including his powerful political poetry in literature courses might encourage students to place poetry in the context of a vital political, racial, and literary history. Students, for whom literature is typically depoliticized, could then think about and perhaps reassess their assumptions about poetry and how to read it. For a range of contemporary readers, the radical Langston Hughes could be a welcome surprise.

Like other gifted writers on the left—my examples are Le Sueur and Herbst, Wright and Rukeyser—Hughes gives his personal accent to a language he shares with those in the movement. Like them, Hughes is not an isolated figure but is an active participant in the cultural dialogue of the thirties left. Rooted in the traditions of jazz and the blues, moreover, and deeply aware from personal experience of what it meant to be poor, black, and oppressed, Hughes is an integral part of a varied history that includes the precedent of his grandmother's first husband, who was with John Brown at Harpers Ferry.[1]

In Hughes's case, at the center of that history is the crucial role of song and music in African culture, in African American slave culture, and in African American culture since abolition. In this oral tradition, song and music were basic to the community, first in the African tribal communities, later in the communities

African Americans created under the pressures of slavery.[2] The basic call-and-response form; the work songs that organized hoeing, tree cutting, and rowing; and the improvisational music that pervaded African American life under slavery into the early years of the twentieth century are reminders that song and music were central and communal.[3] Complex drum rhythms defined the music and the community.[4] Integral to this oral, communal tradition from Africa through slavery were satiric songs, the use of innuendo and wordplay to deflate authority.[5] A related characteristic of the African American oral tradition is the encoded rebelliousness of the many spirituals and work songs that had one meaning for white listeners and quite another meaning for the slave singers.[6]

In his radical political poetry, Langston Hughes reanimates the communal and rebellious tendencies of his African American oral tradition.[7] His left poems use the language of the street, the language of ordinary workers. The tone ranges from the playful to the dignified. Hughes often uses the multiple voices of call and response and the drumbeat rhythms of New Orleans marching music and its African sources. In his radical poems Hughes's persona is typically a representative figure, sometimes black, sometimes a militant worker, sometimes both. In these poems, Hughes speaks for himself and for a community. He expresses the complaints, anger, irreverence, and hopefulness of oppressed people. Hughes repeatedly celebrates black and white workers communally and often militantly triumphing over the pain and injustice of the present. Like the slave spirituals and work songs, these poems serve to build morale: Hughes reassures a dedicated radical audience that ordinary workers, especially black workers, are with them and that the future—on this earth—is theirs. In his political poetry Hughes combines the vernacular language and forms of the African American oral tradition with the language and commitments of the radical left. In the process he rearticulates the communal and rebellious tendencies of the African American tradition in the contemporary 1930s language of Marxist hope and critique.

"Letter to the Academy"

In one of his *International Literature* poems, "Letter to the Academy" (1933), Hughes clears the ground for a reading of his radical poetry in a poem that illustrates the possibilities and satisfactions of engaging this neglected body of work. Reinforcing and reinforced by the Marxist context of *International Literature*, "the subject of the Revolution" is central, so that politics are on the speaker's mind. Equally important, so are cultural politics.[8] The poem opens with a bantering demand that reverses the ordinary power-prestige positions. In a prose form that is part of the subversive message, the speaker, adopting the unlikely stance of a schoolmaster, says

> The gentlemen who have got to be classics and are now old with beards (or dead
>   and in their graves) will kindly come forward and speak upon the subject
> Of the Revolution.

Using mock politeness and the comic implausibility of the dead coming forward to speak, Hughes undermines what he presents as an outdated orthodoxy. He goes on to subvert a depoliticized, idealized poetics of beauty elevated above the conflicts of ordinary life, the poetics of

> the gentlemen who wrote lovely
> books about the defeat of the flesh and the triumphs of
> the spirit that sold in the hundreds of thousands and
> are studied in the high schools and read by the best
> people . . .

For some academic readers a more relevant and challenging antagonist might be the politically reactionary modernism of Eliot and Pound. In the early 1930s, however, the genteel tradition represented by Paul Elmer More, Irving Babbitt, and the humanist movement was also a genuine cultural force. Hughes quietly exposes the material profit involved in what he presents as the genteel, class-based celebration of the spirit and denigration of the flesh. As an alternative to the genteel content of the established canon, Hughes taunts the gentlemen of the academy to "speak about the Revolution," for him a humane, egalitarian vision

> where the flesh triumphs (as
> well as the spirit) and the hungry belly eats, and there are no best people, and
>   the poor are mighty and
> no longer poor, and the young by the hundreds of
> thousands are free from hunger to grow and study and
> love and propagate, bodies and souls unchained . . .

On this view of the Revolution, "the young" are sexually free and intellectually curious, a radical cultural politics at odds with the genteel tradition and more liberated than the conventional morality of official communism. Similarly both radical and independent, for Hughes it is "the poor," not "the proletariat" who, inverting the orthodox class structure, are "mighty." Like the party, Hughes stresses that the revolution will abolish hunger, a basic concern that recurs again and again in his poetry and in the literature of the 1930s left.

Through incantatory repetition, Hughes undercuts the gray-bearded embodiments of cultural hegemony. For the third time he turns to them and with barbed politeness says

> But please—all you gentlemen with
> beards who are so wise and old and who write better
> than we do and whose souls have triumphed (in spite
> of hungers and wars and the evils about you) and
> whose books have soared in calmness and beauty aloof from the struggle to the
> library shelves and the desks of students and who are now classics—come
> forward and speak upon
> The subject of the Revolution.
> We want to know what in the hell you'd say?

Hughes, who early in "Letter to the Academy" uses "I"—"I mean the gentlemen . . ."—now writes as "we," as a member of a new, insurrectionary generation. It is worth stressing that it is not easy to counter the pressure of all those influential wise old men who have dominated the canon and the curriculum. As a young, radical writer challenging the established orthodoxy of the old, Hughes brings into the open, defuses, and turns to his own advantage the feeling that those who set the traditional standards "write better than we do." What constitutes good writing, Hughes reminds us, is not fixed and eternal but is open to question. Hughes is especially acute in aligning genteel standards with the old and in showing that the poetics of the academy may be pure and timeless but at the expense of ignoring the struggle, the hunger, and wars at the center of his own revolutionary vision.

Throughout "Letter to the Academy" the speaker has been insistently polite, has used a middle style, and has avoided dialect and colloquialisms. He has subverted the genteel tradition in something like its own language. In this context, his concluding profanity has intensified impact. At the end, the twist of language, the spice, the shock, the energy of the colloquial profanity is not a shout but a strong insurrectionary intrusion into the quiet decorum of the library, of the hegemonic academy.

Except for the final line, "we want to know what in the hell you'd say," Hughes's language accommodates to genteel standards but his form does not. He not only focuses on struggle, hunger, war, and a liberated view of the sexualized body but he also offers the prose form of "Letter to the Academy" as an example of an alternative poetics. The format on the page makes "Letter" an antipoem, particularly in contrast to the tradition of the old Hughes invokes as his established antagonist. At least in this instance Hughes also deliberately avoids the sweet appeals of rhyme, of regular meter, of conventional poetic devices. Instead, he relies on recurrences, rhythms, and an insistent, ironic challenge to the classics "whose books have soared in calmness and beauty aloof from the struggle," a detachment he counters with his own example throughout the poem and throughout the 1930s.

Hughes was especially engaged by what happened to the Scottsboro Boys. In March and April 1931 eight of the nine were convicted and sentenced to death, allegedly for raping two white women who were hoboing on the same freight train they were on between Chattanooga and Paint Rock, Alabama. In early April 1931 the International Labor Defense (ILD), a Communist organization, demanded a stay of execution and took the lead in organizing a legal and political defense. It soon became apparent that these uneducated black youths—they were between thirteen and twenty years old—had been convicted without benefit of a defense attorney. One of the eight was suffering from such a serious case of syphilis that it would have been unbearably painful for him to engage in sex. Another was practically blind and had not been on the same car as Victoria Price and Ruby Bates. Two southern doctors who had examined the women immediately after the alleged rape found no substantiating evidence of the torn clothing, lacerations, head wounds, blood, or semen they claimed. By January 1933 Ruby Bates, who had made the original rape charge, admitted she had lied, a confession that did not free the accused. They were retried several times, endured mistreatment in Kilby Prison, and were the center of complex legal and political controversy for the rest of the decade.[9]

After the first trial, during the summer and fall of 1931 international protest accelerated as liberal, radical, church, and black groups tried to prevent the electrocutions. Hughes, who was giving readings in the South during fall 1931, did his part with a series of essays, poems, and a verse play about Scottsboro. He visited the Scottsboro Boys in Kilby Prison and had to be talked out of interviewing Ruby Bates. Hughes put together four of his Scottsboro poems and the verse play in a booklet, *Scottsboro Limited*, to raise money for the Scottsboro Defense Fund.[10] The copy I used in the Berkeley library is inscribed to another political prisoner, Tom Mooney, the radical who had probably been framed, who had been imprisoned since 1916 for allegedly bombing the *Los Angeles Times*, and who was the object of repeated "Free Tom Mooney" campaigns. The copy is signed "Langston Hughes."

"Justice," "Christ in Alabama," "Scottsboro Limited"

The collection opens with a four-line poem, "Justice":

That Justice is a blind goddess
Is a thing to which we black are wise.

Her bandage hides two festering sores

That once perhaps were eyes.

The surface is moderate as Hughes quietly subverts the commonplace about Justice as a blind goddess impartially adjudicating. Instead, "we black[s] are wise" to exactly how blind Justice is. Unlike "Letter to the Academy," where the "we" are those in the revolutionary new movement, in "Justice" race is central. Even the apparent typo, "black" instead of "blacks," emphasizes race. Some of Hughes's feelings about southern justice Scottsboro style emerge in the powerful image of the "two festering sores / that once perhaps were eyes." The qualification, "perhaps," opens up an endless prospect of disease, a connotation Hughes underscores in his view of "Dixie justice blind and syphilitic." This prose gloss on the central images of the "blind goddess" and the "festering sores" is from Hughes's Scottsboro essay, "Southern Gentlemen, White Prostitutes, Mill Owners and Negroes," which he wrote at the same time as the republication of "Justice."[11] In the context of Scottsboro is there a subtext in "Justice," a sense that the goddess is not only blind but also white, a white woman with festering syphilitic sores? Has Hughes applied to the deified southern white woman or at least to white justice the stigmata of two of the accused, blindness and syphilis?

For me, "Justice" loses some of its disturbing, subversive power when it is removed from the context of the animating passions and particulars of the Scottsboro case. When Hughes reprinted "Justice" in A New Song, published by the International Workers Order (IWO) in 1938, he did not mention Scottsboro. He did not even connect the poem with Tom Mooney, whose experience deepens the poem, although two pages later Hughes did include his "Chant for Tom Mooney." He also shifted the emphasis from race to class by changing one word: "black" becomes "poor" in A New Song.[12] In the process, we lose the subtext of blind, syphilitic Dixie justice and the specific resonances of Scottsboro, a major instance inspiring and validating the vision of the poem.

"Justice" could usefully be taught along with a group of Hughes's radical poems. This conveniently short, deceptively moderate poem raises the key issue of the importance of historical-political context, of language and energy streaming in from events and circumstances, to paraphrase Josephine Herbst. Scottsboro, the particular historical-political event, is a significant part of what for most students is still the suppressed history of America. In the context of Scottsboro and its suppression, the title, "Justice," invites a complex response. More technically, reading "Justice" in A New Song as part of the sequence "Let America Be America Again" (the 1938, not the usually anthologized version), "Justice," and "Park Bench," gives us a significantly different poem than the one in *Scottsboro Limited*.[13] Working with the two versions raises the general issues of textual reliability ("black"/ "blacks"?) and textual change (from "black" to "poor") and the particular issue of why or to what effect Hughes made the change. In Hughes's case these technical matters are inseparable from the dynamics of the shifting relations of race and class in 1930s left politics generally and the Popular Front in particular. We will return to these concerns when we look more closely at *A New Song*.

"Justice" poses still another interpretive issue, because Hughes first published it in 1923 and thus originally Scottsboro was not involved in the meaning of the poem.[14] Placed in its new context in *Scottsboro Limited*, however, is "Justice" open to the interpretation I have been suggesting or do we ignore the redefinition Scottsboro makes available? How fixed is the meaning of the poem? How do we deal with the different historical contexts, 1923, 1931, 1938? And what role does the interpreter play?

Most interpreters agree that the most powerful poem in *Scottsboro Limited* is "Christ in Alabama." Hughes originally published it on the first page of *Contempo* (December 1931) after the editors asked for his comment on Scottsboro.[15] The unorthodox "Christ, / Who fought alone" is one of the militant martyrs of "Scottsboro," the poem that precedes "Christ in Alabama" in *Scottsboro Limited*. But when Hughes reprinted "Christ in Alabama" in *The Panther and the Lash* (1967), he removed it from the context of Scottsboro, so that an important dimension of the poem is obscured.

In *Scottsboro Limited*,

Christ is a Nigger,
Beaten and black—
O, bare your back.

The compression is daring and subversive. Christ, slaves, abused southern blacks, and especially the Scottsboro Boys all merge. Part of Hughes's achievement is that he implies but does not mention the Scottsboro Boys, at the same time that he places them physically and morally in a history of beating—"*O, bare your back*"— that aligns them with the whip, the worst abuses of slavery, and the Crucifixion. Equally daring and subversive is the use of "Nigger," the most insulting racial epithet in the language, applied to Christ. Particularly in the context of the racial turmoil connected with Scottsboro—contemporary readers can fill in the most recent example of "a Nigger / beaten and black"—imagine the explosive force of the simple statement, "Christ is a Nigger," an insult that dignifies the "beaten and black," in context intensifies the sense of blacks as suffering victims, and simultaneously, through the force of its aggression, qualifies that sense.

In the next stanza

Mary is His Mother—
Mammy of the South,
Silence your mouth.

Hughes subversively taps into another powerful cultural myth, this one involving the black mammy who raised generations of white southerners from slave times to the present of the poem. Juxtaposed with the middle style of "Mary is His Mother," the colloquialism in "Mammy of the South" effects a major cultural appropriation. Hughes jars us into recognizing that this Mary is black, not white, so that he undermines and displaces the entire edifice of white racial superiority justified by a white Christianity presided over by the angelic white woman, the epitome and guardian of religion and morality. In "Silence your mouth" Hughes takes one of mammy's favorite lines and applies it ironically to the complex protest he voices and she now embodies, including the protest against the Scottsboro executions and the perversions of Christianity.

In the third stanza

God's His Father—
White Master above,
Grant us your love.

Hughes continues to retell the Christ story from the perspective of Scottsboro and southern racial practices. The white master below, the model for the sanctioning "White Master above," has granted us the cruel realities Hughes has brought to imaginative life. In the context of "Christ in Alabama," raising the issue of divine love highlights its absence in ordinary relations. Hughes's irony subverts the conventional black subordination to the White Master above and below. Throughout the poem Hughes draws energy from and contributes to a complex discourse subversive of white mastery justified by white Christianity.

Hughes's language and moral passion ignite in the final stanza:

Most holy bastard
of the bleeding mouth:
Nigger Christ
On the cross of the South.

"Nigger Christ" is bad—or good—enough but Hughes compounds it with the unforgivable yes-and-no of "Most holy bastard," an incendiary reminder of insult and celebration. From slave times to Scottsboro to the latest example of the police in the inner city, "the bleeding mouth" embodies the domination, routine humiliation, and abuse of an entire population. In using this simple, physically specific, immediately recognizable phrase, Hughes again shows that he is in touch with everyday language, experience, morality, and history.

As a poet of political protest, moreover, Hughes repeatedly turns to his own subversive uses other central symbols of American culture, nowhere more powerfully than in his compressed indictment,

> Nigger Christ
> On the cross of the South.

As "Nigger Christ" the Scottsboro Boys and all they symbolize are again viewed and evaluated within the basic religious myth of the South. The region and its practices become "the cross of the South," so that the treatment and possible execution of the Scottsboro Boys become another version of the agony of the Crucifixion. Depending on the reader, Hughes is either blasphemous or, in cauterizing a perverted Christianity, deeply religious. In either case, in violating powerful cultural taboos he wins through to one of our most telling works of political exposure.

For all of its strengths, however—perhaps because of them—"Christ in Alabama" is practically unknown. Imagine this poem much more widely disseminated than at present. An Alabama or Iowa or California classroom open to a full discussion of "Christ in Alabama" would be able to engage students in ways rather different from "Prufrock" and "Sunday Morning" or even from the most frequently anthologized of Hughes's poems, "The Negro Dreams of Rivers." Poems like "Christ in Alabama" might or might not compel students indifferent to more conventional poetry; it would be worth finding out. It would also be worth specifying the range of concerns, including the diversity of audience response, poems like "Christ in Alabama" bring alive, particularly for beginning students.

As for the title work in Hughes's Scottsboro booklet, the title of the verse play, "Scottsboro Limited," has a double meaning: it applies literally to the freight train, the scene of the alleged rape, and subversively to the town and the entire prosecution, limited and railroading. In the play Hughes effectively uses jazz rhythms, a simple set—"one chair on a raised platform"—the choreography of "eight black boys," and an imaginative deployment of a white actor playing a series of authority figures. As political theater, the staging is especially compelling. Hughes combines the simplicity of a morality play with the sophistication of innovative twentieth-century stage techniques that allow him to use a limited cast to maximum emotional effect. The play, originally published in *New Masses* in November 1931, is aimed at an audience of sympathizers. "Red voices" speak from and for the audience; the white man who plays the bullying sheriff, prison keeper, and judge also rises from the audience. Even now, interspersed with the Communist Party commonplaces, we can respond to passages of dramatic power. In the context of the Scottsboro case, the left slogans themselves have more than usual energy as Hughes dramatizes now militant racial independence, now the triumph of black and white together under a red flag.

Hughes also enacts a classic left conversion experience as the 8th Boy becomes, in his words, "the new Red Negro." In the process, Hughes gives us insight into a formative, mythmaking moment in which he opens up the ideological possibilities of Scottsboro. Hughes did so even more deeply in "Christ in Alabama." In the poem, Christ–Nigger–Scottsboro Boys experience a martyrdom whose passive implications Hughes qualifies with the aggressive intensity of his rendering. In the play, he confronts and explicitly moves beyond acquiescent martyrdom to celebrate "the new Red Negro" and, in the words and images of the play's concluding call and response,

All: Rise, workers, and fight!
Audience: Fight! Fight! Fight! Fight!
   (The curtain is a great red flag rising to the strains of the Internationale.)

In "Scottsboro Limited" Hughes thus provides a model of the conversion and the militant affirmations Richard Wright engaged and rejected in the climactic jail scenes in *Native Son*.

As political theater "Scottsboro Limited" deserves to be tested and experienced in performance. As a classroom exercise, staging the play would put students in touch with a highly charged political-racial case. Equally useful, it would throw light on the shifting strengths and limits of the play as viewed from different political, racial, and time perspectives. In a contemporary performance, even within the classroom, "Scottsboro Limited" may have a vitality not obvious on the page. In a genuine production, as part of a sequence of radical plays from the 1930s, "Scottsboro Limited" would work instructively along with, for example, performances of Odets's *Waiting for Lefty* and Brecht's *The Secret History of the Third Reich*. In addition to bringing alive a neglected history, staging these plays could generate insight into the unresolved aesthetics of committed art. Either within the classroom or in a college or community production, participants would be able to draw on the insights and enthusiasm of Amiri Baraka, who came to value the radical Langston Hughes and wanted to perform *Scottsboro Limited* along with another neglected African American play of the 1930s, Theodore Ward's *Big White Fog*, in Baraka's judgment "perhaps the most impressive play I've read by an Afro-American."[16]

"August 19th: A Poem for Clarence Norris"

Also bearing on the key issue of the aesthetics of committed art is Hughes's 1938 poem, "August 19th: A Poem for Clarence Norris." Norris, the one Scottsboro Boy who shook Hughes's hand in Kilby Prison in 1931, was scheduled to be electrocuted on August 19, 1938. As part of the protest, Hughes's poem appeared in the *Daily Worker* on August 18 and "was distributed by the Communist party in Birmingham in support of the Scottsboro Defense."[17] Norris is the first-person speaker. In the course of the poem, Hughes has him identify himself in multiple ways. Is he an American, and if so, why shouldn't the red, white, and blue flag fly at half-mast when he dies? Early in the poem, Hughes also establishes that Norris is not one of the privileged, "not the President, / Nor the Honorable So-and-So. / But only one of the / Scottsboro Boys / Doomed 'by the law' to go." Then the bold-faced refrain line, "AUGUST 19th IS THE DATE," a line that recurs with the ever increasing insistence of a drum beat. "When used for public performances," the note heading the poem in the *Daily Worker* instructed, "on the last two verses punctuate the poem with a single drumbeat after each line. AUGUST 19th IS THE DATE. During the final stanza, let the beat go faster, and faster following the line, until at the end the drum goes on alone, unceasing, like the beating of a heart."[18]

"Put it in your book," Norris says, "The date that I must keep with death." In one of his central insights, however, Hughes breaks down the separation between "I" and "you," "for if you let the 'law' kill me," he has Norris stress, "Are you free?" After Norris names himself for the first time—"Charles Norris is my name"—he repeats, "The sentence against me / Against you, the same." Through Norris, Hughes also uses a series of telling concrete instances to body forth the sense of privilege and oppression Scottsboro encodes. The rich who do no work—but rule the land—"sit and fan / And sip cool drinks" framed by the accusation of "AUGUST 19th IS THE DATE." Hughes juxtaposes "The electric chair" and the comfortable summer activities of prosperous people, so that he uses Norris's colloquial language and deprivation to generate pathos through contrast with the upper class— Norris has no wife, no kids, no summer camp or European tours. The contrast also activates both the guilt of the progressive white reader and his or her feelings about the privileges of the wealthy. The refrain line occurs with increasing frequency, the beat and the rhyme underscore the urgency, and Hughes repeats with slight, significant variations his earlier lines, so that the assertion that the rich "rule the land," for example, now turns into a radical protest, a question about "Who shall rule our land?"

Hughes intensifies this protest in his emotionally charged drive to the close of the poem. Norris now addresses the world in the language of Communist militancy. As a poor black shut out and abused by the legal system, Norris identifies his experience as part of the larger injustice and exploitation of international imperialism. Instead of abstractions, however, Hughes has him rely on images, some of them left cliches that are emotionally charged for believers (*"Stop all the leeches / That suck your life away and mine. . . . That drop their bombs on China and Spain"*), some of them verbally and emotionally enlivened by the pervasive threat of lynching facing the Scottsboro Boys (*"Stop all the leeches / That use their power to strangle hope, / That make of the law a lyncher's rope"*).[19]

As in many of Hughes's poems the rhythms are inspired by the role of the drum in African life and ritual and by the drum-time marching music of New Orleans.[20] In the crescendo of the ending, Hughes builds up the drum-beat force of his refrain line juxtaposed with and finally replacing other questions and protests. Complementing his earlier identification of "I" and "you," within his intense concluding rhythmic sequence Hughes subtly varies his pronouns to involve the reader as an individual, as "you," and also as part of a communal movement, as "we":

AUGUST 19TH IS THE DATE.
Can you make death wait?
AUGUST 19TH IS THE DATE.
Will you let me die?
AUGUST 19TH IS THE DATE.
Can we make death wait?
AUGUST 19TH IS THE DATE.
Will you let me die?
AUGUST 19TH IS THE DATE.
AUGUST 19TH IS THE DATE.
AUGUST 19TH IS THE DATE.
AUGUST 19TH . . . AUGUST 19TH . . .
    AUGUST 19TH . . .

"Rising Waters" and "God to Hungry Child"

Well before the Scottsboro case and at the same time that he was writing his bitter-sweet jazz poems about Harlem, in 1925 Hughes was also publishing a group of political poems in the *Workers Monthly*, "The Communist Magazine." They are reminders that beneath the surface of twenties prosperity, rebellious energies were stirring. Years before most of his contemporaries, in "Rising Waters," for example, Hughes used the elemental image of the sea to create a drama of underlying social forces rising to displace the surface foam:

> To you
> Who are the
> Foam on the sea
> And not the sea—
> What of the jagged rocks,
> And the waves themselves,
> And the force of the mounting waters?
> You are
> But foam on the sea,
> You rich ones—
> Not the sea.[21]

Hughes builds suspense by withholding until the end his identification of "you rich ones" with "the foam on the sea." Without actually naming the underlying, opposing forces, Hughes conveys a sense of their threatening power, the power of "the jagged rocks, / And the waves themselves / And the force of the mounting waters." He uses the form of a question to encourage us to fill in a response, to contribute to the sense that "the rising waters" from the depths of the sea will displace the "rich ones" who are a decorative surface, "Not the sea." This way of seeing the rich, as transitory foam, makes it easier to oppose them, particularly given the celebration of "the force of the mounting waters," an image suggesting the power of an unstoppable, insurrectionary working class rising from the lower depths of society.

Four years before the Crash, in the midst of the boom of the 1920s, and at the same time he was writing "Rising Waters," Hughes also exposed one of his country's persistent dirty little secrets. In another 1925 *Workers Monthly* poem, "God to Hungry Child," he has God, speaking as the head of America's corporate wealth, announce that

Hungry child,
I didn't make this world for you.
You didn't buy any stock in my railroad,
You didn't invest in my corporation,
Where are your shares in standard oil?
I made the world for the rich
And the will-be-rich
And the have-always-been-rich.
Not for you,
Hungry child.

Without changing his basic criticism of the rich, Hughes reverses the power relations of "Rising Waters." His language is specific, conversational, and telling. He quietly subverts the conventional view of God and Christianity as on the side of the poor, of children and the weak. Instead, "I didn't make this world for you. / You didn't buy any stock in my railroad." God is usually seen as above buying and selling and He is usually connected with formal language. Simply having God speak is daring enough but Hughes has God speak conversationally to establish His unflattering stand, an irreverent violation of multiple conventions Hughes pulls off without a fuss.

In the lines that follow, Hughes both supports and subverts the deflationary realism of "I didn't make this world for you." He has God imply that *because* "you didn't buy any stock in my railroad," I'm punishing you. Of course, how could the hungry child buy stocks? The deliberately flawed logic exposes the basic cultural myth that the poor deserve what they get because if they were any good they would not be poor. In making God the spokesman for this view, Hughes also brings into the open the usually concealed extent to which the God of established Christianity supports "the rich," "the will-be-rich," and "the always-have-been-rich," an accumulation of riches that adds a delight in idiomatic verbal excess to the political criticism. The innocent "hungry child" is the perfect vehicle for Hughes's exposure of the skewed results of stock ownership, its supporting ideology, and a world made for the rich.[22]

"Merry Christmas," "Pride," "Tired," "A Christian Country"

By the early 1930s, as a result of the depression, Scottsboro, and his own experience, Hughes was increasingly writing political poetry. He became a contributing editor of *New Masses* in September 1930 and in the December *New Masses* he published "Greetings to Soviet Workers" and a Christmas poem, "Merry Christmas."[23] The poem inaugurates the new decade in a style worthy of the Mark Twain of "To the Person Sitting in Darkness":

> Merry Christmas, China,
> From the gun-boats in the river,
> Ten-inch shells for Christmas gifts
> And peace on earth forever.

From a Communist perspective the Japanese assault on China was central to the imperialism of Third Period capitalism (see Introduction and the accompanying note 25). In "Merry Christmas" and throughout the decade, in his repeated skewering of imperialism Hughes is independently and irreverently working within Third Period discourse.

As he moves away from Japan, Hughes continues to open up the discrepancy between Christmas cheer, Christian values, and "the ten-inch shells for Christmas gifts" he shows the Western imperialists bestowing on India, Africa, and, closer to home, Haiti, occupied by U.S. Marines since 1915:

> Ring Merry Christmas, Haiti!
> (And drown the voodoo drums—
> We'll rob you to the Christmas hymns
> Until the next Christ comes.)

For a poet whose livelihood depends on public readings, often in black churches, Hughes takes his chances. He wittily indicates that Christmas hymns support the imperialists' guns and robbery, which in turn help the missionaries suppress voodoo, a competing religion, "until the next Christ comes," surely not a language or insight to endear him to the religiously or politically orthodox. In this irreverent, radical international context, Hughes places the down-and-outers on American streets. In the midst of the depression, they are the recipients not of Christianity but of its secular equivalent, the supposedly impersonal, unchallengeable "economic laws" Hughes deflates by rhyming them nicely with "Santa Claus" in his cheery injunction,

> Oh, eat, drink and be merry
> With a bread-line Santa Claus

At the end of "Merry Christmas," in a passage of restrained satiric passion, Hughes underscores a central contradiction between professed Christian values and capitalistic practice. Using the contrast between Yuletide rhythms and rhymes and the practices of twentieth-century imperialists, in images that look ahead as well as back to World War I, Hughes concludes,

> While Holy steel that makes us strong
> Spits forth a mighty Yuletide song:
> SHOOT Merry Christmas everywhere!
> Let Merry Christmas GAS the air!

For Hughes the actual belief is in "Holy steel," not the Holy Child or the Holy Word. He also achieves a powerful satiric exposure by joining "Merry Christmas" to the incongruous verbs, "shoot" and "gas," so that he gives physical reality to Christianity as a sanction of the gas and guns of imperialist war. This undisguised reality plays off against the professed Christianity of "Merry Christmas" and good-will to men.

In addition to "Merry Christmas" in the *New Masses*, in December 1930 Hughes published three poems in *Opportunity: Journal of Negro Life*, the journal of the National Urban League.[24] The range of tone in his political poetry is illustrated in the contrast between the energy and irreverent, satiric drive of "Merry Christmas" and the dignity of "Pride." The "I" of the poem is Hughes in his role as black spokesman articulating his bitterness at the shame he has to swallow, at the poor pay "you proffer me" for honest work, at "your spit in my face" for honest dreams. Hughes's image of primal insult generates an understandable response:

> And so my fist is clenched—
> Too weak I know—
> But longing to be strong
> To strike your face!

In the radical poems of the next few years Hughes changed this longing into the militancy we have already seen in *Scottsboro Limited*. His revision of "Pride" for the 1938 *A New Song* is an index of his struggle to overcome the taboo against blacks' using force to oppose injustice and, in solidarity, to affirm personal and racial integrity. In the 1938 version Hughes makes the ending much more threatening than he had in 1930. The earlier acknowledgment of weakness is gone; the longed-for future is, starkly, now:

> And so my fist is clenched—
> Today—
> To strike your face.

Black and white hands together are the left symbol of racial solidarity. The clenched fist is a symbol of revolutionary militancy intensified and complicated in "Pride" by the understanding that the fist is black. In one of his most effective juxtapositions in *A New Song*, Hughes placed "Pride" and "Ballad of Ozie Powell" on facing pages, a reinforcing duet of militant response to racial abuse.[25]

At the beginning of 1931, in a medley of poems in *New Masses*, Hughes continued to react against the "meek and humble" stand required of "Certain Negro Leaders."[26] In developing his own response to racial injustice and the depression Hughes is, as he titles one of his poems, "Tired":

> I am so tired of waiting,
> Aren't you,
> For the world to become good
> And beautiful and kind?
> Let us take a knife
> And cut the world in two—
> And see what worms are eating
> At the rind.

This is revolutionary advice in the context of a revolutionary journal. Hughes relies on the powerful images of the world as a piece of rotten fruit, the knife cutting it cleanly and simply in two, and the worms eating at the rind. He uses these tactile, suggestive images to indict the corruption of the world and to advise collectively taking up the knife to change and cut through the rottenness. The knife, the gun, and the razor are three of the most highly charged symbols in the American discourse on race. For readers who see Hughes as African American, he doubly intensifies the sense of threat by turning the knife as a domestic implement into an insurrectionary weapon with a racial subtext. What the worms are Hughes leaves up to us.[27]

On the same page of *New Masses*, reinforcing and reinforced by "Tired," Hughes's "A Christian Country" appeared:

> God slumbers in a back alley
> With a gin bottle in His hand.
> Come on, God, get up and fight
> Like a man.

In dignifying the back-alley wino as God slumbering, Hughes cuts through an entire middle-class discourse morally judgmental of drinking, poverty, and irresponsibility. Whether it is of hopelessness, escapism, or destitution, his spectacle, then and now, indicts "a Christian country." Aside from the contrast between Christian profession and depression American neglect, Hughes also exploits the contrast between Christian respectability and his back-alley God. This God is the direct opposite of the God of "God to Hungry Child" but He is equally unorthodox and, "with a gin bottle in His hand," He is immediately recognizable. Hughes surprises us as, without preamble, he presents the back-alley wino as God slumbering. Hughes then plays on the distinction between God and man, subverting the customary ethic that associates God with turn-the-other-cheek. Instead, in Hughes's idiomatic phrase, straight from the street, "Come on, God, get up and fight / Like a man."

From their classic inscription in the fight between Frederick Douglass and Covey in *Narrative of the Life of Frederick Douglass*, the two words, "fight" and "man" have had a powerful resonance in African American culture. Hughes connects the values and practices they embody with the new revolutionary politics of the depression, with the exposures and injunctions of "Tired," and with the supporting red world of the increasingly militant *New Masses*. In deifying the back-alley down-and-out, Hughes also inverts the usual middle-class view and celebrates the human value and potential power of those at the bottom of society.

Hughes does not specify the race of his God with a gin bottle in his hand—He could be either black or white. But for readers who know Hughes's Harlem poems and know he is an African American poet, the gin bottle may very well be in a black hand as well as a white one, and race probably complicates and intensifies the general revolutionary imperative. To the extent that race enters in, it activates a complex of pejorative stereotypes about improvident blacks, stereotypes Hughes confronts, undermines, and transforms. Finally, however, Hughes subsumes race under the more general category he uses "God" to stand for.

The issue of race needs to be raised as a general issue in Hughes's radical poetry, or, rather, in interpreting the poetry. His sensitivity to the need for revolutionary change is inseparable from his experience as a black person in America. More particularly, when Hughes published poems in *Opportunity* or the *Negro Worker*, regardless of the explicit subject or speaker race is unmistakably involved because of who Hughes was and because of the racial context of the journal. In his *New Masses* poems race is also involved, since Hughes was identified as a prominent Negro poet, so that even in poems without an explicit racial theme there is always a racial dimension that varies from poem to poem, reader to reader. Especially for the *New Masses* poems, the intertwining of race and class in Third Period discussions of "the Negro

Question" and the tendency to place race second to the unity of the working class—
these features of both Third Period and Popular Front discourse are also relevant.

"Union," "White Shadows," "October 16"

In "Union," for example, which appeared in *New Masses* in September 1931, Hughes
speaks explicitly as a black man who has discovered that

> Not me alone
> I know now
> But the whole oppressed
> Poor world,
> White and black,
> Must put their hands with mine
> To shake the pillars of those temples
> Wherein the false gods dwell
> And the worn out altars stand
> Too well defended.[28]

The sentiment represents Hughes's predominant view of race, collective action,
and "the whole oppressed / Poor world," "poor" both economically and as an
object of pity. As in earlier and later poems, the militant hands appear, this time in
a context of images (the temple, the false gods, the worn-out altars) that do their
job but, if not worn out, for me lack the intensity of those in "Pride" and "Christ in
Alabama," the idiomatic irreverence of poems like "Merry Christmas" and "A
Christian Country," or the blasphemous specificity of poems like "Advertisement
for the Waldorf-Astoria" and "Goodbye, Christ." The "false gods" and "the worn
out altars" are not only the gods and altars of conventional religion but also of the
society's most well-defended beliefs and practices, the system of money, racial bias,
and class oppression Hughes is committed to bringing down. In the version he
revised for *A New Song*, Hughes added two final lines: "And the rule of greed's
upheld— / That must be ended" (p. 31). The new concluding lines convey a moral-
political commonplace and a morale-boosting militant imperative that qualifies
the power Hughes attributes to the "too well defended" altars. This revised version
ends both "Union" and the collection, *A New Song*.

In "White Shadows," also published in September 1931 (in *Contempo*), Hughes
develops a much bleaker, less characteristic view of race than he does in "Union."[29]
Beginning with its title, "White Shadows" is also a more suggestive poem than
"Union":

I'm looking for a house
In the world
Where white shadows
Will not fall.

There is no such house,
Dark Brother,
No such house
At all.

The concluding grim recognition emerges from the interplay of racial-political realities and physical impossibilities. "In the world" of racial and political experience, white shadows are everywhere, although "in the world" of physical experience white shadows do not exist. Hughes's imagery moves us back and forth endlessly between physical and racial-political realities, between the world of physics and the world of power. The white shadows that do not exist are at the same time ominous and omnipresent. The spare form answers to and underscores the elemental, inescapable presence of "white shadows" in an unsparing racial landscape.

The speaker is looking for a shelter someplace in the world "where white shadows / Will not fall." The sense of inescapable white power dominating the entire world, including the world of the speaker and the Dark Brother, shows the impact of Hughes's trip to Haiti in spring 1931. One of his essays about the trip is titled "White Shadows in a Black Land." In it Hughes uses his own observation to document specifically who has the power in Haiti. The U.S. Marines are everywhere. The cafés are filled with the "cracker" accents of the Marines, "drinking in the usual boisterous American manner." Beyond the military, "you will discover," Hughes continues, his eye on the other kind of control that counts, "that the Banque d'Haiti with its Negro cashiers and tellers, is really under control of the National City Bank of New York. You will be informed," he goes on, still concentrating on power and money, "that all the money collected by the Haitian customs passes through the hands of an American comptroller. And regretfully, you will gradually learn that most of the larger stores with their colored clerks are really owned by Frenchmen, Germans, or Assyrian Jews. And if you read the Haitian newspapers, you will soon realize from the heated complaints there, that even in the Chamber of Deputies, the strings of government are pulled by white politicians in far-off Washington—and that the American marines are kept in the country through an illegal treaty thrust on Haiti by force and never yet ratified by the United States Senate. The dark-skinned little Republic," Hughes concludes, "has its hair caught in the white fingers of unsympathetic foreigners, and the

Haitian people live today under a sort of military dictatorship backed by American guns. They are not free."[30]

In "White Shadows," as in a politically and racially charged Cubist landscape, Hughes eliminates the particular details and concentrates on the basic power relations and his grim response to them. The Dark Brother of the poem is not only African American but also Haitian and Cuban. He is also a much less hopeful version of "the darker brother" of Hughes's critical and affirmative "I Too Sing America." In "White Shadows" Hughes illuminates the racial impact of the same kind of world-ranging imperialism he had satirized in "Merry Christmas." The extremity of his vision in "White Shadows" is an index of his sense of the power and consequences of American and capitalistic might "in the world." Unlike such works as "Scottsboro Limited," "Tired," and "Union," in "White Shadows" Hughes does not modify his powerful negative criticism with the affirmative promise that black and white workers will make a revolutionary new world.

For readers in the present, Haiti still exists. Hughes's "White Shadows," "White Shadows in a Black Land," and "People without Shoes" take us back to an earlier period of American involvement. The dominance Hughes highlights underlies the current situation even as we have almost totally erased the earlier history from public discourse, so that "White Shadows" and "White Shadows in a Black Land" are involved in both a political and cultural suppression.

The historical context of Haiti in 1931 and the literary-historical context of Hughes's "White Shadows in a Black Land" are necessary to help us understand "White Shadows." The context of Hughes's radical poetry bears on the meaning of "October 16," another of the poems Hughes published in the Fall of 1931, in *Opportunity*.[31] Less extreme in tone and attitude than "White Shadows" and less overtly militant than "Union," "October 16" is a eulogy to John Brown's raid on Harpers Ferry. "Perhaps / You will remember / John Brown," Hughes begins, and then goes on,

John Brown
Who took his gun,
Took twenty-one companions
White and black,
Went to shoot your way to freedom
Where two rivers meet
And the hills of the
North
And the hills of the

South
Look slow at one another—
And died for your sake.

This John Brown is a Christlike bringer of freedom, not the crazed fanatic of liberal discourse. Within the language of the poem, however, Hughes is circumspect about using Brown to validate and encourage armed revolution. Instead, Hughes calmly presents the controversial symbols of the gun, the shooting, and the interracial group. In a gesture of reconciliation that also involves violent disruption, Hughes's landscape brings North and South together even as the integrated black and white band acts "to shoot your way to freedom"—"your," not "his" or "their." Through this shift of pronouns, which subtly merges the reader with Brown and his black and white companions, Hughes involves the reader as an active participant in the violence. In the context of *Opportunity* and what Hughes says throughout about the "you" he is addressing, the audience is first of all African American, although white readers can easily join in.

In what follows, Hughes qualifies the immediacy he has created. His tone becomes retrospective, he celebrates success ("Now that you are / Many years free"), and he unprotestingly acknowledges that "Brown himself / Has long been tried at law, / Hanged by the neck, / And buried in the ground." But in a lovely turn, Hughes also resurrects Brown, brings him again into the present, and concludes,

Since Harpers Ferry
Is alive with ghosts today,
Immortal raiders
Come to town—
Perhaps
You will recall
John Brown.

This elegiac celebration of the "immortal raiders" is not a militant injunction like those in "Union," "Tired," or "Scottsboro Limited," works Hughes was writing at the same time as "October 16." Perhaps that is why, unlike these poems, Hughes included "October 16" in his *Selected Poems*. Read in the context of his other 1930–31 poems, however, "October 16" does have a militant charge centering on the gun, the shooting, the black and white companions, and the celebration of the "immortal raiders." This militant undertow is obscured when the poem is removed from its companion works and placed in collections that filter out Hughes's radical politics, including the context of Third Period "revolutionary upsurge." The reverse also holds. On October 14, 1937, Hughes republished "October 16" in *Volunteer for Liberty*, the Abraham Lincoln Brigades's journal during the Spanish Civil War. Beyond the coincidence of the date, the context of radical involvement in the war to save the republic and defeat Franco intensifies the sense of militant sacrifice in the good fight. What the reader recalls of John Brown, what he or she makes of him as Hughes gives him to us, is not fixed but depends to an extent on context.

"Advertisement for the Waldorf-Astoria"

Several contexts animate "Advertisement for the Waldorf-Astoria," another of the poems Hughes wrote during the fall of 1931. He published it in *New Masses* in December, so that the "CHRISTMAS CARD" ending is, like "Merry Christmas," seasonal. Another occasion for the poem is that, two years into the depression and in the midst of the fight to save the Scottsboro Boys, Hughes read a two-page advertisement in *Vanity Fair*, the most elegant magazine in America.[32] Along with ads for luxury cars, furs, and expensive clothing—the depression did not exist in the world of *Vanity Fair*—Hughes encountered an advertisement announcing the opening of the new Waldorf-Astoria "where," as Hughes noted, "no Negroes worked and none were admitted as guests."[33] In his poem, in place of the bold-faced headings in the ad—"PRIVACY," "FREEDOM FROM RESPONSIBILITY," "MODERN CONVENIENCES"— Hughes substitutes such headings as "LISTEN, HUNGRY ONES," "EVICTED FAMILIES," and "NEGROES."

In a prose format like the ad's, Hughes opens up the absurdities and contrasts between his down-and-outers and the luxury of the rich in their new hotel. His approach is to parody the ad, sometimes by using a left language, sometimes an idiomatic language instead of *Vanity Fair* formality and by directing his flophouse clientele to take advantage of the amenities the hotel provides, to "ankle on down to 49th Street at Park Avenue." Hughes summarizes the "PRIVATE ENTERTAINING" and "PUBLIC FUNCTIONS" the ad describes by intoning of the Waldorf,

> It will be a distinguished background for society.
> So, when you've got no place to go, homeless and hungry ones, choose the
> Waldorf as a background for your rags—
> (Or do you still consider the subway after midnight good enough?)

Under the heading, "ROOMERS," "take a room at the new Waldorf," he advises them, "sleepers in charity's flop-houses where God pulls a long face, and you have to pray to get a bed."

For their edification Hughes reprints a luncheon menu of "GUMBO CREOLE /

CRABMEAT IN CASSOLETTE / BOILED BRISKET OF BEEF / SMALL ONIONS IN CREAM / WATERCRESS SALAD / PEACH MELBA." Then he adds, "Have luncheon there this afternoon, all you jobless. Why not?" To provide an answer, Hughes departs from his dominant tone of high-spirited satiric indignation. He reanimates the left imagery of hands, some cutting coupons while others, exploited by the rich, do hard manual labor. Parodying the ad writer's invitation, Hughes tells his people, "dine with some of the men and women who got rich off of your labor" and then in the emotionally charged, pile-driver rhythms and imagery of left discourse he adds,

> who clip coupons with clean white fingers because your
> hands dug coal, drilled stone, sewed garments, poured
> steel to let other people draw dividends and live easy.
> (Or haven't you had enough yet of the soup-lines and the bitter bread of
>   charity?)
> Walk through Peacock Alley tonight before dinner, and get warm, anyway.
>   You've got nothing else to do.

In one of his most irreverent sections, under the heading "NEGROES" Hughes shifts from the language of left social protest to the language of black vernacular, a language especially incongruous in the upper-class white world of the Waldorf and *Vanity Fair*. "Oh, Lawd, I done forgot Harlem!" Hughes breaks in, using "I" for the first time. Then, in the perfectly rendered idiom of the street, Hughes goes on to contrast the reality of hunger on 135th Street with

> the swell music they got at the Waldorf-Astoria. It sure is a mighty nice place to
> shake hips in, too. There's dancing after supper in a big warm room. It's cold as
> hell on Lenox Avenue. All you've had all day is a cup of coffee. Your pawnshop
> overcoat's a ragged banner on your hungry frame.

Does the last line heighten the emotional impact not only through the contrast between ease and pawnshop poverty but also through the reinforcing contrast between the street idiom of "shake hips" and " cold as hell" and the more formal, literary metaphor, "a ragged banner on your hungry frame"? Hughes often achieves his effects by juxtaposing contrasting languages, although readers unsympathetic to his literary and political project may respond negatively to the slight elevation of the metaphor of the pawnshop overcoat as "a ragged banner on your hungry frame."

In any case, in the pages of *New Masses*, writing explicitly to "you colored folks" within the poem but also to a radical white reading audience, Hughes goes on to subvert the upper-class fascination with things Negro. "You know," he writes, "downtown folks are just crazy about Paul Robeson! Maybe they'll like you, too, black mob from Harlem." Of course. Through the comic and slightly ominous incongruity of the "black mob," Hughes deconstructs the 1920s cult of Harlem, "When the Negro Was in Vogue," as he phrased it in a chapter heading of his autobiography, *The Big Sea*. Hughes cuts even deeper when he invites his "black mob" to

Drop in at the Waldorf this afternoon for tea. Stay to dinner. Give Park Avenue a lot of darkie color—free for nothing! Ask the Junior Leaguers to sing a spiritual for you. They probably know 'em better than you do—and their lips won't be so chapped with cold after they step out of their closed cars in the undercover driveways.
Hallelujah! Undercover driveways!
Ma soul's a witness for de Waldorf-Astoria!

At his most acute, Hughes enters taboo territory and deflates the mix of class privilege and racial condescension at the heart of society's affair with the Negro. At the end he perfectly uses black vernacular to diminish those symbols of class and racial inequity, the underground driveways and the Waldorf itself. In the process, Hughes undercuts the religiously tinged Uncle Tom language he himself turns into a vehicle of hard-hitting comic protest.

In the "CHRISTMAS CARD" that ends the poem, Hughes intensifies his irreverent religious satire. Looking ahead to "Goodbye, Christ" and back to "Christ in Alabama," "Merry Christmas," and "A Christian Country," Hughes exuberantly, provocatively sends his radical greetings:

Hail Mary, Mother of God!
the new Christ child of the Revolution's about to be born.
(Kick hard, red baby, in the bitter womb of the mob.)
Somebody, put an ad in *Vanity Fair* quick!
Call Oscar of the Waldorf—for Christ's sake!
It's almost Christmas, and that little girl—turned whore
because her belly was too hungry to stand it anymore—wants
a nice clean bed for the Immaculate Conception.
Listen, Mary, Mother of God, wrap your new born babe in the red flag of
Revolution: the Waldorf-Astoria's the best manger we've got. For
reservations: Telephone EL.53000.

The censors who a decade later hounded Hughes because of "Goodbye, Christ" somehow overlooked the ending of "Advertisement for the Waldorf-Astoria." In

"CHRISTMAS CARD" Hughes's cultural politics are as radical as his politics. In presenting Mary as a "little girl—turned whore / because her belly was too hungry to stand it anymore," Hughes vividly connects depression hunger and poverty and that of the Holy Family. He does so with a blasphemy—Mary as whore—that he compounds in relating the immaculateness of the Immaculate Conception to the clean bed Mary needs and the manger of the Waldorf can supply. Hughes's radical politics reinforce and are reinforced by his irreverent cultural politics. The brash announcement that "the new Christ child of the Revolution's about to be born," the injunction "kick hard, red baby, in the bitter womb of the mob," and the final imperative, "listen Mary, Mother of God, wrap your new born babe in the red flag of Revolution" are examples of the radical spirit of 1931, hopeful, optimistic, unintimidated. In "CHRISTMAS CARD" and "Goodbye, Christ," Hughes handles communism as the new religion with more verve and idiomatic force than anyone in the decade.

In "Advertisement for the Waldorf-Astoria" Hughes is also one of the pioneering left poets who incorporated and put to unconventional uses the language of the media—advertising, in this case, the documentary in Muriel Rukeyser's, the movies in Kenneth Fearing's. These poets engaged and tapped into the energy of influential "low" forms and turned them from their prevailingly commercial to left uses. As with the black vernacular and jazz rhythms and improvisation that animate his work, Hughes as much as any modernist delights in "low" forms typically excluded from the "high" art of traditional poetry. They contribute to the immediacy, energy, and accessibility of his work, reinforced in the *New Masses* by the drawings that frame "Advertisement for the Waldorf-Astoria." The drawings are fanciful satiric line sketches of limousines, upper-class dowagers and top-hatted gentle-men, and decadent partygoers above a panorama of grim-faced working people.

"Goodbye, Christ"

Between "Advertisement for the Waldorf-Astoria" (December 1931) and "Goodbye, Christ" (*Negro Worker*, November–December 1932), Hughes came out strongly for the 1932 Communist Party ticket of Foster and Ford. In "Goodbye, Christ" he savages the "pawned," "wore out" Christ of the established religions and celebrates His replacement, "a new guy with no religion at all— / A real guy named / Marx Communist Lenin Peasant Stalin Worker ME— / I said, ME."[34] Before we know who he is, using black vernacular and a kind of fearless folk hyperbole, this collective "I" brashly says,

Listen, Christ,
You did alright in your day, I reckon—
But that day's gone now.
They ghosted you up a swell story, too—
Called it Bible—
But it's dead now.

The idiom and good-humored, blasphemous irreverence of "ghosted you up a swell story, too / Called it Bible— / But it's dead now" contribute their distinctive accents to Hughes's culturally and politically radical art.

With a fine indifference to particular denominations, the "I" of the poem goes on to offend the orthodoxies of Catholicism and Protestantism ("the popes and the preachers") and to indict conventional religion for selling out to money, political, military, and cultural power. Of the Bible, the "swell story" they've "ghosted up,"

The popes and the preachers've
Made too much money from it.
They've sold you to too many
Kings, generals, robbers, and killers—
Even to the Tzar and the Cossacks,
Even to Rockefellers Church,
Even to *The Saturday Evening Post*.
You ain't no good no more.
They've pawned you
Till you've done wore out.

Hughes irreverently mixes American references, Russian Communist antagonists, and black street idiom.

In the stanza that gives him his title and identifies the speaker, Hughes continues to build momentum and to mix idiom, irreverence, and communism:

Goodbye,
Christ Jesus Lord God Jehova,
Beat it on away from here now.
Make way for a new guy with no religion at all—
A real guy named
Marx Communist Lenin Peasant Worker ME—
I said ME—

In the balancing lines (Christ Jesus . . . Marx Communist), Hughes intensifies his compound of blasphemy and rebellious Third Period affirmation, as he does when the "new guy" concludes,

Go ahead on now,
You're getting in the way of things, Lord.
And please take Saint Gandhi with you when you go,
And Saint Pope Pius,
And Saint Aimee McPherson,
And big black Saint Becton
Of the Consecrated Dime.
Move!

Don't be so slow about movin'!
The world is mine from now on—
And nobody's gonna sell ME
To a king, or a general,
Or a millionaire.

Close to the start of the nearly decade-long "moment of Marxism," Hughes's concluding brag defines an early, hopeful sense of possibility. Using an idiomatic language accessible to ordinary working people, in "Goodbye, Christ," as in the best of his radical poetry, Hughes mobilizes the energies of believers and expresses his own deeply felt criticism and commitment. Read in the light of subsequent history, however, we can see that selling out to millionaires is not the only pitfall for a radical movement. As with all of Hughes's radical poetry and most of the work of the 1930s left, an entire discourse of disillusion with Soviet-style communism could be brought to bear on "Goodbye, Christ" and its ending. Beyond this single instance, the history of reaction to "Goodbye, Christ" vividly bears out the general view that literary works do not have fixed, unalterable meanings and that to an extent judgments about quality vary with context and the reader's situation.

For movement readers of the November–December Negro Worker, where the poem first appeared, or for sympathetic readers of the reprints in the 1934 left anthology, Negro, and the 1938 The Negro's God, "Goodbye, Christ" had a significantly different meaning than it did for the influential African American ministers who attacked the poem in 1933 in the widely circulated African American newspaper, the Pittsburgh Courier.[35] They did not influence Hughes's political stand but it may not be a coincidence that he never again published the kind of exuberantly blasphemous religious satire that he had in "Goodbye, Christ," "Advertisement for the Waldorf-Astoria," "A Christian Country," "Merry Christmas," and "God to Hungry Child."

The evangelist Aimee Simple McPherson and her publicist were two other readers who had a demonstrably different view of "Goodbye, Christ" than its original movement readers presumably had. On November 15, 1940, the two orchestrated a noisy, well-publicized picketing of an appearance Hughes was to make at a book and author luncheon at the exclusive Vista Del Arroyo Hotel in Pasadena.[36] A month later, in its December 21, 1940, issue, the *Saturday Evening Post*, another recipient of Hughes's attention, repaid the honor by reprinting "Goodbye, Christ" without Hughes's permission. By 1940 not only was the movement increasingly on the defensive but also in the pages of the *Saturday Evening Post* "Goodbye, Christ" had a somewhat different ring than it had in the *Negro Worker*.

The most dramatic contrast in meaning and context was the reading Senator Albert Hawkes gave of "Goodbye, Christ" and "One More 'S' in the U.S.A."[37] By early 1948 when he called Hughes a Communist and entered the poems in the *Congressional Record*, anticommunism was becoming the official American religion and the inquisitors were busy enforcing orthodoxy. "Communist" now signified a traitorous demonism at odds with the thrust of Hughes's usage and commitment. Even more than in the 1930s, in 1948 the energy, irreverence, and critical power of "Goodbye, Christ" were threatening to religiously and politically conservative readers and to liberals touchy about the taint of communism. In ways not obvious on the surface, the very qualities that animated the poem and disturbed some readers were also invaluable. They could have reminded people losing their nerve of an alternative political culture, neither Stalinist nor conformist but impudent, rebellious, and alive. Religious orthodoxy and obsessive anticommunism, however, encouraged a focus on doctrinal issues that made—and perhaps still make—the underlying qualities and implications difficult for some readers to see and value.

"Good Morning, Revolution"

The same holds for another of Hughes's 1932 poems, "Good Morning, Revolution," which he published in the *New Masses* along with "For Tom Moody" at a time of active protest that included the World War I veterans Bonus March on Washington.[38] Hughes takes his title and form from such blues songs as Leadbelly's "Good Morning Blues" and puts them to revolutionary uses.[39] The "I" of the poem emerges as a representative unemployed worker, not specifically African

American but a worker who speaks a racy idiom and brings into the open a rebellious working-class consciousness. If the reader responds to the idiom and speech rhythms as African American, however, Hughes sets up an interplay between the explicit Communist language of "workers" and "tools of production," the celebration of "Revolution" and the "greetings to the Socialist Soviet Republics" and the more specifically African American language encoded in idiom, rhythm, and turns of phrase. For some readers they characterize the speaker not only as a rebellious worker but also as a rebellious black worker. In either case, Hughes shows his marvelous facility for entering diverse points of view. The poem represents his outlook but, like Revolution, the speaker is a personified, representative figure, not Hughes himself.

Treating revolution as a human being instead of an abstraction contributes to the lively immediacy of the poem. From the start the speaker establishes an intimate relation with all of those energies, groups, and forces "Revolution" stands for. Far from the revolutionaries' conspiratorially seeking the workers out, moreover, Hughes has the speaker take the initiative in greeting the new day coming:

> Good morning, Revolution:
>> You're the very best friend
>> I ever had.
> We gonna pal around together from now on.

Hughes speaks to the heart of conservative fears and left hopes. As he continues, Hughes brings into the open the appeal of communism and disposes through contrast and down-home idiom of the stock objection that Communists are "trouble making alien enemies." In a good-humored way Hughes goes on to build up the catalog of what the owners have and do:

> The boss's got all he needs, certainly,
>> Eats swell,
>> Owns a lotta houses,
>> Goes vactionin',
>> Breaks strikes,
>> Runs politics, bribes police,
>> And struts all over the earth—
> But me, I ain't never had enough to eat.
> Me, I ain't never known security—
> All my life, been livin' hand to mouth,
>> Hand to mouth.

Hughes politicizes the concluding blues phrase and repetition by placing the lines in a context of left contrasts. The blues language and sensibility contribute their authenticity to the proletarian politics of the poem. Hughes also reanimates the standard left attitudes through his convincing idiomatic particularity at the start, through the surprise of "eats swell" and "goes vactionin'" juxtaposed with more underground activities—"breaks strikes," "bribes police," and the other examples of what the boss does with his money and power, culminating in the comic spectacle of "Pays off congress, / And struts all over the earth." Hughes compresses into one comic image an entire discourse on owner power, arrogance, and dominance.

In the remainder of the poem Hughes has his working-class speaker tell his "buddy," Revolution, "Together, / We can take everything." The "we" includes all revolutionary workers and the "everything" includes

Factories, arsenals, houses, ships,
Railroads, forests, fields, orchards,
Bus lines, telegraphs, radios
(Jesus! Raise hell with radios!)
Steel mills, coal mines, oil wells, gas,
All the tools of production,
(Great day in the morning!)
And turn 'em over to the people who work.
Rule and run 'em for us people who work.

With a fine sense of timing, Hughes interjects the idiomatic "Jesus! Raise hell with radios!" into his left catalog, just as he playfully uses "great day in the morning!" to undercut a certain pretentiousness in the slogan "all the tools of production."

The radios recur in the final stanza as America joins in,

Broadcasting that very first morning to USSR:
Another member the International Soviet's done come
Greetings to the Socialist Soviet Republics
Hey you rising workers everywhere greetings

As he continues, Hughes combines elliptical street idiom and Communist celebration to reconfirm left readers in their commitment to the revolution, to the Soviet Union, and to the worldwide victory over hunger, cold, and oppression. In stressing at the end that "I been starvin' too long / Ain't you?" Hughes brings together long-term poverty and oppression, the depression, and the immediacy and symbolic force of "starvin'," literally for food and more generally for those intangibles the Revolution is to supply.

In poems like "Good Morning, Revolution" Hughes draws on Third Period Communist slogans and attitudes and infuses them with idiomatic energy and good-humored comic critique and characterization. These poems serve to raise the morale of believers—a small minority in America in 1932—and to express Hughes's personal criticism and beliefs. Readers who choose to dismiss these poems as propaganda have to filter out the play of idiomatic and party language, the frequent irreverence, and the pervasive charge of personal commitment to a common cause. The good-natured treatment of revolution, of course, ignores the blood, suffering, and complexity inseparable from revolution and leaves Hughes open to the charge of naiveté. A less negative view is that Hughes's treatment of revolution expresses the hopefulness of radicals in the early 1930s at a time when the Soviet Union appeared vital and beleaguered and the depression and Scottsboro called for basic, not cosmetic change. With the evidence of collapse all around them, radicals could understandably believe that the breakdown would minimize the need for revolutionary violence. As the contrast between "Good Morning, Revolution" and his antiimperialist poems illustrates, Hughes is much more willing to specify the violence white capitalists inflict on blacks "everywhere" than he is to imagine the violence of revolution. When he does bring that violence to imaginative life, he typically does so in the context of deeply felt racial as well as capitalistic injustice.

"The Same"

And no wonder. Hughes's commitment to revolutionary change is inseparable from his experience as a black man and his understanding of exploitation, a combination that drives another of his fall 1932 poems, "The Same." Hughes published "The Same" in the September–October 1932 issue of the *Negro Worker*, an international journal, "organ of the International Trade Union Committee of Negro Workers, Hamburg, Germany." The motto of the *Negro Worker* was "Workers of the World, Unite!"[40] The editors introduced the poem with a photo and an identifying note that presents the radical Hughes of the 1930s, "the young revolutionary novelist and poet, . . . the author of several volumes of poems describing various phases of Negro working class life in America. He has recently written a play on the infamous Alabama case, called the 'Scottsboro Express' [*sic*]."[41] In this context the "I" of the poem is Hughes speaking first for himself and later as a representative black person. As a merchant seaman and traveler, Hughes can say from direct experience,

It is the same everywhere for me:
On the docks at Sierra Leone,
In the cotton fields of Alabama,
In the diamond mines of Kimberley,
On the coffee hills of Haiti,
The banana lands of Central America,
The streets of Harlem,
And the cities of Morocco and Tripoli.

This opening has a cadence and dignity that appropriately express Hughes's sense of the deep wrong white capitalists have inflicted on blacks, "everywhere":

Black:
Exploited, beaten, and robbed,
Shot and killed.
Blood running into
    Dollars
    Pounds
    Francs
    Pesetas
    Lire
For the wealth of the exploiters—
Blood that never comes back to me again.

The blood that never comes back elides with the money, the international capital, that never comes back. Blood and money fuse. Unlike "White Shadows," however, in "The Same" Hughes voices militant, revolutionary opposition to the imperialistic exploitation he particularizes. When he goes on, the blood—"my blood," Hughes's and all those he represents—is now a symbol of violent revolt against the beating, shooting, killing, and exploiting that precipitate and justify revolution:

Better that my blood
Runs into the deep channels of Revolution,
Runs into the strong hands of Revolution,
Stains all flags red,
Drives away from
    Sierra Leone

Kimberley
Alabama
Haiti
Central America
Harlem
Morocco
Tripoli
And all the black lands everywhere
The force that kills,
The power that robs,
And the greed that does not care.

When he focuses on the violence of white exploiters, for Hughes revolution is no longer the good-natured "pal" of "Good Morning, Revolution." He now stresses that the red flag is inseparable from the blood spilled in "driving away from . . . all the black lands everywhere / The force that kills, / The power that robs, / And the greed that does not care."

Unlike Richard Wright, who had serious problems reconciling the competing claims of race and proletarian unity, Hughes is not troubled. He repeatedly affirms the militant unity of black and white and all the races, as he does at the end of "The Same":

Better that my blood makes one with the blood
Of all the struggling workers in the world—
Till every land is free of
    Dollar robbers
    Pound robbers
    Franc robbers
    Peseta robbers
    Lire robbers
    Life robbers—
Until the Red Armies of the International Proletariat,
Their faces black, white, olive, yellow, brown,
Unite to raise the blood Red Flag that
Never will come down!

Although the radical content compels attention, the form is also worth considering. The reiterated parallel structure and the skillfully varied refrain line of dollars and pounds, Sierra Leone and Tripoli, lire robbers and life robbers, have the emphasis and impact of the African and New Orleans drumbeat Hughes often uses as a rhythmic model, here intertwined with Third Period proletarian slogans. As for the content, "the Red Armies of the International Proletariat" are international, not specifically those of the Soviet Union, although in the context of "Good Morning, Revolution" the red armies of the Soviet Union are themselves international. In the *Negro Worker* the concluding militant affirmation is reinforced by a drawing of a powerful black man above a globe showing the United States, Cuba, Haiti, and Africa. The black man is breaking the chains that shackle these lands.

"Revolution"

In "Revolution," a February 20, 1934, *New Masses* poem, blacks are not the focus, although their enslavement and oppression is in the background.[42] In the foreground Hughes addresses and celebrates the

> Great Mob that knows no fear—
> Come here!
> And raise your hand
> Against this man
> Of iron and steel and gold
> Who's bought and sold
> You—
> Each one—
> For the last thousand years.

Hughes continues his effective practice of personifying large forces, here of the wealthy ruling class as "this man / Of iron and steel and gold." The iron, steel, and gold are prime sources of dominant class power. They also define the antagonist as a power to reckon with, so that in Hughes's drama of rebellion the opposing forces are both significant. Hughes justifies and motivates revolution and brings it home to "You / Each one" on the grounds that "this man" has "bought and sold" each of us, that capitalistic control amounts to slavery in a process that has gone on "for the last thousand years."

The militancy intensifies as Hughes repeats,

> Come here,
> Great mob that knows no fear,
> And tear him limb from limb,
> Split his golden throat

Ear to ear,
And end his time forever,
Now—
this year—
Great mob that knows no fear.

By stressing its courage and characterizing it as "great," majestic, Hughes redefines the mob, undercutting its negative associations, for example, with the mob of the French Revolution and, for middle-class readers, its pejorative suggestion of disorder and the violence of striking workers. In voicing a sense of immediacy, Hughes was also reinforcing a view he shared with the other editors of the *New Masses*. In the same issue with "Revolution," the cover of the February 20, 1934, issue featured "Europe on the Barricades," a drawing of a factory, and the bold letters, STRIKE. The epigraph for the issue was, "For Justice themselves condemnation— / A better world's in birth!" Then the lead editorial began, "Austria! France! Spain! Europe on the barricades. The world is afire with revolution and harbingers of revolution" (p. 3). In Hughes's version the immediacy comes from vivid physical action and the stress on "Now— / This year." But Hughes also distances the violence by using the timeless, biblical imagery of "tear him limb from limb, / Split his golden throat / Ear to ear," a language that simultaneously encourages and validates revolutionary violence, gives it a biblical precedent, and obscures its actual forms in the present.

"Cubes"

The next month, without detracting from his commitment or from the seriousness of his work, Hughes deals playfully with the contradiction between "Liberty, Egality, Fraternity" and "the old game of black and white."[43] In "Cubes" Hughes looks back on the Paris of the 1920s from the vantage point of 1934:

In the days of the broken cubes of Picasso
And in the days of the broken songs of the
Young men
A little too drunk to sing
And the young women
A little too unsure of love to love—
I met on the boulevards of Paris
An African from Senegal.

The African is probably Leopold Senghor.

God
Knows why the French
Amuse themselves bringing to Paris
Negroes from Senegal.
It's the old game of the boss and the bossed,
   boss and the bossed,
Amused
   and
Amusing,
   worked and working
Behind the cubes of black and white,
     black and white,
   black and white

At first "the broken cubes of Picasso" are "cubes," as in "cubism." But Hughes then gives the colors and shapes, "the cubes of black and white," a sense of racial separation and the "old game of the boss and the bossed." Hughes politicizes cubism and also plays a game with blues repetition and line variation, so that he amuses himself by having the form of the poem both conform to and subvert the apolitical Paris world of "broken cubes." The game is even more amusing for readers who see the cubes as dice and the "old game" as a play on craps.

The fun intensifies as Hughes develops the demimonde milieu of the whore-house:

But since it is the old game,
For fun
They gave him the three old prostitutes of
   France—
Liberty, Egality, Fraternity—
And all three of 'em sick
In spite of the tax to the government
And the legal houses
And the doctors
And the *Marseillaise*.

Hughes is worldly, irreverent, and scathing in his exposure of the gap between the basic ideals of French and American democracy and "the old game" of racism and exploitation. The ideals are "a disease . . . the young African from Senegal / Carries back from Paris . . . / To spread among the black girls in the palm huts."

He brings them as a gift
   disease—
From light to darkness
   disease—
From the bossed to the bossed
   disease—
From the game of black and white
  disease
From the city of the broken cubes of Picasso
        d
         i
     s
   e
   a
      s
    e

Hughes, too, gives and takes as he plays riffs on his blues theme, turns "disease" into an indictment and celebration, and breaks up and playfully rearranges the form of his key word so that we can know it fully. Some readers may also see a scatter of dice in the concluding throw of "disease." For Hughes and the *New Masses*, in 1934 it was not all blood and Europe on the barricades.

"One More 'S' in the U.S.A." and "Ballad of Lenin"

Three weeks after "Cubes" appeared in the *New Masses*, Hughes published "One More 'S' in the U.S.A.," a "workers' song on the occasion of the Eighth Convention of the C.P.U.S.A."[44] Hughes originally composed the poem for a Scottsboro rally.[45] The refrain line conveys the force of Hughes's hope and commitment:

Put one more *S* in the U.S.A.
To make it Soviet.
One more *S* in the U.S.A.
Oh, we'll live to see it yet.
When the land belongs to the farmers
And the factories to the working men—
The U.S.A. when we take control
Will be the U.S.S.A then.

Despite its energy and political interest, until the 1995 *Collected Poems* the poem was never reprinted and Donald C. Dickinson does not list it in his *Bio-Bibliography of Langston Hughes*.[46] "One More 'S' in the U.S.A." is Hughes's most overt expression of his support for the Communist Party and for revolutionary change in America.

He develops that support in another of his 1934 poems, "Ballad of Lenin," one of his three selections in *Proletarian Literature in the United States: An Anthology* (1935).[47] In "Ballad of Lenin," as in "Good Morning, Revolution," Hughes tells another leader,

> Comrade Lenin of Russia,
> High in a marble tomb,
> Move over, Comrade Lenin,
> And give me room.

Part of the ongoing drama of the poem is the identity of the speaker. In a poem signed "Langston Hughes," it is significant that the first identification is

> I am Ivan, the peasant,
> Boots all muddy with soil.
> I fought with you, Comrade Lenin,
> Now I have finished my toil.

The command to "move over" does not mean that Lenin is being displaced. Far from it. Lenin is

> Alive in a marble tomb,
> Move over, Comrade Lenin,
> And give me room.

In Hughes's version Lenin is not an authoritarian leader. Instead, in the democracy of the revolution Lenin shares his honors with the workers who, as the composite "I" of the poem, speak to him directly:

> I am Chico, the Negro,
> Cutting cane in the sun.
> I lived for you, Comrade Lenin,
> Now my work is done.

> Comrade Lenin of Russia,
> Honored in a marble tomb,
> Move over, Comrade Lenin,
> And give me room.

Hughes handles the refrain of the ballad so that the speaker is both Ivan and Chico and now

> I am Chang from the foundries
> On strike in the streets of Shanghai,
> For the sake of the Revolution
> I fight, I starve, I die.

> Comrade Lenin of Russia
> Rises in the marble tomb:
> *On guard with the fighters forever—*
> *The world is our room!*

In the omniscient voice of the final stanza, Lenin lives. His rising echoes Christ's but with a militant, revolutionary connotation that gives his sanction and protection to "the fighters forever." At the end the "marble tomb," the "room" of the poem, is transformed into the revolutionary affirmation, "the world is our room." The ballad shows that the room of the world is filled with committed workers of all colors from around the globe.

"Park Bench" and "White Man"

In a lighter but still provocative mode, in another of his *Proletarian Literature* poems, "Park Bench," Hughes idiomatically illuminates and subverts the geography of class in New York and America:

> I live on a park bench,
> You, Park Avenue.
> Hell of a distance
> Between us two.

> I beg a dime for dinner—
> You got a butler and maid.
> But I'm wakin' up!
> Say, ain't you afraid

> That I might, just maybe,
> In a year or two,
> Move on over
> To Park Avenue?[48]

The "I" of the poem is a representative depression figure, bantering and coming into a militant, working-class consciousness. In rendering this change, Hughes appeals to the hopes of his left audience but in a much more understated and playful way than in poems like "Revolution." The qualifications in the final stanza, the play of "might" and "maybe," highlight Hughes's range, as in "Cubes" at the other extreme from the energized left slogans in poems like "Ballad of Lenin" and "Good Morning, Revolution."[49]

In "White Man" Hughes continues his mode of direct, idiomatic address, this time between a black "I" and a White Man "you."[50] The oppositions of rich and poor, good jobs and mean ones, Park Avenue and park bench emerge again, underscored by the opposition of white and black:

Sure, I know you!
You're a White Man,
I'm a Negro.
You take all the best jobs
And leave us the garbage cans to empty and
The halls to clean.
You have a good time in a big house at
Palm Beach
And rent us the back alleys
And the dirty slums.

The details are specific, representative, and unforced, as is the witty contrast,

You enjoy Rome—
And *take* Ethiopia.

From the politics of the fascist takeover of Ethiopia, Hughes moves closer to home:

White Man! White Man!
Let Louis Armstrong play it—
And you copyright it
And make the money.
You're the smart guy, White Man!
You got everything!

Hughes builds to the turning point of "White Man," a contest between the primacy of race and class. During the 1930s the contest was crucial for African Americans in the movement. Hughes resolves it militantly in favor of Marx and

The Communist Manifesto as the speaker experiences another of the conversions that distinguish the literature of the 1930s left:

But now,
I hear your name ain't really White Man.
I hear it's something
Marx wrote down
Fifty years ago—
That rich people don't like to read.
Is that true, White Man?
Is your name in a book
Called The Communist Manifesto?
Is your name spelled
C-A-P-I-T-A-L-I-S-T?
Are you always a White Man?
Huh?

At the end the taunting question rather than an assertion draws in the reader and strengthens the impact of the speaker's insight.

"Air Raid over Harlem"

For Hughes the allusion to Ethiopia was not casual. In "Air Raid over Harlem: Scenario for a Little Black Movie" (1935–36), he fuses the fascist bombing of Ethiopia with another war, the one the white police waged against black people in the Harlem "riot" of 1935. On March 19, 1935, Harlem erupted after a rumor spread that the police had killed a black teenager, a suspect in a minor theft. Although the Manhattan district attorney blamed Communists for the riot, the official report established that the underlying causes were long-term neglect—no new schools in Harlem for over twenty-five years, substandard conditions at Harlem Hospital, and severe depression unemployment, even worse in Harlem than elsewhere. The report focused on police provocation and intense resentment at a long history of racial injustice and conflict with a predominantly white police force as the immediate cause of the uncoordinated window smashing and looting that spread through Harlem.[51] At the same time, throughout 1935 the headlines and newsreels were also filled with the buildup to Mussolini's bombing of Ethiopia, a war that began in October 1935.

In a surreal, incendiary "scenario for a little black movie," Hughes brings together the war in Ethiopia and what he presents as the war on Harlem. In the "scenario" Hughes is more formally experimental than usual. He combines modernist disruptions of the text, surreal dreams and political juxtapositions, and the techniques of the Living Newspaper. "Air Raid over Harlem" is at one extreme in the range of Hughes's politically engaged art. It deserves commentary because of its form and the intensity of Hughes's political involvement, and because, like most of Hughes's radical work, it has received absolutely no critical attention, a neglect that might change after its appearance in the second edition of the *Heath Anthology*.[52]

Hughes begins idiomatically with two speakers discussing the film:

Who you gonna put in it?
Me.
Who the hell are you?
Harlem.
Alright, then.

The moviemaker is Harlem personified; the questioner, also from Harlem, is understandably concerned about "AIR RAID OVER HARLEM," in the words of the first of the Living Newspaper headlines Hughes uses provocatively throughout the poem. "You're not talkin' 'bout Harlem, are you?" the questioner asks, and then brings vividly into the open,

That's where my home is,
My bed is, my woman is, my kids is!
Harlem, that's where I live!
Look at my streets
Full of black and brown and
Yellow and high-yellow
Jokers like me.
Lenox, Seventh, Edgecombe, 145th.
Listen,
Hear 'em talkin' and laughin'?
Bombs over Harlem'd kill
People like me—
Kill ME!

By precisely discriminating the multiple shades of "jokers like me," Hughes deconstructs the racial monolith, "black" or "Negro." He simultaneously drives home the immediacy of the killing of "people like me"—and of ME—so that the "Ethiopian war [that] broke out last night" is not abstract and distant. But Hughes also fuses the Ethiopian war and the police war. The next newspaper headline, "BOMBS OVER HARLEM," acquires a surreal double reference juxtaposed with

Cops on every corner
Most of 'em white

And then another tabloid headline from the riot,

COPS IN HARLEM
Guns and billy-clubs
Double duty in Harlem
Walking in pairs
Under every light
Their faces
WHITE
In Harlem
And mixed in with 'em
A black cop or two
For the sake of the vote in Harlem

Hughes again brings Ethiopia and Harlem together: next to his streetwise portrait of a white occupying army with a token "black cop or two," Hughes places the headline, "GUGSA A TRAITOR TOO." Is Haile Selaisse Gugsa, the black emperor of Ethiopia, a traitor because he flees from his country? Or is the reference to the Ethiopian nobleman, Gugsa Wele, a provincial governor accused of "secret dealings with local rebels and the Italians. He was killed in a clash with the Ethiopian army" in 1930.[53]

In any case, Hughes develops a deadpan joke as the speaker, in the act of denying it, identifies one of the black cops as a traitor:

No, sir,
I ain't talkin' 'bout you,
Mister Policeman!
I know we got to keep
ORDER OVER HARLEM
Where the black millions sleep
Shepherds over Harlem
Their armed watch keep
Lest Harlem stirs in its sleep
And maybe remembers

And remembering forgets
To be peaceful and quiet
And has sudden fits
Of raising a black fist
Out of the dark
And that black fist
Becomes a red spark
PLANES OVER HARLEM
Bombs over Harlem

Hughes mixes street language and the more elevated, biblical language of shepherds who, ironically, are those bombing the sleeping millions. The headline,
"BOMBS OVER HARLEM," becomes "ORDER OVER HARLEM." Through this repetition
with change and his ironic language of radical political insight and protest, Hughes
conjures up a vision of black rage emerging from the socially sanctioned sleep of
black docility. In his version, the anger takes the militant form of a black fist and a
red spark whose full political implications he keeps suspended.

To this rush of words he has the questioner raise the commonsense objection,

You're just making up
A fake funny picture, ain't you?
Not real, not real?

The speaker responds with another question, a powerful appeal to the shared
memory of the violence and oppression of slave times. "Did you ever taste blood /
From an iron heel / Planted in your mouth / In the slavery-time South," he asks. As
he continues without a break, his momentum builds, the violence accelerates, and
Hughes moves back and forth in time and space, fusing the beatings under slavery
in the South with the guns and billy clubs in the riot-present in Harlem:

And not even a *living* nigger
Has a tale to tell
Lest the kick of a boot
Bring more blood to his mouth
In the slavery-time South
And a long billy-club
Split his head wide
And a white hand draw
A gun from its side
And send bullets splaying

Through the streets of Harlem
Where the dead're laying
Lest you stir in your sleep
And remember something
You'd best better keep
In the dark, in the dark
Where the ugly things hide
Under the white lights
With guns by their side
In Harlem?

In this world of liberated rhythms and language, Hughes effects surreal mergings and moves under the surface of consciousness into the dark region of the political unconscious "where the ugly things hide."

In this region another voice idiomatically and ironically says,

Say, what are yuh tryin' to do?
Start a riot?
You keep quiet!
You niggers keep quiet!

Appropriately enough, the hegemonic voice of the cops intrudes to tame the insurrectionary energies of Harlem and of the poem. Hughes then opens up what is involved in the sleep and order the police enforce. Ironically addressing the "BLACK WORLD," the speaker says,

Never wake up
Lest you knock over the cup
Of gold that the men who
Keep order guard so well
And then—well, then
There'd be hell
To pay
And bombs over Harlem.

The "hell to pay," the "bombs over Harlem," contain a threat of race war and retaliation against black people who upset the capitalistic order of money and those who guard it. The bombs at home are like the fascist bombs on Ethiopia, a connection Hughes stresses by repeating his title and headline, "AIR RAID OVER HARLEM."

Instead of being intimidated, however, the speaker first defiantly invokes the "riot" and the police violence, the "bullets through Harlem." He then goes on to imagine the revolutionary response of

And someday
A sleeping giant waking
To snatch bombs from the sky
And push the sun up with a loud cry
Of to hell with the cops on the corners at night
Armed to the teeth under the light
Lest Harlem see red
And suddenly sit on the edge of its bed
And shake the whole world with a new dream
As the squad cars come and the sirens scream
And a big black giant snatches bombs from the sky
And picks up a cop and lets him fly
Into the dust of the Jimcrow past
And laughs and hollers
Kiss my
!x!&!

The thirties imagery of the heroic, larger-than-life black giant snatching bombs from the sky merges to dramatize defiance of the cops of the Jimcrow past and present. For Hughes, black rage expresses itself in the politics of red militancy, of seeing red, in Hughes's political pun. The rhyming, the anger, and the irreverent bravado look ahead to the rappers of the 1990s, a similarity that highlights through contrast Hughes's commitment to the 1930s left.

At another cultural level Hughes's irreverent mergings, his milieu of anger and "riot," and his imagery of sleeping and awakening anticipate the dream techniques, the anger, the riot scenes, and the central motif of awakening in Ralph Ellison's *Invisible Man*. The shared concern with the Communist Party or Brotherhood underscores the contrast between the 1930s and 1950s view of the party, which Ellison's narrator exposes and rejects. Because Ellison helped fix the image of the party for over a generation, it is worth stressing that in contrast to the disillusioned sense of betrayal, expediency, and authoritarianism in *Invisible Man*, in his concluding stanzas Hughes explicitly reaffirms his commitment to the party and its cohesive values. After self-reflexively calling attention to his "Scenario for A Little Black Movie," he uses another headline to play on "black" and "red," to explicate his poem and film, and to advertise "A RED MOVIE TO MR. HEARST." Hughes compounds this affront to the symbol of thirties red-baiting by tapping into the language and idealism of the Communist Party. His speaker invokes a vision of

Black and white workers united as one
In a city where
There'll never be
Air raids over Harlem
FOR THE WORKERS ARE FREE

What workers are free?
THE BLACK AND WHITE WORKERS—
You and me!
Looky here, everybody!
Look at me!

I'M HARLEM!

Hughes's personified Harlem celebrates a world without war, without class conflict, and with the cohesion of free workers, black and white. He combines the down-home idiom of "looky here" with the language of Communist unity to round out his surreal rendering of militant rebellion against capitalistic, police, and fascist bombing and all the bombing comes to represent. The Harlem of Hughes's scenario is a long way from his sometimes exotic, sometimes bittersweet Harlem of the 1920s, just as it differs from Ellison's 1950s version of late thirties Harlem. For contemporary readers, finally, one of the values of reading "Air Raid over Harlem" is that the poem brings into the open the 1935 Harlem "riot," one of a series of typically forgotten urban upheavals that give a vital perspective on current and undercurrent conditions.

"Madrid—1937"

Hughes's involvement in the Spanish Civil War serves the same purpose of recalling the immediacy of one of the crucial experiences of the 1930s left. Like Hughes, in their support of the loyalist cause members of the thirties left tapped into their deepest and most authentic commitments. Hughes does justice to the significance of the War in "Madrid—1937," one of the poems he wrote soon after he arrived in Spain.[54] His epigraph is a simple news item: *Damaged by shells, many of the clocks on the public buildings in Madrid have stopped. At night, the streets are dark.* In the poem, Hughes opens up the full implications of the basic images of the clock and the dark. For Hughes, man himself, an entire view of civilization, progress, "the human heart," are at stake in the fascist attack on Madrid. As the lights go out and the clocks stop, all of "time stand[s] still" and Hughes contemplates a reversion to "the nothingness of barren land," to "the ever minus of the brute" in a total reversal of evolution to "time's end and throw-back" to an aboriginal darkness, a terrifying "birth of darkness." Even more than in World War I,

> Again man mocks himself
> And all his human will to build and grow
> > Madrid!
> The fact and symbol of man's woe.

This bleak prospect is for Hughes inseparable from the dynamics of capital, from the role of England, France, and the United States in selling out loyalist Spain, the

> Emptiness of gold,
> The dullness of a bill of sale:
> BOUGHT AND PAID FOR! SOLD!

Hughes goes on to deepen the sense that time has stopped, that in the fullest sense darkness is taking over and "all lights are out," that man's ability to see and think is being wiped out and that the hard-won light of the mind from its evolutionary origins on is being obliterated

> Beneath the bullets!
> > Madrid!
> Beneath the bombing planes!
> > Madrid!
> In the fearful dark!

In contrast to the earlier light of the "mind of man," Hughes now ironically addresses the "mind of man / Moulded into a metal shell," thus neatly exposing the extent to which humankind has channeled its ability into making deadly weapons, the "left-overs of the past / That rain dull hell and misery / On the world again." For Hughes, "the world" in all its generality is consistently inseparable from the particulars of the fascist bombing and shelling of Madrid,

> These guns,
> These brainless killers in the Guadarrama hills
> Trained on Madrid
> To stop the clocks in the towers

And shatter all their faces
Into a million bits of nothingness
In the city
That will not bow its head
To darkness and to greed again:
That dares to dream a cleaner dream!

Hughes also consistently makes us see the particulars in Spain from the perspective of humanity itself, a perspective that emerges from his repeated use of "the mind of man," of "mankind," and of the suggestive imagery of "light and dark," as in his grim admonition,

Let there be no sense of time,
Nor measurement of light and dark,
In fact, no light at all!
Let mankind fall
Into the deepest pit that ignorance can dig
For us all!
Descent is quick,
To rise again is slow.

Having recalled his earlier vision of the sweep and reversal of evolution, Hughes concludes,

In the darkness of her broken clocks
Madrid cries NO!
In the timeless midnight of the Fascist guns,
Madrid cries NO!
To all the killers of man's dreams,
Madrid cries NO!

To break that NO apart
Will be to break the human heart.

Hughes does not need a theory of negative dialectics to render his sense that the affirmation of hope, of the dream of humanity, emerges from the defiant NO of Madrid. The human heart itself is at stake in the battle. The urgency of Hughes's concluding refrain and, throughout the poem, the sweep of reference into the dark recesses of nothingness suggest the importance the fight for Spain and against fascism had for Hughes as an individual and as a representative of the thirties left.

Except for the four short poems in *Scottsboro Limited* (1932), *A New Song* (1938) is the only collection of political poems Hughes published during the 1930s. The collection was sponsored by the 140,000 member International Workers Order (IWO) "to foster culture, and establish cultural ties between people of various races and nationalities. In this way a better understanding will be created which will help break down the artificial barriers erected between people. Fraternalism means brotherhood; and the poetry of Langston Hughes is a true expression of our ideals because it is an impassioned cry for humanity and brotherhood."[55] As its first publication, the union was making Langston Hughes available to ordinary workers at a price they could afford. The IWO's exemplary ideals, however, result in a principle of selection that unfortunately filters out Hughes's most compelling radical poems, so that the collection does not represent anything like the full power of Hughes's work during the 1930s.

The concern with brotherhood, moreover, led Hughes to revise some of the poems to shift their emphasis away from race, as when he changed "black" to "poor" in "Justice," thereby removing the poem from the passions of the Scottsboro protest and flattening out the full implications of blind, syphilitic Dixie justice. He similarly changed the title of his 1932 poem, "Red Flag on Tuskegee," to the more general "Open Letter to the South," a revision that mutes both the radical and racial emphasis of the original title.[56] In the poem itself Hughes had originally written "migration into force and power— / Tuskegee with a red flag on the tower!" He revised the militant "red flag" to the much tamer "new flag" for "Open Letter to the South." Hughes included "Ballads of Lenin" in *A New Song* but he passed over more irreverent, more energized poems like "Good Morning, Revolution," "Goodbye, Christ," and "One More 'S' in the U.S.A." Could Hughes be responding to the accommodationist tendency of the Popular Front? That tendency seems behind the change at the end of "Ballads of Lenin," from "on guard with the fighters forever" to "on guard with the workers forever" (p. 20), a moderating of the revolutionary implications of the earlier version. For a *A New Song*, on the other hand, Hughes strengthened "Pride." He moves from the 1930 "longing to be strong / To strike your face!" for the racial insults, bitterness, and inequity he experiences to the much more forceful, decisive

And so my fist is clenched—
Today—
To strike your face.[57]

In *A New Song*, Hughes juxtaposes "Pride" (p. 16) and "Ballad of Ozie Powell" (p. 17), a strong, reinforcing sequence. Typically, however, Hughes's sequences defuse rather than intensify, partly because he has eliminated his most provocative poems, partly because he is unwilling to give full play to the drama of race and class, partly because he abstracts the poems from the history that animates them and gives them much of their significance. The Scottsboro poems are an example. Hughes removes "Justice" both from Scottsboro and from the passions of the Tom Moody protest, although he later groups "Chant for Tom Moody" with another chant, "Chant for May Day" (pp. 13–15). The original version of "Justice," "Ballad of Ozie Powell," and "Christ in Alabama," which Hughes did not include, would have made for a powerful sequence.

The poems Hughes wrote responding to the early days of the depression, moreover—"Advertisement for the Waldorf-Astoria," "Good Morning, Revolution," "Goodbye, Christ"—have a range of tone, language, and insight only hinted at in *A New Song*. Hughes may have withheld these poems because of their blasphemous, irreverent treatment of Christianity as much as for their overtly radical politics. Hughes did not include any of his antiimperialist poems or "Air Raid over Harlem" and "Broadcast on Ethiopia." Without the leaven of the omitted poems, with their impudence, anger, and extremity, their idiomatic language and feel for those on the bottom of society, in *A New Song* Hughes relies too much on unenlivened left commonplaces. There is a little too much of

> When the marching feet of the masses
> Will raise for you a living monument of love,
> And joy, and laughter,
> And black hands and white hands clasped together as one,
> And a song that reaches the sky—[58]

But although the cumulative effect is disappointing, *A New Song* has its moments. In "Sister Johnson Marches" (p. 26), Hughes catches the vernacular voice and commitment of Sister Johnson in a call and response focused not on religion but on the workers' alternative, "de first of May":

> Here am I with my head held high!
> *What's de matter, honey?*
> I just want to cry:
> It's de first of May!
>
> Here I go with my banner in my hand!
> *What's de matter, chile?*

Why we owns de land!
It's de first of May!

Who are all them people
Marching in a mass?
Lawd! Don't you know?
That's de working class!

It's de first of May!

Through the religious-based form and in the character of someone usually connected with the church, Hughes has Sister Johnson voice a surprising sense of working-class consciousness. She also conveys a reassuring sense of pride and solidarity. Through her voice, unpretentious and nonthreatening, Hughes affirms that blacks are involved along with the mass of workers in celebrating the workers' symbolic holiday, a May Day march that embodies the cohesion of workers in the present and their victory in the future. The workers are coming into their own—"we owns de land" in that on May Day the streets belong to the workers who, in the communal future, will "own the land" as property. "Sister Johnson Marches" speaks to and for ordinary working people in idiomatic, easily comprehensible language. The call-and-response form is traditional and familiar to African Americans, the rhythms and rhymes are basic and satisfying. The poem conveys a morale-boosting sense of the involvement of blacks, the cohesion of workers, and the nonviolent triumph of the movement. In tone and content "Sister Johnson Marches" exemplifies the ideals of the IWO and the nonrevolutionary side of the Popular Front.

Although a certain muting of Hughes's earlier Third Period militancy predominates in *A New Song*, the collection also reveals the extent to which within the Popular Front moderate and revolutionary tendencies coexisted. For *A New Song*, for example, Hughes made the ending of "Pride" more militant than in the earlier version. He moves from the 1930 "longing to be strong / To strike your face!" for the racial insults, bitterness, and inequity he experiences to the much more forceful, decisive

And so my fist is clenched—
Today—
To strike your face.[59]

In *A New Song*, Hughes also juxtaposes "Pride" (p. 16) and "Ballad of Ozie Powell" (p. 17), a strong, reinforcing sequence. Especially in the title poem, "A New Song" (pp. 24–25), which immediately precedes "Sister Johnson Marches," Hughes strikes a grimmer, more militant note. In giving full expression to the bitterness and black consciousness "of the black millions / Awakening to action," Hughes strains almost to the breaking point the left harmony of black and white united as one in a worker's revolt, or, rather, he does such a powerful job with the black side of the dialectic that the concluding assertion of the black and white worker's world is in danger of seeming tagged on. Hughes in fact altered the original 1933 ending, cutting and adding for his 1938 collection. In both versions the speaker in "A New Song" is Hughes in his explicitly representative character:

I speak in the name of the black millions
Awakening to action.
Let all others keep silent a moment.
I have this word to bring,
This thing to say,
This song to sing:

Bitter was the day
When I bowed my back
Beneath the slaver's whip.
That day is past.

Before he turns to the present, however, Hughes fully dramatizes one of his refrain lines, "bitter was the day," as in his evocation,

Bitter was the day, I say,
When the lyncher's rope
Hung about my neck,
And the fire scorched my feet,
And the oppressors had no pity,
And only in the sorrow songs
Relief was found.
That day is past.

Emerging from this past, the lesson in the present is an affirmation of militant black power:

I know full well now
Only my own hands,
Dark as the earth,
Can make my earth-dark body free.

When Hughes repeats "that day is past," the line reflects not on the assertion of black power and freedom but on the spectacle of the exploiters who can no longer say

> With arrogant eyes and scornful lips:
> "You are my servant,
> Black man—
> I, the free!"

In his concluding sequence, Hughes develops the contrast between past and present, the old song and the new. He continues to bring alive the sense of militant "dark mouths where red tongues burn / And white teeth gleam" but now

> New words are formed,
> Bitter
> With the past
> But sweet with the dream.

"The dream," the "new words," the "new song" are

> Tense,
> Unyielding,
> Strong and sure,
> They sweep the earth—

Revolt! Arise!

> The Black
> And White World
> Shall Be one!
> The Worker's World!

The past is done!

> A new dream flames
> Against the
> Sun!

In "A New Song" the dream is not the American, republican dream Hughes invokes in "Let America Be America Again." The "flames"; the vision of the words and dream, "unyielding, strong and sure, they sweep the earth"; the call to "arise," "revolt"—at the end of "A New Song" Hughes changed his original ending and reanimates the Third Period revolutionary militancy of the early 1930s. In the context of the generally accommodationist tone of *A New Song*, Hughes's title poem is a throwback to an earlier era. What is surprising is that Hughes chose not only to include this poem, originally published in *Opportunity* in 1933, but also to make it his title poem. One result is that "A New Song" contributes a vital, disruptive strain to the collection. The black anger Hughes conveys and affirms is not easily contained within the vision of a unified, rebellious working class. In contrast to his avoidance of the potentially disruptive claims of race and class in most of the poems in *A New Song* and in contrast to his generally successful melding of these claims in such poems as "White Man," "The Same," "Scottsboro Limited," "Air Raid over Harlem," and "Ballad of Lenin," in "A New Song" the intensities at the center of the poem uncharacteristically threaten the militant resolution at the end. In the original 1933 version this problem does not arise because Hughes had sustained his sense of black rage and black power with lines like these, cut in 1938:

Black World
Against the wall,
Open your eyes—
The long white snake of greed has struck to kill!
Be wary and wise!
Before
The darker world
The future lies.[60]

Unlike the focus on blacks and slavery in tension with the revolutionary international vision at the end of the 1938 "A New Song," in the opening poem of his collection, "Let America Be America Again" (pp. 9–11), Hughes balances celebration of American possibility and radical criticism of capitalistic abuses, "of dog eat dog, of mighty crush the weak." The balance is characteristic of the Popular Front at its frequent best. The dissonant energies of "A New Song" and the hopefulness and qualified militancy of "Let America Be America Again" define Hughes's range in his end-of-the decade collection.

"Let America be America again," Hughes begins his poem and collection,

Let it be the dream it used to be.
Let it be the pioneer on the plain
Seeking a home where he himself is free.

(America never was America to me.)

In calling for a renewal of the old republican America, Hughes taps into traditional imagery and values and stresses the American dream of freedom in contrast both to the acquisitive side of the dream and to its failure to include those the speaker represents. As he often does, Hughes defers identifying the speaker, so that at first we see him as a black person committed to the fervently invoked republican dream of a land "where never kings connive nor tyrants scheme / . . . (It never was America to me.)" The speaker also brings alive the republican vision of

> a land where Liberty
> Is crowned with no false patriotic wreath,
> But opportunity is real, and life is free,
> Equality is in the air we breathe.
>
> (There's never been equality for me,
> Nor freedom in this "homeland of the free.")

The protests in the parenthetical intrusions evoke another voice, which breaks in to ask,

> *Say who are you that mumbles in the dark?*
> *And who are you that draws your veil across the stars?*

"The dark" and the "veil," with their racial connotations and echo of Du Bois's famous "life behind the veil," reinforce the implied racial identity of the "you," the original speaker. Hughes, however, plays off against these implications. In the language of the Popular Front, he has the speaker identify himself:

> I am the poor white, fooled and pushed apart,
> I am the Negro bearing slavery's scars.
> I am the red man driven from the land,
> I am the immigrant clutching the hope I seek—
> And finding only the same old stupid plan
> Of dog eat dog, of mighty crush the weak.
>
> I am the young man, full of strength and hope,
> Tangled in that ancient endless chain
> Of profit, power, gain, of grab the land!
> Of grab the gold! Of grab the ways of satisfying need!
> Of work the men! Of take the pay!
> Of owning everything for one's own greed!

In the remainder of the poem Hughes develops his protest against capitalistic values and exploitation and celebration of the dispossessed as "the people," as "Pioneers." His vision grows to include the entire range of Popular Front and New Deal protagonists—"the farmer," "the worker, sold to the machine," "the Negro," "the man who never got ahead," and those who

> left dark Ireland's shore,
> And Poland's plain, and England's grassy lea,
> And torn from Black Africa's strand I came
> To build a "homeland of the free."

Although not as militantly radical as his poems of the early thirties, Hughes structures and energizes "Let America Be America Again" around a dialogue of idealistic, republican celebration and hard-hitting exposure. "The free?" a voice says,

> Who said the free? Not me?
> Surely not me? The millions on relief today?
> The millions shot down when we strike?
> The millions who have nothing for our pay?
> For all the dreams we've dreamed
> And all the songs we've sung
> And all the flags we've hung,
> The millions who have nothing for our pay—
> Except the dream that's almost dead today.

Against this bleak background the speaker affirms,

> Sure, call me any ugly name you choose—
> The steel of freedom does not stain.
> From those who live like leeches on the people's lives,
> We must take back our land again,
> America!
>
> O, yes,
> I say it plain,
> America never was America to me,
> And yet I swear this oath—
> America will be!
>
> Out of the rack and ruin of our gangster death,
> The rape and rot of graft, and stealth, and lies,

We, the people, must redeem
The land, the mines, the plants, the rivers,
The mountains and the endless plain—
All, all the stretch of these great green states—
And make America again!

Playing off against the rape, rot, and lies and the militancy of "we must take back our land again" is the much more moderate sense of "we, the people, must redeem the land." The list—the land, mines, plants—is reminiscent of "Good Morning, Revolution" but instead of invoking "the tools of production," "the International Soviet," and the "rising workers everywhere" Hughes now echoes the language of the Declaration of Independence, the Gettysburg Address, and the panoramic vistas of "America the Beautiful." Hughes substitutes the ideal republican America for the earlier workers' internationalism and the USSR. Without at all ignoring the union busting, "the millions on relief," and the "endless chain / of profit, power, gain, of grab the land," for Hughes "the moment of Marxism" is nonetheless moderating and drawing to a close.

"Let America Be America Again" exemplifies the Popular Front's fervent idealism, critique of grab-and-gain capitalism, and the Popular Front's affinity for and willingness to invoke the traditional republican vision of America. A decade later, in the twilight of the Popular Front, under the pressure of congressional accusations that he was a Communist, and in the context of the developing blacklist, Hughes revised "Let America Be America Again." It says something about the continuing energies of the Popular Front that the year after Henry Wallace ran for president on the Progressive ticket, Langston Hughes included "Let America Be America Again" as one of his representative poems in *The Poetry of the Negro*, the anthology he and Arna Bontemps edited for Doubleday.[61] It says something about the cultural politics of the Cold War that Hughes eliminated the stanza that brought alive the immediacy of depression America and most fully challenged the view of America as the "homeland of the free," the stanza on "the millions on relief," on the strikers shot, on "the millions who have nothing for our pay," on "the dream that's almost dead today." Immediately before his final stanza Hughes also added to the speaker's oath—"America will be!"—the upbeat lines,

An ever-living seed,
Its dream
Lies deep in the heart of me.[62]

At the same time Hughes cut the next two lines, his grim exposure,

Out of the rack and ruin of our gangster death,
The rape and rot of graft, and stealth, and lies

Hughes's agent, Maxim Lieber, understood precisely what was going on and he did not like it. "I am a little amused," he wrote Hughes, "to see that you have revised the poem, bringing it up to date. While I suppose there is no law against such a procedure, it does seem somewhat strange. What would have happened to the original of Shelley's poem to the men of England—and to some of the work of our own American poets written within a certain period? For instance, what would have happened to Francis Scott Key's Star Spangled Banner, if he had a chance to revise it some twenty years later?"[63] Although Hughes did not answer Maxim Lieber directly, he did respond indirectly. During the Cold War he not only eliminated the most radical sections of "Let America Be America Again" but also, even more important, he excluded from his autobiographies and from his literary canon almost all of his left poetry of the 1930s.

As contemporary readers we also need to consider Lieber's question, since we are part of an ongoing process of revision—and of restoration. In my view the point is not to criticize Hughes for accommodating in order to continue as an effective voice for the racial causes he was committed to. Instead, we need to deal with the current and future status of the radical work at the center of Hughes's creative life during the decade in which he came into his own as a mature poet. Is it possible to get this work into anthologies and classrooms so as to correct the image of Hughes shaped during the Cold War?

To do so, readers first of all need to consider alternatives to the modernist poetics that set the standards for poetry for the Cold War generation. The prospects are encouraging, since contemporary readers are willing—perhaps all too willing—to consider these alternatives. Unlike his modernist contemporaries, Hughes wrote in an idiomatic, easily accessible language. His politics were radical, not conservative; his concerns were racial and political, not philosophical or religious. Hughes's readers, moreover, need to understand and value the oral traditions Hughes is rooted in, his way with jazz and blues forms, and the significance of his frequently irreverent engaging with public concerns and the language and attitudes of what is often stigmatized as the Stalinist left.

Working within these traditions, in his radical poems Hughes time and again revitalized the languages that compelled him. He was committed to ordinary speech, to ordinary working people, and to the values of equality and freedom. He exposed the insults, oppression, and anger of black people. Typically, Hughes then moved to a celebration of a black and white worker's world. He had an ear and eye for the deadliest sides of capitalistic imperialism and American capitalism. Sometimes jauntily, sometimes with dignified intensity, he brought a renewing sense of hope, anger, and commitment to movement readers who shared his values and vision. "The time has passed," he wrote in February 1933, "for us to sit by and bemoan our fate. Already we have had too much literature in the vein of the spirituals, lamenting our fate and bemoaning our condition, but suggesting no remedy except humbleness and docility."[64]

For contemporary readers Langston Hughes brings alive the sense of radical possibility that for many on the left characterized the 1930s. In the process Hughes demonstrates the importance of historical context for a full appreciation of public, political poetry. Reading his neglected left poems in the present involves a challenging interplay between current and historical concerns. For a range of contemporary readers, Hughes's radical poetry constitutes an exceptionally useful lens on both present and past. The challenge is to make this poetry physically, intellectually, and pedagogically available.

NOTES

Introduction

1. For representative examples, see Willard Thorp, "American Writers on the Left," in *Socialism and American Life*, ed. Donald Drew Egbert and Stow Persons (Princeton: Princeton University Press, 1952), 1:606–20; Clement Greenberg, "Avant-Garde and Kitsch," *Partisan Review* 6 (Fall 1939): 34–49; Philip Rahv, "Proletarian Literature: A Political Autopsy," *Southern Review* 7 (1939): 616–28; Alfred Kazin, *On Native Grounds: An Interpretation of Modern Prose Literature* (1942; Garden City, N.Y.: Anchor Books, 1956), pp. 283–310; Lionel Trilling, *The Liberal Imagination* (New York: Viking, 1950), esp. "Reality in America"; Robert Warshow, "The Legacy of the Thirties" (1947), in *The Immediate Experience: Movies, Comics, Theatre and Other Aspects of Popular Culture* (Garden City, N.Y.: Anchor Books, 1962), pp. 33–48; Leslie Fiedler, "Hiss, Chambers, and the Age of Innocence," pp. 3–24, and "Afterthoughts on the Rosenbergs," pp. 24–45, in *An End to Innocence: Essays on Culture and Politics* (Boston: Beacon Press, 1955). During the 1930s "proletarian" or "revolutionary" literature was regarded as the most influential movement of the decade. See, for example, Malcolm Cowley, "A Farewell to the 1930s," *New Republic* 101 (November 8, 1939): 44. By 1948 the movement had been erased from the official record: the authoritative *Literary History of the United States*, ed. Robert E. Spiller, et al., 4 vols. (New York: Macmillan, 1948), does not contain a single index reference to "proletarian," "revolutionary," or "Marxist" literature, although individual traces remain—Dos Passos, Farrell, and Wright, for example, receive bibliographical treatment.

2. Readers interested in a particular writer, Meridel Le Sueur or Richard Wright, for example, can find material on career and biography in Chapter 2.

3. I have profited especially from the work of Raymond Williams, *Marxism and Literature* (New York: Oxford University Press, 1977). Williams introduced me to Gramsci and Bakhtin, both of whom are important to me. See particularly Antonio Gramsci, *Selections from the Prison Notebooks*, ed. Quentin Hoare and Geoffrey Smith (New York: International Publishers, 1971); Joseph Femia, *Gramsci's Political Thought: Hegemony, Consciousness, and the Revolutionary Process* (New York: Oxford University Press, 1981); Perry Anderson, "The Antinomies of Antonio Gramsci," *New Left Review* 100 (1976–77): 5–78; Mikhail M. Bakhtin, *The Dialogic Imagination*, ed. Michael Holquist, trans. Caryl Emerson and Michael Holquist (Austin: University of Texas Press, 1981). Ellen Wood, *Mind and Politics: An Approach to the Meaning of Liberal and Socialist Individualism* (Berkeley: University of California Press, 1972), is another key work. See also Terry Eagleton, *Marxism and Literary Criticism* (Berkeley: University of California Press, 1976); Tony Bennett,

Formalism and Marxism (New York: Methuen, 1979); Catherine Belsey, *Critical Practice* (London: Routledge, 1988); Pierre Macherey, *A Theory of Literary Production*, trans. Geoffrey Wall (London: Routledge and Kegan Paul, 1978); Ernst Bloch et al., *Aesthetics and Politics*, trans. Ronald Taylor, afterword by Frederick Jameson (London: New Left Books, 1977); Frederick Jameson, *The Political Unconscious: Narrative as a Socially Symbolic Act* (Ithaca, N.Y.: Cornell University Press, 1981); Richard Ohmann, *The Politics of Letters* (Middletown, Conn.: Wesleyan University Press, 1987); and Paul Lauter, *Canons and Contexts* (New York: Oxford University Press, 1991).

4. See, for example, Louis Menand, "The Hammer and the Nail," *New Yorker*, July 20, 1992, esp. pp. 80, 82, 84 and Harold Bloom, introduction to *Richard Wright's Native Son*, ed. Harold Bloom (New York: Chelsea House, 1988), pp. 1–4.

5. See, for example, E. M. Broner's retrospective essay, "Meridel Le Sueur, 1900–1996," *Nation* 264 (February 17, 1997): 33–35. Broner is unaware that Le Sueur was a principled Communist activist, that she was deeply involved in the political culture of the 1930s left, and that she was the author of such achievements as *Salute to Spring* (1940) and *North Star Country* (1945). Le Sueur's *New York Times* obituary presents her as a "reporter" and children's book author, gives no indication that she was one of the best writers of the 1930s left, ignores her blacklisting during the Cold War suppression of suspect ideas, and passes over her significant contribution to feminist theory and practice (*New York Times*, January 24, 1997, p. 21). Among academic critics, Constance Coiner is critical of what she sees as Le Sueur's totalizing politics, *Better Red: The Writing and Resistance of Tillie Olsen and Meridel Le Sueur* (New York: Oxford University Press, 1995), esp. pp. 100–107. Paula Rabinowitz similarly dismisses Josephine Herbst's political art in *Labor and Desire: Women's Revolutionary Fiction in Depression America* (Chapel Hill: University of North Carolina Press, 1991), pp. 157–70. For more favorable evaluations, see John Crawford's editorial notes in the West End Press editions of Le Sueur's works; Linda Ray Pratt, "Woman Writer in the CP: The Case of Meridel Le Sueur," *Women's Studies* 14 (1988): 247–64; Blanche H. Gelfant, "'Everybody Steals': Language as Theft in Meridel Le Sueur's *The Girl*," in *Tradition and the Talents of Women*, ed. Florence Howe (Urbana: University of Illinois Press, 1991), pp. 183–210; and Elinor Langer, *Josephine Herbst* (New York: Warner Books, 1984).

6. James W. Tuttleson, "The Problematic Texts of Richard Wright," *Hudson Review* 45 (1992): 268.

7. James Baldwin, "Everybody's Protest Novel," *Partisan Review* 16 (1949): 578–85. Geraldine Murphy has perceptively shown that to gain acceptance with the *Partisan Review* critics and to distract attention from his own homosexuality, Baldwin reversed the customary identification of proletarian literature as masculine and instead undermined the "protest novel" and Richard Wright by feminizing them through identification with Harriet Beecher Stowe's *Uncle Tom's Cabin*. "Protesting the Protest Novel: James Baldwin and the Poetics of Cold War Liberalism," paper presented at the American Studies Association annual meeting, Nashville, October 30, 1994. See also Baldwin's "Alas, Poor Richard," in *Nobody Knows My Name* (New York: Dell, 1961), pp. 144–70, and "Many Thousands Gone," in *Notes of a Native Son* (Boston: Beacon, 1955, 1984), pp. 24–445.

8. Houston A. Baker Jr., "Richard Wright and the Dynamics of Place in Afro-American Literature," in *New Essays on Native Son*, ed. Keneth Kinnamon (Cambridge: Cambridge University Press, 1990), pp. 104, 112.

9. Horace Gregory and Marya Zaturenska, *A History of American Poetry, 1900–1940* (New York: Harcourt, Brace, 1946), p. 439.

10. Dismissed, by Virginia Teriss, "Muriel Rukeyser: A Retrospective," *American Poetry Review* 3 (May–June 1974): 10–11; presented as politically moderate by Walter Kalaidjian, *American Culture between the Wars: Revisionary Modernism and Postmodern Critique* (New York: Columbia University Press, 1993), pp. 173–87.

11. In 1973 Faith Berry recovered much of this work in *Good Morning Revolution: Uncollected Social Protest Writings by Langston Hughes* (New York: Lawrence Hill, 1973), but for most readers Hughes remains the race poet of "The Negro Speaks of Rivers" or the bittersweet jazz poet of *The Weary Blues*.

12. See, for example, Mike Gold, "Towards Proletarian Art" (1921), in *Mike Gold: A Literary Anthology*, ed. Michael Folsom (New York: International Publishers, 1972), pp. 62–70; the contrasting articles by Malcolm Cowley, "What the Revolutionary Movement Can Do for a Writer," and Edwin Seaver, "The Proletarian Novel," in *The American Writers' Congress*, ed. Henry Hart (New York: International Publishers, 1935), pp. 59–65, 98–103; the polemical article by Philip Rahv, "Proletarian Literature: A Political Autopsy," *Southern Review* 7 (1939): 616–28; and Josephine Herbst's slashing rejection of the characterizing label "proletarian," quoted by David Madden in introduction to *Proletarian Writers of the Thirties*, ed. David Madden (Carbondale: University of Southern Illinois Press, 1968), pp. xv, xvii, xix–xxii, xxxvi. See also Barbara Foley, *Radical Representations: Politics and Form in U.S. Proletarian Fiction, 1929–1941* (Durham, N.C.: Duke University Press, 1993), esp. pp. 86–127.

13. Quoted by Douglas Wixson, *Worker-Writer in America: Jack Conroy and the Tradition of Midwestern Literary Radicalism* (Urbana: University of Illinois Press, 1994), p. 247, from a 1932 letter by Kalar. The disagreements among Cowley, Seaver, and Rahv indicate that a generally accepted formulation never emerged either in theory or practice. For a powerful negative criticism, see James Farrell, *A Note on Literary Criticism* (New York: Dynamo, 1936).

14. Mike Gold, "A Problem Novel?," *The New Republic* 43 (June 4, 1930): 74.

15. Wixson, *Worker-Writer*, p. 5.

16. Foley, *Radical Representations*, pp. 72–85, 129–69.

17. See, for example, Franklin Folsom, *Days of Anger, Days of Hope: A Memoir of the League of American Writers, 1937–1942* (Niwot: University Press of Colorado, 1994), pp. 96–101. Folsom, who joined the party in 1931 as a Rhodes Scholar at Oxford, was the executive secretary of the League of American Writers between 1937 and 1942. Alexander Trachtenberg was head of the party press, International Publishers, and a member of the Communist Party Central Committee. V. J. Jerome was a "novelist, poet, cultural director of the Communist Party" (Folsom, p. 98).

18. Foley, *Radical Representations*, pp. 71–74, 123–24. See also James Murphy, *The Proletarian Moment: The Controversy over Leftism in Literature* (Urbana: University of Illinois Press, 1991), index entry under "Charkov Conference," and Lawrence Schwartz, *Marxism and Culture: The CPUSA and Aesthetics in the 1930s* (Port Washington, N.Y.: Kennikat, 1980), index entry under "Kharkov Conference."

19. "The Significance of the Comintern Address," *Communist* 8 (June 1929): 295.

20. Earl Browder, "Economic Crisis and the Third Period," *Communist* 9 (March 1930): 237.

21. The quoted phrase recurs in Third Period discourse. See, for example, "Tasks in the Struggle against Hunger, Repression and War: Resolution of the 13th Plenum, Central Committee, C.P.U.S.A., on the Main Tasks in the Organization of Mass Struggles against the Offensive of the Capitalists," *Communist* 10 (October 1931): 820, and I. Amter, "The Revolutionary Upsurge and the Struggle of the Unemployed," *Communist* 12 (February 1933): 112–22.

22. See, for example, J. Zack, "Against the Labor Party (Militant Reformism) in the U.S.A.," *Communist* 9 (January 1930): 67–80; A. B. Magill, "Toward Social-Fascism: The 'Rejunvenation' of the Socialist Party," *Communist* 9 (April 1930): 309–20 and (May 1930): 462–68; Si Gerson, "The New 'Left' Social-Fascism," *Communist* 9 (July 1930): 622–31; William Z. Foster, "The Trade Union Line of Lovestone and Cannon-Muste Auxiliaries," *Communist* 9 (October 1930): 884–99; William Z. Foster, "Museism—'Left' Demagogy à la Mode," *Communist* 10 (June 1931): 483–87; Earl Browder, "How We Must Fight against the Demagogy of Fascists and Social-Fascists," *Com-*

munist 10 (April 1930): 300–304; "Tasks of the Communist Party, U.S.A.," *Communist* 11 (April 1932): 313; Editorial, "The Roosevelt Program—An Attack upon the Toiling Masses," *Communist* 12 (May 1933): 419–25; Carl Reeve, "Lovestonism—Twin of Fascist-Trotskyism," *Communist* 17 (August 1938): 732–42; Gene Dennis and Gil Green, "Notes on the Defense of American Democracy," *Communist* 17 (May 1938): 410–18.

23. Ernst Thaelmann, "Growth of Fascist Dictatorship in Germany," *Communist* 10 (March 1931): 222; "Tactics of the United Front: Leading Article in the July 15th Issue of *The Bolshevik*," *Communist* 11 (October 1932): 932, 939, 942. See also N. Sparks, "The Significance of the German Elections," *Communist* 9 (October 1930): 932–39, and V. Knorin, "The Significance of the German Elections," *Communist* 11 (September 1932): 811–16.

24. "The Imperialist Offensive and the Fourteenth Plenum of the Central Committee," *Communist* 11 (June 1931): 483.

25. See, for example, "The Significance of the Comintern Address," *Communist* 8 (June 1929): 295, 298, 300; William M. Weinstone, "The XI Plenum of the Executive Committee of the Comintern," *Communist* 10 (October 1931): esp. 773–74, 777; "The Imperialist Offensive and the Fourteenth Plenum of the Central Committee," *Communist* 11 (June 1932): esp. 483, 489; Earl Browder, "Place the Party on a War Footing," *Communist* 11 (July 1932): 590–605, esp. 590; Bill Dunne, "The War Offensive—Tightening the Capitalist Dictatorship in the United States," *Communist* 11 (June 1932): 543–52. The emotional and intellectual tone emerge in such statements as Dunne's "a new war for the redivision of the world among the imperialist powers having already begun in the Far East with the murderous onslaught of Japanese imperialism upon the Chinese masses, with invasion of the Soviet Union coming closer each day as a central part of the whole offensive, American imperialists and their hangers-on *are deliberately creating a war atmosphere*" (p. 544). Even after the German elections in 1932, the same emphasis on imperialism, particularly Japanese imperialism as "the spearhead of imperialist intervention against the Soviet Union," goes along with silence on the rise of German fascism. See, for example, "The Sharpening Capitalist Offensive, the Rising Tide of Mass Struggles and the Next Tasks of the Party: Resolution of the Fifteenth Plenum of the Central Committee, C.P., U.S.A.," *Communist* 11 (October 1932): 902–17. The quotation is from p. 903.

26. For authoritative and representative positions, see, for example, the documents in Georgi Dimitroff, *The United Front: The Struggle against Fascism and War* (New York: International Publishers, 1938); Earl Browder, *The People's Front* (New York: International Publishers, 1938); V. J. Jerome, "The People's Front Strikes from the Shoulder," *Communist* 15 (July 1936): 618–28; Clarence A. Hathaway, "Fighting for Democracy in Spain," *Communist* 15 (September 1936): 829–44; Earl Browder, "The Results of the Elections and the People's Front," *Communist* 16 (January 1937): 14–49; V. J. Jerome, "Charting the Course of the Democratic Front: A Review of Earl Browder's *The People's Front*," *Communist* 17 (April 1938): 339–50; Clarence A. Hathaway, "Building the Democratic Front," *Communist* 17 (May 1938): 404–9; Gene Dennis and Gil Green, "Notes on the Defense of American Democracy," *Communist* 17 (May 1938): 410–18; A. B. Magill, *The Perils of Fascism: The Crisis of American Democracy* (New York: International Publishers, 1938). The "People's Front" becomes "the Democratic Front" in 1937. The articles by Hathaway and Dennis-Green clarify that it's not really a shift.

27. Paul Lyons, *Philadelphia Communists, 1936–1956* (Phildadelphia: Temple University Press, 1982), p. 26.

28. "The whole level of thought and discussion, the level of culture itself, had been lowered," Robert Warshow asserted. Writing in 1947 within an influential discourse intitiated by Greenberg's 1939 "Avant-Garde and Kitsch," 34–49, and Lionel Trilling's "Parrington, Mr. Smith and Reality," *Partisan Review* 7 (1940): 24–40, Warshow went on to say that because of Stalinist

vulgarization "the soap-box speech merged with the Fourth of July oration. A poet became Librarian of Congress and denounced American intellectuals for weakening their country's spirit. Father Divine rode in the May Day parade. *The Grapes of Wrath* was a great novel. . . . The mass culture of the educated classes—the culture of the 'middle-brow,' as it has sometimes been called—had come into existence." Robert Warshow, "The Legacy of the 30's" (1947), in *The Immediate Experience: Movies, Comics, Theatre and Other Aspects of Popular Culture* (Garden City, N.Y.: Anchor Books, 1962), p. 34.

29. Judy Kutulas, *The Long War: The Intellectual People's Front and Anti-Stalinism, 1930–1940* (Durham, N.C.: Duke University Press, 1995), deals with the conflict between intellectuals on both of the opposing sides she examines, the People's Front and the anti-Stalinist left, 1930–40. Our work is complementary, since my interest is the reverse of Kutulas's, for whom "it is not the literary expression of politics that interests me as much as the institutions, manifestos, and political activities that [intellectuals] used to express themselves and to oppose one another" (p. 16).

30. Unlike Barbara Foley in "The Politics of Poetics: Ideology and Narrative Form in *An American Tragedy* and *Native Son*," in *Narrative Poetics: Innovations, Limits, Challenges*, ed. James Phelan, Center for Comparative Studies in the Humanities, Ohio State University, *Papers in Comparative Studies* (1987): 55–67, I see classsical realist-naturalistic works as open to disruptive authorial commentary and challenges to middle-class norms and the basic assumptions and practices of capitalism. I accordingly place many writers of the 1930s left within rather than at odds with the conventions of realism-naturalism. For analysis of one of the masters of naturalism, see "Dreiser and the Dynamics of Capitalism," in my *Social Criticism and Nineteenth-Century American Fictions* (Columbia: University of Missouri Press, 1987), pp. 284–316.

31. See my previous discussion and "Coda: A Note on Criticism" at the end of this chapter.

32. James D. Bloom, *Left Letters: The Culture Wars of Mike Gold and Joseph Freeman* (New York: Columbia University Press, 1992).

33. Constance Coiner, *Better Red: The Writing and Resistance of Tillie Olsen and Meridel Le Sueur* (New York: Oxford University Press, 1995).

34. See, for example, Alice Walker's foreword and Nancy Hoffman's afterword to Agnes Smedley, *Daughter of Earth* (New York: Feminist Press, 1929, 1987); Alice Kessler-Harris and Paul Lauter's introduction and Sylvia J. Cook's and Anna W. Shannon's afterwords to Fielding Burke, *Call Home the Heart: A Novel of the Thirties* (1932; Old Westbury, N.Y.: Feminist Press, 1983); Alice Kessler-Harris and Paul Lauter's introduction and Janet Sharistanian's afterword to Tess Slesinger, *The Unpossessed* (1934; Old Westbury, N.Y.: Feminist Press, 1984); Lionel Trilling, "Young in the Thirties," *Commentary* 41 (1966): 43–51 (on *The Unpossessed*); Alan M. Wald, *The New York Intellectuals: The Rise and Decline of the Anti-Stalinist Left from the 1930s to the 1980s* (Chapel Hill: University of North Carolina Press, 1987), pp. 39–40, 64–74 (on *The Unpossessed*); Foley, *Radical Representations*, index entries under Smedley, Burke, Slesinger, Lumpkin, and Page; Barbara Foley's introduction to Myra Page, *Moscow Yankee* (1935; Urbana: University of Illinois Press, 1995, pp. vii–xxviii); Sylvia Jenkins Cook, *From Tobacco Road to Route 66: The Southern Poor White in Fiction* (Chapel Hill: University of North Carolina Press, 1976), index entries under Burke and Lumpkin; Paula Rabinowitz, *Labor and Desire: Women's Revolutionary Fiction in Depression America* (Chapel Hill: University of North Carolina Press, 1991), index entries under Smedley, Burke, Slesinger, and Lumpkin.

35. On Dos Passos, see, for example, Lionel Trilling, "The America of John Dos Passos," *Partisan Review* 4 (April 1938): 26–32, and Trilling's partial retraction in *The Liberal Imagination: Essays on Literature and Society* (New York: Viking, 1950), p. 294; Jean Paul Sartre, "John Dos Passos and 1919," in *John Dos Passos: A Collection of Critical Essays*, ed. Andrew Hook (Englewood

Cliffs, N.J.: Prentice-Hall, 1974), pp. 61–69; Melvin Landsberg, *Dos Passos' Path to U.S.A.* (Boulder: University of Colorado Press, 1974); Townsend Ludington, *John Dos Passos: A Twentieth-Century Odyssey* (New York: Dutton, 1980); Robert C. Rosen, *John Dos Passos: Politics and the Writer* (Lincoln: University of Nebraska Press, 1981); Donald Pizer, *Dos Passos' U.S.A.: A Critical Study* (Charlottesville: University of Virginia Press, 1988); and Foley, *Radical Representations*, pp. 425–37. On Farrell, see Alan Wald, *James T. Farrell: The Revolutionary Socialist Years* (New York: New York University Press, 1978).

36. On Cantwell, see Merrill Lewis, *Robert Cantwell* (Boise, Idaho: Boise State University Press, 1985). On Rolfe, see the basic work of Cary Nelson and Jefferson Hendricks, eds., *Edwin Rolfe: A Biographical Essay and Guide to the Rolfe Archive at the University of Ilinois at Urbana-Champaign* (Urbana: University of Illinois Library, 1990); Cary Nelson and Jefferson Hendricks, eds., *The Collected Poems of Edwin Rolfe* (Urbana: University of Illinois Press, 1993), including a bibliography of works by and about Rolfe; Cary Nelson, "Lyric Politics: The Poetry of Edwin Rolfe," in *Edwin Rolfe, Trees Became Torches: Selected Poems*, ed. Cary Nelson and Jefferson Hendricks (Urbana: University of Illinois Press, 1995), pp. 1–39; and Cary Nelson, *Repression and Recovery: Modern American Poetry and the Politics of Cultural Memory, 1910–1945* (Madison: University of Wisconsin Press, 1989), index entry under "Rolfe, Edwin." On Fearing, see M. L. Rosenthal, "Chief Poets of the American Depression: Contributions of Kenneth Fearing, Horace Gregory, and Muriel Rukeyser to Contemporary American Poetry" (Ph.D. diss., New York University, 1949); Nelson, *Repression and Recovery*, index entry under "Fearing, Kenneth"; and Cameron Barrick, "Social Protest and Poetic Decorum in the Great Depression: A Reading of Kenneth Fearing, Horace Gregory, and Muriel Rukeyser" (Ph.D. thesis, Columbia University, 1994).

37. Walter Rideout, *The Radical Novel in the United States, 1900–1954: Some Interrelations of Literature and Society* (Cambridge, Mass.: Harvard University Press, 1956); Nelson, *Repression and Recovery*; Wald, *The New York Intellectuals*; Foley, *Radical Representations*; Rabinowitz, *Labor and Desire*. Laura Browder, *Rousing the Nation: Radical Culture in Depression America* (Amherst: University of Massachusetts Press, 1998), appeared after I had completed my own work and too late for me to take it into account.

38. Paul Lauter, "American Proletarianism," in *The Columbia History of the American Novel*, ed. Emory Elliott et al. (New York: Columbia University Press, 1991), pp. 331–56.

39. Alan Filreis, *Modernism from Right to Left: Wallace Stevens, the Thirties, and Literary Radicalism* (New York: Cambridge University Press, 1994).

40. Nelson, *Repression and Recovery*, p. 171.

41. Daniel Aaron, *Writers on the Left* (1961; New York: Oxford University Press, 1977).

42. On the *Partisan Review* and the New York intellectuals, see, for example, James B. Gilbert, *Writers and Partisans: A History of Literary Radicalism in America* (New York: John Wiley, 1968); Terry A. Cooney, *The Rise of the New York Intellectuals: Partisan Review and Its Circle, 1934–1945* (Madison: University of Wisconsin Press, 1986); Wald, *The New York Intellectuals*; Alexander Bloom, *Prodigal Sons: The New York Intellectuals and Their World* (New York: Oxford University Press, 1986); and Harvey M. Teres, *Renewing the Left: Politics, Imagination, and the New York Intellectuals* (New York: Oxford University Press, 1996).

43. Foley, "The Politics of Poetics," pp. 55–67.

44. Richard Pells, *Radical Visions and American Dreams: Culture and Social Thought in the Depression Years* (New York: Harper and Row, 1973); Warren Susman, "The Culture of the Thirties," in *Culture as History* (New York: Pantheon, 1984), pp. 150–83; Kalaidjian, *American Culture between the Wars*; and Kutulas, *The Long War*.

45. Warshow, "The Legacy of the 30's," pp. 33, 36.

46. Michael Denning, *The Cultural Front: The Laboring of American Culture in the Twentieth*

Century (London: Verso, 1996). Because it appeared well after I had completed my own study, I have not been able to take Denning's work into account. Because of his emphasis on the CIO rather than the Communist Party as central to the cultural front, when he does concentrate on particular writers Denning focuses on such non-Communist authors as Steinbeck and Dos Passos, whereas I examine writers either in or close to the party. In this sense our work is complementary.

47. Schwartz, *Marxism and Culture*; Maurice Isserman, *Which Side Were You On? The American Communist Party during the Second World War* (Middletown, Conn.: Wesleyan University Press, 1982); Murphy, *The Proletarian Moment*; M. J. Heale, *American Anticommunism: Combatting the Enemy Within, 1830–1970* (Baltimore: Johns Hopkins University Press, 1990); Foley, *Radical Representations*.

48. Harvey Klehr, *The Heyday of American Communism: The Depression Decade* (New York: Basic Books, 1984); Harvey Klehr, John Earl Haynes, and Kyrill M. Anderson, *The Soviet World of American Communism* (New Haven: Yale University Press, 1998); Theodore Draper, *The Roots of American Communism* (New York: Viking, 1957); Ronald Radosh and Joyce Milton, *The Rosenberg File: With a New Introduction and Containing Revelations from National Security Agency and Soviet Sources* (New Haven: Yale University Press, 1997).

49. Ellen Schrecker, *Many Are the Crimes: McCarthyism in America* (Boston: Little, Brown, 1998), and Victor Navasky, "Dialectical McCarthyism(s)," *Nation* 267 (July 20, 1998): 28–31.

50. Navasky, "Dialectical McCarthyism(s)," 28. On the active, principled, effective involvement of those in the middle and on the bottom, see also Lyons, *Philadelphia Communists, 1936–1956*, pp. 109–37.

51. Al Richmond, *A Long View from the Left: Memoirs of an American Revolutionary* (Boston: Houghton Mifflin, 1973); Steve Nelson, James R. Barrett, and Rob Ruck, *Steve Nelson, American Radical* (Pittsburgh: University of Pittsburgh Press, 1981); Vivian Gornick, *The Romance of Communism* (New York: Basic Books, 1977); Victor S. Navasky, *Naming Names* (New York: Viking, 1980); Griffin Fariello, *Red Scare: Memories of the American Inquisition: An Oral History* (New York: Norton, 1995); Mark Naison, *Communists in Harlem during the Depression* (New York: Grove, 1983); Robin D. G. Kelley, *Hammer and Hoe: Alabama Communists during the Great Depression* (Chapel Hill: University of North Carolina Press, 1990), and *Race Rebels: Culture, Politics, and the Black Working Class* (New York: Free Press, 1994), pp. 103–58; Roger Keeran, *The Communist Party and the Auto Workers' Union* (New York: International Publishers, 1980); and Lyons, *Philadelphia Communists, 1936–1956*.

52. Russell J. Reising, "Lionel Trilling, *The Liberal Imagination*, and the Emergence of the Cultural Discourse of Anti-Stalinism," *Boundary 2* 20 (1993): 94–124; Foley, *Radical Representations*, pp. 7–9.

53. See, for example, William H. Chafe, *The Unfinished Journey: America since World War II* (New York: Oxford University Press, 1995), pp. 31–78;, Richard M. Freeland, *The Truman Doctrine and the Origins of McCarthyism: Foreign Policy, Domestic Politics, and Internal Security, 1946–1948* (New York: Knopf, 1972); Daniel Yergin, *A Shattered Peace: The Origins of the Cold War and the National Security State* (New York: Penguin, 1977); William Appleman Williams, *The Tragedy of American Diplomacy* (New York: Delta, 1959), and *The Contours of American History* (Chicago: Quadrangle, 1961); Athan G. Theoharis and John Stuart Cox, *The Boss: J. Edgar Hoover and the Great American Inquisition* (Philadelphia: Temple University Press, 1988); Richard M. Fried, *Nightmare in Red: The McCarthy Era in Perspective* (New York: Oxford University Press, 1990); Peter L. Steinberg, *The Great "Red Menace": United States Prosecution of American Communists, 1947–1952* (Westport, Conn.: Greenwood Press, 1984); and Schrecker, *Many Are the Crimes*.

54. Hilton Kramer, "Who Was Josephine Herbst?," *New Criterion* 3 (1984): 1–14. See also the

more temperate views developed in Stephen J. Whitfield, *The Culture of the Cold War* (Baltimore: Johns Hopkins University Press, 1991).

Chapter One

1. On the IWW see Joyce L. Kornbluh, ed., *Rebel Voices: An I.W.W. Anthology* (Ann Arbor: University of Michigan Press, 1964), and Ralph Chaplin, *Wobbly: The Rough-and-Tumble Story of an American Radical* (Chicago: University of Chicago Press, 1948). For histories of American radicalism, see Donald Drew Egbert and Stow Persons, ed., *Socialism and American Life*, 2 vols. (Princeton: Princeton University Press, 1952); Howard Zinn, *A People's History of the United States* (New York: Harper and Row, 1980); and Nick Salvatore, *Eugene V. Debs: Citizen and Socialist* (Urbana: University of Illinois Press, 1982). For a Cold War history of the Communist Party, see Irving Howe and Lewis Coser, *The American Communist Party: A Critical History (1919–1957)* (Boston: Beacon Press, 1957). On revisionist analysis, see my "Introduction." On the relation between turn-of-the-century women socialists and 1930s women radicals, see Deborah Rosenfelt, "From the Thirties: Tillie Olsen and the Radical Tradition," in *Feminist Criticism and Social Change*, ed. Judith Newton and Deborah Rosenfelt (New York: Methuen, 1985), pp. 216–48.

2. Ralph Chaplin's "Solidarity Forever" (1915) is reprinted in Kornbluh, *Rebel Voices*, pp. 26–27. "You haven't a pot" is from "Dan McGann" by Dublin Dan, in Kornbluh, p. 31. For a stimulating discussion of IWW songs, poetry, and visual art, see Cary Nelson, *Repression and Recovery: Modern American Poetry and the Politics of Cultural Memory, 1910–1945* (Madison: University of Wisconsin Press, 1989), pp. 58–66.

3. Meridel Le Sueur, "Proletarian Literature and the Middle West," in *American Writers' Congress*, ed. Henry Hart (New York: International Publishers, 1935), p. 137, and *I Was Marching: Meridel Le Sueur's First Ninety Years*, PBS documentary, produced and directed by David Shulman, 1991; Josephine Herbst, *The Executioner Waits* (1934; New York: Warner Books, 1985), pp. 98–152; Douglas Wixson, *Worker-Writer in America: Jack Conroy and the Tradition of Midwestern Literary Radicalism* (Urbana: University of Illinois Press, 1994), index entry under "Wobblies"; John Dos Passos, *U.S.A.* (New York: Modern Library, 1937), esp. "U.S.A.," v–vii; the narrative sections on "Mac," and the biographies of Debs ("The Lover of Mankind"), Big Bill Haywood ("Big Bill"), Joe Hill, and Wesley Everest ("Paul Bunyan"), and the framing section at the end, "Vag."

4. Granville Hicks, *John Reed: The Making of a Revolutionary* (New York: Macmillan, 1936).

5. Eric Homberger, "Proletarian Literature and the John Reed Clubs, 1929–1935," *Journal of American Studies* 13 (1979): 221–44, gives an unflattering analysis of the John Reed Clubs and what Homberger presents as the dominance over "proletarian literature" of Soviet literary policy.

6. John Trumbold, "John Dos Passos's U.S.A. Trilogy: Political Futurism and Popular Culture" (Ph.D. diss., Columbia University, 1995).

7. "Journey to Revolution," Josephine Herbst Papers, Scribner's Box, Beinecke Rare Book and Manuscript Library, Yale University. See also Donald Drew Egbert, "Socialism and American Art," in *Socialism and American Life*, ed. Donald Drew Egbert and Stow Persons (Princeton: Princeton University Press), 1: 672–73.

8. Mike Gold, "Towards Proletarian Art," in *Mike Gold: A Literary Anthology*, ed. Michael Folsom (New York: International Publishers, 1972), pp. 62–70; Langston Hughes, "Rising Waters," in *Good Morning Revolution: Uncollected Social Protest Writings by Langston Hughes*, ed. Faith Berry (New York: Lawrence Hill, 1973), p. 19.

9. Wixson, *Worker-Writer*, pp. 102, 171, 420.

10. Mark Naison, *Communists in Harlem during the Depression* (Urbana: University of Illinois

Press, 1983), pp. 3–25. For a study of the Communist Party from the perspective of a significant black leader who operated at the highest levels of the party, see Gerald Horne, *Black Liberation/ Red Scare: Ben Davis and the Communist Party* (Newark: University of Delaware Press, 1994). See also Earl Ofari Hutchinson, *Blacks and Reds: Race and Class in Conflict, 1919–1990* (East Lansing: Michigan State University Press, 1995).

11. Robin D. G. Kelley, *Race Rebels: Culture, Politics, and the Black Working Class* (New York: Free Press, 1994), p. 11.

12. Naison, *Communists in Harlem*, pp. 203–4.

13. Quoted by Elinor Langer, *Josephine Herbst* (New York: Warner Books, 1984), p. 59.

14. Joseph Freeman, "Social Trends in American Literature," *Communist* 9 (July 1930): 651.

15. Granville Hicks et al., eds., *Proletarian Literature in the United States: An Anthology* (New York: International Publishers, 1935). On the congress, see "Our First Congress of Writers," *New Masses* 15 (April 30, 1935): 9; the 1935 published version, Hart, *American Writers' Congress*; the retrospective "Thirty Years Later: Memories of the First American Writers' Congress," *American Scholar* 35 (1966): 495–516; and Richard Wright's memories in *Black Boy (American Hunger)* (1944; New York: Library of America, 1991), pp. 300–333.

16. "Revolutionary Symbolism in America," in Hart, *American Writers' Congress*, pp. 88, 89. Subsequent quotations are cited by page parenthetically in the text.

17. See Kenneth Burke's recollections in "Thirty Years Later: Memories of the First American Writers' Congress," *American Scholar* 35 (1966): 501, 504, 506–7. See also Kenneth Burke, "My Approach to Communism," *New Masses* 10 (March 20, 1934): 16–20.

18. Donald Drew Egbert, "Socialism and American Art," *Socialism and American Life*, p. 682. Egbert himself does not fully endorse the view he summarizes.

19. On Rolfe and Hurwitz and Rolfe, Maltz, and Odets, see Cary Nelson, "Edwin Rolfe: Poet on the Left" in *Edwin Rolfe: A Biographical Essay and Guide to the Rolfe Archive at the University of illinois at Urbana-Champaign*, ed. Cary Nelson and Jefferson Kendricks (Urbana: University of Illinois Press, 1990), pp. 6–12, 14–15. On Hurwitz, Copland, Blitzstein, and the Workers Film and Photo League and the Nykino group, see William Alexander, *Film on the Left: American Documentary Film from 1931 to 1942* (Princeton: Princeton University Press, 1981), pp. 15, 97, 152, 213. On Copland and Clurman and Copland's work on the left, see Aaron Copland and Vivian Perlis, *Copland: 1900 through 1942* (New York: St. Martin's Press, 1984), pp. 38, 51–52, 185, 219, 224–25, 289–91. Clurman's tribute to Copland is on p. 61. For the text and score of "Into the Streets May First," see *New Masses* 11 (May 1, 1934): cover and 16–17.

20. Clement Greenberg, "Avant-Garde and Kitsch," *Partisan Review* 6 (Fall 1939): 34–49; Robert Warshow, *The Immediate Experience: Movies, Comics, Theatre and Other Aspects of Popular Culture* (Garden City, N.Y.: Anchor Books, 1964), esp. "The Legacy of the 30's" (1947).

21. Anthony Dawahare, "Modernity and 'Village Communism' in Depression-Era America: The Utopian Literature of Meridel Le Sueur," *Criticism* 39 (1997): 416–17.

22. See, for example, Harry Alan Potamkin, *The Eyes of the Movies* (New York: International Pamphlets, 1934), and *The Compound Cinema: The Film Writings of Harry Alan Potamkin*, ed. Lewis Jacobs (New York: Teachers' College Press, 1977); Alexander, *Film on the Left*; Herbert Kline, ed., *New Theatre and Film 1934 to 1937: An Anthology* (New York: Harcourt Brace Jovanovich, 1985); Wendy Smith, *Real Life Drama: The Group Theatre and America, 1931–1940* (New York: Knopf, 1990); on the Living Newpaper, see Laura Browder, *Rousing the Nation: Radical Culture in Depression America* (Amherst: University of Massachusetts Press, 1998), pp. 117–55; on folk music, folklore, and the blues, see the published version of the 1939 American Writers' Congress, *Fighting Words*, ed. Donald Ogden Stewart (New York: Harcourt, Brace, 1940), esp. B. A. Botkin's "At the Listening Post" and "Folklore and Folksay," a session featuring Hyde

Partnow, Aunt Molly Jackson, Victor Campbell, Alan Lomax, and Earl Robinson; on the contributions of Woody Guthrie, Earl Robinson, Charles and Pete Seeger, B. A. Botkin, and Alan Lomax, see Robbie Lieberman, *My Song Is My Weapon: People's Song, American Communism, and the Politics of Culture, 1930–1950* (Urbana: University of Illinois Press, 1989). See also Mark Naison, *Communists in Harlem during the Depression* (Urbana: University of Illinois Press, 1983).

23. Trumbo's *Johnny Got Your Gun* assumed a special meaning when it was serialized in the *Daily Worker* in 1940 during the period of the Hitler-Stalin Pact. The party at that time opposed U.S. involvement in the war against the Nazis.

Cantwell and Newhouse both left the movement during the 1940s, Cantwell for *Time* and *Sports Illustrated*, Newhouse for the *New Yorker* and the suburbs of the 1950s. Dalton Trumbo, Albert Maltz, and John Howard Lawson, however, are among the gifted writers who stayed with the party, moved to Hollywood, and took their stand as members of the Hollywood Ten. They remind us that contrary to the Cold War version, the Communist Party continued to compel the allegiance of talented writers well after the Hitler-Stalin Pact of 1939. See Larry Ceplair and Steven Englund, *Inquisition in Hollywood: Politics in the Film Community, 1930–1960* (Garden City, N.Y.: Anchor Press/Doubleday, 1980), and Victor S. Navatsy, *Naming Names* (New York: Viking, 1980), pp. 388–407.

24. *Time*, March 28, 1938, p. 63.

25. Malcolm Cowley, "A Farewell to the 30's," *New Republic* 101 (November 8, 1939): 43.

26. Langston Hughes, "Advertisement for the Waldorf-Astoria" (1931), in *Good Morning Revolution: Uncollected Social Protest Writings by Langston Hughes*, ed. Faith Berry (New York: Lawrence Hill, 1973), p. 22.

27. On the contemporary bias against realism, see, for example, Catherine Belsey, *Critical Practice* (London: Routledge, 1988); Tony Bennett, *Formalism and Marxism* (New York: Methuen, 1979); Constance Coiner, *Better Red: The Writing and Resistance of Tillie Olsen and Meridel Le Sueur* (New York: Oxford University Press, 1995), pp. 23–25, 91–94, 116–17. On the Cold War hostility to realism, recall the emphasis on myth and symbol, archetypes, Freud, and formalism in the orthodox criticism of the period.

28. In Ernst Bloch et al., *Aesthetics and Politics*, trans. Ronald Taylor, afterword by Frederick Jameson (London: New Left Books, 1977).

29. Maurice Isserman, *Which Side Are You On? The American Communist Party during the Second World War* (Middletown, Conn.: Wesleyan University Press, 1982).

30. For insight into the Spanish Civil War and into the class and political antagonisms and class alignments before and during the war, see Robert Colodny, *Spain: The Glory and the Tragedy* (New York: Humanities Press, 1970), and Hugh Thomas, *The Spanish Civil War* (New York: Harper, 1961).

31. As one of countless examples, the front page of the *Daily Worker* was dominated by stories about the Spanish Civil War, particularly during 1937 and 1938: "Fierce Battle Rages for Key Basque Hills" (June 7, 1937, p. 1); "Fascists Bomb Suburbs of Bilbao" (June 14, 1937, p. 1); "Franco Guns Bomb Madrid Civilians" (Feb. 4, 1938, p. 1). Rallies, lectures, and films, in addition to the almost daily headlines and stories about Spain, made the war immediate and unforgettable .

32. For the Communist point of view, see Robert Minor, "The Change in Spain," *Communist* 16 (August 1937): 697–708; "Open Letter on Communist-Socialist Unity in Spain," *Communist* 16 (September 1937): 848–55.

33. Naison, *Communists in Harlem*, pp. 140–45; *The Complete Report of Mayor LaGuardia's Commission on the Harlem Riot of March 19, 1935* (1935; New York: Arno Press, 1969).

34. Naison, *Communists in Harlem*, pp. 216–17.

35. "Resolution on the Negro Question in the United States, Final Text, Confirmed by the Politi-

cal Commission of the E.C.C.I.," *Communist* 10 (February 1931): 153–67. For the debate and vary-ing interpretations, see, for example, Jos. Prokopec, "Negroes as an Oppressed National Minor-ity," *Communist* 9 (March 1930): 239–45; N. Nasonov, "Against Liberalism in the American Negro Question," *Communist* 9 (April 1930): 296–308; Jim Allen, "Some Rural Aspects of the Struggle for the Right of Self-Determination," *Communist* 10 (March 1931): 249–55; Earl Browder, "For Na-tional Liberation of the Negroes! War against White Chauvinism," *Communist* 11 (April 1932): 295–309; B. D. Amis, "For a Strict Leninist Analysis on the Negro Question," *Communist* 11 (Octo-ber 1932): 944–49, a review—and correction of—James Allen's *The American Negro*; Harry Hay-wood, "The Struggle for the Leninist Position on the Negro Question in the U.S.A.," *Communist* 12 (September 1933): 888–901. Haywood was one of the shapers of the line. See his account in Harry Haywood, *Black Bolshevik: Autobiography of an Afro-American Communist* (Chicago: Liberator Press, 1978), pp. 218–44, and Barbara Foley, *Radical Representations: Politics and Form in U.S. Proletarian Fiction, 1929–1941* (Durham, N.C.: Duke University Press, 1993), pp. 174–80, 183–87.

36. Philip S. Foner and Herbert Shapiro, introduction to *American Communism and Black Americans: A Documentary History, 1930–1934* (Philadelphia: Temple University Press, 1991), p. xv.

37. For a rebuttal of these and other criticism and for a thorough examination of such issues as self-determination and the oppressed nation thesis, see James S. Allen, *The Negro Question in the United States* (New York: International Publishers, 1936).

38. See, for example, James W. Ford's summary for the twentieth anniversary of the founding of the CPUSA, "The Struggle for the Building of the Modern Liberation Movement of the Negro People," *Communist* 18 (September 1939): 817–28, esp. pp. 818, 824–26, and Israel Amter, review of James W. Ford, *The Negro and the Democratic Front*, *Communist* 18 (January 1939): 82–84. Amter stressed that for Ford, the party program emphasized the organization of Negro workers into the trade unions, in unity with white workers in the industry: "the C.I.O. represents in the main the broad base for the organization of the Negro workers" (pp. 82–83). Without ever mentioning the separate nation thesis, Amter concludes that there is "only one solution . . . through the forging of the democratic front against fascism and the extension of that front until it reaches the goal of true democracy which is socialism" (p. 84). See also James W. Ford, "The United Front in the Field of Negro Work," *Communist* 14 (February 1935): 158–74; James W. Ford and Louis Sass, "Development of Work in the Harlem Section," *Communist* 14 (April 1935): 312–25; Nat Ross, "Some Problems of the Class Struggle in the South," *Communist* 14 (January 1935): 61–75; Nat Ross, "The Next Step in Alabama and the Lower South," *Communist* 14 (September 1935): 968–76; "The Development of Struggle for Negro Rights" [Resolution Adopted by the Chicago Commit-tee of the C.P. on Work in Chicago South Side (Sections 2, 7, and 11)], *Communist* 14 (June 1935): 569–76; Ben Davis Jr., "The Negro People in the Elections," *Communist* 15 (October 1936): 975–87; James W. Ford, "The Negro People in the Elections," *Communist* 16 (January 1937): 63–73; James W. Ford, "Uniting the Negro People in the People's Front," *Communist* 16 (August 1937): 725–34; James W. Ford, "Forging the Negro People's Sector of the Democratic People's Front," *Communist* 17 (July 1937): 615–23; James W. Ford, "Rally the Negro Masses for the Democratic Front," *Communist* 17 (March 1938): 266–71.

Chapter Two

1. Meridel Le Sueur, "Corn Village," *Scribner's* 90 (August 1931): 133–40.

2. Jack Conroy, introduction to *Writers in Revolt: The Anvil Anthology*, ed. Jack Conroy and Curt Johnson (New York: Lawrence Hill, 1973), p. xiv.

3. Horace Gregory, "One Writer's Position," *New Masses* 14 (February 12, 1935): 20–21; Meridel Le Sueur, "The Fetish of Being Outside," *New Masses* 14 (February 26, 1935): 22–23.

4. Meridel Le Sueur, *I Was Marching: Meridel Le Sueur's First Ninety Years*, PBS documentary, produced and directed by David Shulman, 1991.

5. Linda Ray Pratt helpfully observes that although Le Sueur's party identification prevented her from reaching a mainstream audience during the 1950s, the party helped sustain her creativity by providing *Masses and Mainstream* as an outlet for her work. "Woman Writer in the CP: The Case of Meridel Le Sueur," *Women's Studies* 14 (1988): 261.

6. See esp. Paula Rabinowitz, *Labor and Desire: Women's Revolutionary Fiction in Depression America* (Chapel Hill, N.C.: University of North Carolina Press, 1991), index entry under "Le Sueur."

7. Elinor Langer's *Josephine Herbst* (New York: Warner Books, 1984) is the source for biographical information throughout my account. Herbst draws extensively on her own and her family's life in her fiction and memoirs. For an accessible version of a portion of the memoirs, see Josephine Herbst, *The Starched Blue Sky of Spain and Other Memoirs*, introd. Diane Johnson (New York: Harper-Collins, 1991).

8. Mary Anne Rasmussen, "Rewriting the Thirties: Feminist Representation and Radical Ideology in Josephine Herbst's 'A Year of Disgrace,'" paper presented at the American Studies Association annual meeting, 1990.

9. Josephine Herbst, "Literature in the U.S.S.R.," *New Republic*, April 29, 1931, p. 306.

10. Josephine Herbst, letter to Burroughs Mitchell, October 22, 1959, Josephine Herbst Papers, Scribner's Box, Beinecke Rare Book and Manuscript Library, Yale University.

11. Carbon of a letter headed "South America" and "League of Am. Writers" (1939), Herbst Papers.

12. Rebecca Pitts, review of *Rope of Gold*, *New Republic* 98 (March 22, 1939): 202.

13. Carbon of a letter headed "South America" and "League of Am. Writers" (1939), Herbst Papers.

14. Josephine Herbst, "Yesterday's Road," *New American Review* 3 (1968): 84–105, and Langer, *Josephine Herbst*, pp. 271–88.

15. On Cowley, see Langer, *Josephine Herbst*, p. 276; on Rukeyser, see Kate Daniels, "Searching/ Not Searching: Writing the Biography of Muriel Rukeyser," *Poetry East* 16–17 (1985): 83; on Wright, see Arnold Rampersad, "Chronology," in *Richard Wright: Early Works*, ed. Arnold Rampersad (New York: Library of America, 1991), p. 896.

16. Langer, *Josephine Herbst*, pp. 277–83. Langer reprints Herbst's FBI file on pp. 278–81.

17. Hilton Kramer, "Who Was Josephine Herbst?," *New Criterion*, September 1984, pp. 1–14, esp. pp. 8–11, 13–14; Stephen Koch, *Double Lives: Spies and Writers in the Secret Soviet War of Ideas against the West* (New York: Free Press, 1994), pp. 231–36, 324. See also Elinor Langer's review of Koch's *Double Lives*, "The Secret Drawer," *Nation* 259 (May 30, 1994): 752–60; Koch's reply, "Spy vs Spy," *Nation* 259 (August 22–29, 1994): 182; and Mary Anne Rasmussen's defense of Herbst, *Nation* 259 (August 22–29, 1994): 182, 212.

18. Quoted by Langer, *Josephine Herbst*, p. xii, from a February 17, 1966, letter.

19. "Hunter of Doves," *Botteghe Oscure* 13 (Spring 1954): 310–44; "Ruins of Memory" (1956), in *A View of the Nation: An Anthology*, ed. Henry M. Christman (New York: Grove, 1960), pp. 19–24.

20. See Chapter 4, "Coda: A Note on Criticism."

21. Richard Wright, *Black Boy (American Hunger)* (1945; New York: Library of America, 1991), p. 235.

22. *Black Boy (American Hunger)*, pp. 235–39, 269; *Conversations with Richard Wright*, ed. Keneth Kinnamon and Michel Fabre (Jackson: University of Mississippi Press, 1993), pp. 32, 38, 81, 116, 159, 214.

23. Richard Ohmann, *Politics of Letters* (Middletown, Conn.: Wesleyan University Press, 1987), pp. 68–91.

24. Natalie Robins, *Alien Ink: The FBI's War on Freedom of Expression* (New York: William Morrow, 1992), pp. xi, 79, 285.

25. Rampersad, "Chronology," p. 856.

26. Ibid., p. 902.

27. As an instance of reassessment, see John M. Reilly, "Richard Wright and the Art of Non-Fiction: Stepping Out on the Stage of the World," *Callaloo* 29 (1986): 507–20.

28. See the citations in Chapter 5, note 17.

29. Louis Menand, "The Hammer and the Nail," *New Yorker*, July 20, 1992, esp. pp. 80, 82, 84. See also Donald Gibson, "Richard Wright: The Politics of a Lone Marxian," in *The Politics of Literary Expression: A Study of Major Black Writers* (Westport, Conn.: Greenwood, 1981), pp. 21–57. For an opposing emphasis, see John M. Reilly, "Giving Bigger a Voice: The Politics of Narrative in *Native Son*," in *New Essays on Native Son*, ed. Keneth Kinnamon (New York: Cambridge University Press, 1990), pp. 35–62.

30. See, for example, Harold Bloom, introduction to *Richard Wright's Native Son*, ed. Harold Bloom (New York: Chelsea House, 1988), pp. 1–4.

31. Addison Gayle, *Richard Wright: Ordeal of a Native Son* (Garden City, N.Y.: Anchor Press/Doubleday, 1980), pp. xiii–xv, 152–300.

32. Muriel Rukeyser, "Under Forty," *Contemporary Jewish Record* 7 (1944): 6. Subsequent page references will be cited parenthetically in the text. For biographical information I have also relied on *Current Biography, 1943*, ed. Maxine Block (New York: H. W. Wilson, 1944), pp. 645–47; Rukeyser's autobiographical essay in *Twentieth Century Authors: A Biographical Dictionary of Modern Literature*, ed. Stanley Kunitz and Howard Haycraft (New York: H. W. Wilson, 1942), pp. 1210–11; her eloquent "Migrations," the introduction to *An American Portrait*, ed. Alex Rosenberg (New York: Transworld Art, 1976), n.p.; Muriel Rukeyser, "The Education of a Poet," in *The Writer on Her Work*, ed. Janet Sternburg (New York: Norton, 1980), pp. 217–30; and Kate Daniels, "Searching/Not Searching: Writing the Biography of Muriel Rukeyser," *Poetry East* 16–17 (1985): 70–93.

33. See, for example, the advertisement for *Student Review* in *New Masses* 10 (January 2, 1934): 32.

34. Muriel Rukeyser, "The Trial," *New Masses* 11 (June 12, 1934): 20.

35. Review of Faulkner's *Dr. Martino and Other Stories*, *New Masses* 11 (May 22, 1934): 27; review of John Wheelwright's *Rock and Shell*, *New Masses* 11 (July 10, 1934): 28; review of Kurt Hamsun's *The Road Leads On*, *New Masses* 11 (July 24, 1934): 27–28.

36. Leonard Bernstein, interview, in Aaron Copland and Vivian Perlis, *Copland: 1900 through 1942* (New York: St. Martin's/Merek, 1984), pp. 336–37.

37. Muriel Rukeyser, "Death in Spain: Barcelona on the Barricades," *New Masses* 20 (September 1, 1936): 9–11; "Barcelona, 1936," *Life and Letters Today* 15 (Autumn 1936): 28–33.

38. See, for example, Edna Lou Walton, "Muriel Rukeyser's Poems: Review of *U.S. 1*," *New York Times Book Review*, March 27, 1938, p. 19; Kerker Quinn, "A Modern Poetic Realist: Review of *U.S. 1*," *New York Herald Books*, February 20, 1938, p. 12; review of *U.S. 1*, *Time*, March 28, 1938, p. 63; William Rose Benet, "Four American Poets," *Saturday Review of Literature*, April 30, 1938, p. 16; Philip Blair Rice, "The Osiris Way: Review of *U.S. 1*," *Nation* 146 (March 19, 1938: 335–36; William Carlos Williams, "Muriel Rukeyser's *U.S. 1*," *New Republic*, March 9, 1938, pp. 141–42; Louis Untermeyer, "New Books in Review," *Yale Review*, n.s. 26 (Spring 1938): 608–9; Willard Maas, "Lost between the Wars: Review of *U.S. 1*," *Poetry* 52 (May 1938): 101–4; John Wheelwright, review of *U.S. 1*, *Partisan Review* 4 (March 1938): 54–56; Morton D. Zabel, "Two Years of Poetry," *Southern Review* 5 (1939–40): 600.

39. "Grandeur and Misery of a Poster Girl," *Partisan Review* 10 (1943): 471, 472.

40. Rebecca Pitts, "The Rukeyser Imbroglio," *Partisan Review* 10 (1943): 125–27.

41. F. O. Matthiessen, "The Rukeyser Imbroglio (cont'd)," *Partisan Review* 10 (1943): 217.

42. John Malcolm Brinnin, "Muriel Rukeyser: The Social Poet and the Problem of Communication," *Poetry* 61 (January 1943): 566, 567.

43. Horace Gregory and Marya Zaturenska, *A History of American Poetry, 1900–1940* (New York: Harcourt, Brace, 1946), p. 439.

44. Daniels, "Searching/Not Searching," p. 83 and n. 23.

45. *Mid-Century American Poets*, ed. John Ciardi (New York: Twayne, 1950), pp. 50–66; Kimon Friar and John Malcolm Brinnin, eds., *Modern Poetry: American and British* (New York: Appleton-Century-Crofts, 1951), pp. 368–71; Oscar Williams, ed., *A Little Treasury of Modern Poetry, English and American* (New York: Scribner's, 1952), pp. 685–89); George P. Elliott, ed., *Fifteen Modern American Poets* (New York: Rinehart, 1956), pp. 163–82; *The American Tradition in Literature*, ed. Sculley Bradley, Richard Croom Beatty, and E. Hudson Long (New York: Norton, 1956), 2:1544–51. On the Bollingen Prize Committee, Daniels, "Searching/Not Searching," p. 87.

46. M. L. Rosenthal, "Muriel Rukeyser: The Longer Poems," *New Directions in Prose and Poetry*, ed. James Laughlin, 14 (1953): 202–29.

47. Virginia R. Terris, "Muriel Rukeyser: A Retrospective," *American Poetry Review* 3 (May–June 1974): 10, 11.

48. Louise Kertesz, *The Poetic Vision of Muriel Rukeyser* (Baton Rouge: Louisiana State University Press, 1980); Walter Kalaidjian, *American Culture between the Wars: Revisionary Modernism and Postmodern Critique* (New York: Columbia University Press, 1993), pp. 160–75, 183–87.

49. Cameron Barrick, "Social Protest and Poetic Decorum in the Great Depression: A Reading of Kenneth Fearing, Horace Gregory, and Muriel Rukeyser" (Ph.D. diss., Columbia University, 1994); Anne Frances Herzog, " 'Faith and Resistance': Politics and the Poetry of Muriel Rukeyser" (Ph.D. diss., Rutgers University, 1993); Daniels, "Searching/Not Searching," esp. p. 85.

50. Kate Daniels, "Preface: 'In Order to Feel,' " in Muriel Rukeyser, *Out of Silence: Selected Poems* (Evanston, Ill.: TriQuarterly Books, 1992), p. xiv.

51. *New York Times*, November 14, 1958, p. 11.

52. Langston Hughes, "The Negro Artist and the Racial Mountain," *Nation* 122 (June 1926), in *Voices from the Harlem Renaissance*, ed. Nathan Irwin Huggins (New York: Oxford University Press, 1976), p. 308. Hughes's *Worker Monthly* poems are "Drama for Winter Night (Fifth Avenue)," March 1925, p. 225; "God to Hungry Child," March 1925, p. 234; "Rising Waters," April 1925, p. 267; "Poem to a Dead Soldier," April 1925, p. 267; "Park Benching," April 1925, p. 261.

53. The Communist Popular Front opposition to "war and fascism" was central to the original call for the 1935 meeting of the American Writers' Congress, *New Masses* 14 (January 22, 1935): 20. The quotation is from Waldo Frank, foreword to *American Writers' Congress*, ed. Henry Hart (New York: International Publishers, 1935), p. vi. Hughes's "To Negro Writers" is on pp. 139–41.

54. See, for example, "About the USSR," *International Literature*, no. 2 (July 1933): 155; "Moscow and Me," *International Literature*, no. 2 (July 1933): 61–66; "Negroes in Moscow: In a Land Where There Is No Jim Crow," *International Literature*, no. 4 (October 1933): 78–81; "Going South in Russia," *Crisis* 41 (June 1934): 162–63; and, as late as 1946, the series for the *Chicago Defender*, Summer 1946, reprinted in *Good Morning Revolution: Uncollected Writings of Social Protest by Langston Hughes*, ed. Faith Berry (New York: Citadel Press, 1992), pp. 84–98.

55. The best biographical treatment of Hughes during his radical years and their aftermath is Faith Berry, *Langston Hughes: Before and after Harlem* (Westport, Conn.: Lawrence Hill, 1983). See also Arnold Rampersad, *The Life of Langston Hughes*, vol. 1 (New York: Oxford University Press, 1986).

56. "Lenin," *New Masses* 5 (January 22, 1946): 5. The essays on the Soviet Union appeared in the

Chicago *Defender* in June, July, and August 1946. The essays and "Lenin" are reprinted in Berry, *Good Morning Revolution*, pp. 84–98.

57. *Life* 20 (April 4, 1949): 42.

58. Hughes published a summary of his testimony as "Langston Hughes Speaks," *Crisis* 60 (May 1953): 279–80, reprinted in Berry, *Good Morning Revolution*, pp. 147–48. See also Berry, *Langston Hughes*, pp. 317–20.

59. The poem was published in *The Panther and the Lash* (New York: Knopf, 1967), the year Hughes died and a decade and a half after the investigation.

60. The poems in *The Panther and the Lash: Poems of Our Times* are "Christ in Alabama," p. 37; "Militant" (previously "Pride"), p. 39; "Florida Road Workers," p. 41; and "Justice," p. 45. As late as 1967, in the midst of the civil rights struggle, Hughes still does not group his Scottsboro poems so as to give them the historical and reinforcing poetic context they deserve.

61. Walter C. Daniel, "Langston Hughes versus the Black Preachers in the *Pittsburgh Courier* in the 1930s," in *Critical Essays on Langston Hughes*, ed. Edward J. Mullen (Boston: G. K. Hall, 1986), pp. 129–35.

62. The comprehensive *Collected Poems of Langston Hughes*, ed. Arnold Rampersad and David Roessel (New York: Knopf, 1994), provides useful, understated notes, helpful to the informed reader but in their content and the formal arrangement of the poems tending to minimize the full force of Hughes's political involvement.

63. Christopher C. DeSantis, "Rage, Repudiation, and Endurance: Langston Hughes's Radical Writings," *Langston Hughes Review* 12 (1993): 31.

64. James O. Young, *Black Writers of the Thirties* (Baton Rouge: Louisiana State University Press, 1973), pp. 178, 179.

65. See, for example, Richard K. Barksdale, *Langston Hughes: The Poet and His Critics* (Chicago: American Library Association, 1977), pp. 40–70; Onwuchekwa Jemie, *Langston Hughes: An Introduction to the Poetry* (New York: Columbia University Press, 1976), pp. 14–15, 112–13, 120–23; and R. Baxter Miller, *The Art and Imagination of Langston Hughes* (Lexington: University of Kentucky Press, 1989), pp. 67–74. James Edward Smethurst, *The New Red Negro: The Literary Left and African American Poetry, 1930–1946* (New York: Oxford University Press, 1999), pp. 93–115, 144–63, appeared too late for me to take it into account.

Chapter Three

1. To complement the discussion and citations in Chapter One, for accessible, representative examples of the discourse Le Sueur contributed to and developed within, see Granville Hicks et al., eds., *Proletarian Literature in the United States: An Anthology* (New York: International Publishers, 1935); Henry Hart, ed., *American Writers' Congress* (New York: International Publishers, 1935); Joseph North, ed., *New Masses: An Anthology of the Rebel Thirties* (New York: International Publishers, 1969); Jack Conroy and Curt Johnson, eds., *Writers in Revolt: The Anvil Anthology* (New York: Lawrence Hill, 1973); Joyce L. Kornbluh, ed., *Rebel Voices: An I.W.W. Anthology* (Ann Arbor: University of Michigan Press, 1964); and V. J. Jerome, "Toward a People's Culture," in *Culture in a Changing World: A Marxist Approach* (New York: New Century Publishers, 1947), pp. 47–64.

2. Sacvan Bercovitch, "The Rites of Assent: Rhetoric, Ritual, and the Ideology of the American Consensus," in *The American Self: Myth, Ideology, and Popular Culture*, ed. Sam B. Girgus (Albuquerque: University of New Mexico Press, 1981), p. 17.

3. In "The Politics of Bibliography," Deborah Rosenfelt argues that traditional formalist criticism privileges genres like poetry and fiction and devalues others like autobiography and essay

because they invoke the artist and history. Quoted in Paul Lauter, "Race and Gender in the Shaping of the American Literary Canon: A Case Study from the Twenties," *Feminist Studies* 9 (Fall 1983): 462, n. 37. For an illuminating essay on "Corn Village," an analysis informed by the rhetorical theories and views of Bakhtin, Kenneth Burke, Rorty, Iser, and Greene, see James M. Boehnlein, "Meridel Le Sueur, 'Corn Village,' and Literary Pragmatism," *Midamerica* 21 (1994): 82–97.

4. Meridel Le Sueur, "Corn Village," in *Salute to Spring* (1940; New York: International Publishers, 1989), pp. 7, 14, 22–23. Subsequent page references to "Corn Village" and the other stories in *Salute to Spring* will be cited parenthetically in the text.

5. Meridel Le Sueur, "The Fetish of Being Outside," *New Masses* 14 (February 26, 1935): 22.

6. Annette Kolodny, *The Lay of the Land: Metaphor as Experience and History in American Life and Letters* (Chapel Hill: University of North Carolina Press, 1975).

7. See, for example, "Women on the Breadlines," *New Masses* 8 (January 1932): 5–7; "Women Are Hungry," *American Mercury* 32 (March 1932): 316–26; "Cows and Horses Are Hungry," *American Mercury* 33 (September 1933): 53–56; "The Farmers Face a Crisis," *New Masses* 20 (July 21, 1936): 9–10; "How Drought Relief Works," *New Masses* 20 (August 18, 1936): 14–16. Except for the last two, these reports are reprinted in Meridel Le Sueur, *Ripening: Selected Works, 1927–1980*, ed. Elaine Hedges (Old Westbury, N.Y.: Feminist Press, 1982).

8. Meridel Le Sueur, "Women on the Breadlines," in *Harvest Song: Collected Essays and Stories by Meridel Le Sueur*, rev. ed. (Albuquerque, N.M.: West End Press, 1990), p. 166. Subsequent page references to this edition are cited parenthetically in the text. On hunger and starvation, see the citations in n. 7.

9. Le Sueur, "The Fetish of Being Outside," p. 20. Subsequent quotations will be cited by page parenthetically in the text. "The Fetish of Being Outside" is also reprinted in *Harvest Song*, pp. 199–203.

10. "Corn Village," p. 21.

11. In the PBS documentary *I Was Marching: Meridel Le Sueur's First Ninety Years*, produced and directed by David Shulman, 1991, Le Sueur relates an anecdote from the early 1930s. On a visit to Minneapolis, Anna Louise Strong, instead of admiring Le Sueur's two young daughters, chastised Le Sueur for having them because they would prevent her from becoming a party organizer. The episode illustrates a basic attitude that Le Sueur indicates changed during the Popular Front.

12. See, for example, Albert Maltz's representative "Man on the Road," which also involves a middle-class person who picks up a working-class hitchhiker. Hicks et al., *Proletarian Literature in the United States*, pp. 116–22.

13. In overlooking the role of the imagination and creativity, Anthony Dawahare perpetuates Paula Rabinowitz's view that, in Dawahare's words, "by identifying the female self almost exclusively with maternity, Le Sueur plays into the idea that women were best suited to be mothers, an idea that prolonged the struggle for women's suffrage and equal rights well into the mid-twentieth century." See Anthony Dawahare, "Modernity and 'Village Communism': The Utopian Literature of Meridel Le Sueur," *Criticism* 39 (1997): 417, and Paula Rabinowitz, *Labor and Desire: Women's Revolutionary Fiction in Depression America* (Chapel Hill: University of North Carolina Press, 1991), p. 123. Rabinowitz and Dawahare ignore (or, to use Dawahare's word, are "blind" to) the imagination and its creations—that is, to what the mind, not the body, produces (Le Sueur herself pervasively counters this mind-body division). In his treatment of Le Sueur, Dawahare unfortunately filters out the imagination, metaphoric language, the full implications of Le Sueur's nonlinear form, and her insights into the politics, complexities, and centrality of the creative process. Dawahare instead views Le Sueur through the lenses of a totalized concept, "economism," and an equally monolithic "proletarian literary movement."

14. As applied to Le Sueur in particular, see Harvey Swados, *The American Writer and the Great Depression* (Indianapolis: Bobbs-Merrill, 1966), p. 181.

15. In addition to "Women on the Breadlines," see the citations in note 7.

16. A year later Le Sueur and Horace Gregory reenergized these issues in their exchange in the *New Masses*. See my earlier discussion in this chapter.

17. Constance Coiner, *Better Red: The Writing and Resistance of Tillie Olsen and Meridel Le Sueur* (New York: Oxford University Press, 1995), p. 106.

18. In contrast to readers who believe she privileges " 'mass feeling' over individual consciousness as the subjective basis of community" (Dawahare, "Modernity and 'Village Communism,' " p. 423), Le Sueur says the exact opposite. She stresses that her involvement in communal activity intensifies her individual consciousness so that "I know everything that is going on." For the history and philosophical basis of the tradition of Marxist or socialist individualism that Le Sueur reanimates in "I Was Marching," see Ellen Wood, *Mind and Politics: An Approach to the Meaning of Liberal and Socialist Individualism* (Berkeley: University of California Press, 1972).

19. Dorothy Parker, "Incredible, Fantastic . . . and True," in North, *New Masses: An Anthology of the Rebel Thirties*, pp. 172–77.

20. Karl Marx and Frederick Engels, "The Communist Manifesto," in *Selected Works in One Volume* (New York: International Publishers, 1968), p. 44.

21. John Murray Cuddihy, *The Ordeal of Civility: Freud, Marx, Levi-Strauss and the Jewish Confrontation with Modernity* (New York: Basic Books, 1974), pp. 5–10.

22. Meridel Le Sueur, *The Girl*, rev. ed. (1935; Albuquerque, N.M.: West End Press, 1990), pp. 4, 10. Subsequent page references to *The Girl* are cited parenthetically in the text.

23. In a nuanced and probing essay, Blanche H. Gelfant focuses on the complexities, contradictions, and syntheses in the language of *The Girl* in the context of thirties radicalism and contemporary feminist theory. " 'Everybody Steals': Language as Theft in Meridel Le Sueur's *The Girl*," in *Tradition and the Talents of Women*, ed. Florence Howe (Urbana: University of Illinois Press, 1991), pp. 183–210.

Chapter Four

1. Edwin Seaver, "The Proletarian Novel," in *American Writers' Congress*, ed. Henry Hart (New York: International Publishers, 1935), p. 101.

2. Josephine Herbst, "Literature in the U.S.S.R.," *New Republic*, April 29, 1931, p. 306. For the more customary interpretation of the Kharkov platform, see A. Elistratova's critical assessment of the 1931 *New Masses* in "New Masses," *International Literature* 1 (1932): 107–14, and the studies cited in my Introduction, note 18. Herbst was close to the party but unlike her husband, John Herrmann, she did not join. Although *Pity Is Not Enough* (1933) and *The Executioner Waits* (1934) were written during the Third Period, as her remarks on Kharkov indicate, Herbst was not writing from a party point of view. In contrast to her emphasis, the central role of the party was a basic feature of the Kharkov platform. In the infighting on the left, however, in his unflattering review of *The Executioner Waits*, Lionel Abel aligns Herbst with the party in his "A Technician of Mediocrity," *Nation* 139 (October 31, 1934): 514–16.

3. Josephine Herbst, *Rope of Gold: A Novel of the Thirties* (1939; Old Westbury, N.Y.: Feminist Press, 1984), p. 428. Subsequent quotations from *Rope of Gold* are from this edition and are cited by page parenthetically in the text. Winifred Farrant Bevilacqua gives a lucid survey of Herbst's narrative method in *Josephine Herbst* (Boston: Twayne, 1985), pp. 13–15.

4. Josephine Herbst, "What Is Americanism: A Symposium on Marxism and the American Tradition," *Partisan Review* 3 (April 1936): 5.

5. Ibid.

6. Josephine Herbst, *Pity Is Not Enough* (1933; New York: Warner Books, 1985), p. 167. Subsequent quotations are cited by page parenthetically in the text.

7. I have relied on Ruth Currie-McDaniel, *Carpetbagger of Conscience: A Biography of John Emory Bryant* (Athens: University of Georgia Press, 1981), pp. 80–117, for information about Reconstruction Georgia and the politicians and financiers Herbst uses as her models.

8. Herbst, *Pity Is Not Enough*, pp. 40–42; Currie-McDaniel, *Carpetbagger of Georgia*, p. 108.

9. Lenore "stood there with her greenish rather small eyes shining in her pointed freckled face, her straw colored hair pulled tight back giving her high white forehead a precocious plucked and rather forlorn look that made Joe look twice and then turn to Lucy who stood easy and graceful with nothing to feel sorry for" (pp. 54–55). This vivid portrait has elements of authorial self-irony, since Lenore bears a striking resemblance to Josephine Herbst, with her pointed face, green eyes, and lively intelligence. The theme of two sisters, one the beauty, recurs in the Rosamund-Vicky relation, a version of Herbst's relation to her sister, Helen, although, as early as Penelope and Irene in Howells's *Hazard of New Fortunes* (1890), variations on this theme were almost archetypal.

10. bell hooks, *Feminist Theory: From Margin to Center* (Boston: South End Press, 1984), p. 25.

11. For a valuable treatment of Herbst's feminist probing of her women characters, see Laura Browder, *Rousing the Nation: Radical Culture in Depression America* (Amherst: University of Massachusetts Press, 1998), pp. 89–116.

12. Richard Maxwell Brown, *No Duty to Retreat: Violence and Values in American History and Society* (New York: Oxford University Press, 1991), index entries under "incorporation" and "Western Civil War of Incorporation."

13. Josephine Herbst, *The Executioner Waits* (1934; New York: Warner Books, 1985), p. 144. Subsequent quotations are cited by page parenthetically in the text.

14. Josephine Herbst, "A Year of Disgrace," *Noble Savage* 3 (1961): 145.

15. This relation is central to "the story she could never tell," in the words on the cover of Elinor Langer's exemplary biography, *Josephine Herbst* (New York: Warner Books, 1984), index entry under "Greenwood, Marion."

16. Herbst's friend, Mary Heaton Vorse—they had gone together to cover the Flint sit-down strike in 1936—reviewed *Spy Overhead*, by Clinch Calkins, *New Republic*, November 3, 1937, pp. 378–79. The book and the review brought to a focus the results of the Senate Civil Liberties Committee revelations about, in Calkins's words, "the American industrial worker caught in a trap of commercialized espionage and violence" (quoted by Vorse, p. 378). Vorse stresses "the chapter 'Is Gas Politer Than Guns? . . . It contains the revelations of Mr. Ignatius McCarty of the Lake Erie Chemical Company of Cleveland, Ohio, manufacturers of tear gas and tear-gas equipment, and his rivalry with his competitors, Federal Laboratories and Manville Manufacturing Company." The review is full of details about the delight the manufacturers take in using "the D. M. and C. N. gas projectiles (sickening, nauseating and tear gas)" in the milk strikes and the Imperial Valley strike. "One sees the munitions buzzards stirring up trouble, leading mobs, competing jealously with one another for the sale of True-Flight shells and gas—'more effective and terrifying because it is not possible for the rioters to determine where the gas cloud begins or ends, and whose pain from the high concentration of this gas in the eyes, nose and throat is almost unbearable'" (pp. 378–79). Ed Thompson emerges from the threat brought into the open by the Senate hearings and the Calkins book and Vorse review.

17. Paula Rabinowitz, *Labor and Desire: Women's Revolutionary Fiction in Depression America* (Chapel Hill: University of North Carolina Press, 1991), p. 160. Subsequent page references are cited parenthetically in the text.

18. Langer, *Josephine Herbst*, index entry under "Herrmann, John."

1. Richard Wright, *Native Son*, Library of America restored text (1940; New York: HarperPerennial, 1993), p. 22. Subsequent page references are cited parenthetically in the text.

2. Richard Wright, *Black Power: A Record of Reactions in a Land of Pathos* (New York: Harper, 1954), dedication page.

3. For a discussion of the party line on "the Negro Question," see Chapter 1 and the accompanying citations (notes 35–38).

4. The quotations are from Wright's important theoretical essay, "Blueprint for Negro Writing," *New Challenge* 2 (Fall 1937): 59–60.

5. For Wright's account of his relation to the party, see "I Bite the Hand That Feeds Me," *Atlantic* 165 (June 1940): 826–28 (the title does not refer to the party; the article is a forceful statement of Wright's commitment); "I Tried to Be a Communist," *Atlantic* 159 (August 1944): 61–70 and (September 1940): 48–56; *Black Boy (American Hunger)* (New York: Library of America, 1991), pp. 271–365; *Black Power*, pp. xi–xii. See also Ralph Ellison, "Remembering Richard Wright," in *The Collected Essays of Ralph Ellison*. ed. John F. Callahan (New York: Modern Library, 1995), pp. 659–75. Dan McCall analyzes the pressures and, particularly during 1939–42, the shifts in party policy that led to Wright's 1942 break with the party. Dan McCall, *The Example of Richard Wright* (New York: Harcourt, Brace, 1969), pp. 58–60.

6. Quoted by Alfred Davis, "The Story of a Winner—Richard Wright, Negro WPA Writer, Wins Nation Fiction Contest," *Daily Worker*, February 25, 1938, p. 7.

7. See Ben Davis Jr.'s negative review, misleadingly titled "Richard Wright's *Native Son* a Notable Achievement," *Sunday Worker*, March 14, 1940, pp. 4, 6, and Samuel Sillen's two perceptive, favorable reviews, "Richard Wright's *Native Son*: A Distinguished First Novel," *New Masses* 34 (March 5, 1940): 24–25, and "The Meaning of Bigger Thomas," *New Masses* 35 (April 30, 1940): 26–28, in part a response to Davis. See also Mike Gold, "Dick Wright Gives America a Significant Picture in *Native Son*," *Sunday Worker*, March 31, 1940, p. 7, and "Some Reflections on Richard Wright's Novel, *Native Son*," *Daily Worker*, April 17, 1940, p. 7.

For generally negative assessments of Wright's relation to Communism, see, for example, Robert Bone, *The Negro Novel in America* (New Haven: Yale University Press, 1958), pp. 143–44, 150–52; Edward Margolies, *Native Sons: A Critical Study of Twentieth-Century Negro American Authors* (New York: J. B. Lippincott, 1968), pp. 69–70, 72, 79–81; McCall, *The Example of Richard Wright*, pp. 46–62, 90–96, 100–101; Russell Carl Brignano, *Richard Wright: An Introduction to His Work* (Pittsburgh: University of Pittsburgh Press, 1970), pp. 50–86; Keneth Kinnamon, *The Emergence of Richard Wright: A Study in Literature and Society* (Urbana: University of Illinois Press, 1973), pp. 50–74, 125, 147–49; Michel Fabre, *The Unfinished Quest of Richard Wright* (New York: William Morrow, 1973), pp. 95–107, 125–31, 140–46, 183–87, 192–93; Donald Gibson, *The Politics of Literary Expression: A Study of Major Black Writers* (Westport, Conn.: Greenwood, 1981), pp. 25–27, 31–33, 36–39. For more favorable views, see Barbara Foley, *Radical Representations: Politics and Form in U.S. Proletarian Fiction, 1929–1941* (Durham, N.C.: Duke Univeristy Press, 1993), pp. 206–12, and "The Politics of Poetics: Ideology and Narrative Form in *An American Tragedy* and *Native Son*," in *Narrative Poetics: Innovations, Limits, Challenges*, ed. James Phelan, Center for Comparative Studies in the Humanities, Ohio State University, *Papers in Comparative Studies* 5 (1987): 55–67. Except for Foley most of these critics associate the party with simplistic, reductive propaganda. To the disadvantage of the novel, some see Max as Wright's Communist spokesman; others present Wright as heroically rejecting the party line.

8. Developing a hint in Irving Howe's "Black Boys and Native Sons," in Irving Howe, *A World More Attractive* (New York: Horizon Press, 1963), pp. 98–122, Louis Tremaine sees *Native Son* as

expressionist in plot, characterization, and narrative voice. Tremaine, however, disapproves of what are for him the resulting excesses and solipsism. "The Dissociated Sensibility of Bigger Thomas" (1986), in *Richard Wright's Native Son*, ed. Harold Bloom (New York: Chelsea House, 1988), pp. 95–104.

9. What Craig Werner calls "the modernist blues novel inside the realist protest novel" I refer to as Wright's expressionism intertwined with and inseparable from his realism-naturalism. Similarly, what Eugene E. Miller discusses as Wright's surrealism I call expressionism. For some purposes the differences are important but as applied to *Native Son* the differences are less significant than our shared stress on what I refer to as Wright's innovative, avant-garde version of realism-naturalism. Craig Werner, "Bigger's Blues: *Native Son* and the Articulation of Afro-American Modernism," in *New Essays on Native Son*, ed. Keneth Kinnamon (New York: Cambridge University Press, 1990), p. 120; Eugene E. Miller, *Voice of a Native Son: The Poetics of Richard Wright* (Jackson: University Press of Mississippi, 1990), pp. 61–94. In her suggestive essay, "The Politics of Poetics," pp. 55–67, Barbara Foley places *Native Son* outside the tradition of naturalistic fiction. For my reasons for disagreeing, see my Introduction, note 30.

10. John M. Reilly examines these uses as he subtly develops his insight that "in the record of black resistance, *Native Son* has a special place as an instance of direct challenge to the power of prevailing discourse. It not only questions the factuality of received views, but also carries the challenge into the mechanisms of discourse itself with skill and artistry that give readers a great deal more news than they bargained for." "Giving Bigger a Voice," in Kinnamon, *New Essays on Native Son*, pp. 37–62. Craig Werner, for his part, nicely observes that "Wright does not speak *about* the blues; he speaks the blues." For insight into the blues tradition and for a view of the ending similar to mine, see Werner's "Bigger's Blues," pp. 117–51, esp. pp. 150–51.

11. See, for example, Alfred Kazin, "Richard Wright," *New York Times Book Review*, December 29, 1991, pp. 3, 18–19; Louis Menand, "The Hammer and the Nail," *New Yorker*, July 20, 1992, pp. 79–84; and Laura E. Tanner, "Uncovering the Magical Disguise of Language: The Narrative Presence in Richard Wright's *Native Son*," *Texas Studies in Language and Literature* 29 (1987): 412–31. Tanner reifies "the master language" so that it says one monolithic thing unlike the implied narrator who enters and interprets Bigger's inner life and expresses a range and complexity of meanings.

12. In responding to Ben Davis Jr.'s criticism that Wright's Communists, Jan and Mary, are "atypical" and are presented negatively, Samuel Sillen discusses their positive role in "Book Two" and "Book Three" and points to their development—or the changes in Bigger's view of them—from scenes like this in "Book One." Sillen concedes, however, that the power of the negative portrayal in this part of the novel stays with readers and colors our view of the characters. Davis, "Richard Wright's *Native Son*," p. 4, and Sillen, "The Meaning of Bigger Thomas," pp. 26–27.

13. Helen Lynd, *Shame and the Search for Identity* (New York: Harcourt, Brace, 1958).

14. Harriet Jacobs explores this territory in Dr. Flint's possessive pursuit of Linda in *Incidents in the Life of a Slave Girl* (1861). Rebecca Harding Davis engages the feelings centering on "the gorilla and the dove" in her April 1862 *Atlantic* story, "John Lamar." Du Bois touches on related issues in "The Story of John," in *Souls of Black Folk* (1903), and Chesnutt deals with a version in *The House Behind the Cedars* (1900), as does Nella Larsen in *Quicksand* (1928). But it is generally accepted that Wright opens up the passions and complexities of interracial sex and the powerful myths of black and white sexuality more fully than any of his predecessors, that he moves the discourse to a new depth and complexity.

15. Winthrop Jordan, *White over Black: American Attitudes Toward the Negro, 1550–1812* (Baltimore: Penguin, 1969), pp. 3–43, 255–59.

16. McCall, *The Example of Richard Wright*, p. 73.

17. For the view that, as in his treatment of Bessie, Wright presents demeaning portraits of black women, stereotypes that are "both extremely racist and sexist," see Sherley Anne Williams, "Papa Dick and Sister-Woman: Reflections on Women in the Fiction of Richard Wright," in *American Novelists Revisited: Essays in Feminist Criticism*, ed. Fritz Fleischmann (Boston: G. K. Hall, 1982), pp. 394–417, and, for example, Maria K. Mootry, "Bitches, Whores, and Women Haters: Archetypes in the Art of Richard Wright," in *Richard Wright: A Collection of Critical Essays*, ed. Richard Macksey and Frank E. Moorer (Englewood Cliffs, N.J.: Prentice-Hall, 1984), pp. 117–27; Sylvia Keady, "Richard Wright's Women Characters and Inequality," *Black American Literature Forum* 10 (1976): 124–29, and Alan W. France, "Misogyny and Appropriation in Wright's *Native Son*," *Modern Fiction Studies* 34 (1988): 413–23. In her biography, Margaret Walker argues that Wright personally was hostile to black women; see *Richard Wright: Daemonic Genius* (New York: Warner Books, 1987). Michel Fabre questions Walker's interpretation in "Margaret Walker's Richard Wright: A Wrong Righted or Wright Wronged?," *Mississippi Quarterly* 42 (1989): 429–50. Joyce Ann Joyce challenges the negative view in "Richard Wright's 'Long Black Song': A Moral Dilemma," *Mississippi Quarterly* 42 (1989): 379–85, as does Kathleen Ochshorn, "The Community of *Native Son*," *Mississippi Quarterly* 42 (1989): 387–92, and Trudier Harris, "Native Son and Foreign Daughters," in Kinnamon, *New Essays on Native Son*, pp. 63–84.

18. To ride "roughshod over her whimpering protests" is Wright's revision for the Book-of-the-Month Club version ("Notes," p. 591).

19. "A Red Love Note," *Left Front*, no. 3 (January–February 1934): 3; "Strength," *Anvil*, no. 5 (March–April, 1934): 20; "Everywhere Burning Waters Rise," *Left Front*, no. 4 (May–June 1934): 9.

20. See, for example, "Brick Slayer Is Likened to Jungle Beast," *Chicago Sunday Tribune*, June 5, 1938, pt. 1, p. 6; "Science Traps Moron in 5 Murders: Admits a Third Chicago Killing and 2 in West," *Chicago Tribune*, June 3, 1938, pp. 1, 8 (banner headline, lead story); "Brick Moron Tells of Killing 2 Women: Solves Latest Sex Slaying and 1936 Case," *Chicago Tribune*, May 29, 1938, p. 1; "Rapist Slayer Acts Out 2 More Savage Attacks: Shows Police How Nurse Was Slain with Brick," *Chicago Tribune*, June 4, 1938, p. 6; "Beats Slayer of Wife; Own Life Menaced: Nixon Makes Attempt to Strangle Fireman," *Chicago Tribune*, June 8, 1938, p. 3; "Murderer Dies in Chair; Stays Granted to 2," *Chicago Tribune*, June 16, 1939, p. 1.

A different narrative emerges in the reports in the leading black newspaper, *Chicago Defender*. See, for example, "'Police Beat Us,' Say Hicks, Nixon," *Chicago Defender*, June 18, 1938, City Edition, pp. 1–2; "'Powder Keg' in City after Police Fiasco," *Chicago Defender*, June 18, 1938, City Edition, p. 19; "Robert Nixon Attacked by Irate Hubby: Vicious Newsstories Are Blamed for Courtroom-Flare-up," *Chicago Defender*, June 11, 1938, p. 6; "Nixon Goes on Trial: Frame-up Theory Is Strong," *Chicago Defender*, July 30, 1938, City Edition, p. 1.

21. Paul N. Siegel identifies Max as an ILD lawyer but believes he is not a Communist because, although he is sympathetic to the party, he is "neither a revolutionist nor a Stalinist" and hopes to avert the racial cataclysm he forsees. Siegel analyzes Ben Davis Jr.'s review of *Native Son* to demonstrate the extent to which Max deviates from orthodox Communist positions and expectations. "The Conclusion of Richard Wright's *Native Son*," in Macksey and Moorer, *Richard Wright: A Collection of Essays*, pp. 106–16, quotation from p. 108. Samuel Sillen, however, as editor of *New Masses*, was also an influential Communist theoretician and spokesman. He wrote two favorable reviews of *Native Son*, one a response to and rebuttal of Davis. Party positions were not as monolithic as Siegel assumes. For citations and analysis of Davis's and Sillen's reviews, see the previous discussion with note 7. Using the same evidence and line of reasoning as Siegel, moreover, we would have to conclude that Wright was not a Communist, although he was. "Revolutionist" also presents problems for a Popular Front Communist, because the moderate strains within the Popular Front were more pronounced than the revolutionary.

22. Notable exceptions are Reilly, "Giving Bigger a Voice," pp. 56–60, and Foley, "The Politics of Poetics," pp. 55–67. See also Yoshinobu Hakutani, *Richard Wright and Racial Discourse* (Columbia: University of Missouri Press, 1996), pp. 73, 78–79, 82–83. For more customary views even in the work of generally perceptive critics, see, for example, McCall, *The Example of Richard Wright*, pp. 52–53, 54, 57, 90–96, 100–101; Margolies, *Native Sons*, pp. 79–81, and *The Art of Richard Wright* (Carbondale: Southern Illinois University Press, 1969), pp. 112–15; Brignano, *Richard Wright*, pp. 80–86; Kinnamon, *The Emergence of Richard Wright: A Study in Literature and Society*, pp. 125, 141–43; Robert B. Stepto, "I Thought I Knew These People: Richard Wright and the Afro-American Literary Tradition," *Massachusetts Review* 18 (1977): 531–32; Donald Gibson, *The Politics of Literary Expression: A Study of Major Black Writers* (Westport, Conn.: Greenwood, 1981), pp. 36–38; Joyce Ann Joyce, *Wright's Art of Tragedy* (Iowa City: University of Iowa Press, 1986), pp. 114–16; Houston Baker Jr., "Richard Wright and the Dynamics of Place in Afro-American Literature," in Kinnamon, *New Essays on Native Son*, p. 112; Robert Butler, *Native Son: The Emergence of a New Black Hero* (Boston: Twayne, 1991), pp. 54–57, 107–11; James W. Tuttleson, "The Problematic Texts of Richard Wright," *Hudson Review* 45 (1992): 268. Although he does not focus on Max in particular, James Baldwin's influential essays set the tone for dismissing the courtroom speech and the concluding sequences in *Native Son*. See Baldwin's "Everybody's Protest Novel," *Partisan Review* 16 (1949): 578–85; "Alas, Poor Richard," in *Nobody Knows My Name* (New York: Dell, 1961), pp. 144–70; "Many Thousands Gone," in *Notes of a Native Son* (1955; Boston: Beacon, 1984), pp. 24–45. For context see Introduction with note 7.

23. For a representative example of the 1930s Communist analysis of slavery, see James S. Allen, *The Negro Question in the United States* (New York: International Publishers, 1936), esp. pp. 19–54. See also Herbert Biel, "Class Conflicts in the South—1850–1860," *Communist* 18 (February 1939): 170–81 and (March 1939): 274–79, and Herbert Biel, "A Bourbon Defense of Slavocracy: Review of Arthur Y. Lloyd, *The Slavery Controversy*," *Communist* 18 (December 1939): 1169–70. Written from a Marxist but not Communist point of view, see also W. E. B. Du Bois, *Black Reconstruction* (New York: Harcourt, Brace, 1935), index entry under "slavery."

24. For a discussion of the party's discourse on "the Negro Question," see Chapter 1 with notes 35–38.

25. Davis, "Richard Wright's Native Son a Notable Achievement," p. 4; Ralph Ellison, "The World and the Jug," in *Shadow and Act* (New York: Random House, 1964), pp. 119–20, 140–41.

26. "Joe Lewis Uncovers Dynamite" (1935), in *New Masses: An Anthology of the Rebel Thirties*, ed. Joseph North (New York: International Publishers, 1969), pp. 175–78.

27. Reilly, "Giving Bigger a Voice," esp. pp. 52–54.

28. To gauge the extent to which Wright was both working within and going deeper than the prevailing Popular Front discourse on the American Revolution and the Declaration of Independence, see, for example, Earl Browder, "Communism Is the Americanism of the Twentieth Century," *Daily Worker*, July 3, 1937, p. 7 (above Browder's article is a banner headline, "With the Spirit of '76 Let Us Defeat Tory Vigilantes of 1937." Pictures of Jefferson, Washington, Franklin, and Paine are on one side of the article, pictures of William Z. Foster, Earl Browder, James W. Ford, and Ella [Mother] Bloor are on the other, above quotations from Lenin and Stalin. Beneath the article is a handsomely printed Declaration of Independence); Louis Budenz, "The Great Epic of American History," *Daily Worker*, July 3, 1937, p. 8; "July 4th and the 150th Anniversary of the Constitution," *Communist* 16 (July 1937): 668–71; A. B. Magill, "Interpreting the Constitution," *Daily Worker*, September 16, 1937, pp. 3, 6; Earl Browder, "Revolutionary Background of the United States Constitution," *Communist* 16 (September 1937): 793–807; the 1938 ten-page July 4th issue of the *Daily Worker*, including Earl Browder's "The American Tradition and Socialism,"

Milton Howard's "The Declaration of Independence—Birth Certificate of American Democracy," Harry Gannes's "1776—A World Torch of Freedom," Ben Davis Jr.'s "Thomas Jefferson, the First Abolitionist," Art Shields's "Thomas Paine and the Pamphleteers of 1776," "The International Brigades of 1776 and 1938," and special drawings by staff artists and contemporary engravings of the American Revolution; Francis Franklin, "July 4th—Birthday of American Democracy," *Communist* 17 (July 1938): 630–41; Milton Howard, "Jefferson's Principles—Democratic Weapons against Bigoted Attacks on People's Rights," *Daily Worker*, July 4, 1939, p. 3; "Jefferson, Madison Bitterly Fought Tory Alien and Sedition Bills: Led American Fight on Reactionary Drive as Peril to Democracy," *Daily Worker*, July 4, 1939, p. 4; "Negroes Died for U.S. Freedom—July 4 Is Reminder of Their Fight," *Daily Worker*, July 4, 1939, p. 6; "Our Founding Fathers Hailed Role of Jews; Their Principles Betrayed by Anti-Semites," *Daily Worker*, July 4, 1939, p. 6.

29. For examples of this scholarship, see Herbert Aptheker, *Negro Slave Revolts in the United States, 1526–1860* (New York: International Publishers, 1939); Joseph Cephas Campbell, *Slave Insurrections in the United States, 1800–1860* (Boston: Chapman and Grimes, 1938), reviewed by Herbert Biel, *Communist* 18 (February 1939): 381–83; Elizabeth Lawson, "He Led Slaves' Fight for Freedom: 106 Years Ago Nat Turner Organized Revolt," *Daily Worker*, August 21, 1937, p. 7; N. Stevens, "The 100th Anniversary of the Nat Turner Revolt," *Communist* 10 (August 1931): 737–43. Herbert Aptheker was doing research for his book during the period Wright was working for the *Daily Worker* as head of the Harlem bureau. I am not suggesting that Wright drew specifically on any one of these authors but I am arguing that Wright was active in a Communist intellectual milieu that featured their scholarship and that, as an engaged Communist intellectual, he was aware of their pioneering work. The language and values in this key passage of *Native Son* did not emerge from thin air but from a Communist discourse Wright supported and that stimulated him.

30. Frederick Douglass, *Narrative of the Life of Frederick Douglass, An American Slave, Written by Himself*, ed. David W. Blight (1845; Boston: Bedford Books, 1993), p. 46.

Chapter Six

1. To avoid confusion with the similarly titled concluding section, I am italicizing the long poem as *The Book of the Dead*, pp. 9–72, in Rukeyser's *U.S. 1* (New York: Covici, Friede, 1938). Subsequent quotations are from this edition and are cited by page parenthetically in the text.

2. For a thorough study of the Gauley tragedy, including the contemporary response, see Martin Cherniack, *The Hawk's Nest Incident: America's Worst Industrial Disaster* (New Haven: Yale University Press, 1986), and David Rosner and Gerald Markowitz, *Deadly Dust: Silicosis and the Politics of Occupational Disease in Twentieth-Century America* (Princeton, N.J.: Princeton University Press, 1991), pp. 96–101.

3. On the connection with Isis, see M. L. Rosenthal, "Muriel Rukeyser: The Longer Poems," *New Directions in Prose and Poetry*, ed. James Laughlin, 14 (1953): 218.

4. Philip Blair Rice, "The Osiris Way," *Nation* 146 (March 19, 1938): 336.

5. Muriel Rukeyser, *The Life of Poetry* (New York: A. A. Wyn, 1949), p. 159.

6. Muriel Rukeyser, *Twentieth-Century American Authors: A Biographical Dictionary of Modern Literature*, ed. Stanley J. Kunitz and Howard Haycroft (New York: H. H. Wilson, 1942), p. 1211. See Chapter 2 for biographical details of Rukeyser's involvement in documentary film and photography.

7. Rukeyser, *The Life of Poetry*, p. 148.

8. John Wheelwright, "*U.S. 1*," *Partisan Review* 4 (March 1938): 55, 56.

9. Ben A. Franklin, "In the Shadow of the Valley," *Sierra* 71 (May–June 1986): 41–42. See also "Grim Cloud of Worry Reaches U.S.," *U.S. News and World Report* 97 (December 17, 1984): 27; and *New York Times Index, 1985*, "Institute, W. Va.," p. 612, and "Pesticides," pp. 931–32.

10. U.S. Congress, House Committee on Labor, 74th Congress, 2nd Session, *Investigation Relating to Health Conditions of Workers Employed in the Construction and Maintenance of Public Utilities: Hearing* (Washington, D.C.: U.S. Government Printing Office, 1936), p. 1. Subsequent references are cited parenthetically in the text as *Investigation*.

11. Dorothy Emerson, "Poetry Corner," *Scholastic*, April 1, 1939, p. 29E.

12. Muriel Rukeyser, *Out of Silence: Selected Poems*, ed. Kate Daniels (Evanston, Ill.: TriQuarterly Books, 1992).

13. See, for example, *The Ancient Egyptian Book of the Dead*, trans. Raymond O. Faulkner, ed. Carol Andrews (London: British Museum Publications, 1985), Spell 125, pp. 31–32.

14. Ibid., p. 27.

15. David Kadlec convincingly points to a 1936–37 New York exhibit of the Heart Amulet of Hatnofer as the source for connecting the heart and the Egyptian *Book of the Dead*. David Kadlec, "X-Ray Testimonials in Muriel Rukeyser," *Modernism/Modernity* 5 (1998): 32.

16. *Congressional Record*, 2d session, 74th Congress, vol. 80, pt. 5, April 1, 1936, pp. 4752–53.

17. Walter Kalaidjian, *American Culture between the Wars: Revisionary Modernism and Postmodern Critique* (New York: Columbia University Press, 1993), p. 173. Subsequent page references are cited parenthetically in the text.

18. In the context of Kalaidjian's discussion of the "heroic," larger-than-life figures of 1930s muralists, this characterization is misleading if it implies that, like the muralists, Rukeyser renders her characters on a heroic scale.

19. Kadlec, "X-Ray Testimonials," esp. 38.

20. Ibid., p. 28.

21. Ibid., pp. 29, 27.

22. Ibid., pp. 23–47, esp. pp. 28–29.

Chapter Seven

1. On jazz and the blues, see, for example, Langston Hughes, *First Book of Jazz* (New York: Franklin Watts, 1955), and Steven C. Tracy, *Langston Hughes and the Blues* (Urbana: University of Illinois Press, 1988). On Hughes's relation to the raid at Harpers Ferry, see Langston Hughes, *The Big Sea: An Autobiography* (New York: Knopf, 1940), p. 12.

2. On Africa, see John Miller Chernoff, *African Rhythm and African Sensibility: Aesthetics and Social Action in African Musical Idioms* (Chicago: University of Chicago Press, 1979). On the African American slave communities, see Lawrence W. Levine, *Black Culture and Black Consciousness: Afro-American Folk Thought from Slavery to Freedom* (New York: Oxford University Press, 1977), and John Lovell Jr., *Black Song: The Forge and the Flame: The Story of How the Afro-American Spiritual Was Hammered Out* (New York: Macmillan, 1972).

3. In addition to Levine and Lovell, on communal work and singing, see Roger D. Abrahams, *Singing the Master: The Emergence of African American Culture in the Plantation South* (New York: Pantheon Books, 1992), and John F. Szwed and Roger D. Abrahams, "After the Myth: Studying Afro-American Cultural Patterns in the Plantation Literature," in *African Folklore in the New World*, ed. Daniel J. Crowley (Austin: University of Texas Press, 1977), pp. 65–86.

4. See esp. Chernoff, *African Rhythm and African Sensibility*.

5. See, for example, William D. Piersen, "Puttin' Down Ole Massa: African Satire in the New World," in Crowley, *African Folklore in the New World*, pp. 20–34.

6. See, for example, Frederick Douglass, *Life and Times of Frederick Douglass* (1892; New York: Collier-Macmillan, 1962), pp. 157–60; Lovell, *Black Song*, pp. 133–34, 168–80; and Levine, *Black Culture*, pp. 49–53. See also Henry Lewis Gates, *The Signifying Monkey: A Theory of African-American Literary Criticism* (New York: Oxford University Press, 1988).

7. This tradition extends from Africa through slavery to New Orleans jazz and into Hughes's poetry and beyond. To the considerable extent that Walter Benn Michaels discredits or overlooks these continuities, Hughes's poetry and its tradition call into question underlying tendencies in Michaels's argument in "Race into Culture: A Critical Genealogy of Cultural Identity," *Critical Inquiry* 18 (Summer 1992): esp. 675–85.

8. In the same issue with "Letter to the Academy" were "A Discussion: Soviet Literature and Dos Passos"; Sergei Tretyakov, "Hans Eisler: Revolutionary Composer"; A. Lunacharsky, "On Dostoyevsky"; and Alex Keil, "Six German Revolutionary Posters—Drawings." The quotations from "Letter to the Academy" are from *Good Morning Revolution: Uncollected Writings of Social Protest by Langston Hughes*, ed. Faith Berry (1973; New York: Citadel Press, 1992), pp. 1–2.

9. On Scottsboro, see esp. "Opinion of Judge James E. Horton Granting a Motion for a New Trial," reprinted as "Appendix 5," in Haywood Patterson and Earl Conrad, *Scottsboro Boy* (1950; New York: Collier, 1969).

10. Langston Hughes, *Scottsboro Limited: Four Poems and a Play in Verse, with Illustrations by Prentiss Taylor* (New York: Golden Stair Press, 1932). Quotations from *Scottsboro Limited* are from this edition. The pages are unnumbered.

11. The quotation and chronology are from Faith Berry, *Langston Hughes: Before and After Harlem* (Westport, Conn.: Lawrence Hill, 1983), p. 135. The quotation was originally published in *Contempo*, December 1, 1931, p. 1.

12. Langston Hughes, *A New Song* (New York: International Publishers, 1938), pp. 11, 13.

13. Ibid., pp. 9–12.

14. "Justice" originally appeared in *Amsterdam News*, April 25, 1923, p. 12. *The Collected Poems of Langston Hughes*, ed. Arnold Rampersad and David Roessel (New York: Knopf, 1994), p. 614.

15. Rampersad and Roessel, *Collected Poems of Langston Hughes*, p. 632.

16. Ve Ve Clark, "Restaging Langston Hughes's *Scottsboro Limited*: An Interview with Amiri Baraka," *Black Scholar* 10 (July–August 1979): 63.

17. Berry, *Langston Hughes*, p. 345, n. 10, and Rampersad and Roessel, *Collected Poems of Langston Hughes*, p. 639. My quotations from "August 19th: A Poem for Clarence Norris" are from Berry, pp. 143–46.

18. *Daily Worker*, June 28, 1938, p. 7.

19. Along with stories about Scottsboro, throughout 1937 and 1938 stories about the Japanese assault on China and the fascist attacks on Spain dominated the front page of the *Daily Worker*. See, for example, such banner headlines as "Japan Guns, Planes Fire Tientsin" (July 31, 1937, p. 1) or "Fascist Airplanes Machine-Gun, Bomb Fleeing Refugees" (June 15, 1937, p. 1).

20. Hughes, *First Book of Jazz*, pp. 3–4.

21. *Workers Monthly*, April 1925, p. 267; Berry, *Good Morning Revolution*, p. 21.

22. See also Hughes's other 1925 *Workers Monthly* poems, "Drama for a Winter Night" in the March issue; "Poem to a Dead Soldier" and "Park Benching" [not "Park Bench"] in the April issue; "To Certain 'Brothers'" in the July issue. "Poem to a Dead Soldier" and "To Certain 'Brothers'" are reprinted in Berry, *Good Morning Revolution*, pp. 29–30, 47.

23. "Merry Christmas" is reprinted in Berry, *Good Morning Revolution*, pp. 33–34.

24. "Pride," "Black Seed," and "Negro Servant," *Opportunity* 8 (December 1930): 371.

25. Hughes, *A New Song*, pp. 16–17.

26. "To Certain Negro Leaders," "Tired," and "A Christian Country," *New Masses* 6 (February 1931): 4, reprinted in Berry, *Good Morning Revolution*, pp. 16–17, 48, 49.

27. In her severe evaluation of the 1931 *New Masses*, Anne Elistratova quotes "Tired" as an example of "the passive registration of facts of class 'oppression,' [which] amounts to complete repudiation of the revolutionary class struggle, to an advocacy of passiveness and non-resistance." She says of "Tired" in particular that "a distinctively decadent and passive mood characterizes" the poem (*International Literature* 1 [1932]: 111). Her reading and evaluation reveal as much about her own preference for overt statement, her insensitivity to irony, and her distance from American racial discourse as they do about Hughes's "decadence" and "passivity."

28. Reprinted in Berry, *Langston Hughes*, p. 131.

29. "White Shadows" is reprinted in Berry, *Good Morning Revolution*, p. 16.

30. "White Shadows in a Black Land," *Crisis* 39 (May 1932): 157, quoted in Berry, *Langston Hughes*, p. 122. See also Langston Hughes, "People without Shoes," *New Masses* 7 (October 1931): 12, a nuanced treatment of the power of the occupation and of the class lines within Haiti; and Hughes's lively postcard to *New Masses*, "A Letter from Haiti," *New Masses* 4 (July 1931): 9. The "Letter" is reprinted in Berry, *Langston Hughes*, p. 123. On his way to and from Haiti, Hughes visited Cuba. See Hughes's "To the Little Fort of San Lorenzo," *New Masses* 6 (May 1931): 11, reprinted in Berry, *Good Morning Revolution*, p. 34.

31. "October 16," reprinted in *Selected Poems of Langston Hughes* (New York: Knopf, 1959), p. 10.

32. Hughes, *The Big Sea*, pp. 320–21. Hughes reprinted "Advertisement for the Waldorf-Astoria" in *The Big Sea*, pp. 321–23, but he did not include the militant ending, "CHRISTMAS CARD." The original *New Masses*'s version is reprinted in Berry, *Good Morning Revolution*, pp. 23–26.

33. Hughes, *The Big Sea*, p. 321. The ad was in the October 1931 issue of *Vanity Fair*.

34. Reprinted in Berry, *Good Morning Revolution*, pp. 49–50.

35. Walter C. Daniel, "Langston Hughes versus the Black Preachers in the *Pittsburgh Courier* in the 1930s," *Critical Essays on Langston Hughes*, ed. Edward J. Mullen (Boston: G. K. Hall, 1986), pp. 129–35.

36. Berry, *Langston Hughes*, p. 295.

37. Ibid., p. 316.

38. "Good Morning, Revolution," *New Masses* 8 (September 1932): 5; reprinted in Berry, *Good Morning Revolution*, pp. 2–4. "For Tom Mooney," *New Masses* 8 (September 1932): 16. For *A New Song* Hughes gave "For Tom Mooney" a new title, "Chant for Tom Mooney," pp. 13–14. The revised title, like the next poem in *A New Song*, "Chant for May Day," emphasizes Hughes's affinity with the left aesthetic of the communal, of the militant poem to be chanted communally in public, not read in private as the work of a single writer. On the Bonus March, see Howard Zinn, *A People's History of the United States, 1492–Present* (New York: Harper Perennial, 1995), pp. 381–82, 454.

39. Walter Kalaidjian, *American Culture between the Wars: Revisionary Modernism and Postmodern Critique* (New York: Columbia University Press, 1993), pp. 100–101.

40. *Negro Worker* 2 (September–October 1932): contents page and 1.

41. Ibid., p. 31. The poem is on pp. 31–32 and is reprinted in Berry, *Good Morning Revolution*, pp. 9–11.

42. "Revolution," *New Masses* 10 (February 20, 1934): 28, reprinted in Berry, *Good Morning Revolution*, p. 7.

43. "Cubes," *New Masses* 10 (March 13, 1934), 22, reprinted in Berry, *Good Morning Revolution*, pp. 14–15.

44. "One More 'S' in the U.S.A.," *Daily Worker*, April 2, 1934, p. 7.

45. Arnold Rampersad, *The Life of Langston Hughes* (New York: Oxford University Press, 1986), 1:285–86.

46. Donald C. Dickinson, *A Bio-Bibliography of Langston Hughes, 1902–1967* (Hamden, Conn.: Archon Books, 1972).

47. "Ballad of Lenin," in *Proletarian Literature in the United States: An Anthology*, ed. Granville Hicks et al. (New York: International Publishers, 1935), pp. 166–67.

48. "Park Bench," in ibid., p. 168.

49. Ibid. The poem probably has a biographical basis in Hughes's relation to his Park Avenue patron, Mrs. Charlotte Mason.

50. "White Man," *New Masses* 21 (December 15, 1936): 34; reprinted in Berry, *Good Morning, Revolution*, pp. 4–5.

51. Richard Hofstadter and Michael Wallace, eds., *American Violence: A Documentary History* (New York: Vintage, 1971), pp. 258–62, and *The Complete Report of Mayor LaGuardia's Commission on the Harlem Riot of March 19, 1935* (New York: Arno Press, 1969).

52. "Air Raid over Harlem: A Scenario for a Little Black Movie," *New Theater* 3 (February 1936): 19–21. The poem appeared in the "Film" section of *New Theater*, a high-quality left arts journal. The poem is reprinted in Berry, *Good Morning Revolution*, pp. 37–40. It is not listed Dickinson's *A Bio-Bibliography of Langston Hughes* but it appears in *The Heath Anthology of American Literature*, 2d ed., ed. Paul Lauter et al. (Lexington, Mass.: D. C. Heath, 1994), 2:1403–6.

53. Rampersad and Roessel, *Collected Poems of Langston Hughes*, p. 637.

54. "Madrid—1937," inscribed "to Arthur Spingarn, Sincerely, Langston Hughes," was first published in Berry, *Good Morning Revolution*, pp. 111–13.

55. Max Bedacht, general secretary of the International Workers Order, quoted in Mike Gold's introduction to Hughes, *A New Song*, p. 8. Subsequent page references to poems in this edition are cited parenthetically in the text.

56. "Red Flag on Tuskeegee," *Afro-American*, June 25, 1932; reprinted in Berry, *Langston Hughes*, pp. 140–42. "Open Letter to the South," in Hughes, *A New Song*, pp. 27–28.

57. "Pride," *Opportunity*, December 1930, p. 371; Hughes, *A New Song*, p. 16. When he republished "Pride" in the midst of the renewed radicalism of the 1960s, Hughes entitled it "Militant." *The Panther and the Lash: Poems of Our Times* (New York: Knopf, 1967), p. 39.

58. "Kids Who Die," in *A New Song*, p. 19.

59. See note 57.

60. *Opportunity*, January 1933, p. 23; quoted in Berry, *Langston Hughes*, p. 183.

61. Langston Hughes and Arna Bontemps, eds., *The Poetry of the Negro, 1746–1949* (New York: Doubleday, 1949), pp. 106–8.

62. Ibid., p. 108.

63. Quoted in Berry, *Langston Hughes*, pp. 316–17.

64. Quoted in ibid., p. 183.

INDEX

Gilligan, Carol: *In a Different Voice*, 207

Gold, Mike, 7, 8, 9, 14, 19, 26, 135, 136; *Jews without Money*, 3, 17; "Towards Proletarian Art," 3, 13–14

Gordon, Carolyn, 26

Gornick, Vivian: *The Romance of Communism*, 10

Gorz, George, 167

Gramsci, Antonio, 8, 134

Greenberg, Clement, 6–7, 17, 33. *See also* Communist Party: criticism of; Modernism; New York intellectuals

Greenwood, Marion, 27

Gregory, Horace, 15, 17, 36, 51–53

Group Theatre, 16, 17, 35

Haiti, 258, 263–64

Harlan County, Ky., 181

Harlem, N.Y., 285–91, 295. *See also* Naison, Mark

Harper's Bazaar, 23

Hart, Henry, 15

Hayes, Alfred, 13, 16, 17

Haymarket anarchists, 87, 101–2, 107–8

Haywood, Big Bill, 106, 107, 112

Heale, M. J., 10

Hemingway, Ernest, 20, 26, 27

Herbst, Josephine, 1, 2, 13, 14, 31, 32, 33, 40, 112, 140, 183, 244, 249; career and reputation of, 25–30; criticism of, 27, 28; *The Executioner Waits*, 4, 87, 89, 91, 102, 103–21, 127, 128, 134, 136; "Hunter of Doves," 30; memoirs, 30; *Money for Love*, 26; *Nothing Is Sacred*, 26; "Ruins of Memory," 30; *Satan's Sergeants*, 29; *Somewhere the Tempest Fell*, 29; "A Year of Disgrace," 30, 111

—*Pity Is Not Enough*, 4, 87, 88–103, 105, 136; family history in, 25; and organizing centers, 89; Reconstruction Georgia in, 92–94

—*Rope of Gold*, 30, 86, 87, 89, 91, 98, 110, 111, 112, 114, 117, 118, 119, 121–33; and Cuba, 128, 131, 135; and form, 122; ideological range in, 129–31; and Lincoln Brigade, 131; love and politics in, 125, 132, 133; and fascism, 130–31, 132, 133; Rabinowitz on, 133–36; sexual politics in, 124

—Trexler trilogy: and American history, 108, 110, 111; and American Revolution, 107–8;

childbirth and abortion in, 108–10; Christianity and Marxism in, 101–2, 130; Cuba in, 87, 132; Haymarket anarchists in, 87, 101–2, 107–8; literary languages in, 97, 99, 132; and Marxian theory of class in, 26–27, 86, 233; money and capital in, 88, 90, 99, 103, 105, 114, 115, 116; narrative style in, 87, 88, 89, 90, 91, 102, 132–33; patriarchs in, 129; and political art, 107, 121; publishers of, 27; radicalism in, 87–88; sexuality in, 95–96, 103–4, 113; and "the woman's sphere," 96, 97. *See also* International Workers of the World; Left avant-garde; Marxism; Modernism; Political persecution; Realism/naturalism

Hermann, John, 26, 27, 112, 135

Hicks, Granville, 9, 19; *John Reed*, 13

Hill, Joe, 112

hooks, bell, 96

Hughes, Langston, 1, 3, 14, 15, 17, 34, 38, 245; and black oral and musical traditions, 244–45, 255, 273, 278, 303–4; and black/white unity, 245, 264, 265, 277–78, 291; career and reputation of, 37–40; and context as issue, 40, 249–50, 260, 264, 271–72, 295, 304; criticism of, 40, 254, 272, 282, 330 (n. 27); and cultural politics, 245–46, 269; and Ethiopian War, 284, 285–91; and Haiti, 258, 263–64; and Harlem riot of 1935, 285–91; and imperialism, 255, 258–59, 264, 275–79, 303–4; and lynching, 251–52, 255, 297; and McCarthy Committee, 3, 39; overview of, 303–4; patrons of, 39–40; and race, 249, 250, 260, 260–62, 280, 284–85, 286, 294 297–99; and religious satire, 250–52, 256–59, 260–61, 268–72; and revolution, 246–47, 268–69, 272–75, 276–79, 298; and self-censorship, 3, 39, 295; and slavery, 250–51, 278, 288, 297–98, 299; and violence, 275, 288, 294, 296, 299

—works of: "Advertisement for the Waldorf-Astoria," 39, 262, 266–69, 295; "Air Raid over Harlem," 285–91, 295; "August 19th: A Poem for Clarence Norris," 254–55, "Ballad of Lenin," 282–83, 284, 294; "Ballad of Ozie Powell," 260; *The Big Sea*, 39; "Broadcast on Ethiopia," 295; "Chant for May Day," 295; "Chant for Tom Mooney," 249, 295; "A Christian Country," 260–61, 262; "Christ in

and reader's role, 51, 74–75; and reportage, 51, 67, 183; and *Scribner's* prize, 23, 42; and sexuality, 44, 46, 59–60, 65–66, 81–82, 83; and sexual politics, 54–55, 74; and women in party, 66–67; and writing as value, 59–61
—works of: American organicism in, 60; "Annunciation," 44, 53, 57–61, 63, 66, 74; childbirth and revolution in, 59, 61, 63–64, 81, 85; "Corn Village," 41–47, 53, 65, 73, 74, 183; epistemology in, 82; "The Fetish of Being Outside," 51–53, 54; form and language in, 47, 57–58, 77–78, 80, 81–83; *The Girl*, 17, 24, 25, 41, 74–85; "The Girl," 53–57, 58, 183; imagination in, 59, 63; "I Was Marching," 4, 44, 46, 53, 65, 66, 67–73, 74, 80, 84; language in, 18, 41–42, 46–47, 57–58, 62–63, 74, 76, 77–78; *North Star Country*, 24, 43; *Salute to Spring*, 18, 23, 24, 25, 42, 46, 47, 51, 57, 58, 67, 74; "Salute to Spring," 47, 64–67; "Tonight Is Part of the Struggle," 5, 18, 47, 61–64, 66, 67; versus fixed genres, 42, 46–47; "Women Are Hungry," 46; "Women on the Breadlines," 4, 46, 47–51. *See also* American Writers' Congress; Capitalism; Communist Party; Left avant-garde; Marx; Marxism; Political persecution; Popular Front
Lewis, H. H., 16
Lewis, Sinclair, 31, 42
Liberal discourse, 72–73
Liberator, 14
Lieber, Maxim, 24, 303
Liebnecht, Karl, 111, 119
Lincoln, Abraham, 22, 44, 45, 46, 131
Little Red Song Book, 12
Living Newspaper, 17, 199, 286
London, Jack, 13
Long, Huey, 130
Lumpkin, Grace, 8
Luxembourg, Rosa, 111, 119
Lyons, Paul: *Philadelphia Communists, 1936–1956*, 6, 11

McCall, Dan, 152
McCarthy, Joseph, 29
McCarthy Committee, 3, 39
Malcolm X, 156
Maltz, Albert, 16, 181, 183; "Man on a Road"

Marx, Karl, 16, 50, 73, 185, 269, 270, 284; *The Communist Manifesto*, 75, 284
Marxism: and Marxist art, 9–10; and Herbst, 26–27, 86, 87, 98, 108–9; and Hughes; 284; and Le Sueur, 41–42, 47–51, 52–53, 54, 57–58, 63, 68–69, 70, 72–73, 74, 75, 78–79, 85, 321 (n. 18); and Rukeyser, 196, 197, 224, 229; and Wright, 138, 157, 160, 168–69, 171
Mass culture, 17
Matthiessen, F. O., 9, 36
Mellon, Andrew, 215
Menand, Louis, 33
Mencken, H. L., 31
Midland Left, 13
Milton, John: *Paradise Lost*, 222, 223, 224
Modernism, 13, 246; and anti-Stalinism, 6–7, 17, 33; and Herbst, 13, 26, 89, 132; and Hughes, 303; and Rukeyser, 181, 196, 197, 216, 230. *See also* Communist Party: criticism of; New York intellectuals
Mooney, Tom, 231, 248, 249, 295
Moore, Richard B., 14
Murphy, Geraldine, 306 (n. 7)
Murphy, James, 10

Naison, Mark: *Communists in Harlem during the Depression*, 10, 21
Naumburg, Nancy, 181, 242
Navasky, Victor, 10
Nelson, Cary: *Repression and Recovery*, 8, 9
Nelson, Steve, 10
New Deal, 5, 18, 242. *See also* Popular Front
Newhouse, Edward, 8, 17–18, 314 (n. 23); *This Is Your Day*, 8, 18; *You Can't Sleep Here*, 8, 18
New Masses: 9, 13, 14, 17, 34; and Hughes, 38, 253, 257–59, 261–62, 267, 278–79, 281; and Le Sueur, 23, 24, 47, 51–53, 74, 320 (n. 7); and Rukeyser, 34–35, 181, 182
New Theatre, 17
New York intellectuals, 9, 17, 22, 33, 306 (n. 7), 308 (n. 28). *See also* Communist Party: criticism of; Modernism
Nykino group, 16

O'Connor, Harvey, 30, 215
Odets, Clifford, 16
Ohmann, Richard, 32
Olsen, Tillie, 8

Tried to Be a Communist," 32; *Lawd Today!*, 17, *The Outsider*, 32; pan-African nonfiction, 32; "A Red Love Note," 104; "Strength," 164; *12 Million Black Voices*, 29, 32; "Transcontinental," 183; *Uncle Tom's Children*, 18, 19, 31

—*Native Son*: anticommunist view of, 2, 33, 168; and black political consciousness, 152–53, 155, 174; and black pride, 163, 164, 165, 170, 175; and black self-hate, 144, 155; Book-of-the Month Club edits, 142–46, 148–49; and Christianity, 156, 163, 164, 166; and consumerism, 170; criticism of, 2, 28, 33, 139, 152, 170, 171; and drama of belief, 165–66, 175–76, 178–80; and expressionism, 18, 32, 139, 140, 147, 151–52, 158–60, 161, 162, 167, 324 (n. 9); and fear, 144, 145, 147–48; film project, 33; and hatred, 141, 144–45, 147, 154, 173–74; and language, 140–41, 159–60, 161, 163, 165–68, 175, 180; and manhood, 142, 145, 166; narration of, 140–41; and oppression, 159, 168–69; and political psychology, 143–47, 153–60, 163, 169, 173; and power, 137–38, 141–42, 144, 148, 150, 151, 152, 153, 155, 158–59, 161, 162; and race, 144, 150, 153–54, 162; and rape, 149–51, 159, 163, 168; and traditions, 31–32; and violence, 143, 144–45, 149–50, 153, 170; and women, 33, 157–60, 173. *See also* Blues, Communist Party; Federal Bureau of Investigation; Left avant-garde; Marxism; Political perscution; Popular Front